Play with Sound

Play with Sound: Manual for Electronic Musicians and Other Sound Explorers offers a thorough introduction to music technology by centering on curiosity and creativity in the exploration of the fundamentals of sound.

With color illustrations throughout, this book covers topics regarding audio software, acoustical principles, electroacoustic systems, audio processing, sound synthesis, and communication protocols. Each chapter features creative exercises that utilize live electronics, production, and composition to unearth the theories presented and develop technical and musical creativity. Additionally, interactive graphics and lesson slides are available as digital resources to enhance learning inside and outside the classroom.

Play with Sound is an ideal textbook for beginners of all backgrounds looking for an introduction to music technology, production, and live electronics. By engaging with this book, everyone, including traditional students as well as those learning outside the traditional classroom setting, will be able to expand their musical skills and professional opportunities into the world of music technology.

Tommaso Rosati is an Italian sound artist who explores creativity halfway between an academic and a pop approach. He loves augmented instruments, adores music tech design and visualization, and constantly hunts for sounds and musical gestures.

Timothy Hsu is a faculty member in Music Technology at Indiana University – Indianapolis. He loves to mentor students to explore the intersection of musical creativity and technical innovation. His research interests center on aspects of human and environmental sustainability through music technology and acoustics.

PLAY WITH SOUND

MANUAL FOR ELECTRONIC MUSICIANS AND OTHER SOUND EXPLORERS

TOMMASO ROSATI
TIMOTHY HSU

Routledge
Taylor & Francis Group
LONDON AND NEW YORK

Designed cover image: Laura Meffe and Tommaso Rosati

First published in English 2025
by Routledge
4 Park Square, Milton Park, Abingdon, Oxon OX14 4RN

and by Routledge
605 Third Avenue, New York, NY 10158

Routledge is an imprint of the Taylor & Francis Group, an informa business

Published in Italian by Volontè & Co. 2023 as *Suono elettronico. Manuale per studenti di tecnologie musicali e altri esploratori di suoni*

British Library Cataloguing-in-Publication Data
A catalogue record for this book is available from the British Library

ISBN: 978-1-032-79683-3 (hbk)
ISBN: 978-1-032-79682-6 (pbk)
ISBN: 978-1-003-49337-2 (ebk)

DOI: 10.4324/9781003493372

Publisher's Note
This book has been prepared from camera-ready copy provided by the authors.

Access the Support Material:
https://www.tommasorosati.it/play-with-sound

TO **DAVIDE LUFRANO**
great musician, companion in music, life, and even more easy things.

TO **AVERY**
curious explorer of the world

TABLE OF CONTENTS

Table of contents 1

Foreword 4

How this book works 5
The types of audio software 8
Music notation software 8
DAW 9
VST and AU 10
Music programming languages 10
What you can do with electronic music 11
Production 12
Performance 13

Acoustics and Psychoacoustics 18

Sound production and propagation 19
The source 20
Speed of sound 21
Sound representation 22
Period 22
Wavelength 23
Periodic wave - aperiodic wave 23
Frequency 24
Amplitude 30
Phase 34
Timbre 37

Electroacoustic Systems 45

Analog or Digital? 46
Analog 46
Cables 47
Input 50
Signal Levels 50
Impedance 51
DI-Box 53
Microphones 53
Types of microphones 53
Frequency response 58
Polar pattern 59
Stereo microphone techniques 62
Magnetic pickups 69
Processing 73
Mixer 73
Output 76
Monitors 76
Headphones 78
Digital 78
Computer 78
Software 81

Files 82
Audio interfaces 83
Output 85
Monitors and Headphones 85
Sampling and Quantization 86
Sampling - Quantization (ADC) 86
Reconstruction (DAC) 89
Issues in the sampling-reconstruction process 90

Communication Protocols 92

MIDI 93
Connections 94
Types of messages 95
Channel Voice Message 95
System Message 97
MIDI controllers (connection and mapping) 98
.mid files 99
MPE 100
OSC 101

Sound Processing 103

Filters, EQ, and related effects 105
Low-pass and High-pass 105
Band-pass and Notch 107
Low-shelf, High-shelf, and Bell EQ filters 108
Filter order 109
Q 110
All-pass 111
Wah-wah 112
Phaser 113
Delay and related effects 114
Fixed delay times 114
Echo 114
Multiple echo 116
Comb filter 117
Multitap delay 118
Multitap multiband delay 120
Ping pong delay 121
Varying delay times 122
Flanger 122
Chorus 123
Reverb 125
Natural acoustic reverb 125
Impulse response 128
Reverberation time: RT60 128
Artificial acoustic reverb 129
Electromechanical reverb 130
Classic digital reverb 130

Digital convolution reverb 135
Dynamic processors 139
Envelope follower 139
Compressor 140
Multiple compressor 143
De-esser 144
Limiter 144
Expander 145
Gate 146
Distortion 147
Overdrive 148
Fuzz 149
Resampling 150
Bit crushing 151
Waveshaping 152
Spatialization 153
Psychoacoustics of spatial perception 154
Spatialization systems 156
Ambisonics 156
Spatialization playback systems 158
Spatialization control 159
Panning 160
Space as a compositional-performative parameter 161

Sound Synthesis **163**

Introductory concepts 164
Filters 165
Envelopes 165
LFO 166
CV (Control Voltage) 166
Hardware or Software, Analog or Digital, Standalone, Modular or Semi-Modular 167
Linear and Nonlinear synthesis algorithms 168
Additive synthesis 168
Subtractive synthesis 170
AM-RM synthesis 172
FM synthesis 174
Waveshaping 179
Phase distortion 181
Physical modeling 183
Granular synthesis 185
Sampling synthesis 188
Wavetable synthesis 192
Vector synthesis 193
Software 195
Free resources 197
Bibliography 198
Thanks to 199
Index 200

FOREWORD

HOW THIS BOOK WORKS

The chapters and sections in this book are designed to be approached in any order you wish. Designed to be an "open work" in full ***Umberto Eco*** style, each module contains theory, insights, and practical exercises designed to live on their own and to make students approach them as intuitively and creatively as possible.

SLIDES

The topics will be addressed on a theoretical level through the text, examples, and graphs with the idea that what you learn can be assessed through hands-on exercises and other creative activities. PDF slides—that expound on the themes that may be taught in a classroom—were created as a compendium of this book and are available free of charge by scanning the QR code.

www.tommasorosati.it/en/play-with-sound/

DOWNLOAD SLIDES

INTERACTIVE GRAPHICS

There are a variety of interactive graphics online for you to work with. Play with the various concepts, listening to how parameters affect the sound. You can find the interactive graphics by scanning the QR code and looking for the PLAY icons.

www.tommasorosati.it/en/play-with-sound/

INTERACT WITH THE ILLUSTRATIONS

CHAPTERS	SLIDES
FOREWORD How this book works The types of audio software What you can do with electronic music	LESSON 0 MUSIC and COMPUTER ELECTROACOUSTIC COMPOSITION MIXED SEQUENCE and MASHUP
ACOUSTICS AND PSYCHOACOUSTICS Sound production and propagation Sound representation Timbre	SOUND 1 WAVE AND PERIOD SOUND 2 FREQUENCY SOUND 3 AMPLITUDE SOUND 4 PHASE SOUND 5 TIMBRE AUDITORY SYSTEM
ELECTROACOUSTIC SYSTEMS Analog Digital Sampling and quantization	ELECTROACOUSTIC SYSTEMS MICROPHONE and PICKUP DIGITAL SYSTEMS SAMPLING AND QUANTIZATION
COMMUNICATION PROTOCOLS MIDI OSC	COMMUNICATION PROTOCOLS
SOUND PROCESSING Filters, EQ, and related effects Delay and related effects Reverb Dynamic processors Distortion Spatialization	FILTERS DELAY DYNAMIC PROCESSORS DISTORTION REVERB SPATIALIZATION
SOUND SYNTHESIS Additive synthesis Subtractive synthesis AM-RM synthesis FM synthesis Waveshaping Phase distortion Physical modeling Granular synthesis Synthesis by sampling Wavetable	SOUND SYNTHESIS

DOWNLOAD SLIDES

www.tommasorosati.it/en/play-with-sound/

KEYWORDS

In the magenta boxes scattered throughout the book, there will be suggestions on music to listen to, videos to watch, software to experiment with, and artists to learn more about. These suggestions come in the form of **keywords** that should be searched for on the Internet using your favorite search engine. These keywords should lead to articles, audio recordings, and videos. These suggestions are not meant to be merely optional; rather, they are complementary parts of the learning process. Try to look up, or experience, at least one item for each list of keywords you see in a section. An instructor, of course, may propose new keywords based on their own experience and taste.

EXPERIMENT

In the orange boxes, activities aimed at developing your creative thinking are proposed, trying as much as possible to be software agnostic. In other words, these exercises were designed to be able to be completed in one of many software programs and not depend on any one piece of potentially proprietary software. Generally, these activities presented will be done in one of two types of audio software: digital audio workstations (DAWs) and visual object programming environments.
Often, a theme is suggested in the exercises. These themes can be varied as desired from time to time and are intended to trigger research into suggested topics that lead to compositions, stimulating creative thinking. You can navigate from the original suggestion to the final sound in many ways, including by visual association, by imitation of parameters extracted from the theme, or by numerical analogies in a serialist style. Try to choose a theme and a criterion to complete the composition.
Sometimes, a suggestion is made for the kind of sound that should be chosen and used in the "experiments." These sounds can be created independently, sourced from online libraries (freesound.org, for example), provided by the instructor, or downloaded from the link below.

www.tommasorosati.it/files/SOUNDS.zip

DOWNLOAD SOUNDS

SONGS

Another essential activity suggested in this book is reconstructing songs, or parts of songs, with a DAW to practice the theoretical concepts in each section. This supports the discovery of some of the "secrets" behind music composition and production. Deliberately, there is no suggestion for specific pieces in this book, as you can be challenged by any piece of music, be influenced by current music trends, or be curated pieces of music by a teacher or peer. The goal is to support you as you develop your original musical path, keeping your interest in music making healthy and alive.

Recommended free or cost-effective software*.
DAW: Reaper, Audacity, Soundtrap
PROGRAMMING: Pure Data, VCV Rack 2, SuperCollider, ChucK
WRITING: Musescore
PROCESSING: SPEAR
ANALYSIS: EAnalysis, Acousmographe, Sonic Visualiser, Praat
VIDEO EDITING: Openshot

For some video (Italian with English automatic subtitles) support on using these software programs, you can refer to the video lessons found in the following QR codes.

*The authors have no relationship with any of these companies and the inclusion of any software here is not an endorsement.

YOUTUBE:
Tommaso Rosati
@t0mm3

REAPER AUDACITY PURE DATA SPEAR

THE TYPES OF AUDIO SOFTWARE

Music notation software

These are the software programs that allow us to write in musical notation. They work similar to word processing software, but instead of text entry, they enable us to input musical notes, articulations, and all other musical score markings. The notes can be entered in several ways: clicking with a mouse, typing on a computer keyboard, or playing on a MIDI keyboard controller. Once you have created your sheet music, you can export it to PDF for printing, or MIDI and music XML for use in other audio software, such as DAWs.

Among the most widely used music notation software are ***Finale***, ***Sibelius***, and ***Musescore***.

.compose four bars of music for your instrument in a music notation software program. Use at most four different pitches and experiment with other parameters like rhythm and articulations. Generate a listenable WAV version and then play it using an exported PDF. ***Theme: "The four evidences of evolution"***

DAW

DAW (Digital Audio Workstation) software programs are environments in which sounds of all kinds can be recorded, manipulated, and combined. They are used for all stages of the production of a song, especially recording, mixing, and mastering. At the core of any DAW is a horizontal timeline that keeps track of the elapsed time of the music, and a series of vertically stacked tracks that can play simultaneously, each representing an instrument or sound.
When we hit play on a track, a "virtual playback head" (which is essentially a vertical cursor on the screen), reads all the sounds it encounters in the tracks while scrolling from left to right. In addition, there is a mixer that allows us to adjust parameters such as the volume and pan of the various tracks we are handling.

DAWs usually handle both audio clips (sound files) and MIDI clips (music files that give instructions to the computer on what notes to play and how to play them). These MIDI clips are played by any virtual instrument that we get to choose. The DAW allows us to apply effects of all kinds to our tracks and manage their parameters. These effects include delay, reverb, filters, etc. A DAW can also include virtual instruments and effects by using external plugins such as the VST or the Audio Unit (AU).

We can save our work as a project or export a final audio file (WAV or MP3). In the former case, we can reopen it to work on it again. In the latter, while we have a file that we can distribute or publish, it is impossible to continue working on it after we export it.
Cubase, ***Pro Tools***, ***Ableton Live***, ***Logic Pro***, and ***Reaper*** are widely used DAWs.

.download a DAW software program (e.g., Reaper), open the software, and look for where the DAW is similar to a physical mixer or some other music equipment you know. Mark everything down on a screenshot of the DAW you have chosen

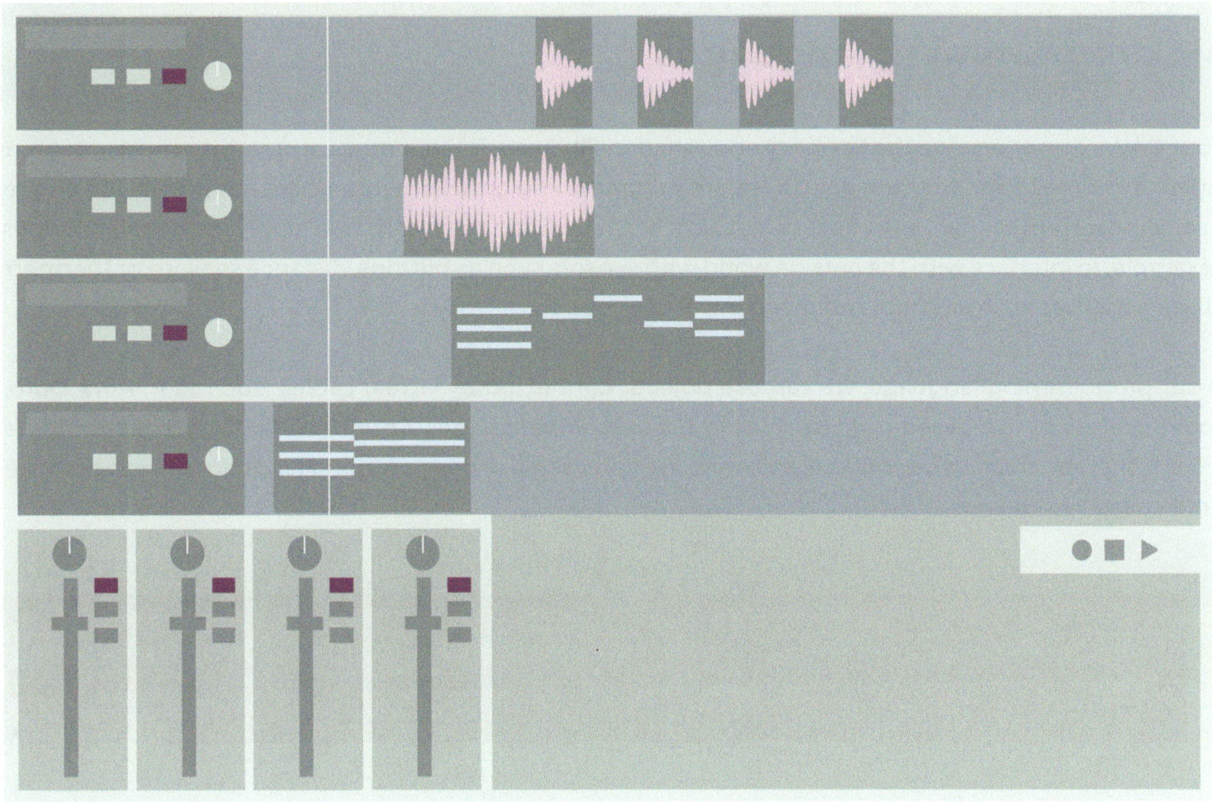

VST and AU

VSTs (Virtual Studio Technology) and **AUs** (Audio Unit) are plugins, meaning they are additional components that integrate into our DAW software. They can be virtual instruments (synthesizers of all kinds, samplers, etc.) or effects that process the sound or MIDI notes.

VSTs and AUs need to comply with programming and audio standards so that they can be supported and opened by different DAWs, and even some music programming languages such as Max (Max/MSP/Jitter). Some plugins are free, while other commercial ones can be found at different price ranges, depending on the plugins' functionality and popularity.

.download a free VST synthesizer of your choice and make a 40-second micro-composition using only that newly acquired synthesizer. Play, at most, four notes of your choice that you can repeat as many times as you like. Experiment with the various timbres you can create from the synthesizer. ***Theme: "Leaves of an oak tree"***

.download a free VST effect of your choice and make a 40-second micro-composition, applying only that effect to a recording of your voice. ***Theme: "On saturn"***

Music programming languages

When our DAWs do not provide the flexibility and functionality to satisfy our musical creativity, music programming languages can come in and save the day. These are programming environments where it is possible to create, from scratch or almost from scratch, any effect or instrument that we can think of. These highly versatile languages allow us, for example, to interface with the outside world with sensors such as buttons, distance sensors, or thermometers, or to utilize actuators such as lights and mechanical devices such as robots.

Within our programming language, we can use objects, connected by virtual cables (such as in ***Pure Data, Max, VCV Rack***), or lines of text-based code (such as in ***Csound, Supercollider, ChucK, SonicPi***), to issue computational instructions, thereby creating our musical software. We can even use programming languages in live performances in a genre called live coding.

Jonny Greenwood Max/MSP ~ pure data organelle ~ mark fell max msp ~ tidal cycles live coding ~ Miller Puckette ~ Autechre ~ Christian Fennesz

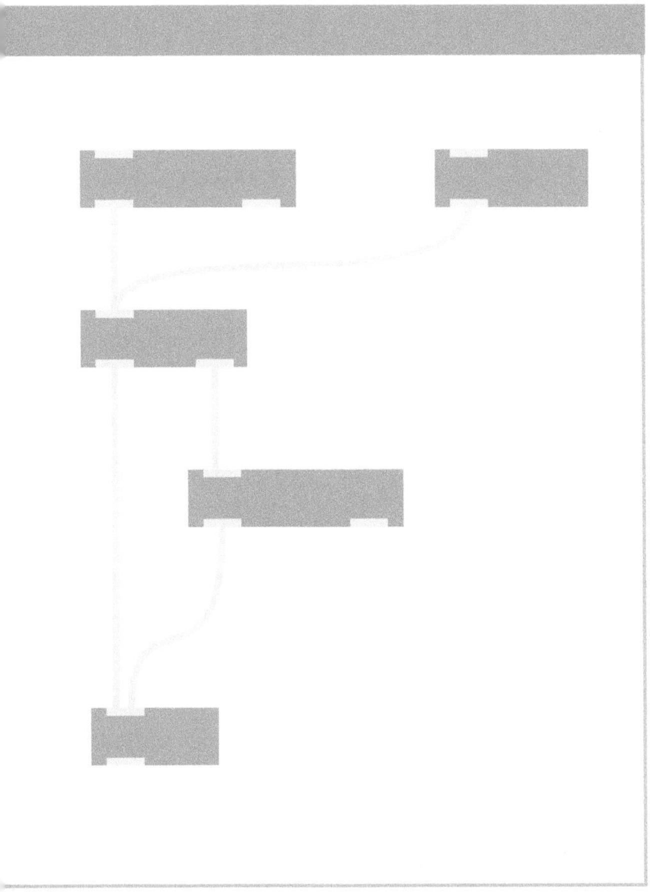

```
instr 1        ;additive synthesis
;p4 = amplitude
;p5 = frequency
;p6 = tab function
;p7 = phase
;p8 = stereo position
;p9 = attack
;ipt = 10 ; tremolo depth
;kfreq        randi ipt, 4
;kcps = kfreq +ipt+2
;atremolo  oscili 1000, kcps, p6

ipt = 2000
atremolo   oscili ipt,5,2        ; generate control
message
;kinviluppoexpseg
.001,p3/2*p9+.01,1,.04,.3,p3 -.05-p3/2*p9,.001
;generate amplitude envelope

kinviluppo expseg
.001,p3/3*p9+.01,1,.04,.7,p3/3,.7,p3-.05-p3/3-
p3/3*p9,.001

asuono       oscili (p4+atremolo)*kinvilup-
po,p5,p6,p7 ;generate sound
             outs          asuono*(1-p8), asuo-
no*p8
             endin
```

WHAT YOU CAN DO WITH ELECTRONIC MUSIC

This next section discusses the endless kinds of things you can do with electronic music, both from an academic and non-academic perspective. This section will briefly highlight some of the "new" possibilities that electronic music can offer us. We use the word "new" a bit loosely and not in a historical context since the concepts of electronic music go back more than a century. However, compared to the traditional methods employed by Western music composers, we are still sonic explorers, complementing and broadening the way music is made through traditional and electronic methods.

Production

When we talk about music production today, we define it as the complete realization of a composition, from inception to the finalization of the piece's audio waveform. We can divide the process of production into five distinct stages.

Composition is the stage where the parts of the piece are conceived and written. This can be done in traditional or graphic notation, on paper, or within a music notation software program. Usually, the writing of the piece is preceded by some research and listening, in order to gather all the elements and information necessary for developing the idea. The writing may lead to precise and detailed sheet music or a series of less specific musical ideas that will need to be developed later in subsequent stages. The former occurs most frequently in contemporary classical music composition, and the latter in contemporary, non-classical music. This vast category of contemporary non-classical music includes pop, rock, dance, hip-hop, etc.

Recording is the stage where the various instruments are recorded, whether acoustic, electric, or electronic (programming or live recording). A basic mix of the tracks occurs at this stage.

Arrangement is the stage where we choose the best takes (i.e., the recordings of the same part that came out the best), decide on how to layer the parts together, and create the structure of the song by deciding what parts happen in what order. You can also create and integrate additional electronic parts to complement the recorded sounds. This stage is, therefore, very rich in decision making moments. In some genres, several of these decisions are made before the recording process. For example, in contemporary classical music, composers and arrangers usually have decided on the structure, textures, and the inclusion of any electronic parts or effects before the recording stage. However, in other genres, many of these decisions are made during or after the recording process.

Mixing is the stage where the various instruments' levels and their position in space are specified, which, as we shall see in the spatialization chapter, page 153, can either be a simple placement in the left-right stereo field or in the complex, three-dimensional space. In this stage, various audio effects that are not musically structural, such as reverberation, compression, or equalization, can be used to "color" sounds.

Mastering is the last stage where the piece's waveform is finalized, aiming to make it easily usable in whatever scenario in which it is played. We use audio processors such as compressors, equalizers, and limiters, to accomplish this task, while trying not to affect any musical or artistic aspects of the piece or the general balance of levels between the audio tracks. We are only trying to affect the final waveform's "playability." In a nutshell, the job of the mastering engineer is to optimize the piece so that it sounds good no matter how the music is experienced—whether it is played back on headphones from a vinyl record or played back through studio monitors from an online streaming service.

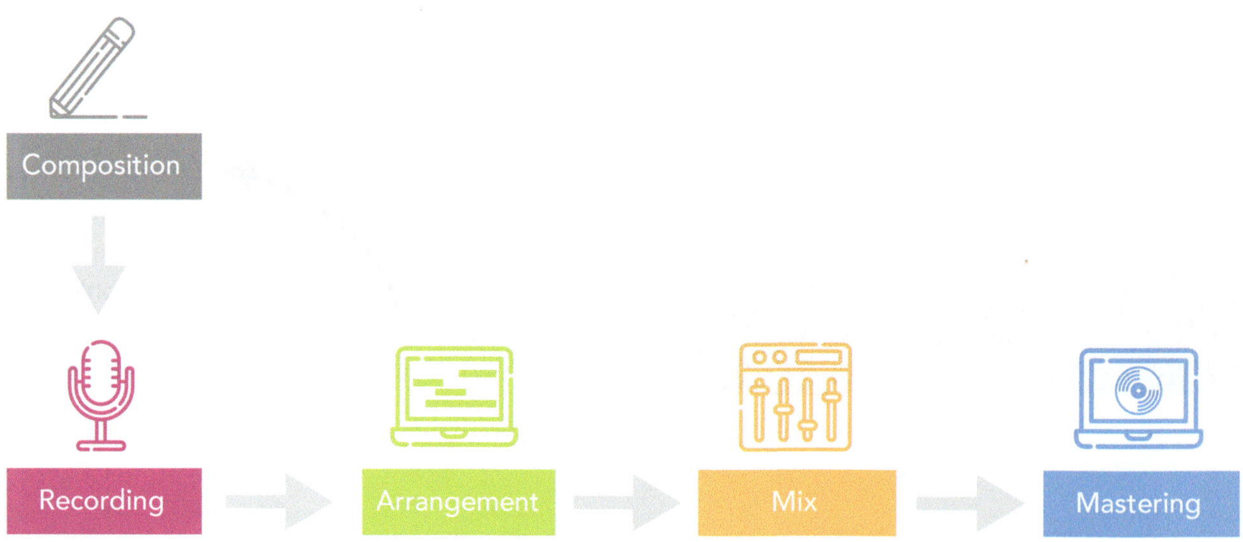

Performance

There are a variety of implementation and performance possibilities that take advantage of electronics. The integration of electronics can range from a minimal trifle to a significant structural contribution, with every kind of nuance in between these extremes.

DJ set is a type of performance where the disc jockey (DJ) plays back recorded tracks and controls the transitions between tracks so that there is no break between them. Traditionally, the tracks have been played from vinyl records. Today, we can find entirely digital workflows, where the songs are files that are played on a computer and the DJs interact with controller devices. Usually, DJ sets are designed to make people dance in particular settings (discos or clubs), so the types of music that may be suitable for this purpose include ***EDM*** (***electronic dance music***), techno, house, swing, or Latin.

DJ SET

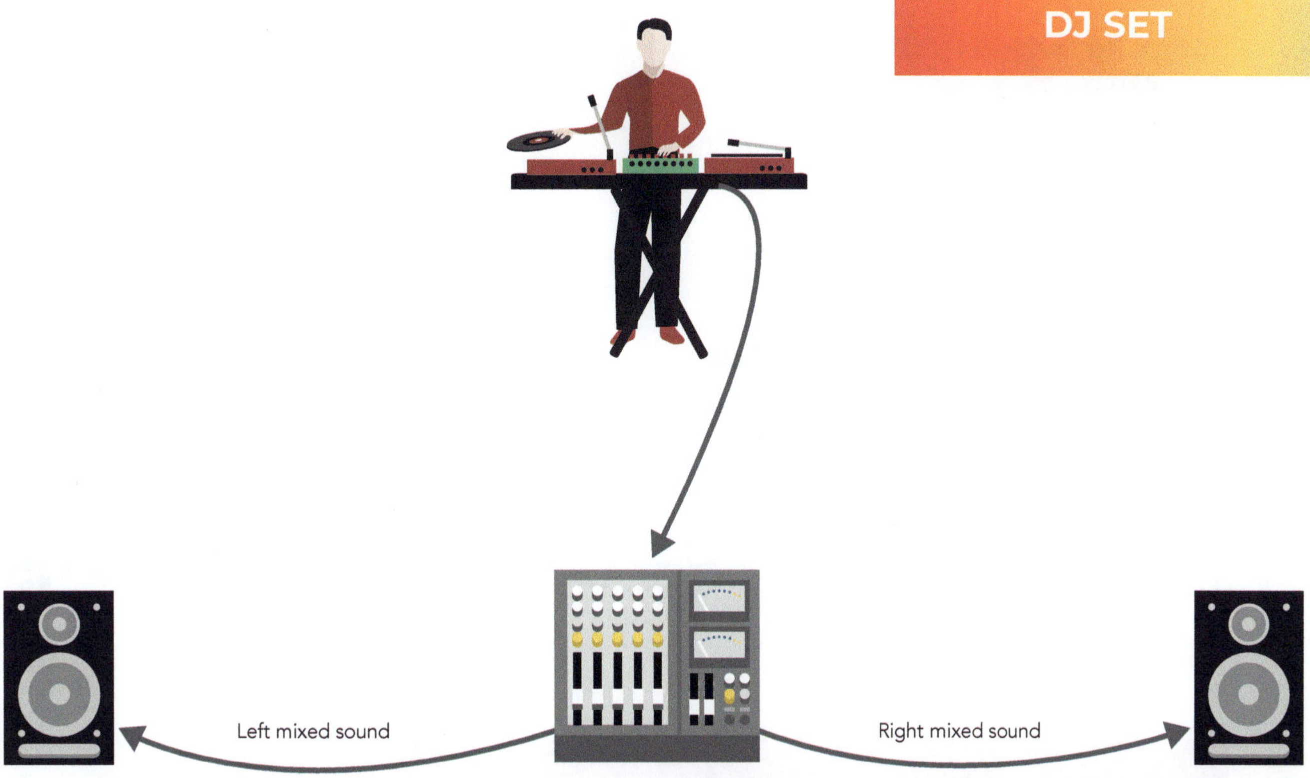

Fourtet dj-set ~ Jeff Mills dj-set

Acousmatic Music is a style of music that does not involve live performers, but rather focuses on sound in its most physical nature. Thus, often in acousmatic concerts, there is no light and the sound is played into the room through multiphonic spatialization systems involving more than two speakers and dynamic spatial placement of the various sounds of the composition.

ACOUSMATIC MUSIC

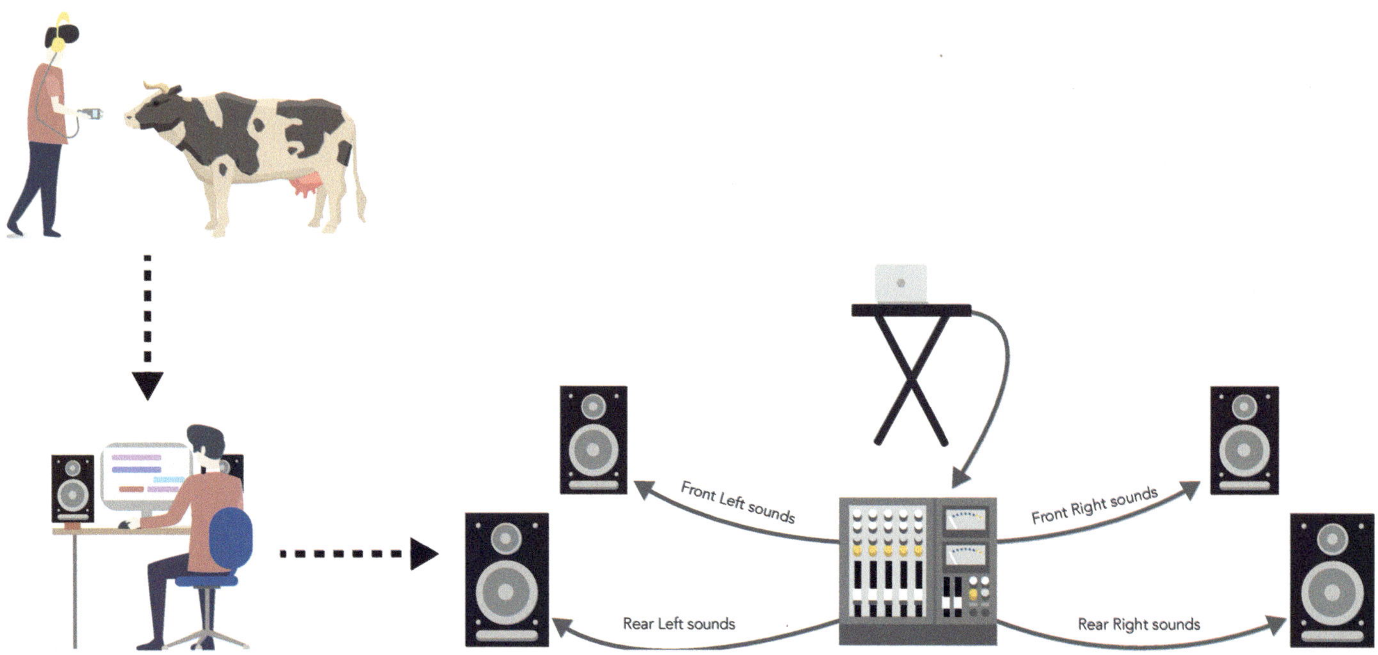

Pierre Schaeffer ~ GRM Parigi ~ Bernard Parmegiani

Live electronics: In these pieces, a sound is processed in real-time. This practice is used across broad styles of music that span contemporary classical, jazz, and popular music. This kind of musical performance has existed—and has steadily evolved—since the dawn of electronic music. There was a boom of live electronic musicians and performances beginning in the late 1980s due to the advent of increasingly lightweight, stable, and powerful computers.

LIVE ELECTRONICS

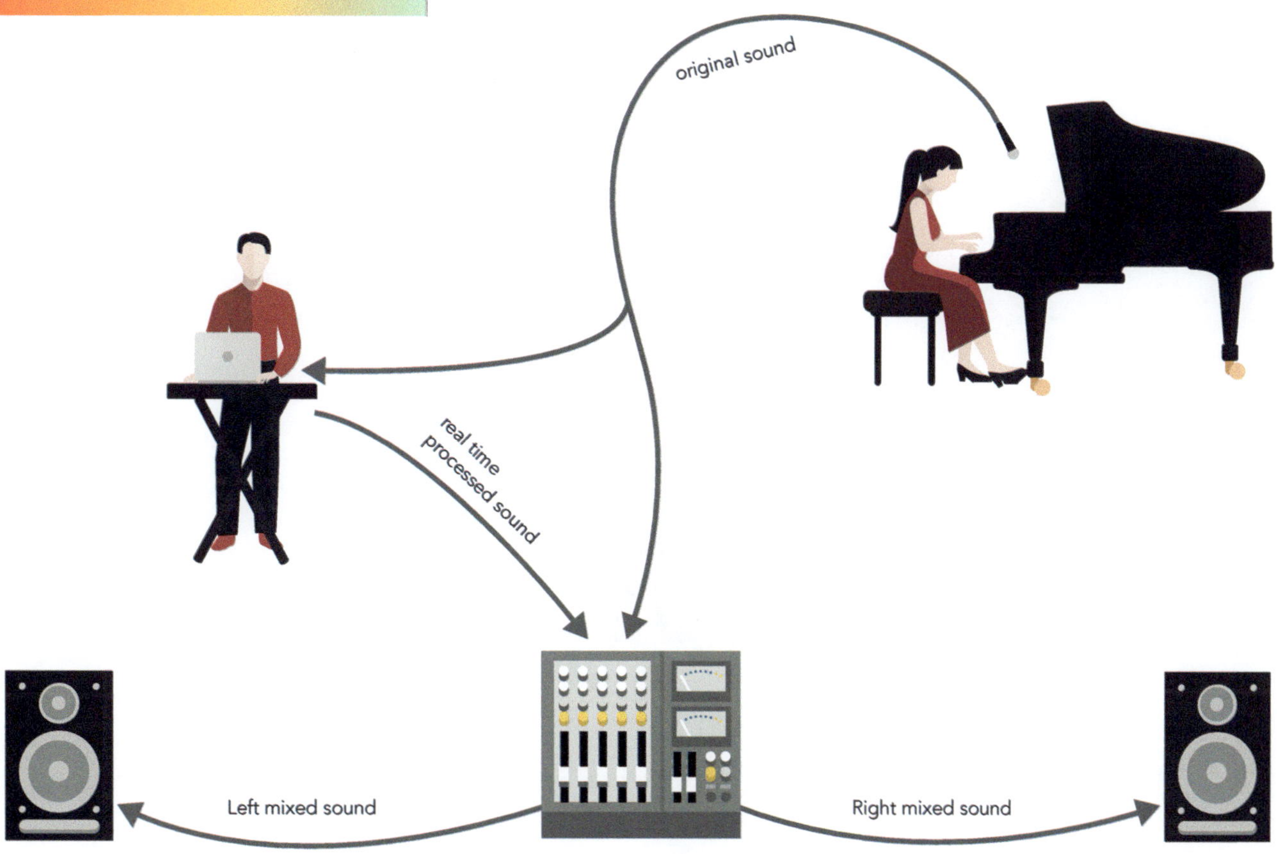

Kaija Saariaho ~ Repòns Pierre Boulez ~ Nicoletta Andreuccetti Notturno Sole ~ Luigi Nono ~ Samuele Strufaldi Tommaso Rosati

A **liveset** is a generic performance in which acoustic, electric, electronic, or mixed instruments can be integrated in any combination. In this kind of concert, electronics are often used to produce live sounds (e.g. sound synthesis). There may also be live electronics components that act upon acoustic, electric, or even electronic instruments. Virtually all performances of present-day non-classical music contain livesets, whether it be pop, dance, hip-hop, trap, or rock music.

LIVESET

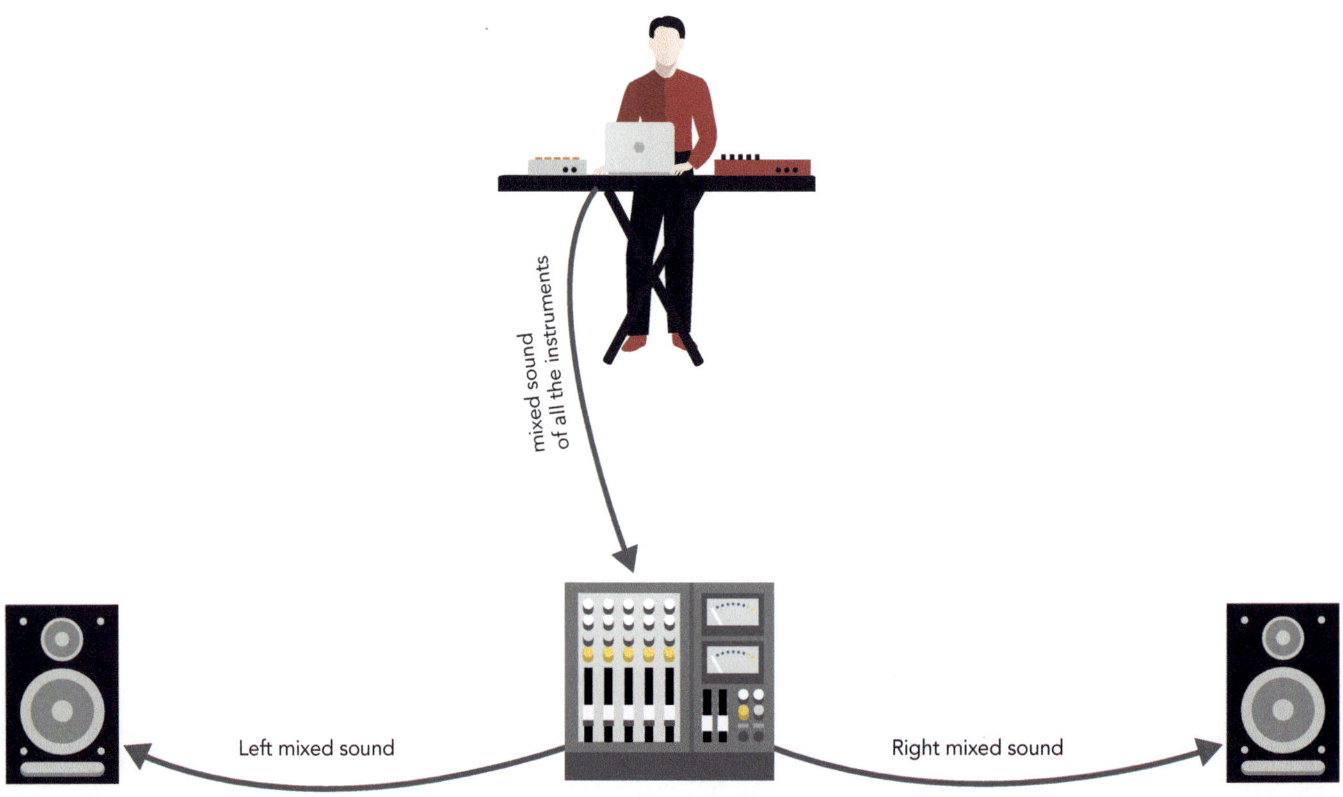

Apparat band ~ Jon Hopkins live ~ Bon Iver live ~ Imogen Heap live ~ St Vincent live ~ Tycho live ~ 7 Live Set Tips from Billie Eilish's Drummer

ACOUSTIC AND PSYCHO-ACOUSTIC

SOUND PRODUCTION AND PROPAGATION

Sound (from the Latin ***sonum***) is the pressure vibration that originates from an oscillating body that travels through the air to reach our ears. Our ears collect these vibrations, and our auditory system, along with our brain, then interprets them as sounds.

In order to exist, a sound needs:

- **a source**, a physical body that creates vibrations, such as a drum
- **an elastic medium**, a fluid, solid, or gas that pressure waves travel through, such as air
- our **auditory system**, a human sensory system that acts as a transducer, converting pressure waves into electrical signals that our brains process

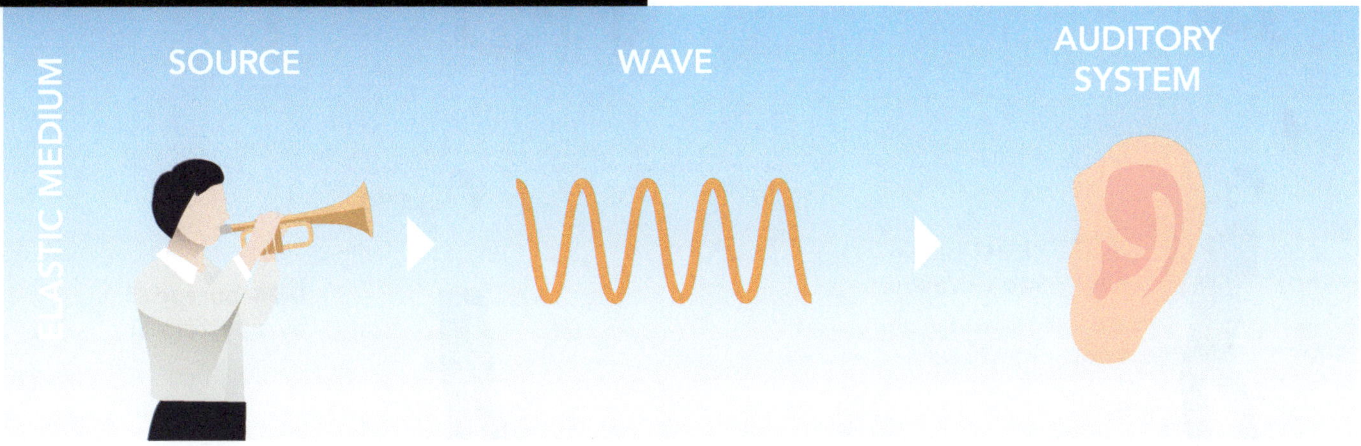

The **elastic medium**, whether it is a gas (like air), a liquid, or a solid, is made up of many molecules that are close together. As the **vibrating body** oscillates, it first pushes the molecules that are closely adjacent to the body closer together causing compression. Compressions exhibit higher pressures. Since it is an elastic medium, the molecules then return to their original position. Next the vibrating body pulls on the molecules, causing the molecules to spread apart into a state of rarefaction, before returning to the original state. Rarefactions are areas of lower pressure. These steps happen cyclically, creating a sound wave. When the vibrations stop, then we return to silence.

Sound energy is thus a mechanical process that begins at the vibrating source and propagates as sound waves through an elastic medium toward the listener.

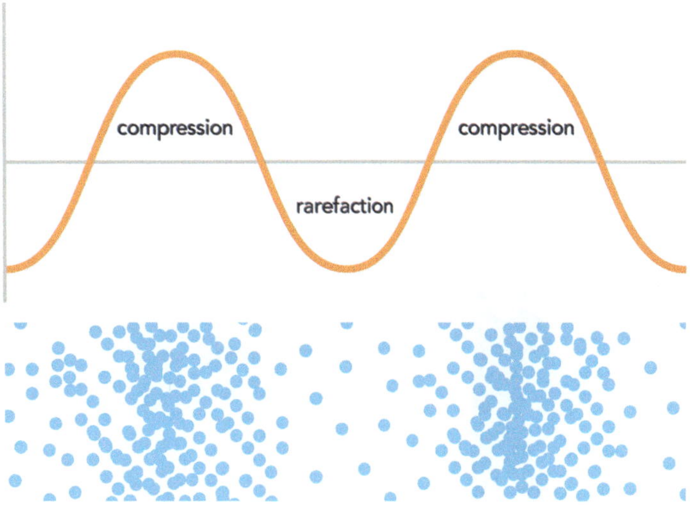

The **wave** is often represented as a graph depicting pressure, describing what happens as the pressure variations travel through the air. When the pressure rises above the equilibrium, the molecules are in a state of compression. On the other hand, when the pressure falls below the line of the equilibrium, the molecules are in a state of rarefaction. It is important to note that the equilibrium is usually atmospheric pressure. For convenience, we can utilize an offset and consider the equilibrium as zero pressure.

The source

The source, as mentioned earlier, is a vibrating body that cyclically compresses and rarefies the molecules of the elastic medium. For example, in air, these compressions come in the form of higher pressures that stem from the air displaced by the vibrating body. We will discuss later how the speed at which the pressure cycles from compression to rarefaction relate to frequency; however, you might already know that it must produce at least 20 cycles per second in order for us to hear it. Not only can musical instruments be sources of sound waves, but the flapping of a mosquito's wing, the beating of a hammer on an anvil, and the ringing of a bell on a bike can all also act as sound sources.

Speed of sound

As stated earlier, an elastic medium capable of propagating sound is necessary. If the medium is not elastic, then there can be no sound since the molecules cannot move. In other words, if we cannot transmit the vibration through a medium, then the energy stops at the source and cannot reach the listener. For this reason, there is no sound that travels in a vacuum.

One key property that can change from one elastic medium to the next is the speed of propagation. Beware that the speed of sound does not depend on how loud a drum is played or what pitch is played on the flute. Instead, the speed of sound depends only on the properties of the medium that the musical instrument plays in. The three main factors of the medium that affect the speed are its density, temperature, and elasticity.

The denser the medium, the slower the speed of sound will be because the molecules are more massive. Regarding temperature, we know from chemistry that temperature is related to the amount of kinetic energy of the molecules. Since the molecules are more active with higher temperature, collisions that propagate a wave occur more quickly, resulting in a faster speed of sound. The greater the elasticity, the faster the speed of sound. Solids are more elastic than liquids, and liquids are more elastic than gasses. This generally explains why the speed of sound is faster in water than it is in air.

For example, in air at 20° C (~68° F), the speed of sound is 343 meters per second (1,125 ft/s), while in 20° C water, the speed of sound is 1,480 meters per second (4,855 ft/s).

temperature

	0°C - 32°F	20°C - 68°F	80°C - 176°F
GAS			
air	331	343	375
helium	972	1007	1105
LIQUIDS			
water	1403	1481	1555
SOLIDS			
iron	*	4910	*

* = differences in solids at temperature changes are negligible

density

elasticity

.plunge your ears into a swimming pool or a tub full of water and try listening to the sound of a metal object slammed by one of your friends on the edge of the pool farthest from you. It will sound much closer to you than it is. Why?

SOUND REPRESEN-TATION

As we have said, the wave we see graphed represents what happens to the molecules within the elastic medium. It shows a representation of the compressions and rarefactions caused by a vibrating body. Now we will analyze the wave to highlight a whole set of properties that will allow us to say more about sound.

Period

All the waves we have represented so far are exceptional because they have the characteristic of cyclically repeating themselves. As we will see in a moment, not all waves are like this, but for now, let's focus on this special case.

The complete oscillation of the wave, that repeats over and over again, from a point in a repetition to the same point in the next repetition, is called a **cycle**. We define **period**, usually measured in milliseconds, as the time it takes for the wave to complete one cycle. A period is represented by the variable T. The period can also be defined as dividing 1 by the frequency of our cyclical wave. We will revisit this relationship when we discuss frequency.

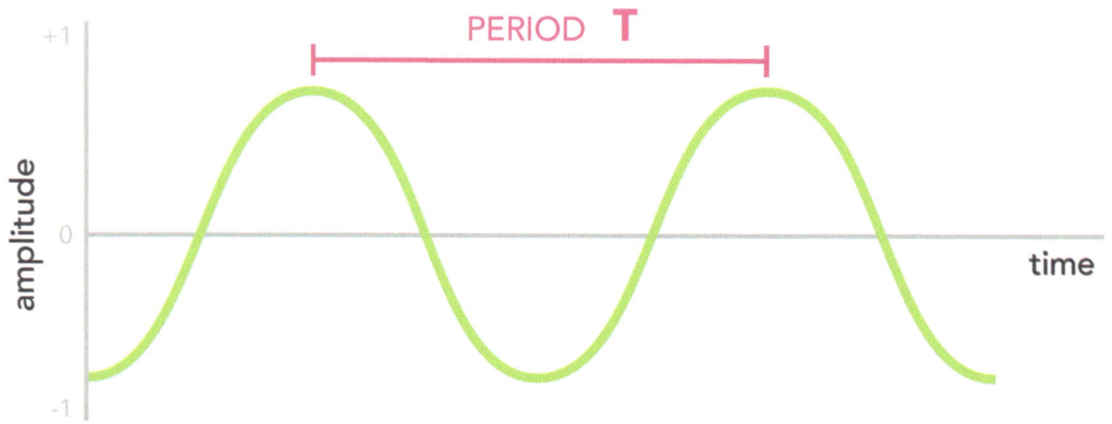

$$T = \frac{1}{f}$$

period — represents 1 second of time — wave frequency

Wavelength

If I visualize a wave propagating in front of my eyes and then freeze the motion, I will see that a cycle occupies a specific length of space. How long this wave is can be defined as the **wavelength** and is represented by the variable λ (***lambda***). Wavelength is the length or distance that one cycle of a wave occupies in a space. It is usually measured in units that represent distances, such as meters, and it is dependent on the speed of sound and the wave frequency. Since the speed of sound varies depending on the elastic medium, this length that the wave occupies can also vary. If the speed of sound is slow, then the length is smaller than if the speed of sound were fast.

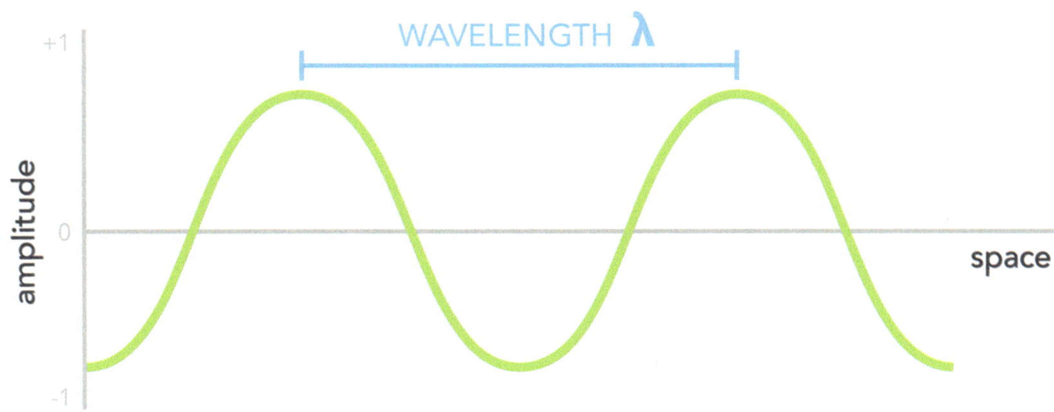

wavelength $$\lambda = \frac{v}{f}$$ speed of sound in the given elastic medium; wave frequency

Periodic wave - Aperiodic wave

If a wave consists of exact copies of a cycle that repeats over and over again, it is called a **periodic wave**. In other words the period, that we discussed above is replicated. When listening, the periodic wave is a pitched sound that can be used in a melody, for example. Not all periodic waves are the same though, as there are simple patterns that repeat and there are very complex patterns that can also repeat. So far, all we have seen in this chapter are simple sine waves.

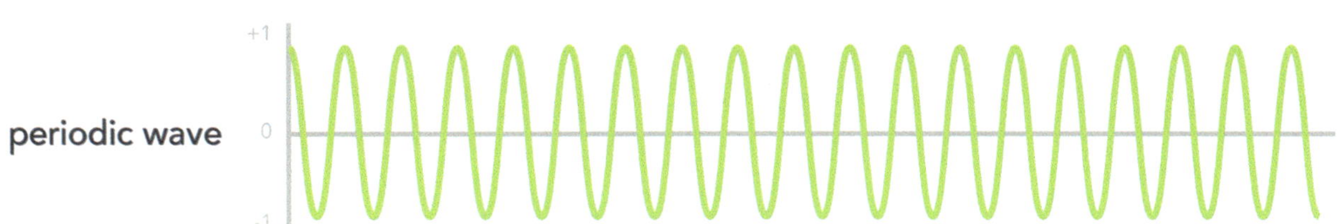

A wave is an **aperiodic wave** if there are no repeating segments or recognizable cycles. As nothing repeats, there is no period, thus the term aperiodic. This type of wave is often produced by instruments such as a snare drum or an orchestra cymbal. The most prominent aperiodic wave is called ***white noise*** (a totally random signal), and, as we shall see later, it (spoiler alert!) contains all frequencies within the sound itself.

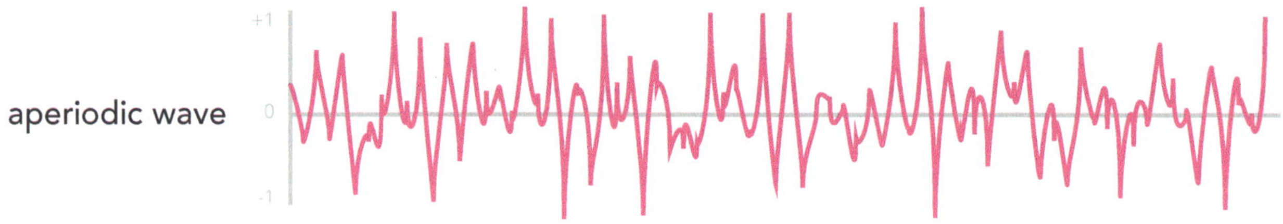

Practically, most instruments are non-ideal and perfect periodicity is very difficult to achieve, particularly with the time-varying nature of musical notes. We can approximate small portions of the sound to be approximately periodic in pitched instruments, whereas in unpitched instruments, even small portions of the sound will be aperiodic. Thus, instruments like the violin and French horn create approximate periodic waves, while cymbals and snare drums do not.

.generate a sine wave, at a frequency of your choice, and white noise. Cut small fragments of the two waves and create an interesting rhythm by using only these fragments, repeating patterns if you desired. Duration 20 seconds

Frequency

The pitch of that D on the violin, the strange scale you have to play in unison with your bandmate, the impossible extension of *Demetrio Stratos*' voice, the out-of-tune string on your new 5-string bass—these are aspects of music that have to do with frequency.

Frequency is the wave property that is directly related to the pitch of the notes that we play on our instruments. In the branch of physics known as acoustics, frequency is defined as the number of times a wave cycle occurs in one second and is expressed in hertz (Hz). For example, 440 Hz refers to 440 oscillations or cycles per second and is equivalent to the note A4 (middle octave A note).

Since frequency represents the number of cycles that happen in one second, we can infer that frequency is the reciprocal of period, expressed mathematically as $\mathbf{f = 1 / T}$.
Of course, with a little algebra, we see that that the period is the reciprocal of the frequency: $\mathbf{T = 1 / f}$.

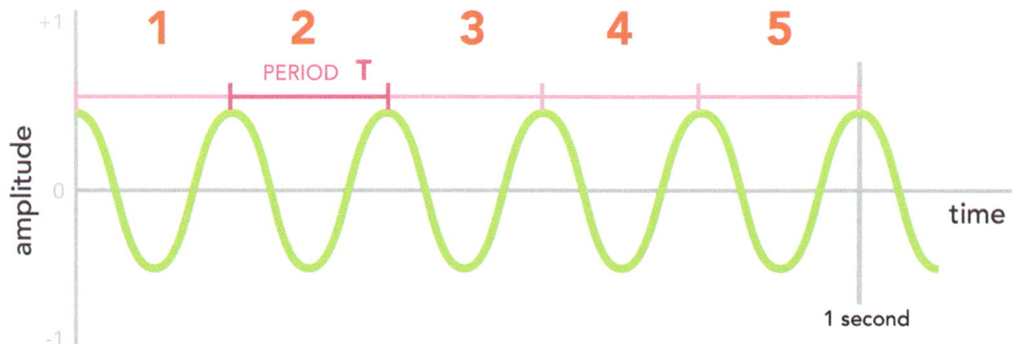

frequency $f = \dfrac{1}{T}$ (1 stands for one second of time; T wave period)

Humans do not perceive the entire range of possible frequencies but only a portion: from 20 Hz to 20,000 Hz. Frequencies below this audible range are known as infrasound and frequencies above are called ultrasound. Other animals have different ranges and can, for example, perceive what to us are infrasonic or ultrasonic. But for the sounds and music that we hear on a daily basis, the frequencies that we are interact with are between 20 Hz and 20,000 Hz.

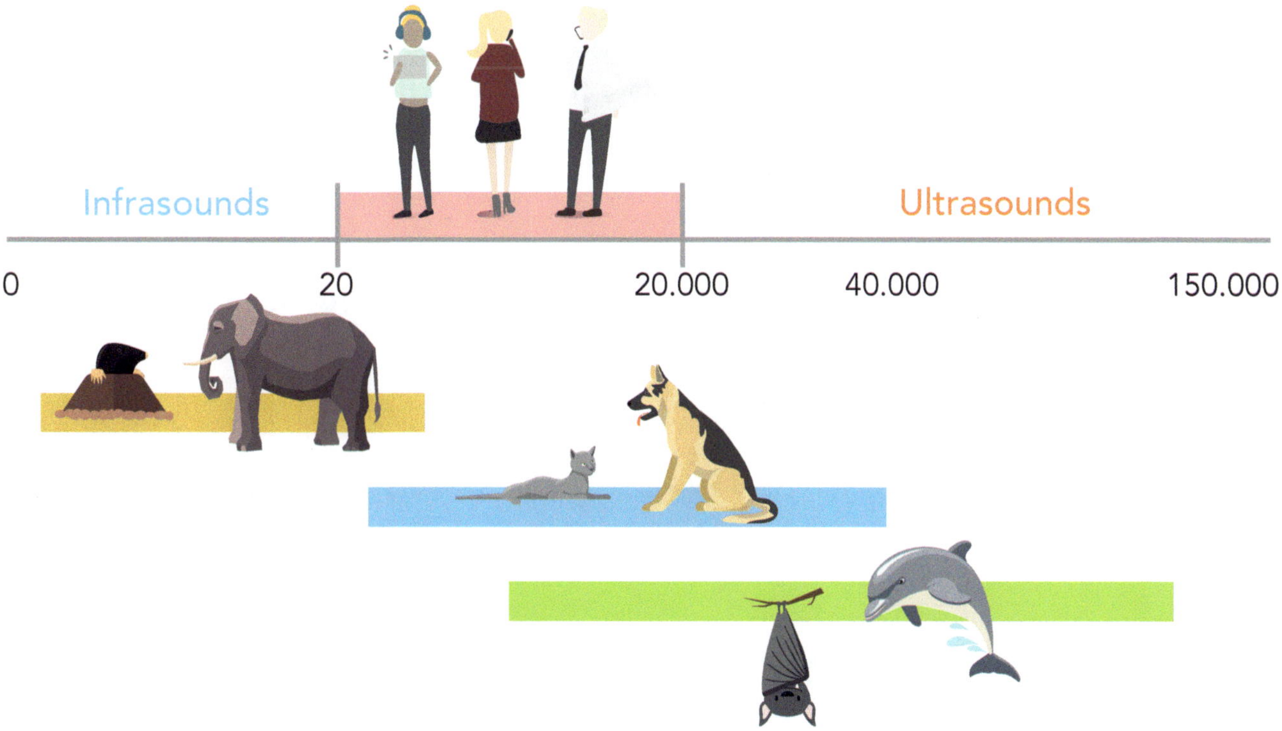

Every instrument we know has a frequency range that limits it to a certain of range of possible notes. Some instruments, such as the double bass or bassoon, primarily play in the low frequency range (40-600 Hz), while others, like the violin or piccolo flute, are optimized for high frequencies (200-5000 Hz).

However, we notice something strange when we investigate the relationship of frequencies with the notes that we perceive and associate them with.

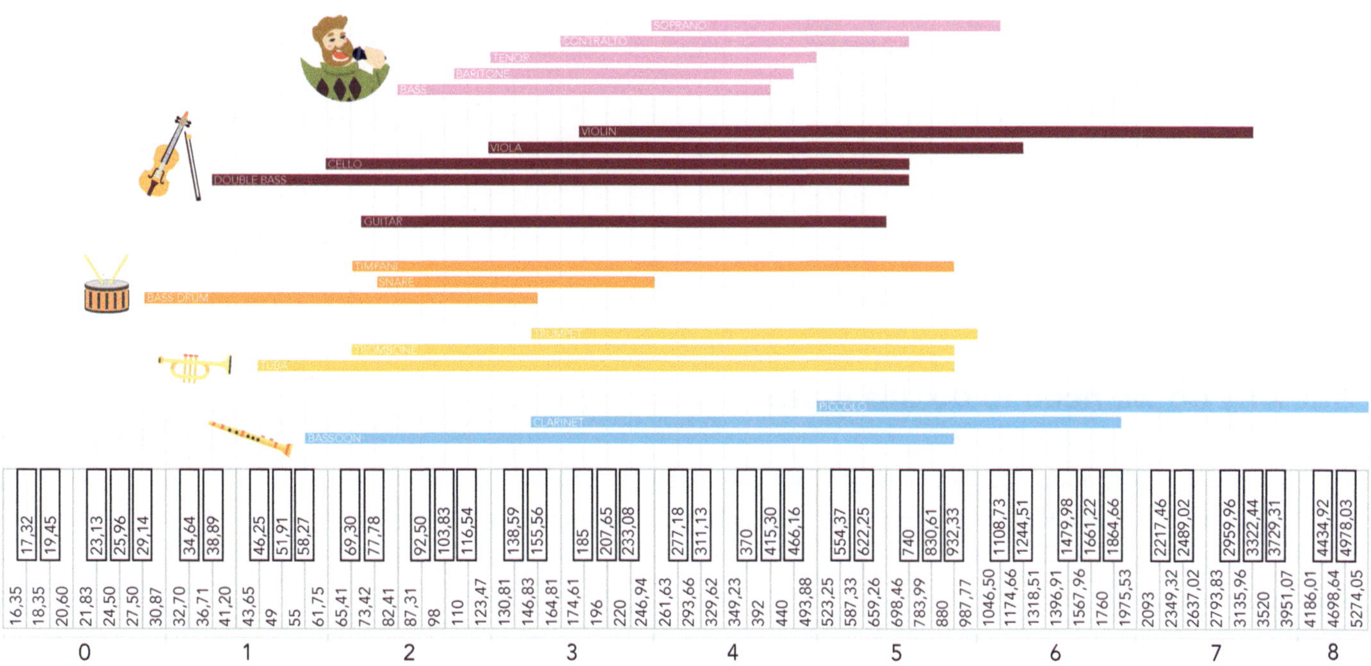

When we form a chromatic scale—a sequence of 12 rising notes each separated by a semitone (C, C#, D, D#, E, F...)—we perceive each semitone to be equal in size. In other words, we consider the distance between C and C# to be the same as G and G# or even C and C# in another octave. However, if we look at look at the difference in frequency (in hertz) between these same notes, rather than the interval, we find that these differences in frequency are not the same. Each semitone actually gets wider, in hertz, the higher we go up the musical scale.

For example, let's look at the interval of an octave. The distance between C1 and C2 is 32.7 Hz, thus, we can say that the octave measures 32.7 Hz. Now let's look at a higher octave, from C6 to C7. Here the distance is 1046.5 Hz, making this octave much bigger. We may wonder in this case then, is the octave 32.7 Hz or 1046.5 Hz? What we realize is that the width of an octave is variable.

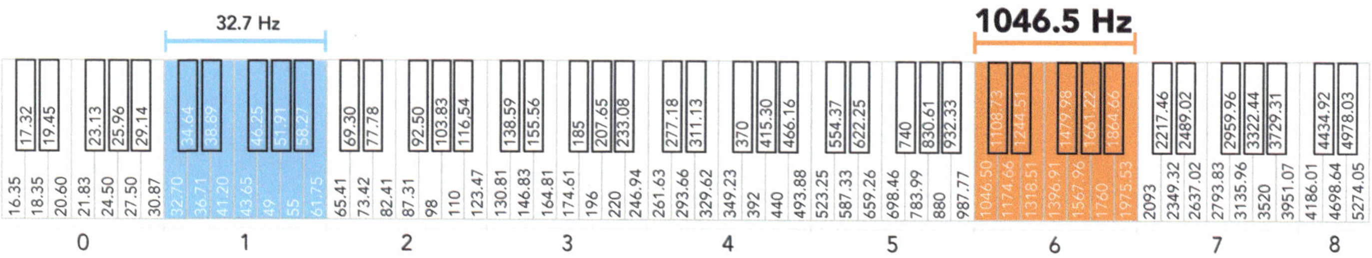

The measure of an octave, or any other musical interval, grows as frequency increases. Practically, the steps between notes that we perceive to be all the same actually correspond to frequency values, in hertz, that grow larger and larger. They follow an exponential trend (larger and larger steps) rather than a linear trend (steps that are all the same).

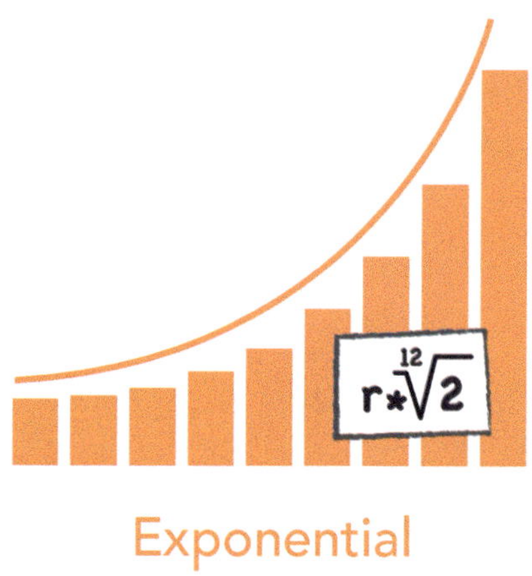

But why do we need to do this math?

Because our auditory apparatus, and many of our other senses, do not respond linearly to stimuli but rather in a logarithmic manner. In logarithmic relationships, the steps at low frequences are large and decrease in size with each successive step, opposite of an exponential trend.

Let's consider the sense of smell as an example. With a single rose in front of me, my sense of smell will perceive an intense rose smell. Now, if I place a second (identical) rose next to the first one, how much more intense will smell be? The result is that we will not perceive twice the intensity of the original rose, but rather we will perceive a little more, but not twice, the intensity of the scent. If we then have three roses, there will again by a more intense scent, but the difference in intensity between the second and third rose will be less than the difference between the first and second rose. The perception of frequencies (and amplitudes, as we shall see) works in a similar way.

If I want to perceive equal steps in frequency, we cannot use equal frequency jumps between notes since our ears perceive frequencies generally logarithmically. Thus, to compensate for our logarithmic perception, this chromatic scale, mentioned earlier, will need to be constructed using an exponential relationship.

So **to summarize**: I construct a scale that is exponential (with larger and larger frequency steps) to compensate for the logarithmic way our hearing works in order to perceive notes with a linear pattern (with steps that are all perceived the same).

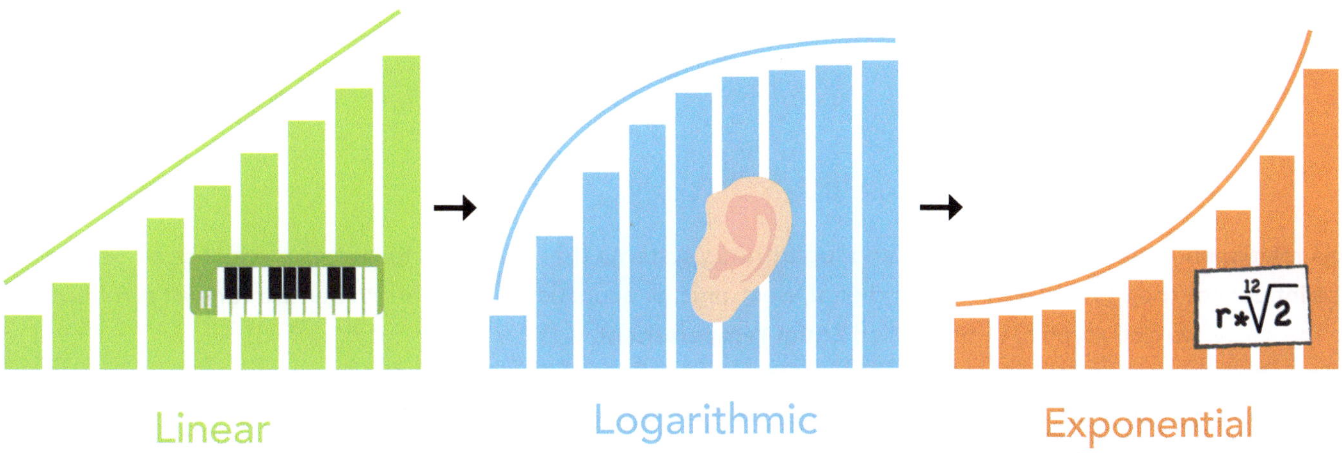

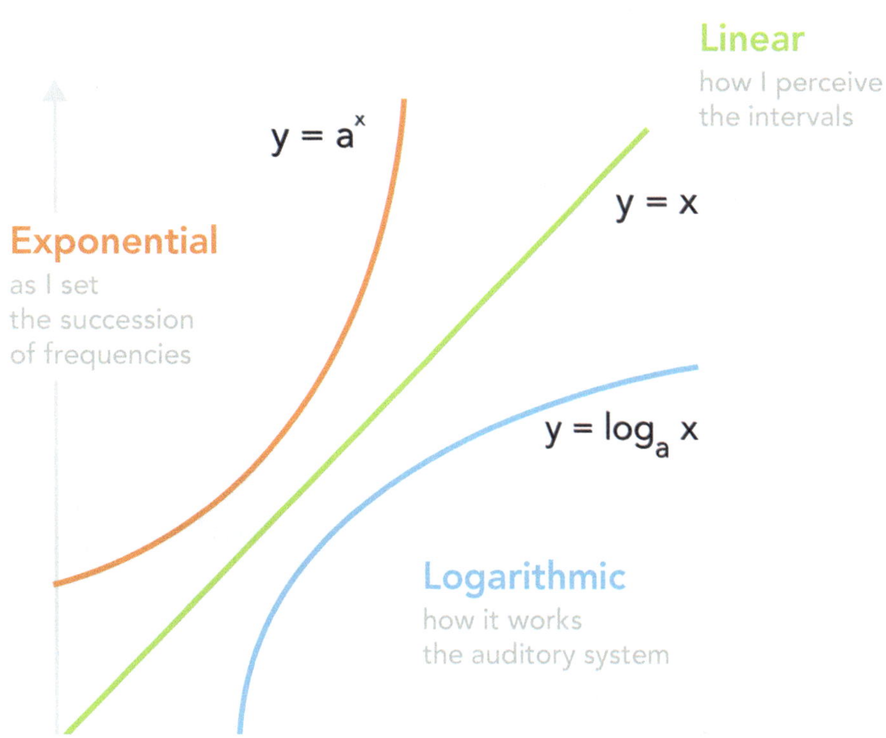

These are the graphical representations of the exponential, linear, and logarithmic functions.

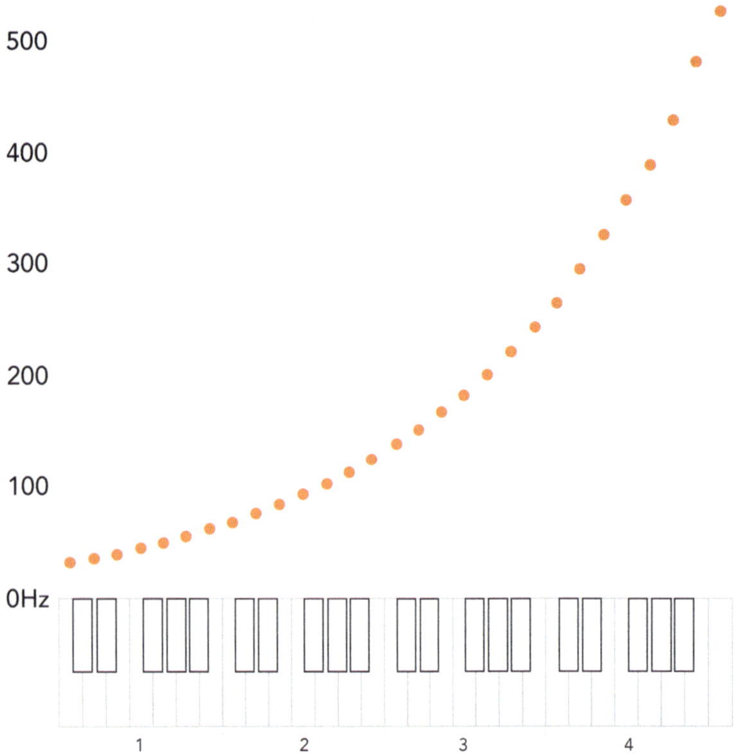

So, if I take the keys of a piano and graph their corresponding frequency (Hz) values, I will notice that the curve is not linear like the layout of the keyboard, but rather exponential in nature.

This relationship between exponential and logarithmic systems that allows us to perceive equal-sized semitones also influences the the way we tune our digital, electronic, or acoustic instruments. When we tune all semitones to be the same, we get a type of tuning called **Equal Temperament**.

The mathematical calculations needed for equal temperament are computationally hard to do by hand, so even though the concept has been known for a long time, the calculations needed for the precise frequencies are relatively recent. Historically, there were approximations with logarithms, square roots, and exponentials, but we now have the ability to precisely calculate all the frequencies with calculators.

Since the shape of acoustic musical instruments and, in particular, the vibrating parts of them (strings, organ pipes, metal bars of the vibraphone, etc.) are direct expressions of the note they are supposed to play, it becomes clear why the frets of a guitar are not all the same distance apart or the length of the organ pipes are not all the same from one semitone to the next. These relationships are exponential, rather than linear.

How is the frequency of a note calculated?

The ratio between the frequencies of two notes is defined as r. For example, if A4 is 440 Hz, and A3 is 220 Hz, the frequency ratio, r, for these two notes is r=440:220 or 2:1. In equal temperament, we can calculate a specific r_{ET} so that the frequency ratio between two successive semitones is always the same. In this case, r_{ET} is the twelfth root of 2, or approximately 1.05946:1. The twelfth root of two can also be expressed as: $\sqrt[12]{2}$

The number twelve is used because the octave, in western music, consists of 12 semitones; thus, we need to divide the octave into 12 steps. If I want to split my octave differently, as we do in microtonal music, I have the freedom to change the number of steps from 12 to anything I want. For example, if I want to divide the octave into 20 equal parts, I use the ratio of twentieth root of 2 instead.

Back to equal tempered scale, I can calculate the frequency of any note x semitones away from a reference note or base frequency, f, using the following formula:

$$f * r_{ET}^{X} \quad \text{where } r_{ET} = \sqrt[12]{2}$$

EXAMPLE

C1	= 32.7		
C#1	= 32.7 * r		
D1	= 32.7 * r * r	= 32.7 * r^2	
D#1	= 32.7 * r * r * r	= 32.7 * r^3	
E1	= 32.7 * r * r * r * r	= 32.7 * r^4	
...	= ...	= ...	
C2	= 32.7 * r^{12}	= 32.7 * 2	

Note that the octave is made up of 12 semitones, so if I raise a twelfth root of 2 to the twelfth power, then I get simply 2. Thus, for an octave, the higher note is exactly twice the frequency (in hertz) of the lower note.

.create our 1-second sine waves at the following frequencies: 35 Hz, 220 Hz, 440 Hz, 10000 Hz. Generate different pitch sequences and subsequently creatively change the order of the notes during the course of a short 30-second song. Avoid putting the same frequency twice in a track

Amplitude

When your neighbor yells at you to play quieter, when your new amplifier lets you play at incredible volumes, when they shut down your favorite club because the music is too loud, when you are listening to frogs croaking, and when a deafening motorcycle passes by you on these and many other occasions, amplitude plays a vital role in how you experience sound.

First of all, let's define the term: **amplitude**.
Amplitude is the acoustical term for the maximum pressure deviation from zero pressure. Remember that zero pressure is a simplistic way to describe the equilibrium, or atmospheric pressure. In other words, the amplitude represents the largest magnitude of the compression or rarefaction in the elastic medium that my vibrating body produces. Amplitude is a quantifiable parameter that you can measure precisely and scientifically with a pressure sensor.

Dynamics, on the other hand, is the musical term for how loudly we should play. It is expressed on a qualitative scale using words, ranging from ***pianissimo*** to ***fortissimo***, and, unlike amplitude, dynamics are relative to context. If, for example, there is an E marked ***pianissimo*** in your score, you might play it very softly if only one listener is in the room with you. However, if you are playing that same note at La Scala Opera House in Milan for the season premiere, you will probably play that ***pianissimo*** a little louder in order to project it to the 2000 people in the audience. Even at slightly different volumes, both are musically still ***pianissimo*** and not ***forte***.

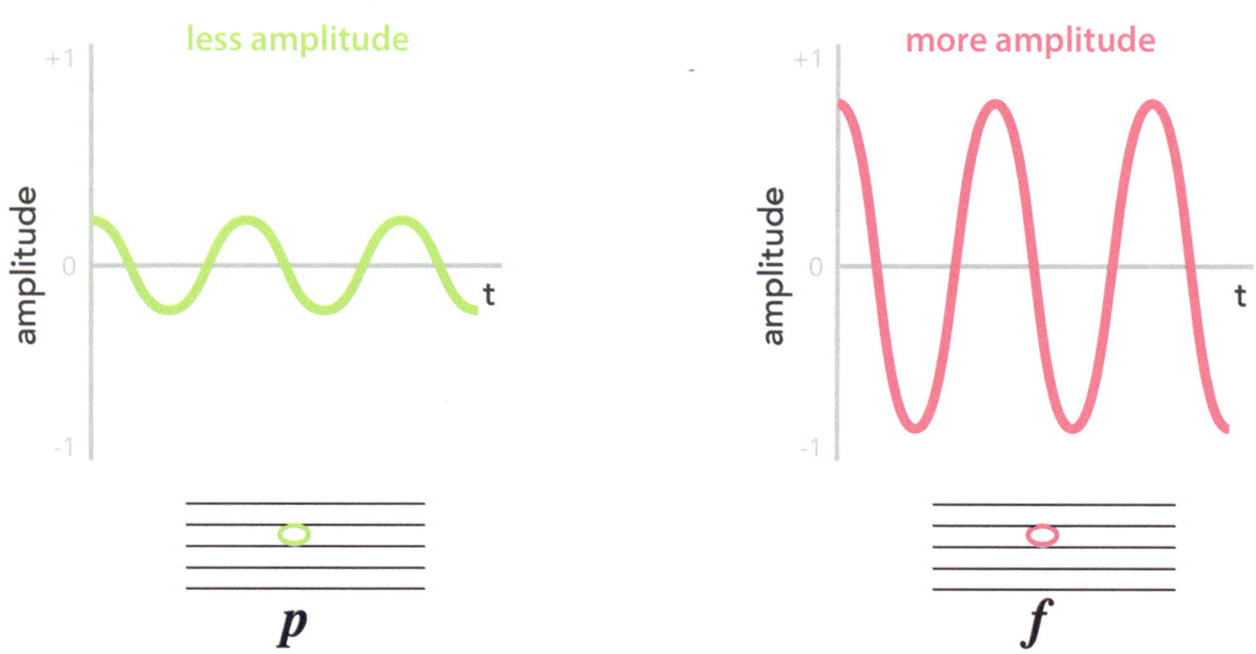

The last term worth clarifying is loudness. **Loudness** refers to our perceived (psychoacoustic) sensation of amplitude, or the amount of air compression-rarefaction. While loudness depends mostly on amplitude, our auditory system also takes cues from pitch and duration to determine how loudly we perceive sound. Volume, on the other hand, is a term that is used in non-technical contexts, that sometimes can refer to amplitude, but can also sometimes refer to loudness. As we turn the volume knob up, we are increasing the measurable amplitude, but also turning it based on our perception of loudness. So we can say that the amplitude (a technical term) of my wave influences the dynamics (a musical term) and the loudness (a psychoacoustic term).

In the graphical representation of a wave, I can see its amplitude by measuring the deviation between the equilibrium line and the maximum peak, whether taken in the positive part (compression) or in the negative part (rarefaction).

There are two ways amplitude can be represented. One method represents the amplitude of a waveform as numbers between -1 and 1. This is what we may see in our DAW, where values that approach 1 (or -1), are louder than values that are close to 0. This scale can also be thought of as voltage values of an analog signal. For example, the value of 0.5 indicates that we are at half the maximum voltage. The other way we represent amplitude is through a unit of measurement called the **decibel (dB)**. Decibels are calculated with a reference, which gives us a meaningful measure of sound that allows us to compare its amplitude to other sounds.

The decibel (abbreviated as dB) is a somewhat peculiar unit of measurement because there are many different varieties. Usually, after the letters "dB," we will find the description of which decibel type (i.e., dBmV, dBu, etc.). In particular, we will discuss two types of decibels: **SPL (sound pressure level)** and **FS (full scale)**. dB SPL is used mainly in the analog domain, and dBFS is used the digital domain, like within audio software. They differ only in one detail, which we will see later. For now, let us first describe how a decibel is calculated and measured.

Pressure in physics is a measure of the force applied to a surface (**F / S**) and is therefore measured in Newton/m^2, or in pascals (Pa).
We can imagine that the pressure a string imparts in the air will be different than the pressure a drum may create in air. We can measure these pressures and start to realize that the string will be heard at a particular loudness, which may be different than the loudness caused by the drum.

Let's try an example. We can measure the pressure exerted by beating a mosquito's wings (one of the weakest audible sounds) at a certain distance. We can also measure the pressure caused by the roar of a jet airplane engine (the loudest sound), also at the same distance. We likely get extremely different values, possibly 0.000025 N/m^2 for the mosquito and 30 N/m^2 for the jet. This huge range of numbers becomes a bit cumbersome to handle; thus, mathematics can help us out by transforming our numbers into something more usable. A logarithm allows us to "squash" this large range and make these numbers easier to use and understand. First, I take the measured pressure (say, that of my cello string) and divide it by the minimum audible pressure (a bit less than that of the mosquito's wings). I then take the logarithm of that result, and multiply that number by 20. Voila! Now I have computed how loud the cello is in dB SPL. The minimum audible pressure, sometimes known as the threshold of hearing, serves as our reference pressure and is 0.000020 Pa, 20 uPa.

measured pressure

$$\mathbf{SPL} = 20\mathbf{log}\left(\frac{p}{p_0}\right)\ \text{dB}$$

reference pressure

dBW

Sound power describes the source, but not how a sound wave travels to the listener. We will see that speaker specification sheets report a sound power level that tells us how much acoustic power comes from the speaker. Sound power level is often shown in **dBW** or L_W.

dB SIL

Sound intensity describes how power is spread out at a distance from the source. For intensity, the further you are from the source, the smaller the intensity. This change has a 1/(distance^2) relationship and is the basis behind the inverse square law. The sound intensity level (in dB) metrics are called **SIL** or L_I.

By using decibels, we get two essential advantages.

1) A **smaller numerical scale** which is more agile to use

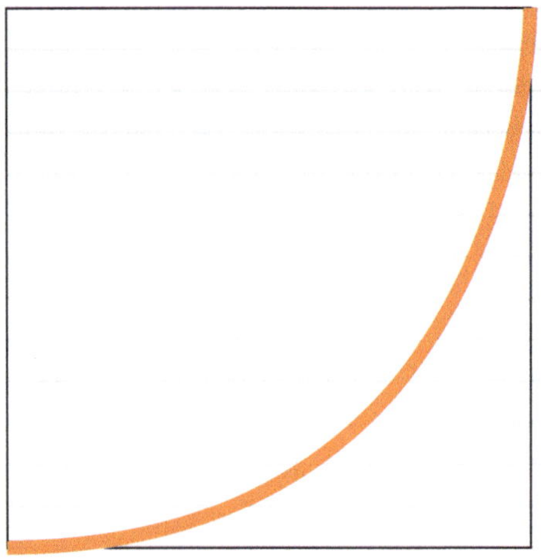

μPa sound pressure	dB
63.400.000	130
20.000.000	120
6.340.000	110
2.000.000	100
634.000	90
200.000	80
63.400	70
20.000	60
6340	50
2000	40
634	30
200	20
63	10
20	0

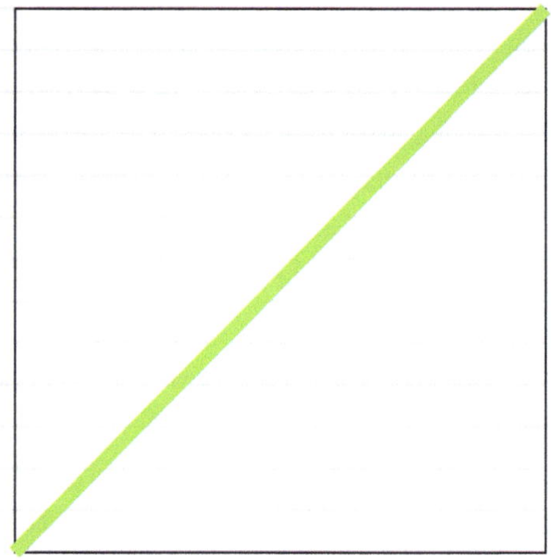

2) Decibels relate more to how our **auditory system functions**. As with frequencies, our perception of amplitude does not follow a linear relationship; instead, we perceive loudness in a logarithmic way. If the pressure doubles, I do not perceive it as a doubling of loudness. That's why we use the decibel, as it allows us to describe loudness in a more perceptually relevant way.

So if I want to double the amplitude of a sound, all I have to do is multiply its dB value by 2? **Absolutely not!**
A significant practical consideration of using a logarithmic scale is when you want to increase the amplitude of your signal using a fader. If we want to double the amplitude of the sound, we do not double the position of the fader, but rather we would push up the fader by +6 dB. This would correspond to +3 dB SIL, but SIL is not usually used in musical contexts. When we adjust the fader by -6 dB (down), then the amplitude is halved. It is worth noting here that perceptually, a doubling of sound is related to +10 dB, instead of 6 dB. So, if you want to double the loudness, then you will need to adjust the fader by 10 dB.

The reason I need to add, instead of multiply, becomes apparent when analyzing the graph representing the addition of coherent sounds.

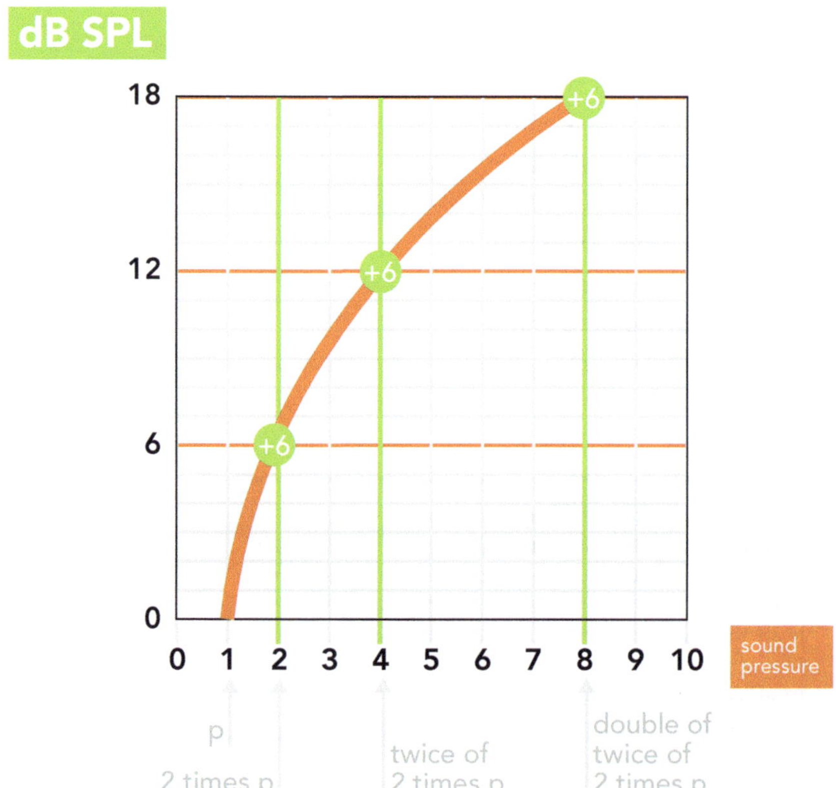

The sound pressure level scale, in decibels, ranges between two extreme values: the threshold of hearing (0 dB) and the threshold of pain (140 dB). Sound pressures are not to be joked with. A sound approaching the threshold of pain can seriously, and permanently, damage our auditory system because the energy that makes our eardrum move may instead overload and harm our eardrum and internal hearing organs. Not only that, even lower sound pressures over an extended amount of time can still lead to hearing damage. Just think of those who work in noisy environments. Without proper hearing protection devices, they risk losing their hearing quickly. While frequencies that exceed the upper range of hearing are generally harmlessly inaudible, amplitudes that exceed the upper range of comfort can cause serious damage and must be carefully managed. We must preserve our hearing and that of our listeners by avoiding exaggerated peaks or prolonged exposure to moderate sound pressures.

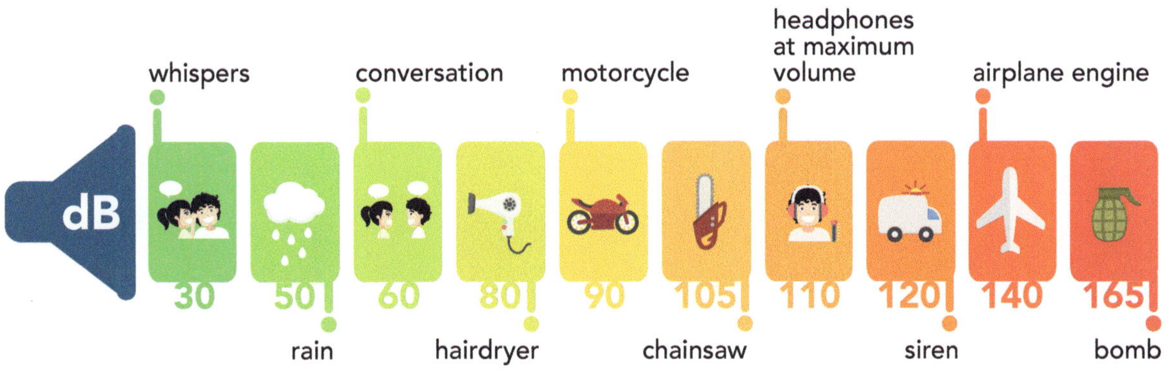

But there is more. *Have you ever wondered why the first thing that jumps out to our ears when we hear a song is the melody? Or why police and ambulance sirens are glissando sounds focused mainly on high frequencies?* This is not by chance. These sounds capitalize on how our auditory system works. We are more sensitive to medium to high frequencies rather than low frequencies or very high frequencies. If I produce two waves of different frequencies but equal amplitude, I will perceive them as having different loudnesses. For example, a 5000 Hz sine wave is perceived to be louder than a 90 Hz sine wave.

Our ears are not equally sensitive to all frequencies. The two physicists who studied this phenomenon created a graph that represents this phenomenon: the **Fletcher-Munson diagram**. How do we read it? Each orange line represents a given perceived loudness (expressed in **Phon**). The graph illustrates how many decibels, at a given frequency, is equivalent to that loudness level. In other words, if I pick an orange phon curve and follow it from the lowest to the highest frequencies on the graph, the perceived loudness will appear to be constant throughout. For example, to perceive the same loudness of 40 phons, a 1000 Hz wave needs to be at 40 dB, while a 30 Hz wave needs to be 80 dB.

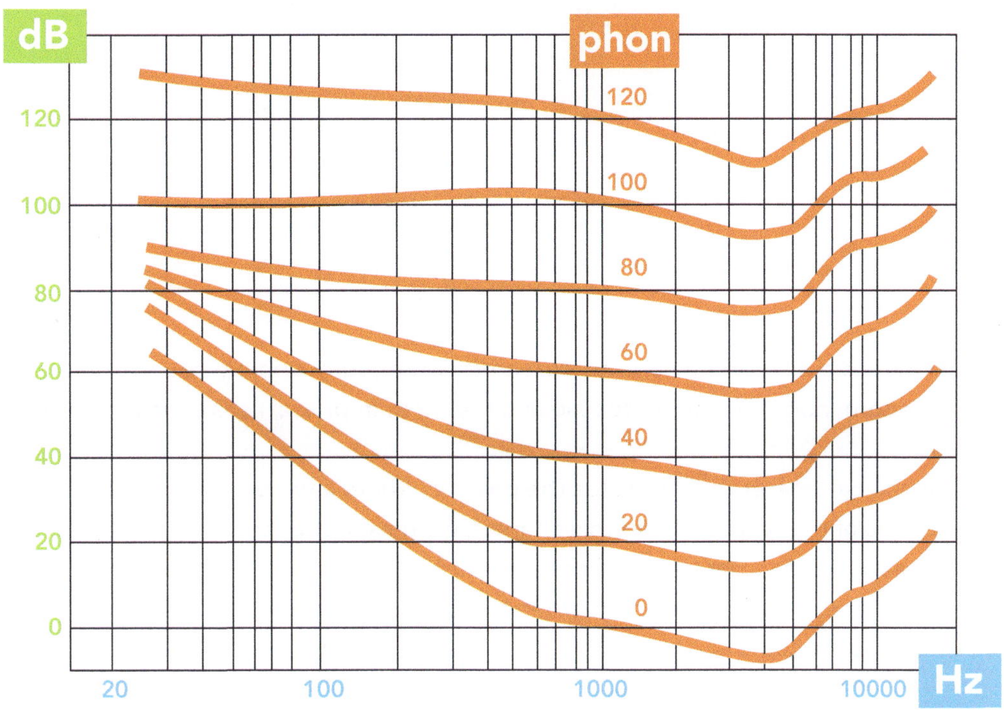

In the digital domain, we use **dBFS** (full scale). dBFS differs from SPL in the reference value. While for SPL, the reference was 0.000020 Pa (the threshold of hearing) the reference for dBFS is the maximum possible loudness for a digital binary number. If we have a 16-bit binary number (see the section on digital audio, page 82), the maximum loudness is when all 16 digits are 1, or 1111111111111111. When I plug this into the decibel equation, I find that 0 dBFS is the maximum ampitude possible in the digital domain without distortion. By having the loudest sound as the reference, all quieter sounds will have a negative decibel value. The extreme case is silence, which has a value of dBFS = -∞. Otherwise, everything is similar to SPL. + 6 dB to double and - 6 dB to halve coherent sounds. dBFS can be found in DAW software and all other software that handles digital audio and has a meter, the indicator of the amplitude level present in a given audio stream.

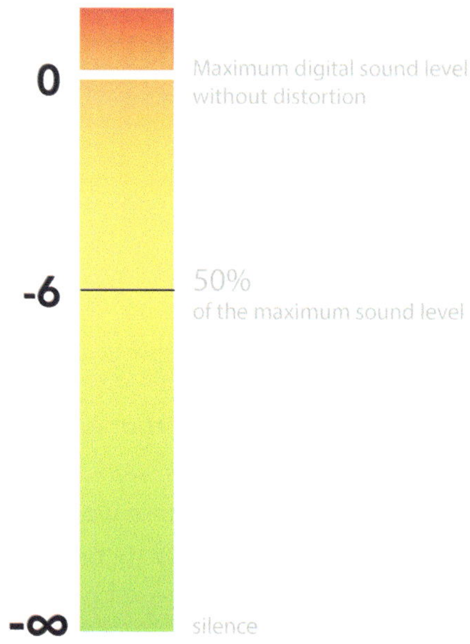

.generate crescendos of white noise of at least 10 seconds each. Arrange them, at will, in a timeline so that no definite rhythm is perceived. Complete a piece by playing live on your instrument, freely creating notes with dynamics that behave in an opposite way to the dynamics of the white noise. As the amplitude of the white noise increases, the note you are playing should decrease in amplitude at the same rate

.download a song of your choice from the internet and import it into a DAW. Halve the amplitude and mark on a sheet of paper how many dB you reduced it by and observe how the dBFS values on the meter change. Halve the amplitude again and compare these values with your first measurements

Phase

Do you know that there is a scenario where we can emit two equally audible sounds and the listener hears no sound at all? This phenomenon is possible because of differences in phase. Let's start with a definition.

The **Phase ϕ (phi),** is the parameter that indicates the position where a wave is in its cycle at a given instant. In the previous representations of the wave so far in this chapter, we have not been concerned with the starting point of our wave, but we are about to discover that this is very important. Phase is not an audible parameter when we only have a single wave, but it becomes very evident when there are multiple waves. When these waves with different phases interact, "magic" can occur.

We measure phase in degrees (0°, 90°, 180°, etc.) because our simple sine wave has trigonometric properties. Imagine that you have in front of you a very long horizontal sheet of paper that is being pulled from the left to the right at a constant rate. If you try to draw a circle on it in a counterclockwise direction, your circle will be transformed into a sinusoidal wave due to the moving paper. Now for each point in the period of this wave, think about where you were in your circle, and the angle from the center of the circle to this point is the phase of your wave.

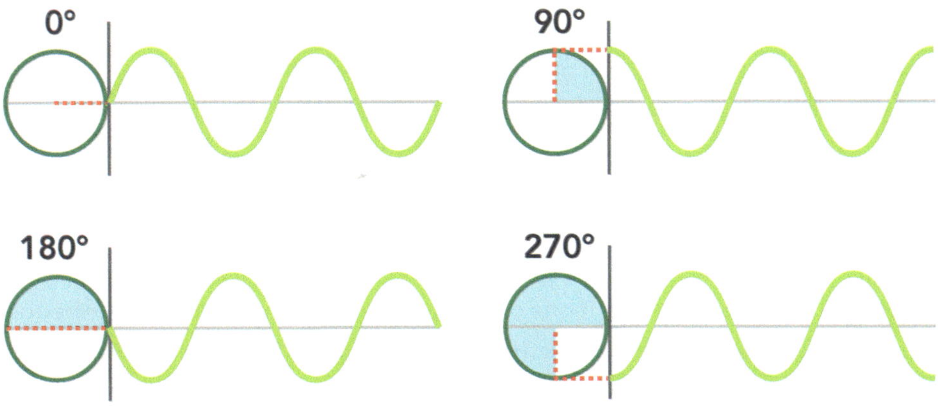

Let's see what happens when now consider two waves. Adding two waves together results in a wave that is the algebraic sum of the amplitude values of the two initial waves, taken instant by instant. This, in some instances, leads to two extreme cases (amplitude doubling or total silence) or more general intermediate outcomes. Let us look at some important examples:

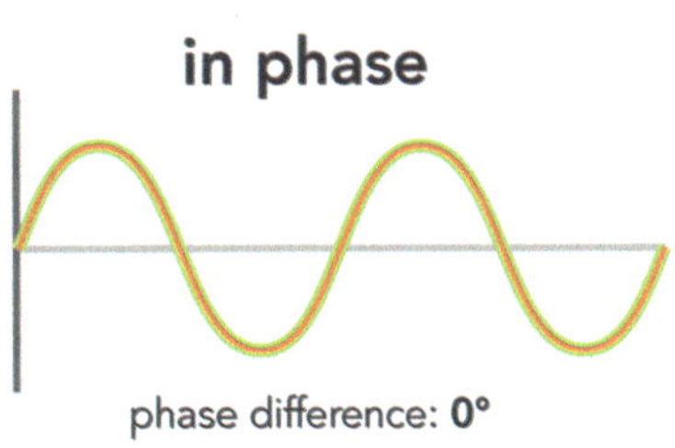

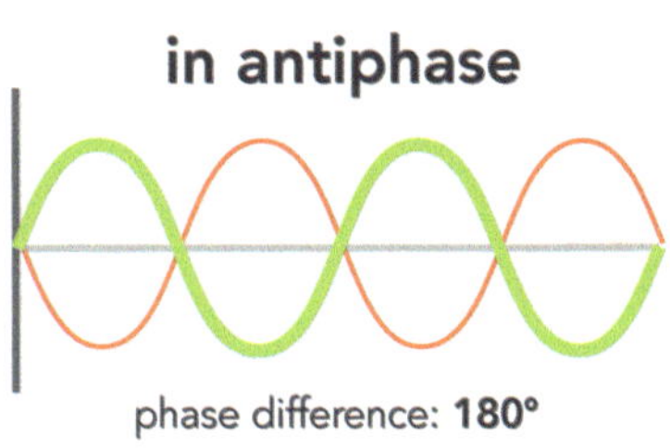

When two waves of equal amplitude and frequency have identical phases, adding them together results in a wave with the same frequency and phase but **twice the amplitude.**

When two waves of equal amplitude and frequency have a phase difference of 180° or odd number multiples of 180°, "magic" occurs when we add them together. The positive portion of one wave is cancelled out completely by the negative portion of the wave that is in antiphase. The result is **silence**, where all values of the resultant wave are zero.

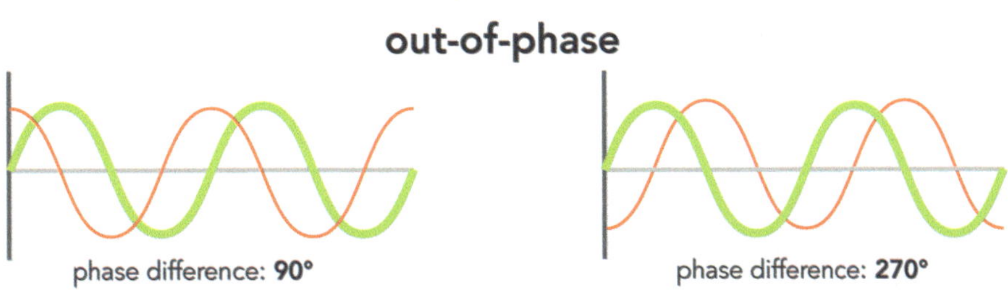

The term **out of phase** applies to all other cases when the phase difference between the two waves is between 0° and 180°. The resultant wave you get when you sum these two waves depends on how close the two initial waves are to being in phase or having an antiphase relationship. When they are close to in-phase, you get an increase in amplitude; when the close to antiphase, you get a decrease in amplitude.

Beats are a phase-related physical phenomena that occur when two waves with **equal amplitudes and very close but not equal frequencies** are added together. This results in a rhythmic increase and decrease in loudness that can potentially be used for creative purposes to create precise rhythmic effects. On some instruments, like the guitar, the elimination of beats is used for tuning purposes. This is because the presence of beats, while playing the same note on two different strings, indicates that the one string is not in tune with the other.

The number of beats the combined sound makes per second is calculable and corresponds to the difference in frequency of our two initial sine waves. For example, if I have a 440 Hz wave and a 441 Hz wave, I will get one beat per second when I add the two waves up. If we want to translate this into musical terms, this is the speed of quarter notes at 60 BPM. It is clear that the phenomenon of beats ends when the frequency difference between the two waves becomes so large that it creates a rhythm that is too fast to be perceived. At this point, we perceive two distinct notes.

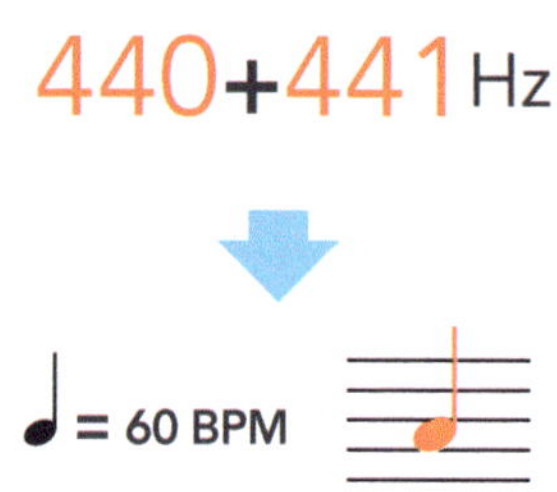

Why this phenomenon occurs can be intuitive. If one of the two waves has a slightly higher frequency than the other, the two waves will start off in phase with each other. However, the higher frequency wave will get ahead of the other wave, to the point where they are completely out of phase for a moment. The higher frequency wave continues to move ahead, and becomes back in phase with the other wave, albeit now it is one entire cycle ahead. In other words, the two waves start off in phase, find themselves in antiphase, then back in phase again. Correspondingly, the amplitude doubles, becomes zero, and then returns to a doubling, respectively. This is what creates beating.

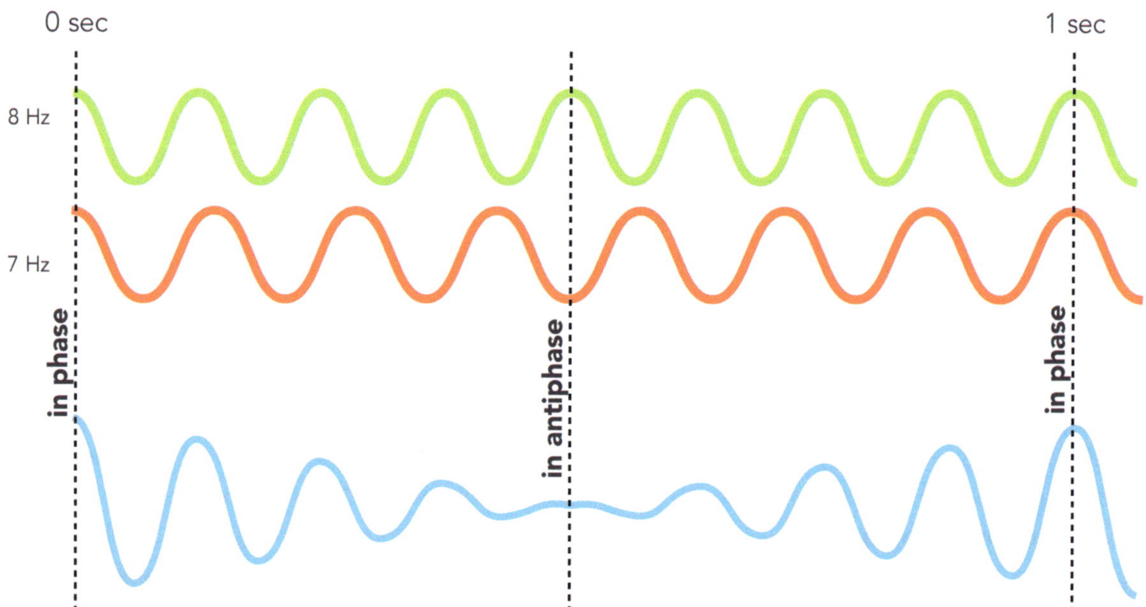

.generate a sine wave that, when combined with a 200 Hz sine wave, creates a resultant wave that beats twice per second and simultaneously beats once per second when combined with a 400Hz sine wave. Keep an eye on the amplitudes of your sine waves to avoid distortion in the resulting sound

.create a 50-second micro-song in which you use beats to create rhythms. There must be at least one section in the piece where the number of beats steadily increases. Use a glissando (in frequency) to produce it. ***Theme: "Biking on the clouds"***

Piano phase - Steve Reich ~ pure data organelle ~ Nicoletta Andreuccetti c p d (In two minds) for soprano sax and live electronics ~ Pietro Grossi - Battimenti

Timbre

Why does the sound of Chet Baker's trumpet on My Funny Valentine excite me? Why does the sound of Keith Emerson's synthesizer sound better than my new plugin? Do I buy a Stradivarius or a low-cost violin from your favorite online shop? Many of the answers to these questions stem from the study of timbre.

Timbre, by definition, is the characteristic of sound that makes one instrument distinguishable from another, even if they play the same note at the same dynamic level. Let's dig a little deeper to see how we might describe and characterize our sound more accurately and scientifically. Immediately we find a complication. Timbre is not measurable as frequency, amplitude, or phase by themselves; it actually needs multiple factors to describe it. Herein (perhaps) lies the appeal of timbre. I cannot make a direct comparison of any two timbres by using only a single metric, as no one metric describes timbre. While I can say that an orange is half as heavy as a grapefruit, I cannot say that a violin is half as "timbral" as a trumpet. I can, however, start to describe timbre scientifically if I break it down into the two parts which describe each instrument's unique timbral characteristics: the **dynamic envelope** and the **spectrum** (or frequency content).

The **dynamic envelope** is a detailed look at the dynamics of a note played by an instrument, describing the amplitude of a note from the moment it is excited to when the note fades away to nothing. The dynamic envelope for acoustic instruments is bound by the physics of instrument construction, while for electronic instruments, the musicians can alter the various parameters that control the dynamic envelope. For example regarding acoustic instruments, suppose I compare bowing a string on a violin with striking a snare drum with a stick. I notice that with the violin, it takes a little longer for the sound to reach its peak amplitude when compared to the sound of the snare, which reaches the maximum peak amplitude quickly. We could say that the snare's dynamic envelope is one reason the sound can be described as "percussive." In another example, if I pluck the string of a ukulele and simultaneously play a sustained note on the piano, the sound of the ukulele will end considerably earlier than piano sound.

The dynamic envelope of acoustic instruments can be complex. However, we can simplify this and make it a little bit more manageable for electronic instruments. For electronic instruments, the dynamic envelope is broken into four time segments: the Attack, Decay, Sustain, Release. This type of dynamic envelope is known generally as **ADSR**.

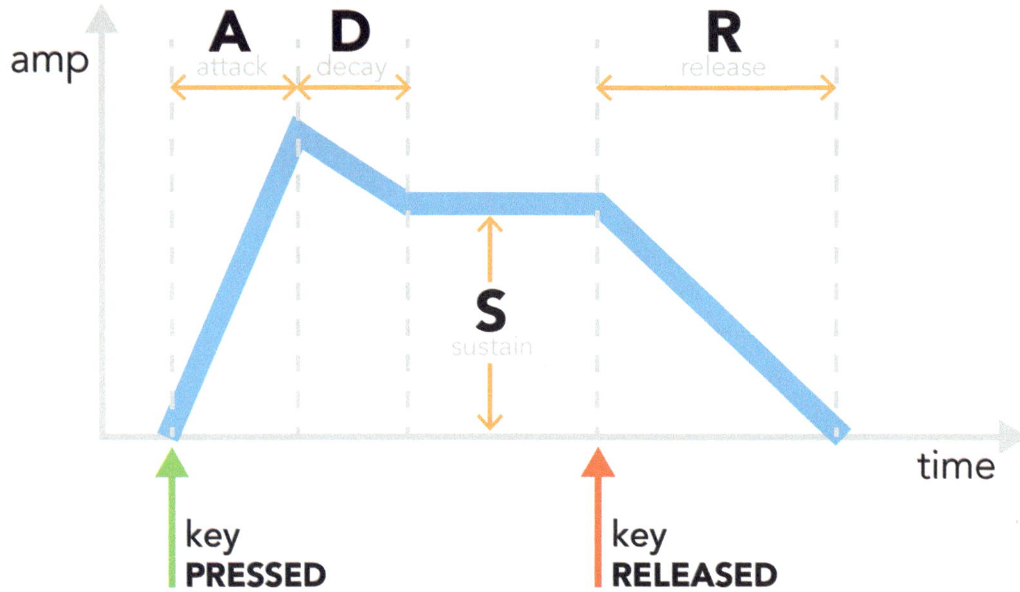

Attack is the time between the start of a note and the peak amplitude of the sound. It is a crucial stage because it determines, for example, the percussiveness of a sound.

Decay is the time it takes for the natural decay of an instrument's sound after the peak amplitude. For sustained instruments, the amplitude tends to rapidly get softer after the peak before stabilizing at the amplitude in which the note is sustained.

Sustain is the amplitude that the instrument is kept at as the note is being held. It is important to note that sustain is not a time measurement. How long the note is sustained depends on how long the musician holds the note, and is not a parameter of ADSR. The controllable parameter for sustain is thus amplitude. Note that some instruments, such as the guitar and percussion instruments, do not have a sustain stage.

Release is the time it takes the instrument to reach silence once the musician stops playing the note.
In instruments without sustain, the decay time from peak to silence is sometimes called the decay or the release.

Every sound we hear, even the most complex, can be thought of as the sum of simple sine wave components of varying frequencies. A **spectrum** is essentially the description, or graph, of sound using these frequency components, also known as partials or harmonics. The partials can be harmonic or inharmonic, meaning they can be integer multiples of a fundamental wave or non-integer multiples respectively. The mathematician and physicist who theorized and proved this concept was *Jean Baptiste Fourier*, and the theorem that describes this is named after him: **Fourier's Theorem**. From this, we can analyze simple and complex sounds and uncover what simple sine waves they are comprised of using the Fourier Transform. While the Fourier Transform's mathematics are beyond the scope of this book, let's try to extrapolate the practical aspects of the Fourier Transform.

Thanks to Fourier's concepts, I can represent the spectrum of a sound by constructing an amplitude spectrum. The amplitude spectrum depicts the amplitude of all of the sound's frequency components, where the X-axis is frequency and the Y-axis is amplitude. It's a kind of "photograph" of an instant of sound, or an average across a time region of sound, that shows and identifies the frequency and amplitude of each sine wave frequency component. If instead of the amplitude, I represent the phase, the new graph is the phase spectrum. In both cases, I can decide the visualization precision level, showing the sinusoids of the analyzed sound schematically or not. When the spectrum is simplified and shown on a bar graph, the height of the bar shows the amplitude of the entire frequency band; thus, the width of the bar and spacing in between the bars is not important.

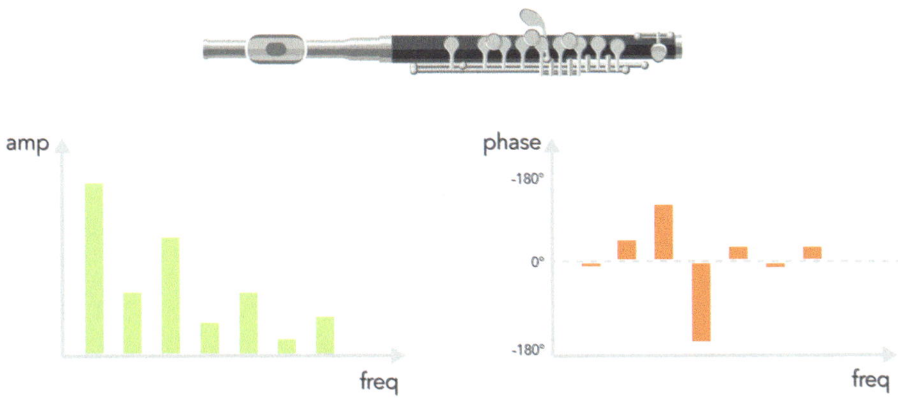

AMPLITUDE SPECTRUM **PHASE SPECTRUM**

> Be careful to distinguish the amplitude or phase spectrum from the time domain wave representations that we saw earlier. In the time domain, we have time flowing on the X-axis and the wave's amplitude on the Y-axis, as we see with the cycles of a sine wave. On the other hand, when we talk about amplitude or phase spectrum, we are in the frequency domain where we show frequency on the X-axis and amplitude/phase on the y axis, as we see with filter responses.

The limitation of these representations is that they photograph an instant or an average. It does not allow you to see what happens with the frequency components from one moment to the next. For sounds that never change, this is not an issue. However, most sounds we are familiar with are "alive" in that they evolve over time (i.e., the timbre changes from one moment to the next). These amplitude or phase spectrums, as we have seen, cannot capture the time-changing nature of the sound. Take, for example, a piano note: if we analyze it at the moment of attack, we notice many partials. However, if we take the spectrum near the end of a piano note's sustain, the amplitude spectrum will show very few partials. There is a representation that allows us to see an evolving spectrum: the spectrogram. In a spectrogram, time is depicted on the X-axis, the Y-axis shows frequency, and the color (more or less intense) describes the amplitude of that given partial.

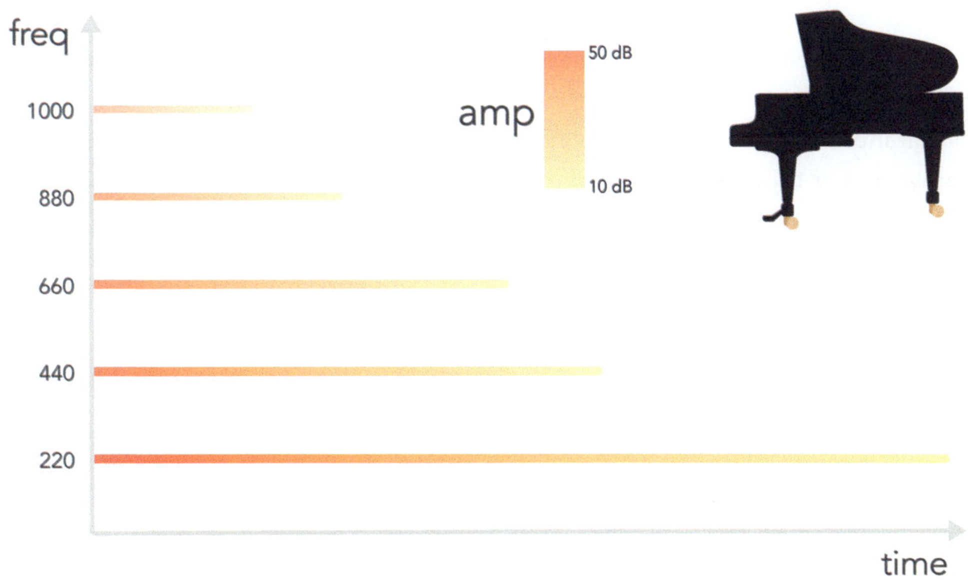

Let's analyze a musical instrument's note. We notice an oddity – one partial appears to have a large amplitude, and above it, we find a series of other partials, often at regular distances from each other, with smaller and smaller amplitudes than the first. We call the most significant and lowest partial in the spectrum the **fundamental,** and all the **partials** above the fundamental are known as **overtones**. The term partial is used to describe all the frequency components. If I look at the relationship between the fundamental and the overtones in a spectrum, I can identify two distinct cases of **harmonic** and **inharmonic**.

Harmonic Spectrum occurs when the overtones are integer multiples of the fundamental. In other words, the harmonics have frequencies that correspond to the fundamental frequency multiples by 1, 2, 3, 4, etc. In this case, the overtones are specifically called harmonics. When an instrument has well defined harmonics, the sound will have a defined pitch for a specific note. This is, therefore, the case with all instruments that can make distinct notes such as violins, flutes, pianos, etc.

An **Inharmonic Spectrum** occurs when the overtones are NOT integer multiples of the fundamental. In this case, the fundamental is multiplied by numbers that have fraction values or numbers that have digits after the decimal point (floating point numbers), such as 1.4 or 2.1. Instruments that have an inharmonic spectrum are not as tunable and have a less defined pitch (e.g. drums, bells, gongs, etc.).

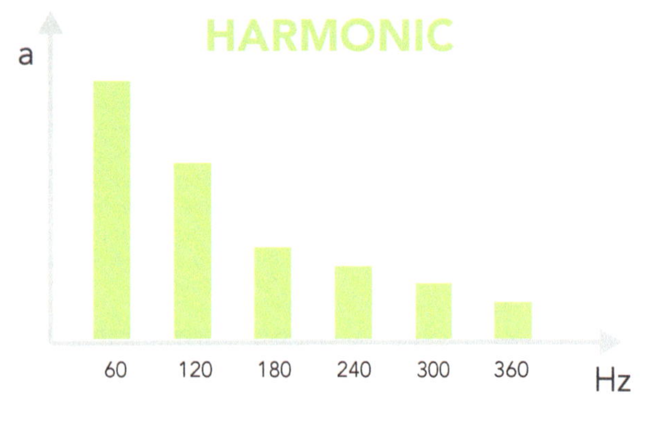

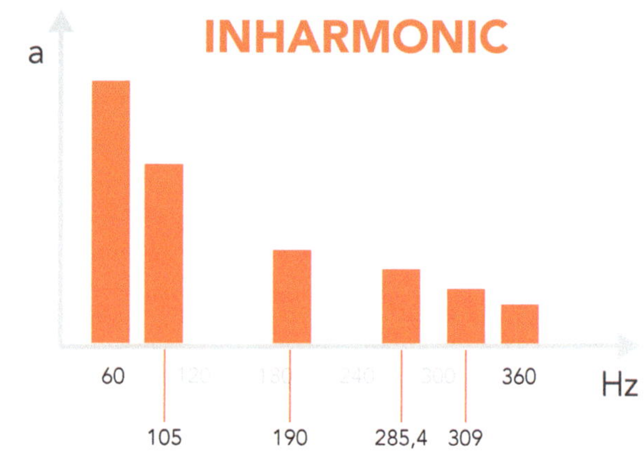

As we have said, overtones, plus the fundamental, make up the Harmonic Spectrum. Harmonics are produced directly by the natural physics of the instrument. When I play an A4 on the piano, I might hear the 440 Hz frequency that the A4 is tuned to. But actually inside this sound, there are many frequencies and components (harmonics) actually contained within this piano sounding A4. The components above 440 Hz (the fundamental frequency) are smaller in amplitude and not as evident, but they are vital to create the instrument's timbre.

If we look specifically at the fundamental frequency and the integer multiple frequencies of the harmonics above the fundamental, the succession of these frequencies creates intervals that sound like a chord that can play simultaneously with our fundamental. In order, the intervals between the first eight harmonics are: octave, fifth, octave, major third, fifth, septimal minor seventh, and octave. If I play a C2 on a string, within the note, I will have the following harmonics within the note: C3, G3, C4, E4, G4, approximately Bb4, and C5. Clearly, these harmonics do not end with the eighth harmonic but go on infinitely. In the illustration, you will find notes going up to the 16th harmonic number. With most instruments, the amplitude of each harmonic gets smaller as we go up the harmonic series.

There is, however, a slight difference in pitch between these notes and those played on our instruments. This is because some of our instruments with fixed tuning (e.g. piano, organ, guitar), as we saw in the section on frequency,

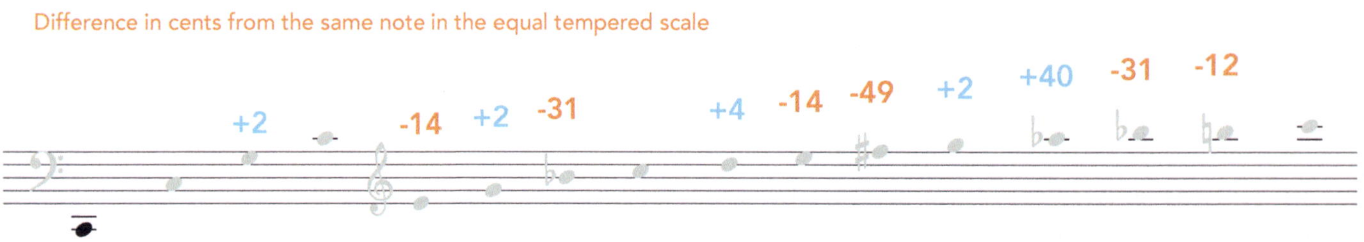

are tuned to equal temperament, featuring a perfectly exponential scale so that the semitones are always equal to each other. We can divide this equal semitone into 100 small (exponential) steps, also known as cents. If one semitone is made up of 100 cents, then one octave is made up of 1200 cents. Because the integer multiples of the fundamental frequency do not line up with equal temperament, we get some slightly "out of tune" intervals, the difference of which can be described in cents.

Not found in acoustic instruments, some artificial timbres, used by synthesizers and computers in sound syntheses, are essential because they help us understand the relationship between time domain representations and frequency domain representations. These waves are named after their wave shape in the time domain, but in the diagram, we also see how they are formed by summing a fundamental frequency with select harmonics at specific amplitudes.

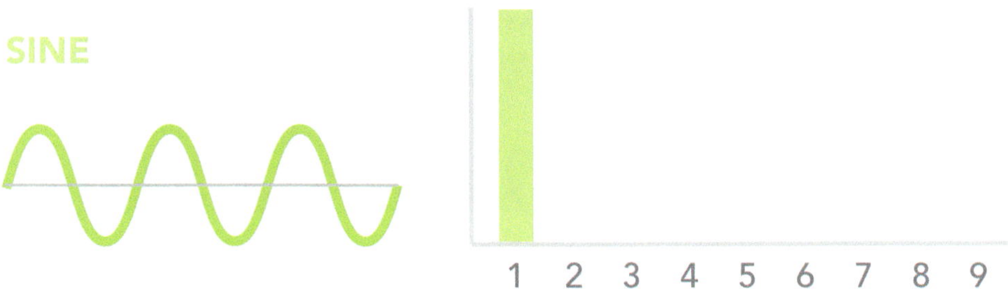

The simplest example is the sine wave, but it is made up of only one harmonic (itself!).

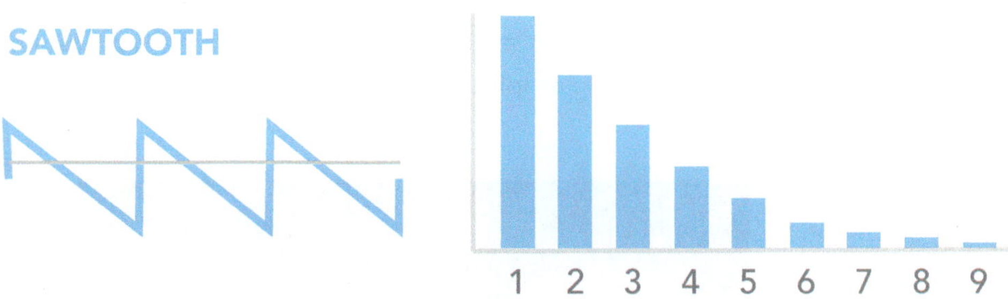

It is made up of all harmonics with amplitudes that get smaller and smaller as you get further away from the fundamental.

The amplitudes for the Nth harmonic can be calculated as 1/N.

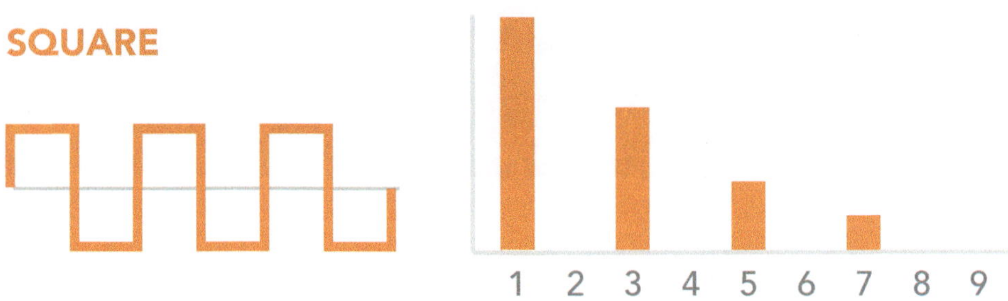

It has only odd harmonics components that all start in phase with each other. The amplitude of the harmonics gradually decreases with the same relationship as the sawtooth wave. For the Nth harmonic, the amplitude is 1/N. Here, N are the odd numbers—N= 1, 3, 5, 7, 9,...

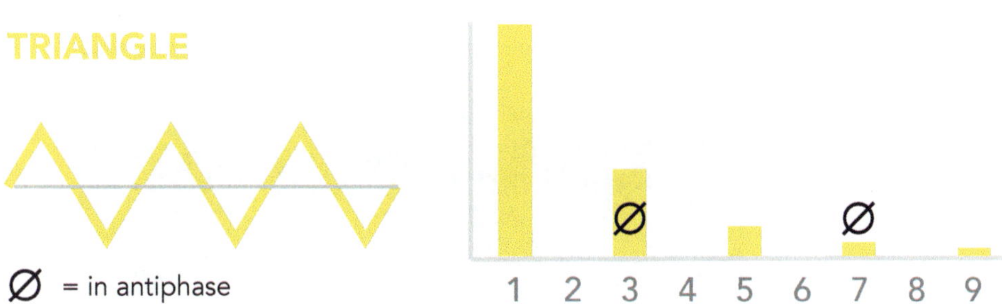

It, too, has only odd harmonic components. Here though, the harmonics have phases that alternate from in phase to antiphase. In other words, the fundamental is in phase, the 3rd harmonic is in antiphase, the 5th in phase, the 7th in antiphase, and so on. The amplitudes also get smaller at a faster rate in triangle waves. The amplitude for the Nth harmonic is $1/N^2$.

Finally, let's analyze some sounds to determine how their timbre affects the spectrogram and waveform representations.

Again, we start with the simplest timbre: the sine wave. We notice the perfect periodic cycles and cleanliness of the waveform. In the spectrogram, we see only one harmonic throughout the entire length of the note, which is the wave's frequency. This is a special timbre; we rarely find pure sine wave sounds, by themselves, in nature. However, they are useful in electronic music and we can artificially create these sine waves with software or hardware synthesizers.

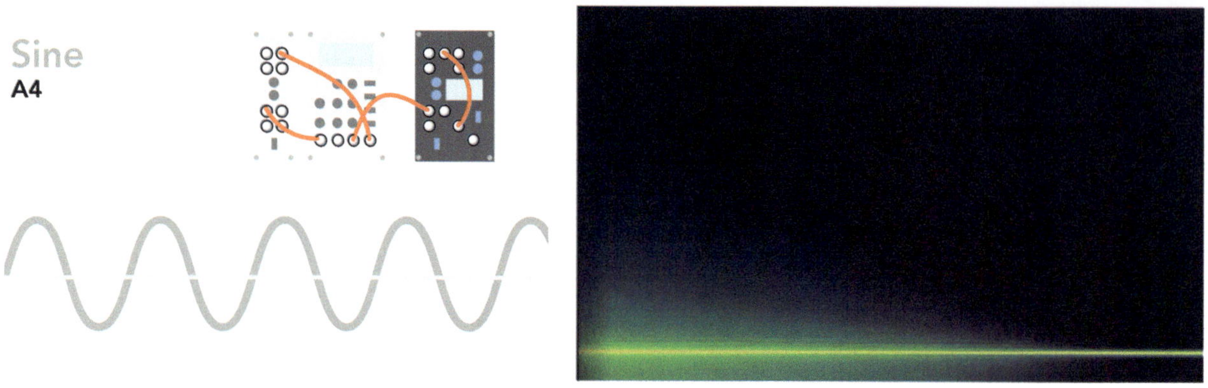

In the french horn, we can see the periodic nature of the waveform, where the period is easy to identify. This periodicity indicates that the sound should be harmonic in nature and have a relatively tunable timbre. Additionally, since the waveform is not overly complex, we do not expect the sound to be very rich or have many strong harmonic components. This can be confirmed by the spectrogram, which shows a regular distribution of a relatively few number of harmonics. Note how the vertical spacing of the harmonics is even, indicating that the harmonics are multiples of the fundamental. As with other acoustic instruments, the amplitude of the harmonics decreases with increasing frequency.

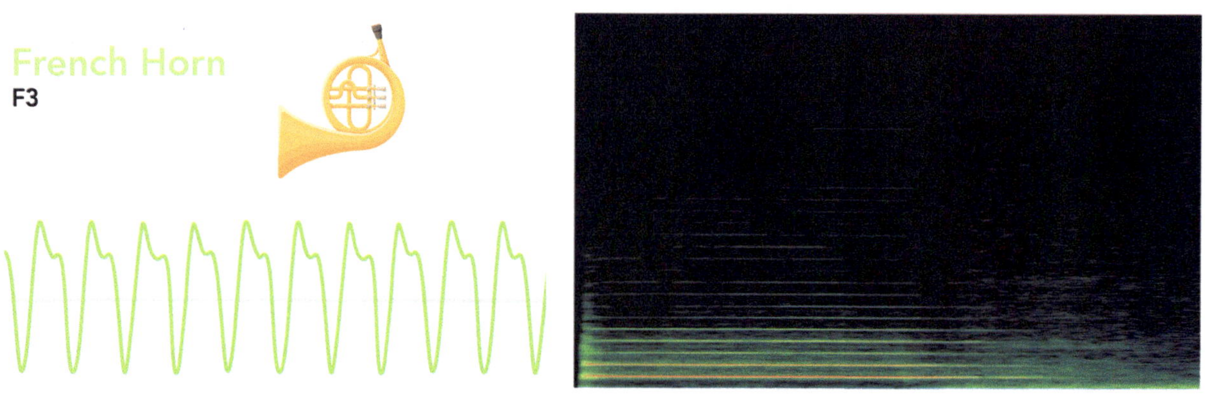

The harmonicity of the timbre is also evident in the viola, seen again by the regularity of the periods in the waveform and the even distribution of harmonics in the spectrogram. The timbre is richer than the previous example because we see more harmonics present in the spectrogram. The more harmonics that are present, the more complex the waveform.

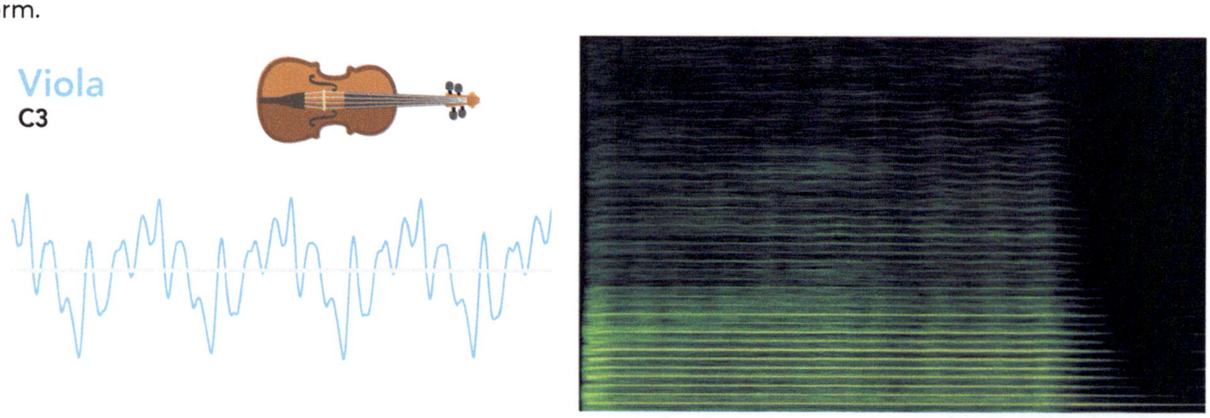

On the other hand, the gong shows us an irregular waveform that has a tone that does not have a defined, tunable pitch. This indicates that the gong has an inharmonic timbre. This inharmonic nature is confirmed by the spectrogram in which the partials, though well-defined, are not distributed in regular frequency intervals to each other.

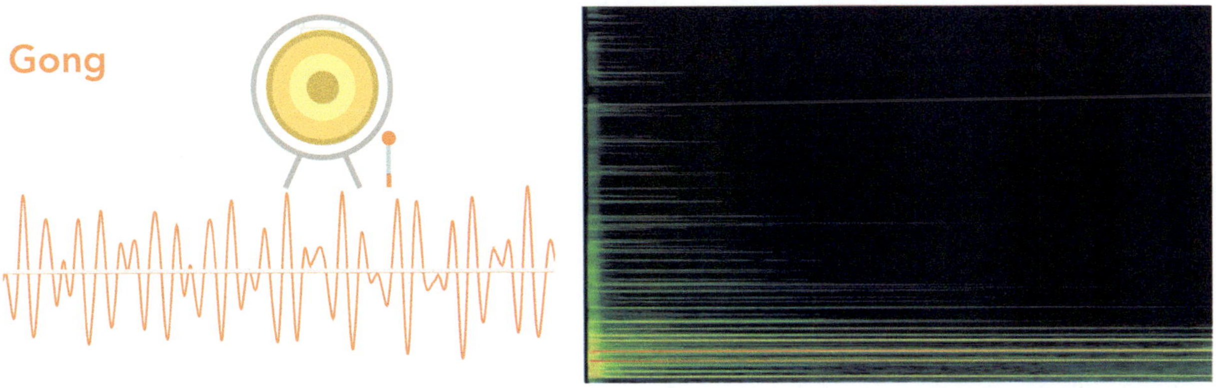

Let's now analyze the crash of a drum cymbal. We see that these graphs are quite different from the previous results. The waveform is very irregular, and although the spectrogram shows somewhat defined frequency bands, the frequencies are irregular in their distribution and amplitudes. The graph actually has quite a bit more color everywhere, indicating that there is energy in many frequencies. This tells us that the crash has a timbre close to white noise but differs from noise because it possesses energy in distinct frequency bands. These distinct frequency bands help us distinguish one crash cymbal from another. For example, for "darker" crashes, there is more energy in frequency bands in the lower-middle part of the spectrum, and for "brighter" crashes, there is more amplitude in the upper-middle harmonics. These differing characteristics are a key factor of why the whole drum cymbal market exists!

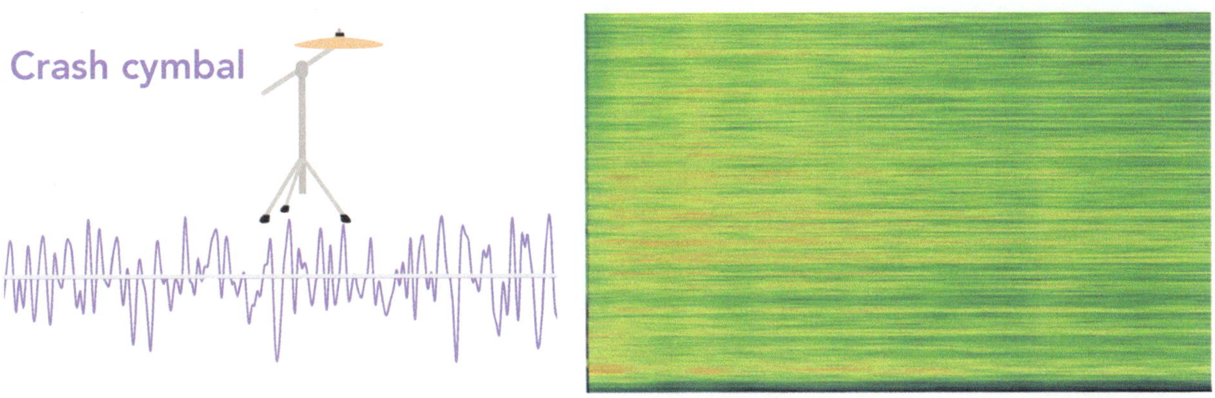

Let us consider a sound of nature that we all know and appreciate: the sound of the sea. From a timbral point of view, we are dealing with a sound very close to white noise, a sound that contains all frequencies represented at the same amplitude. This is because the drops of water collide on the shoreline chaotically and randomly, and this causes infinite frequencies to add up in the overall sound. Thus we have a very irregular waveform and a spectrogram saturated with overtones on all frequencies, almost equally distributed in amplitudes, with concentrations at the points where the sound is loudest.

Finally, we come to the most extreme example of complexity: white noise, the richest timbre of all. Like with light, the term "white" indicates the presence of all colors or frequencies. In white noise, we have all frequencies represented, all at the same amplitude, as shown in the spectrogram. In the time domain, the waveform is made up of infinite random variations that will never have any repeating portions. Like the sine wave, it is an extreme example because pure white noise does not generally acoustically exist in nature but can be produced artificially by software or hardware synthesizers.

.analyze a bell's timbre. Note how the frequency components are not integer multiples of the fundamental. With a partial editing, analysis, and resynthesis software, transform this bell's sound by making the harmonic components be integer multiples of the fundamental

.take a note from an instrument of your choice, filter it five different ways, and use these five versions of this note to construct a 1:00 micro-song. ***Theme: "Disturbed transmissions"***

.choose a note and have eight different instruments play it. These instruments can be virtual, real, synthesized, or acoustic instruments. With all eight versions of the note, try to compose a 1:00 micro-song. ***Theme: "First contact"***

.analyze the sound of a bell and write down all the frequencies of the overtones found within it. Compose a piece using only the frequencies found. ***Theme: "Bronze casting"***

Pierre Schaeffer Treatise on Musical Objects ~ GRM Parigi ~ Chrome music lab ~ Bernard Parmegiani - Conjugaison Du Timbre ~ Spear software ~ EAnalysis software ~ Acousmographe software ~ Sonic Visualiser ~ Spectralism ~ Partiels Gérard Grisey

ELECTRO-ACOUSTIC SYSTEMS

What cables do I need to connect my home studio loudspeakers? Do I use a DI-Box or can I plug my keyboard for tomorrow's gig directly into the system? Should I buy an audio interface with two or four outputs?
This chapter will answer these and many other questions. We will discuss various cables, connectors, mixers, microphones, pickups, computers, and all the other equipment we need to create electroacoustic systems.

An electroacoustic system is a set of devices that, as a whole, receive, transmit, or store sound signals in analog or digital formats. Its purpose can be diverse, depending on the situation, device, cable, or configuration chosen.
The two terms, an analog signal, and a digital signal, indicate two different ways of representing a given "message" so it can be handled by electroacoustic systems. In our case, the message almost always represents a sound.

ANALOG OR DIGITAL?

An **analog signal** is an electrical signal that is modulated to take on a waveform similar (analogous, in fact) to the waveform of the sound wave it represents. The analog wave, because it is a continuous signal, contains an infinite number of possible values. On the other hand, a **digital signal** is a symbolic representation composed of a finite, discrete number of steps, ultimately represented as a series of 1s and 0s. This representation in 1s and 0s has no apparent similarity with the original sound wave until it is decoded and translated back into an analog wave that can be played to become a sound wave.

The devices we use daily for talking on the telephone, playing music, and recording sounds continuously switch between analog to digital signals and vice versa to exploit the advantages offered by each type of signal.

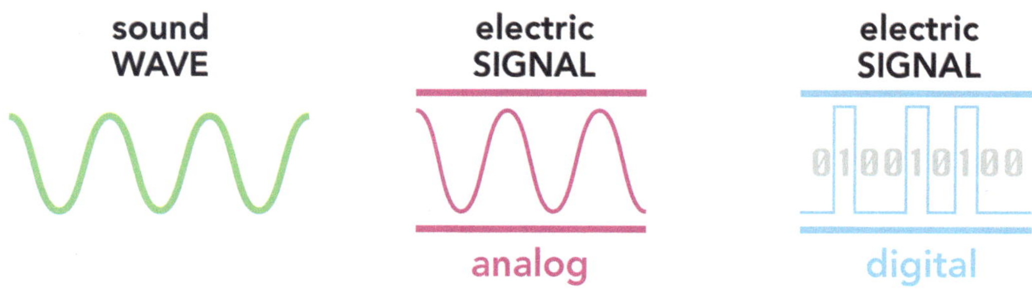

ANALOG

The first signal domain that we discuss here is the analog signal, due to the prevalence of devices that handle analog audio and because digital signals often are directly related to analog sounds. We also start with analog out of chronological respect since analog was born much earlier than digital. When we discuss digital sounds later, we need an understanding of analog sound in order to grasp the concepts around digital sound. For example, the digital sound in your DAW was recorded as an analog sound that was converted to digital sound before entering your DAW. Additionally, as you playback sounds from your DAW, another conversion happens to turn that digital sound back to analog in order for your headphones or loudspeakers to create an audible sound wave.

For example, this figure represents very common configuration of sound devices, consisting of a voice that is amplified with loudspeakers into a room.

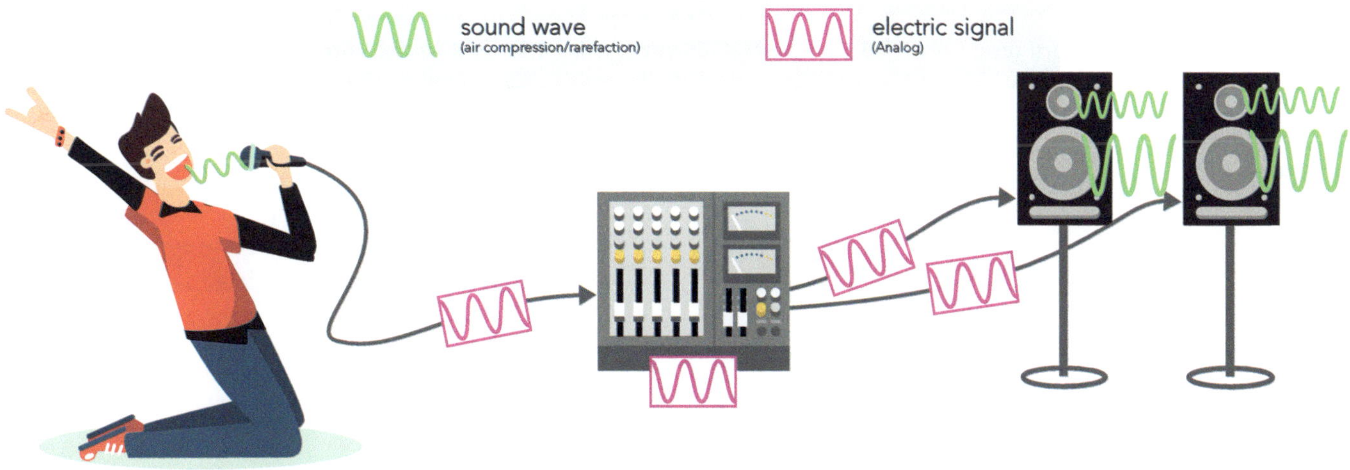

In this system, the microphone translates a sound wave (compressions and rarefactions in air) into an analog electrical signal. The signal passes through the cable and goes to the mixer. The mixer adds it to other inputs, potentially making small amplitude changes or timbral alterations by applying equalization. Finally, the signal is transmitted to the powered loudspeakers, which amplifies it and transforms the electrical signal back into sound waves (compressions and rarefactions in air).

The microphone and loudspeakers can be thought to be inverses of each other, where microphones are transducers that turn sound waves into electrical energy and loudspeakers are transducers that turn electrical energy into sound waves. This can be seen directly, with the right devices, when we use a microphone as a loudspeaker and vice versa. For example, *Edison's phonograph* was considered to be not only a playback device, but also as the first sound-recording instrument (1877).
Let us first analyze the essential components of a generic analog electroacoustic system chain.

Cables

Cables transmit signals from one point of the audio chain to another. A cable, generically, consists of a sheath or jacket containing several wires insulated from each other. The cable is terminated by two connectors, one at the beginning and one at the end of the cable.
Audio cables are divided into two main categories: 2-pin and 3-pin cables. This also means that there are either two or three electrical wires inside the cable and two or three pins on each of the two connectors.
In these two categories, we find different types of cables distinguishable by the configuration of the connector plugs on the ends.
The main 2-pin connectors varieties are **TS (1/4-inch, 6.35mm)**, **mini-TS (1/8-inch, 3,5mm)**, and **RCA**s. TS (Tip-Sleeve) cables are used, for example, to connect guitars or electric basses to amplifiers.

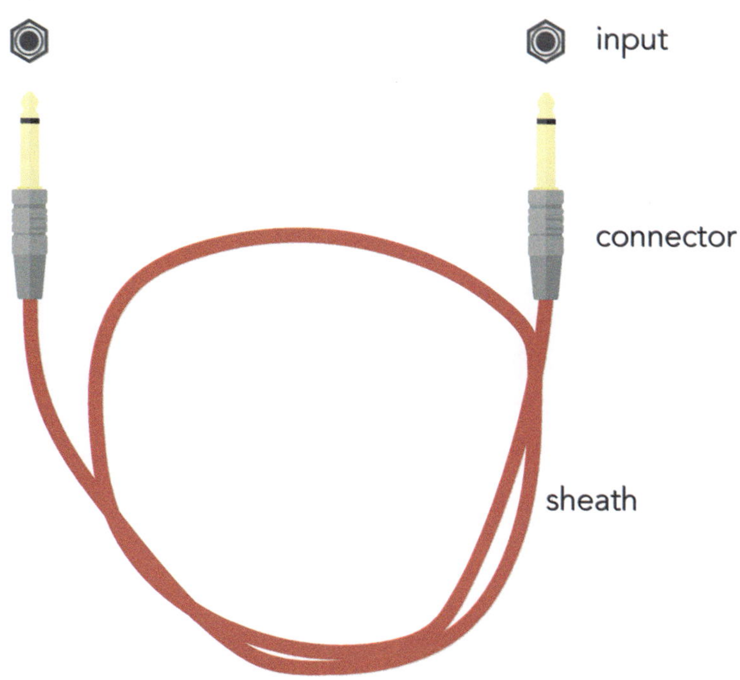

Mini-TS cables are used with small synthesizers with mono outputs or as patch cords for modular synthesizers and recording studios. We most commonly use RCA cables to connect analog audio from a TV to a HI-FI system or to send audio out of some audio interfaces through unbalanced outputs.

The main 3-pin connectors types are **TRS (1/4-inch, 6.35mm)**, **mini-TRS (1/8-inch, 3.5mm)**, and **XLR (cannon)**. TRS (Tip-Ring-Sleeve) is explicitly used for balanced connections with audio interfaces, mini-TRS are used for stereo connections with audio players or smartphones, and XLR are used for balanced signals from microphones or loudspeakers.

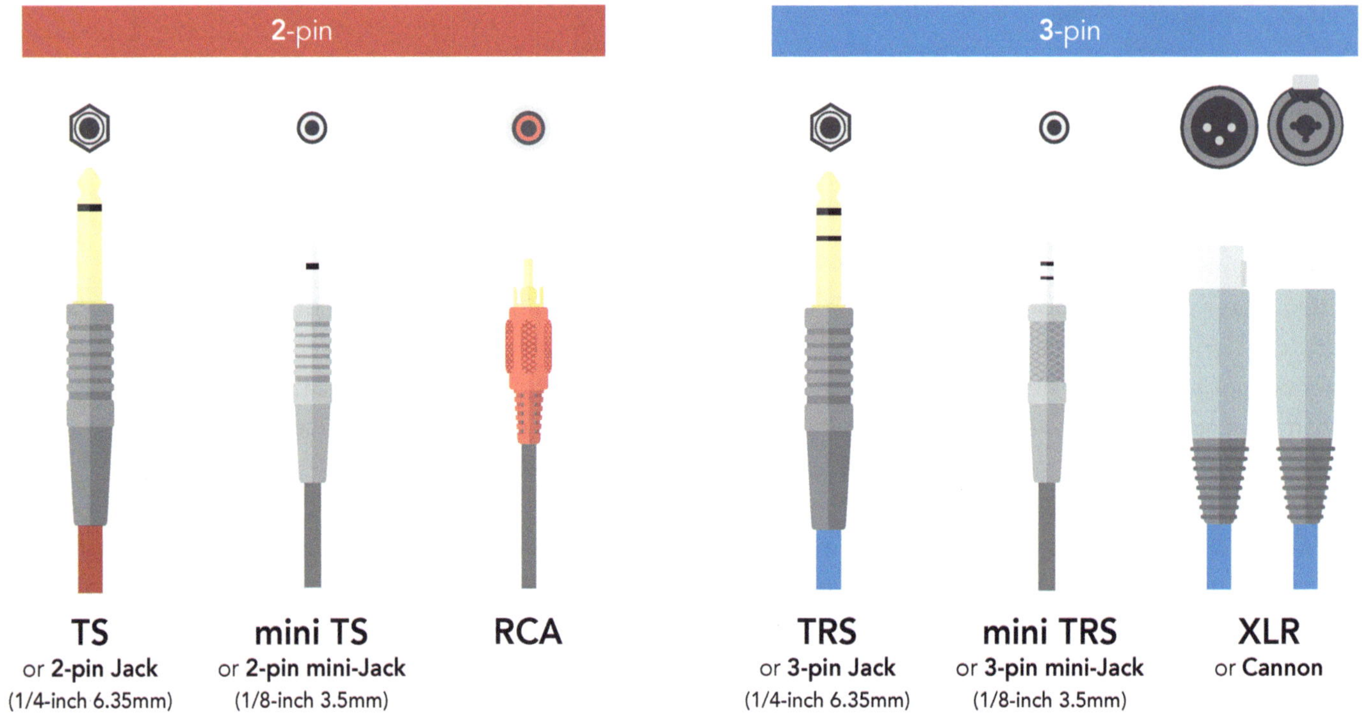

To find the number of cable pins, we need to check how many separate contacts the connector or plug has. In the case of TS and TRS, we can count the metal parts divided by the insulators, the dark rings that encircle the connector. The contacts are named **Tip**, **Ring**, and **Sleeve**. Generally, the Tip and Ring carry signal and the Sleeve represents ground. In the case of RCA plugs, the tip (the pole in the center) carries the signal and the cylindrical metal component surrounding the space around the tip, is the sleeve that carries ground. In XLRs, we see the three contacts are either holes in the female connector or pins in the male connector. Pin 1 carries the ground, pin 2 transmits the positive signal, and pin 3 transmits the negative signal.

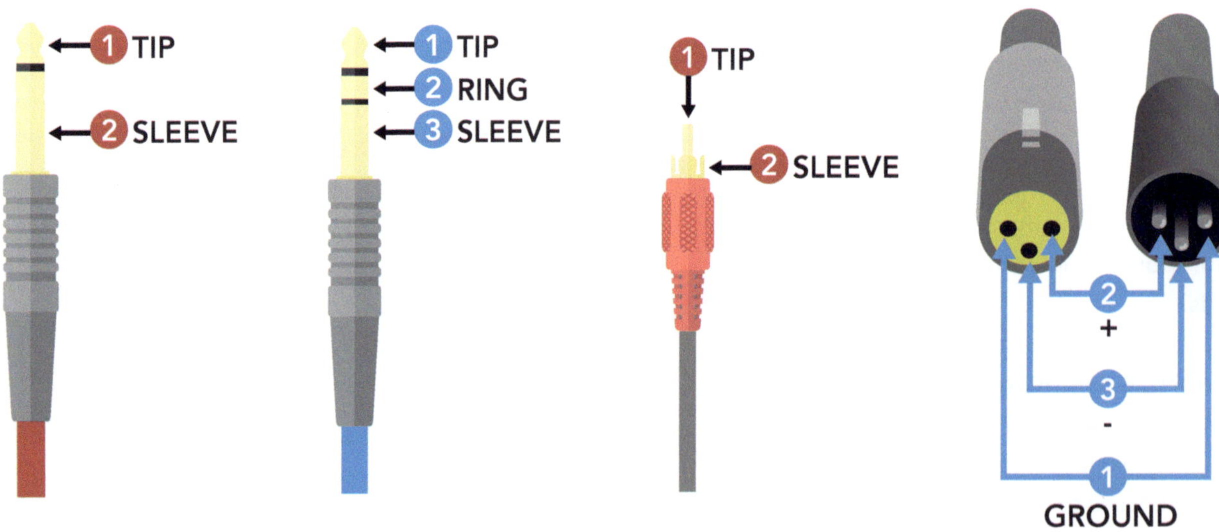

Each cable can carry different types of signals, depending on the user's preferences and the devices that the cables are connected to. 2-pin cables are used solely for unbalanced mono signals, and 3-pin cables can be used either for balanced mono signals or unbalanced stereo signals.

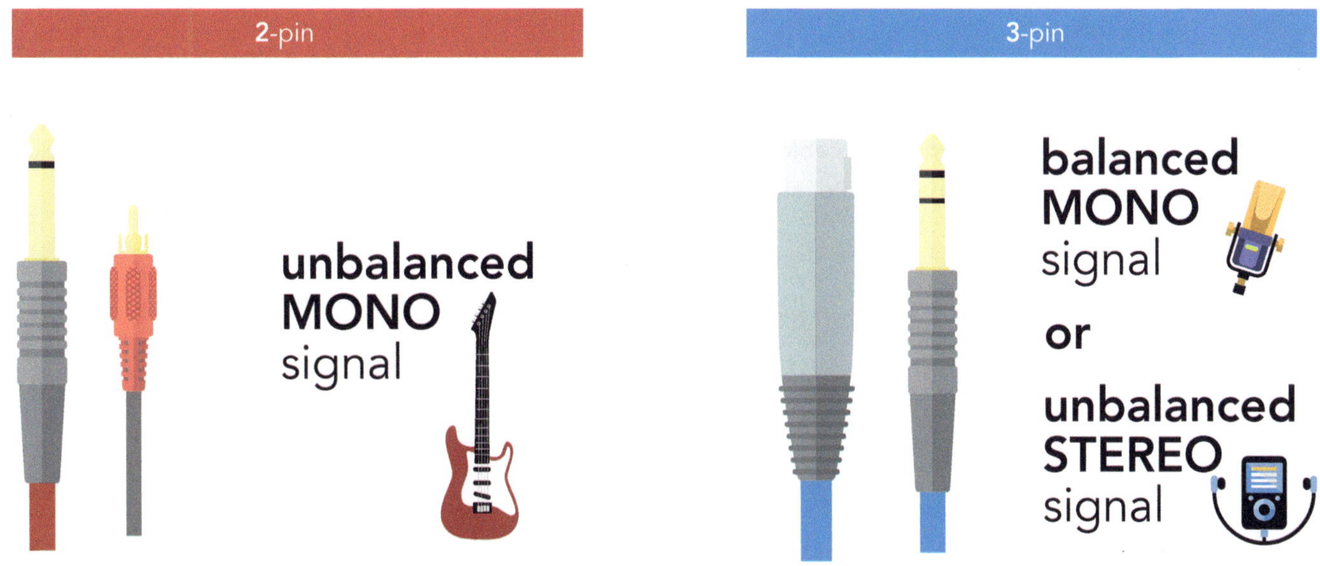

A **balanced connection** is a method of preserving the audio signal, even over long distances, by minimizing and canceling out external noise-inducing interference. This is possible because balanced connections reverse the polarity of one of the wires within the cable (i.e., the wire associated with pin 3 of an XLR cable), effectively cancelling out the shared noise carried within the cable. The audio signal is preserved while the noise is silenced and cancelled out due to the superposition of two noise profiles of opposite polarity.

For balanced audio, we need the devices to play together as a team. This means that we need balanced outputs (for example, a microphone) to be connected to balanced inputs (for example, a mixer).

The microphone, in this case, outputs two "hot" signals: one regular signal through Pin 2 (+) and the signal that is identical except it is inverted in polarity in Pin 3 (-). Throughout the length of the cable, the two signals will be impacted by electrical interference from the surrounding environment that ultimately creates noise within the cable. Within the two "hot" wires inside the cable, the noise is identical in signal and in polarity. At the end of the cable at the mixer, the signal from Pin 2 (-) is then inverted in polarity once more and added to the signal from Pin 1 (+). This causes the original signal to be retained and the noisy electrical interference to be eliminated since the two identical noisy signals are now of opposite polarity and are added together.

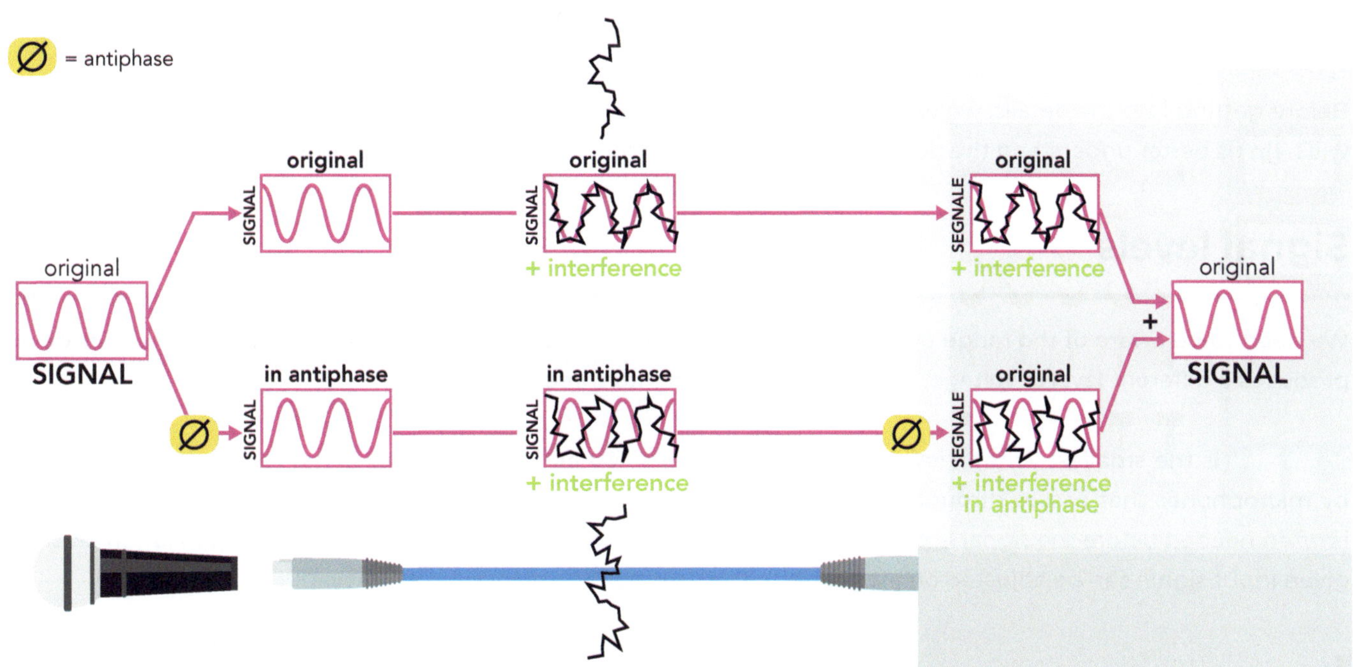

We need to discuss one other element that cables carry: ground. The ground (also called "earth") represents 0V and is the reference for not only the audio signals, but it is also the common electrical reference for all the devices in our electroacoustic system. For this reason, ground is always carried by the cable between devices. When two devices have mismatched ground signals, then we get a buzzy noise at 50 Hz or 60 Hz, also known as ground loop noise.

At this point, we can review the roles cables play within electroacoustic systems. A 2-pin cable carries only **unbalanced mono signals** because one of the cables passes the signal and the other the ground. In a 3-pin cable, on the other hand, we either have an **unbalanced** stereo cable consisting of a left signal, a right signal, and ground; or a **balanced** mono cable, consisting of "hot" signal, a "cold" signal which has its polarity flipped, and a ground connection.

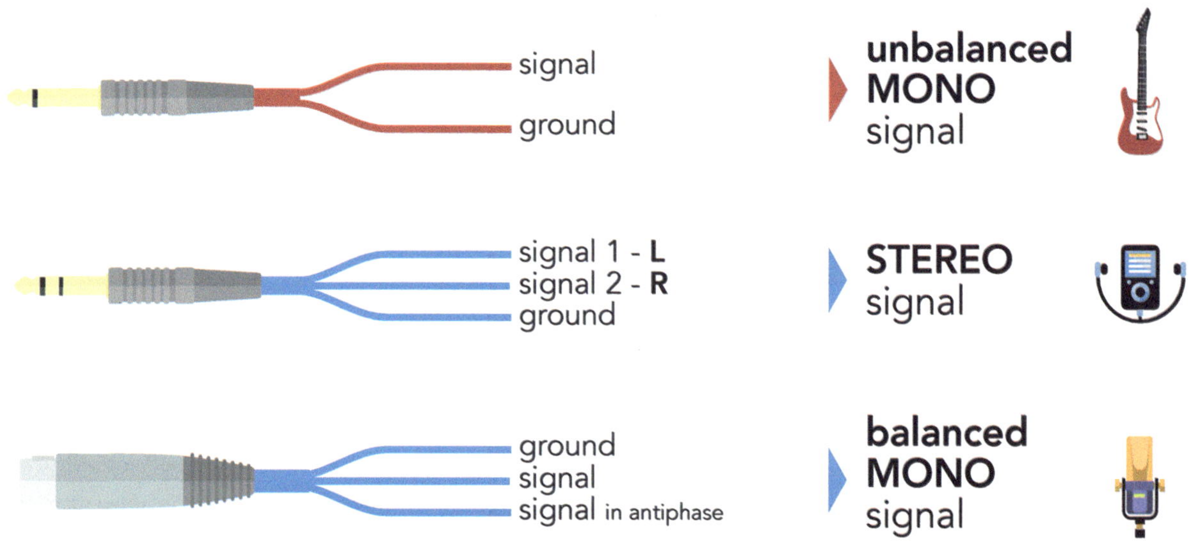

In an electroacoustic system, all devices can have one (or more) of three possible functions: an **Input** device, a **Processing** device, or an **Output** device.

Input

Input devices introduce or import audio signals into the electroacoustic system. This category of devices includes not just microphones, but also instruments such as electric guitars, electric basses, electric pianos, synthesizers, *Blu-ray* players, and even smartphones that input streaming songs into the system.

Before getting into the details, we will look at some general audio specifications of input devices. This information will help us better understand the devices and how we connect them together in our electroacoustic system chain.

Signal levels

We need to be aware of the range of voltages that our devices output into our system. Each instrument or device produces a different level of voltage, which can be divided into three categories:

Mic level is the smallest voltage level, outputting between -60 and -40 dBV. This is the voltage range produced by microphones that passes through the 3-pin XLR cables. Because these voltages are so small, preamplification is often needed before the signal is processed or recorded. We will discuss later how the preamplification level of a given input signal can be adjusted on a mixer with the gain pot.

Instrument level is an intermediate voltage level, approximately -20 dBu*, that is used mainly in instruments that use magnetic pickups: guitars, basses, and electric pianos. It runs through 2-pin cables with TS connectors. Sometimes the signal coming in at instrument level can require preamplification.

Line level is the largest level of electric voltage and does not require preamplification. Within line level, there are two categories: **Consumer** (-10 dBV*) and **Professional** (+4 dBu). The consumer category includes, for example, digital audio players and *Blu-ray* players. While the professional category can include synthesizers and drum machines. Cables carrying line level are usually 2- or 3-pin with TS, TRS, or even RCA connectors.

Mixers and other devices that receive multiple signals have different types of inputs, each intended to receive different levels. For example, in mixers, we will often find XLR inputs with built in preamplifiers, because it is assumed that we will apply gain to the microphone level to make it usable within the mixer. Conversely, with a stereo TS input, the mixer expects to receive line level, and no amplification is usually needed.

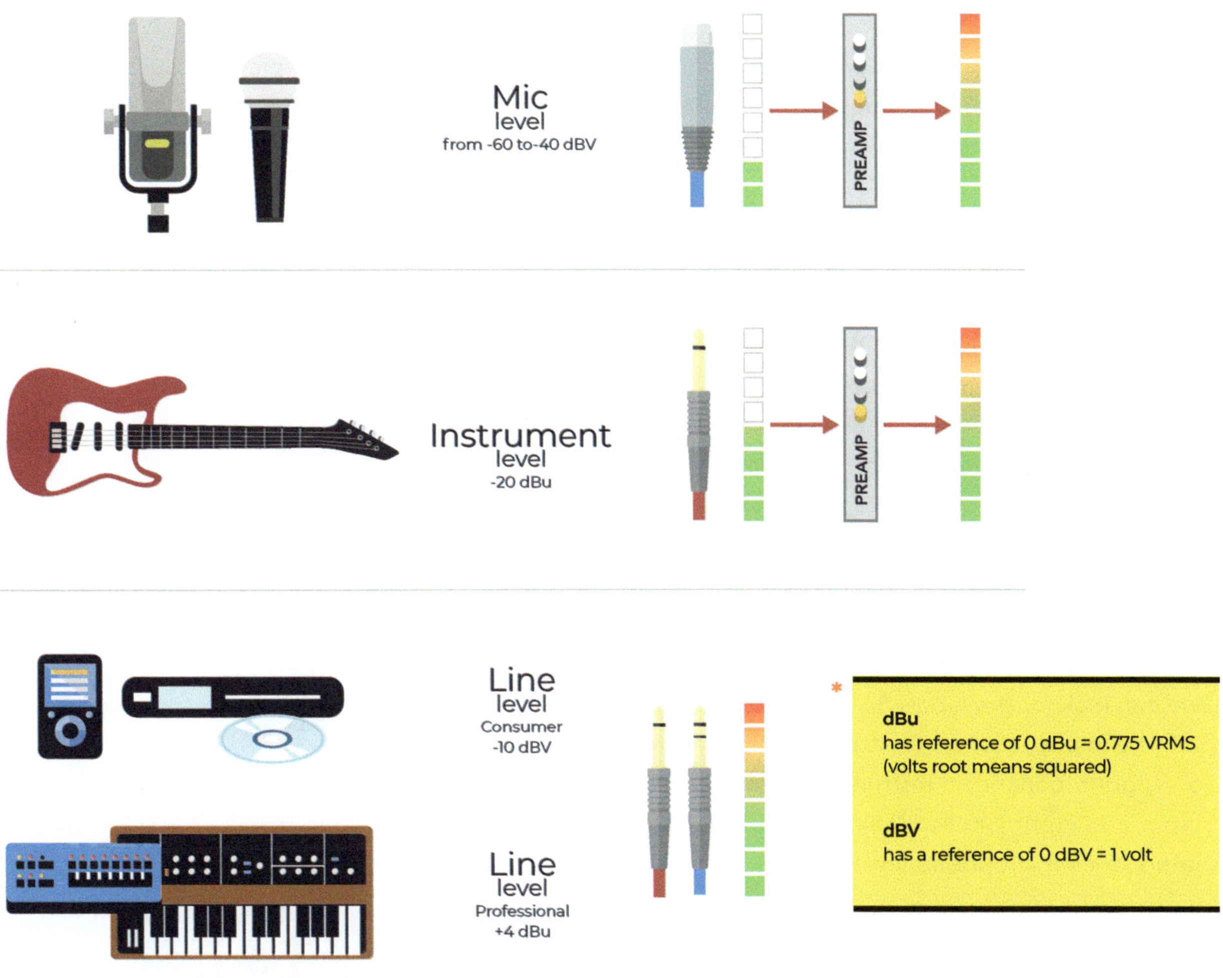

both dBV and dBu measure the Volts of our signal but related to different values: 1V for dBV and 0.775V for dBu

Impedance

In electricity, **impedance (Z)** is the opposition to alternating current caused by the resistance and reactance of elements in an electric circuit. Impedance is generally a complex number (a+bi) and has a magnitude and phase component. The units of impedance are Ohms (Ω) and understanding how impedance works is essential in electroacoustic musical systems because, if not handled properly, signal loss or unintentional harmonic distortion can occur.

Every device has an **Output Impedance** and a **Load Impedance**. The output impedance refers to what resistance an external device experiences when plugged into the instrument. Load impedance refers to the impedance presented to an audio device from an external load, such as a speaker. This is related to input impedance. A microphone has an output impedance that a mixer sees. The mixer has an input impedance that the microphone sees. And the mixer applies a load impedance to the microphone. Typically the load impedance must be at least 10 times higher than the impedance of the sound source. This is known as "bridging impedance", where there is maximum voltage transfer, while minimizing signal degradation, from the one device to another. For example, if I connect a microphone to a mixer, I should ensure that my microphone's output impedance is ten times lower than the mixer's input impedance.

Fortunately, on a practical level, there is a simplification that we can use in most cases. Most audio device impedances fall into two broad categories:

Low Impedance (Lo-Z) is the typical impedance of professional grade microphones and line level devices, such as synthesizers and digital audio players. Typically, the impedances range between 50 and 600 Ω. As such, it is less prone to interference.

High Impedance (Hi-Z) is typically found on instruments with magnetic pickups, such as guitars, basses, and electric pianos (Fender Rhodes style). The impedances range between 10 kOhm and 100 kOhm and the audio signal may be subject to degradation and interference. Typically, long cables need to be avoided to avoid losses and signal degradation.

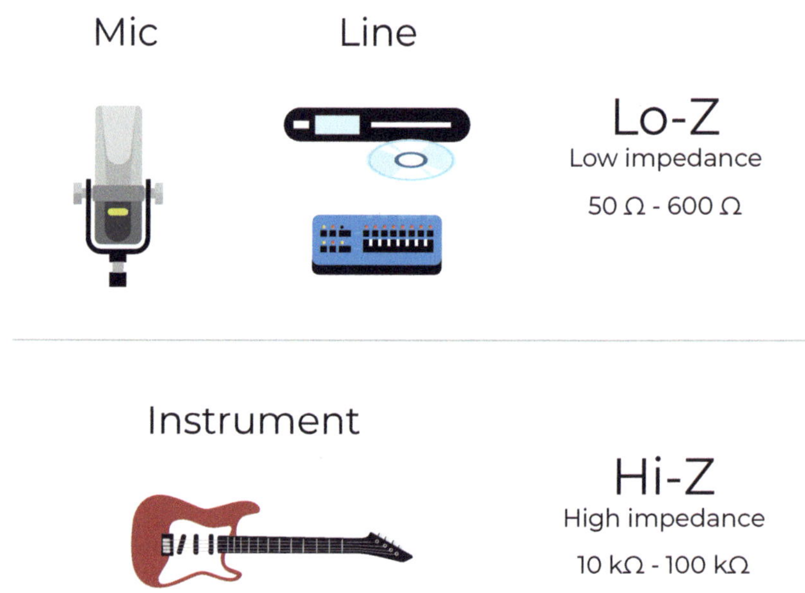

These two impedance categories tell us how to connect our devices together. Typically, if we have a Lo-Z device, we want to connect it to a Lo-Z input. Likewise, if we have a Hi-Z device, we prefer to use a Hi-Z input. For example, a Lo-Z microphone will be plugged into a Lo-Z input, while still maintaining the 10x rule from above. Conversely, a Hi-Z electric guitar will need to be connected to a Hi-Z input. To recognize the inputs, we can look for the labels "Hi-Z" or "Lo-Z." The input labelled "Instrument" is a high-impedance instrument-level input and input labelled "Mic" is a low-impedance microphone-level input.

Some audio interfaces or mixers have only one input for microphones, line level devices, and instruments, sometimes called a "combo" input. These combo inputs are usually paired with a button (Mic/Line or Inst) to select the type of input, whereby if you select instrument, you change the input to expect an Hi-Z device.

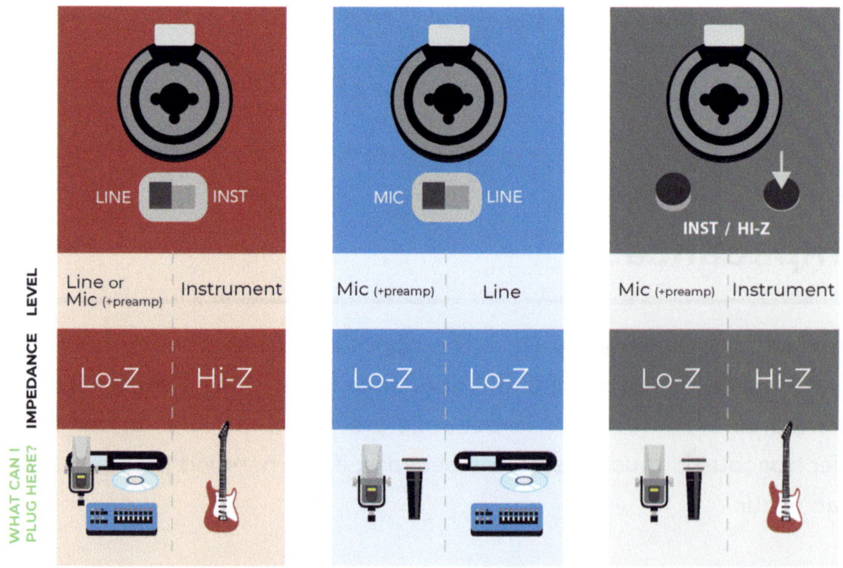

DI-Box

DI-Box (or Direct Inject Box) is a "little box" that transforms an unbalanced high-impedance signal into a balanced low-impedance signal. This conversion allows our signal to make long runs without losing quality. Active DI-Boxes make some preamplification possible, while passive DI-Boxes do not have this ability. DI-Boxes can be mono or stereo, depending on if they can handle one or two channels. They are also used, for example, on stages to transform the unbalanced signal of an instrument, such as a synthesizer, to balanced signal in order to use an XLR cable to make the long cable run (longer than ten meters) to the mixer. Using a DI-Box in this application ensures the quieter balanced connection that prevents noise, interference, and degradation that can occur with long unbalanced cables.

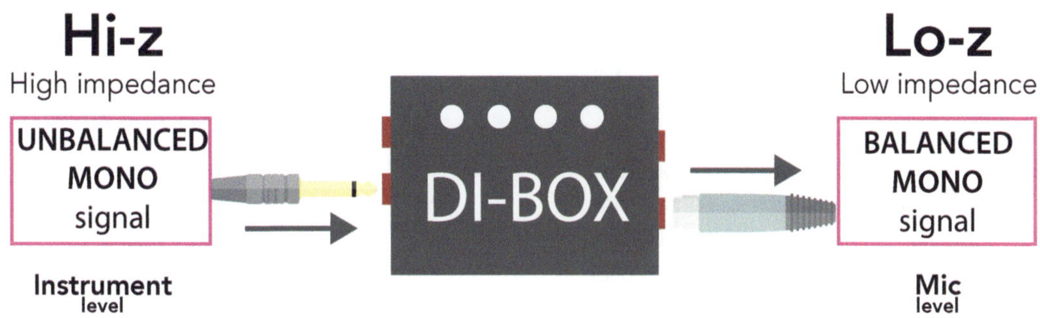

Microphones

Types of microphones

A microphone is a transducer, transforming an acoustical sound wave that propagates in the elastic medium (air or water) into an analogous electrical signal. There are three main types of microphones, each differing in how the acoustical wave to electrical voltage transduction is carried out.

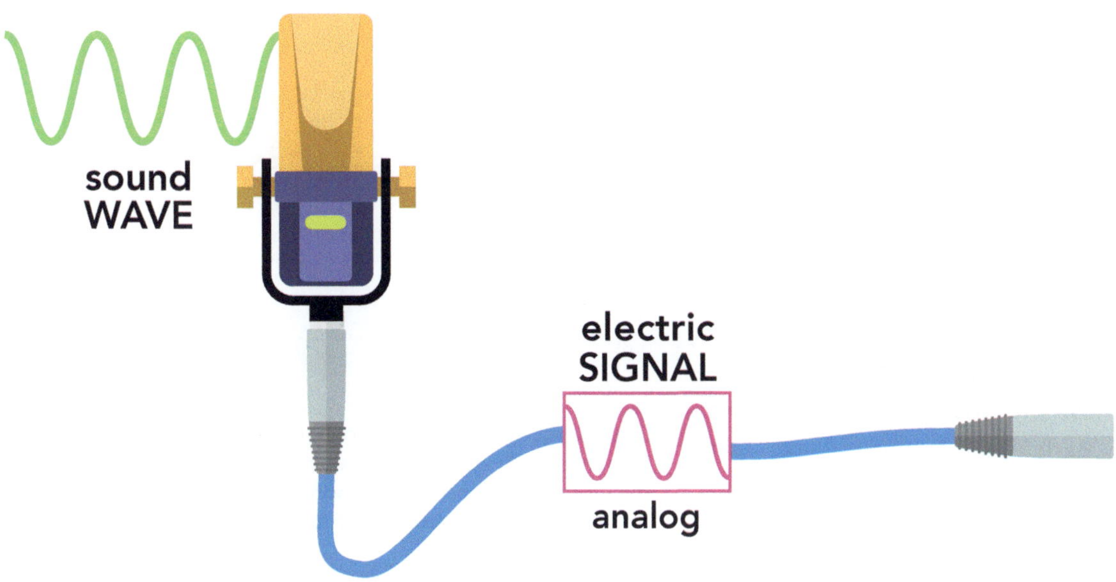

Balanced signal: as we clarified in previous sections, most microphones found in recording studios generate a balanced signal. To do this, they have a small transformer that takes the signal and creates two versions, the original signal and one with inverted polarity, that are transmitted through two of the wires within a 3-pin cable.

Larsen effect: Before proceeding further, it is appropriate to introduce the Larsen effect, also known as acoustic feedback. We may already have experienced this phenomenon. This effect happens when the speaker and microphone or pickup are physically close to one another, creating a feedback loop. The sound of a speaker is picked up by a microphone or a pickup and then the sound is amplified again and retransmitted from the microphone or pickup through the same speaker, creating a loop of sound that can only be stopped if the feedback is interrupted. This effect can produce a distinct high pitched tone or whistling. Sometimes, especially in electric guitars, it is intentionally triggered and controlled by the musician who uses the Larsen effect as an artistic choice.

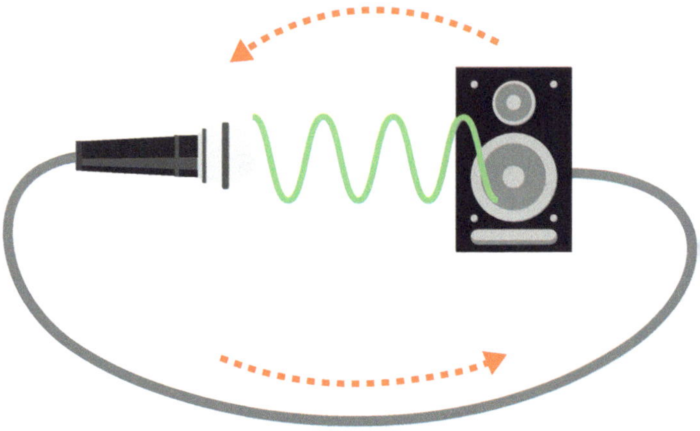

DYNAMIC MICROPHONE

Dynamic microphones are popular in live concert situations because it is more "selective" in capturing sounds and consequently less subject to the Larsen effect. While it is, on average, less sensitive than a condenser mic, dynamic mics are more durable to mechanical shocks and drops and can withstand the rigors of extremely high sound pressure levels. Additionally, unlike condenser mics, dynamic mics do not require phantom power to operate.

Operation Dynamic microphones consist of a diaphragm that is rigidly connected to a moving coil that surrounds a fixed magnet. Faraday's law* is the electromagnetic concept that states that when a coil moves around a magnet, the magnetic field changes, thereby inducing a voltage change. This precisely explains the mechanics of a dynamic microphone. When the acoustic wave hits the diaphragm, the coil moves around the fixed magnet, inducing a voltage change. This induced voltage, drawn at the ends of the coil, is proportional to the sound wave that makes the diaphragm move. Another way to think about dynamic microphones is as the inverse of dynamic speakers. Both use Faraday's law, but whereas a speaker uses changing voltage to move a coil, the dynamic microphone uses a moving coil to generate a voltage.

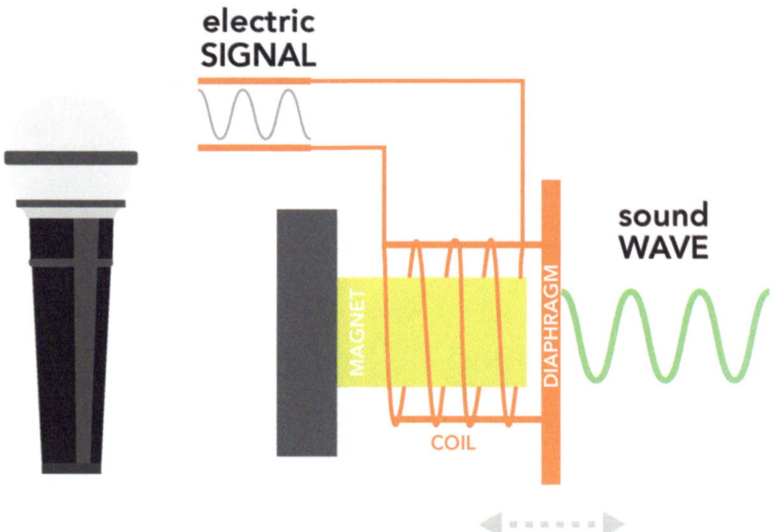

* Faraday's Law of Electromagnetic Induction is the principle that helps us turn movement into electricity. Another example of this law in action is the bicycle dynamo, which consists of a magnet and a coil of copper wire. As the magnet and the coil move around each other, an electrical voltage is generated by induction.

CONDENSER MICROPHONE

Condenser microphones are the most popular microphone in recording studios due to the high quality, sensitivity, and versatility. Hundreds of different models exist, optimized for different instruments and varying recording situations. These microphones exhibit high sensitivity, making them less useful in live music settings since they might capture too much unwanted background noise and be more susceptible to the Larsen effect. Condenser microphones also require auxiliary power, called **phantom power**. Typically, phantom power is +48V, which can be supplied by the mixer or mic preamp to which the microphone is connected. Alternatively, it can be powered by batteries inside the microphone itself, although this is less common.

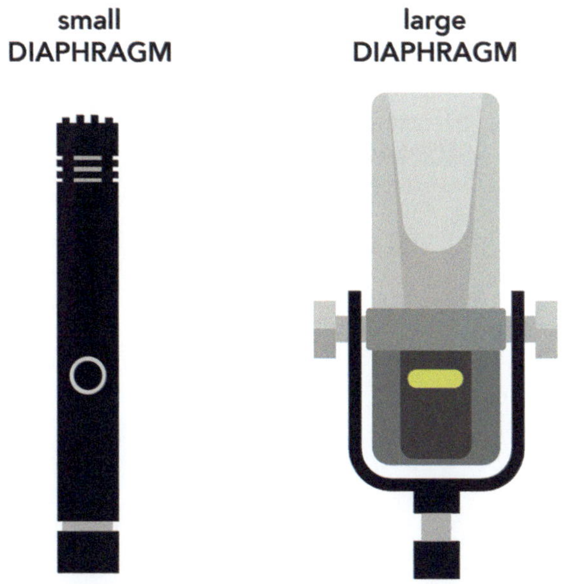

Condenser microphones fall into two broad categories, based on capsule size or diaphragm diameter: **small-diaphragm** (equal to or smaller than 1 inch, about 2.5 cm) and **large-diaphragm** (larger than 1 inch). Small diaphragm microphones are, on average, less sensitive and have more self-noise but have the advantage of a more neutral frequency response and better transient response. In contrast, large-diaphragm condenser microphones are more sensitive and exhibit lower self-noise. Thus, they are excellent in making rich sounding recordings that capture low frequency sounds well, but they need to be placed away from excessively noisy sound sources. Small diaphragm condenser mics can sometimes be found on stage in live music performances (e.g., the overhead mics of a drum kit), while large-diaphragm microphones are usually kept in more controlled environments like recording studios.

Operation A condenser microphone is, at its core, a capacitor that reacts to acoustic energy. A capacitor is an electrical component consisting of two conducting plates separated by an insulating dielectric. In a condenser microphone, a capacitor is formed by the diaphragm, sometimes made from gold-plated mylar sheets, and the back plate. As the diaphragm moves in and out when being impacted by an acoustic sound wave, the distance between diaphragm and the back plate varies, analogous to the pressure variations of the sound wave.

Between the two plates, an electric field is formed when +48V is supplied to the capacitor. This electric field is inversely proportional to the distance between the plates. As the diaphragm vibrates proportionally to the sound wave hitting it, the electric field, and thus the electric voltage, also varies accordingly. The output voltage is then usually sent to a preamplifier and then to a mixer or a DAW, where it is recorded.

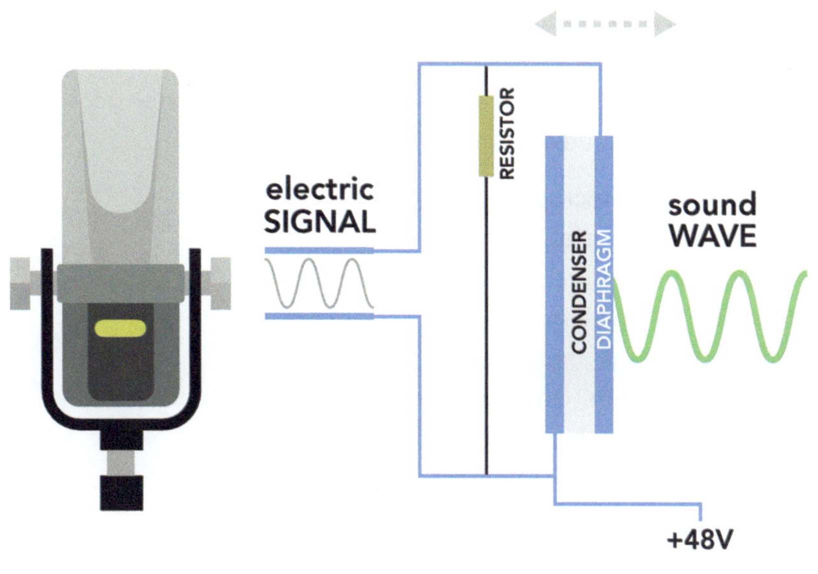

RIBBON MICROPHONE

Ribbon microphones are electromagnetic microphones known to be very precise and accurate, while being fragile to mechanical shock. These properties make ribbon microphones optimal for recording studio situations. Ribbon microphones do not require phantom power because their operation is similar to moving coil dynamic microphones. In fact, with many ribbon microphones, accidentally applying phantom power may permanently damage the microphone. Ribbon microphones may also require preamplification within the microphone itself.

Operation Ribbon microphones are also based on Faraday's law, taking advantage of the induced voltage that occurs when the metal ribbon and a magnet move relative to each other. The significant difference here is that in ribbon microphones, the corrugated metal ribbon acts as the diaphragm, instead of a metal coil as seen in dynamic microphones. This ribbon-diaphragm vibrates analogously to the sound wave that strikes it, while the magnet remains stationary. The voltage is output at the ends of the metal ribbon and can be recorded into a DAW as our analog audio signal.

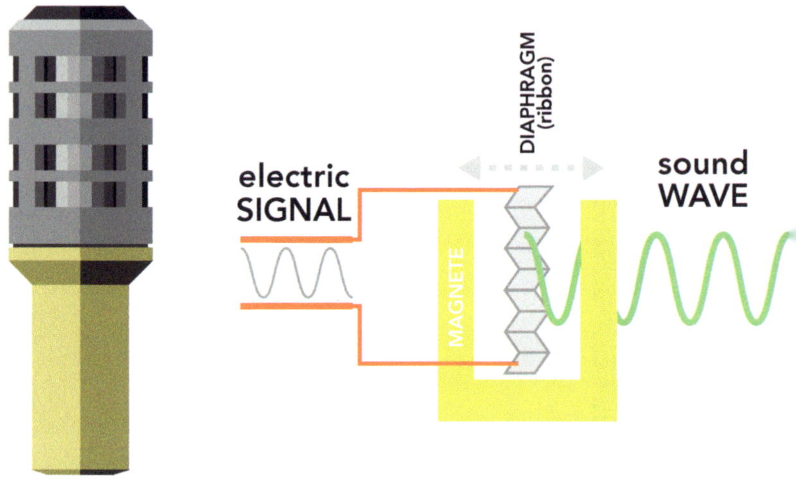

Special Microphones

CONTACT PIEZO MICROPHONE

Contact piezo microphone generally physically attach to the vibrating body of an instrument, directly transforming mechanical vibrations into an electrical signal. In this case, the sound does not need to propagate in air for the piezo microphone to capture the sound. These piezo microphones are generally more affordable and can even be built as DIY projects. Generally, the sound it produces is not as high in quality or detail as the previously mentioned microphone types. It is, however, excellent in live music situations because the Larsen effect can be avoided because piezo microphones react only to mechanical vibrations, and not the acoustic energy radiating from a speaker, thereby breaking the feedback cycle. Piezo microphones are commonly used, for example, to pick up string instruments in a live pop or jazz concert setting, where they can offer good sound isolation as the acoustic energy from the instrument is not loud enough on its own.

Operation Piezo microphones utilize piezoelectric crystals, special crystals that generate an electric charge when pressure is applied to it, causing a deformation. In this case, the mechanical vibration of an instrument body creates a mechanical compression onto the piezoelectric crystal, resulting in a changing voltage that is the analog audio signal. Piezo microphones can be subject to the vibration properties of the instrument itself, making the placement of the microphone important. Usually, these microphones, unlike those seen above, output an unbalanced signal.

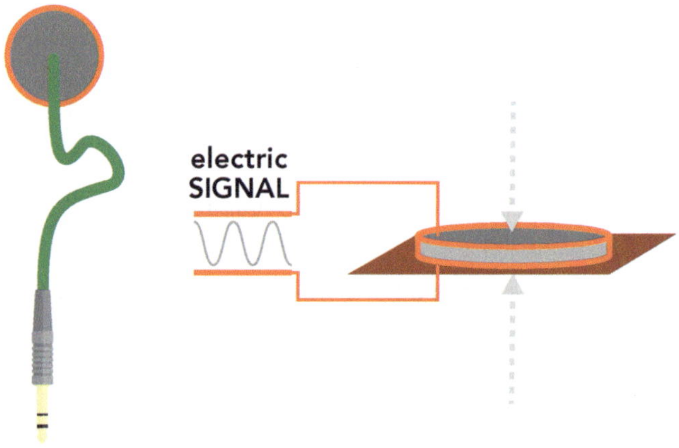

ELECTRET MICROPHONE

Electret microphones are a subset of condenser microphones that do not require phantom power. Instead, the electric field is created with a permanently charged back plate. These microphones are versatile and can be used in a variety of situations because no phantom power is needed. While less popular in recording studios, electret microphones are commonly used in the lavalier microphones you see on TV. Additionally, electret microphones are used in laptops, cell phones, and other small devices.

Operation In 1962, James West and Gerhard Sessler invented the electret microphone at ***Bell Laboratories***. As we saw earlier, a capacitor needs +48V to create the electric field between the plates. In this case, the back plate is made up an electret material, which holds a permanent electric charge that powers the capacitor. There may be other components within an electret microphone, such as a preamplifier, transmitter, or other internal components, that require external power.

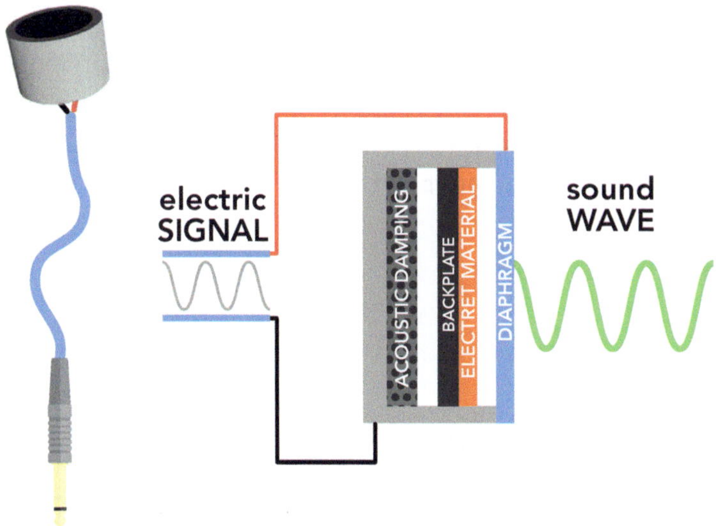

BOUNDARY LAYER MICROPHONE

Boundary layer microphones (or pressure zone microphones, PZM) are a type of microphone that sits in very close proximity to a large flat surface. These microphones are used on stages, on walls, and along other flat surfaces such as piano lids. One of the most common non-musical uses is in conference rooms, where a boundary layer microphone sits on a large table.

Operation A small microphone, either omnidirectional or cardioid, is mounted very close to a surface and is pointed toward the surface. Often, a piezo or condenser microphone is used. The microphone then picks up the air pressure variations sitting on the surface (not the surface vibrations), rather than the changing pressures traveling through the air like traditional microphones. When a sound wave hits a boundary, there is a pressure maximum at the boundary, leading to an amplitude boost when using this kind of microphone. The larger the plate, or boundary, that this microphone sits on, the better the bass frequency response.

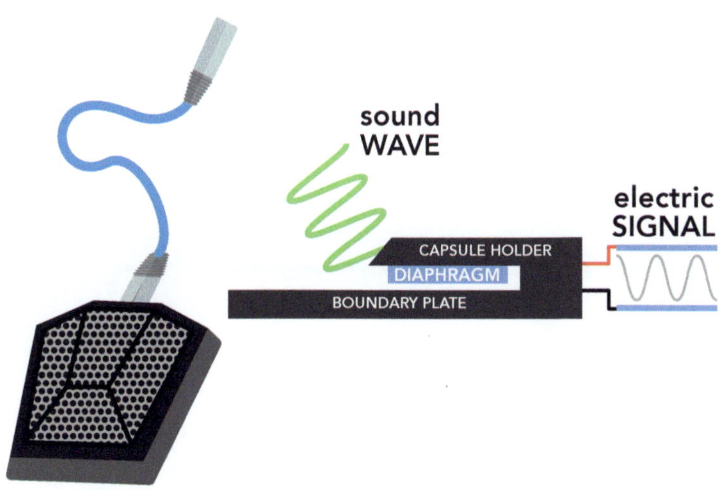

HYDROPHONE

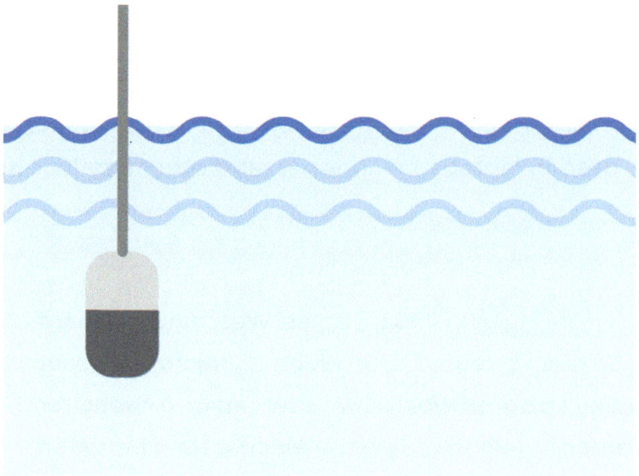

Hydrophones are used to pick up sound underwater and are often used for scientific research and musical or sound design effects. Many hydrophones have capsules that are so physically durable that they can be frozen or placed in boiling water, greatly expanding the kinds of sounds that they can capture.

Operation Hydrophones can be dynamic or condenser microphones. The only difference with these hydrophones, from the traditional varieties described above, is that they have a protective waterproof capsule.

Frequency response

Only an "ideal" microphone would be able to equally capture all frequencies in the spectrum of a sound. Each microphone is characterized by a different preference for some frequency bands in the real world. This causes each microphone to have its own identity, its own "color," which it applies each time to the sound it picks up, transforming it slightly or noticeably from the original acoustic sound. This ultimately is a spectral distortion caused by the frequency response of the microphone.

The **frequency response** of a microphone is defined as its sensitivity to different frequencies. We can find a microphone's frequency response by examining the graph that is included with the microphone instructions, or by finding the microphone's datasheet. The frequency response is a curve that represents the frequency on the graph's X-axis and the corresponding amplitude, usually in dB, on the Y-axis. Flat frequency responses have essentially the same amplitudes across all frequencies, i.e., they react more or less the same across all frequencies. Optimized frequency responses can tailor or customize frequency responses to emphasize or attenuate certain frequencies in order to achieve a desired sound of specific instruments. Microphones can, for example, favor mid-high frequencies, making the microphone more suitable for capturing a live voice. Flat frequency responses, on the other hand, are ideal for studio recording because they offer a sound more closely conforming to the original by not favoring any particular frequency band.

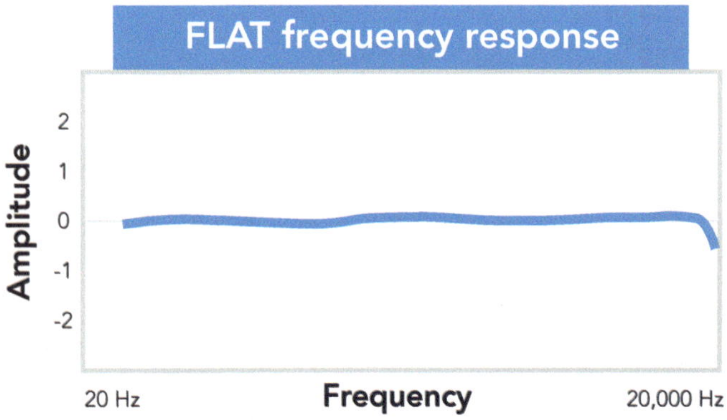

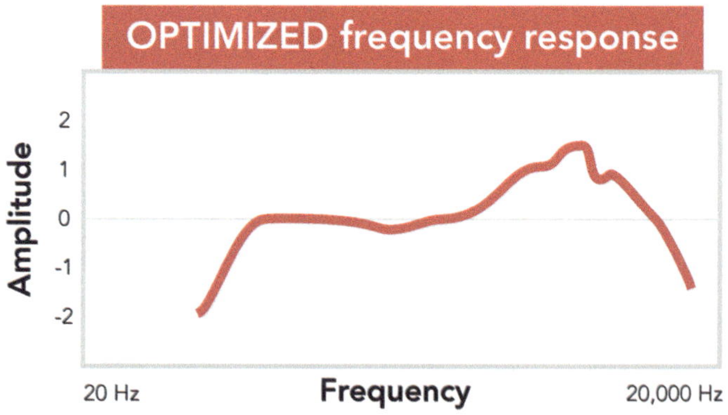

PAD A Passive Attenuation Device (PAD) can be used on a microphone when the incoming sound wave is excessively loud and needs to be attenuated to prevent overloading the microphone and causing distortion. A PAD essentially makes the microphone less sensitive. Usually, we can choose between 0 dB, i.e., no attenuation, and one or more negative dB values (e.g. -10 dB) to attenuate the loud input sound before the preamplification stage.

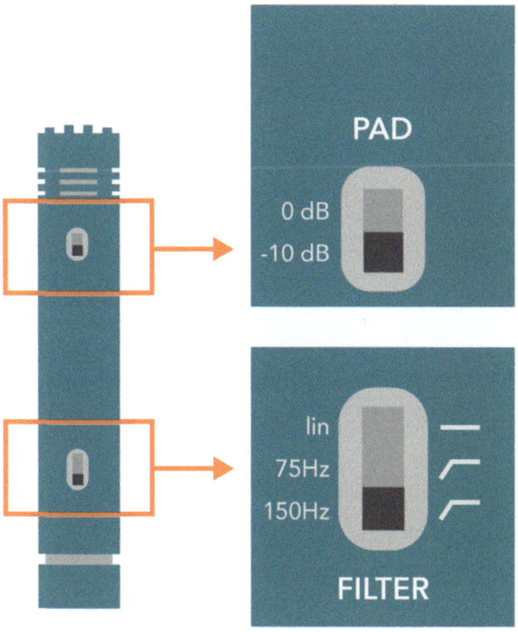

LOW-CUT FILTER This filter allows us to choose whether to attenuate low frequencies by activating a ***high-pass*** filter (see the chapter on filters, page 105) on the entire input sound. Some microphones even give several options for cutoff frequency. We often use these ***low-cut*** filters to reduce wind interference in outdoor recordings or attenuate rumbly building or vibration noises that can enter our recordings. In vocal recordings, the ***low-cut*** filter can help reduce the punchiness that comes from plosive sounds and other sounds associated with high-velocity air.

Polar pattern

What would happen if the singer during the concert sings behind the microphone? Surely we would hear the voice with less volume. This is because each microphone has preferred pick-up angles based on directionally characteristics of the microphones. We show the microphone's directionality with its **polar pattern** or describe it with its polar characteristic.

This directionality describes how the microphone picks up sounds from various directions, relative to the orientation of the diaphragm and, thus, the microphone itself. It can be defined and illustrated through polar graphs, showing us the amplitude (in dB) relative to an angle around a circle. The microphone is represented by the origin of the graph and is pointed at 0°. The higher the amplitude, the further the line is from the center. Likewise, curves that approach the center of the circle are attenuated. While there are an infinite number of possible polar patterns, the most commonly used ones fall into four ideal types:

CARDIOID

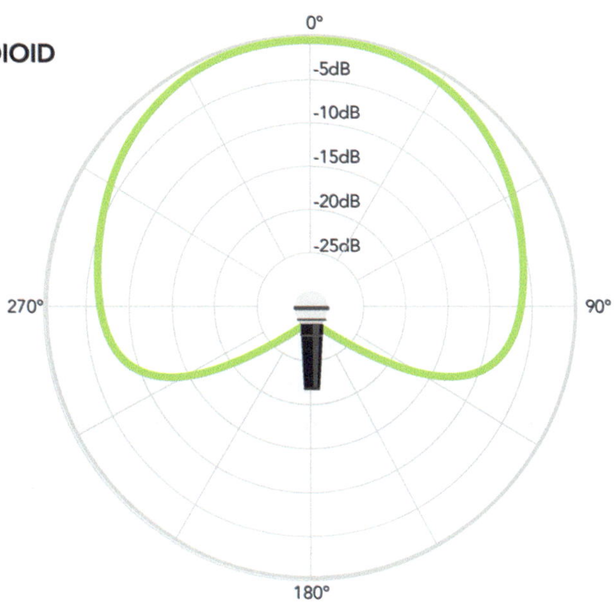

The typical directional microphone has a **cardioid** polar pattern. It has the highest sensitivity directly on-axis in front of the capsule (0°) and the lowest sensitivity at 180°, behind the capsule. Theoretically, there is a null point at 180°, meaning that there is infinite attenuation for sounds coming from behind the microphone. Practically, cardioid microphones will pick up sound well from the front while sounds from the rear will be quite quiet. Since the polar pattern is relatively wide on-axis, a singer can have some flexibility to move a few inches left or right from the microphone. The null point at 180° allows us to isolate unwanted sound sources by placing them behind the microphone. This null point can also provide excellent immunity to triggering the Larsen effect as compared to omnidirectional microphones. Thus, a cardioid microphone is a common choice for live musical performances that have high sound pressures on stage.

SUPERCARDIOID

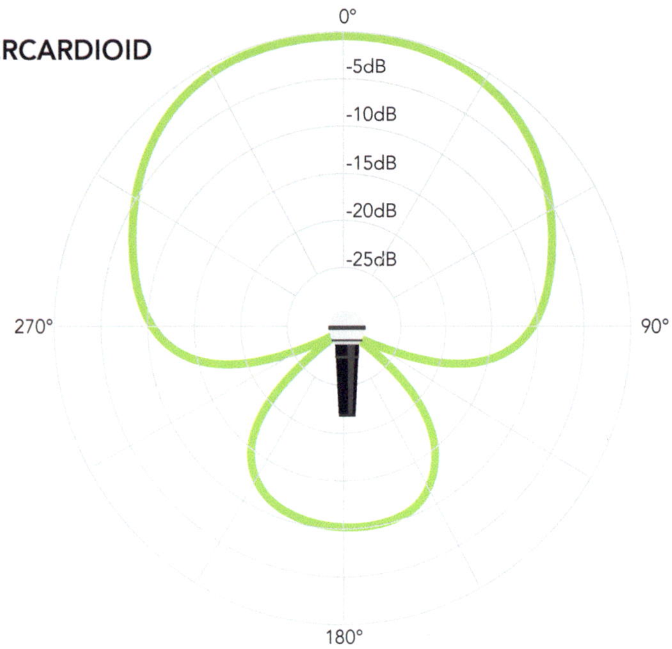

HYPERCARDIOID

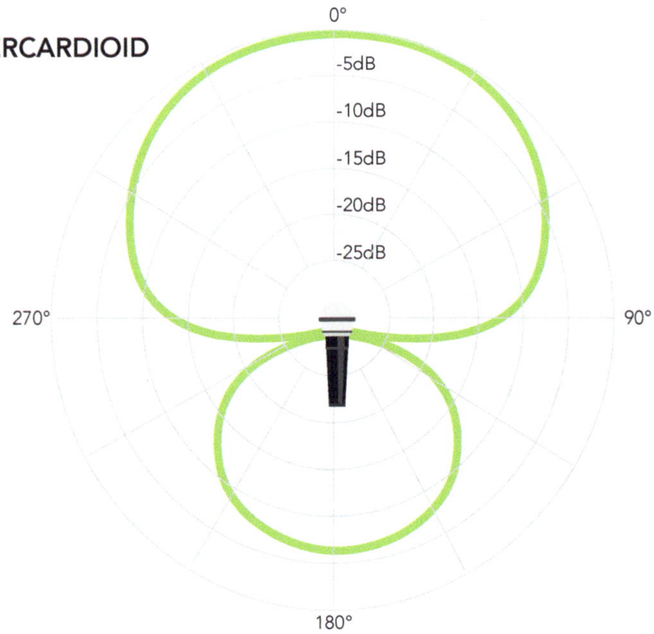

Supercardioid and **Hypercardioid** microphones exhibit similar patterns that exhibit a narrower on-axis pick-up angle, when compared to cardioids, and have two null points slightly displaced from 180°. At 180°, the microphone's sensitivity is less than the on-axis response, but it is not completely null as with cardioid microphones. Supercardioids have null angles at 126° and 234°, and hypercardioids have null angles at 110° and 250°. The null points can be quite useful on stage when positioning a stage microphone in front of a wedge monitor. If the wedge monitor is placed at the null point of a supercardioid or hypercardioid microphone, then the Larsen effect can be avoided. Furthermore, the narrower on-axis response makes the microphone more sensitive to only on-axis sounds, also helping with preventing the Larsen effect.

OMNIDIRECTIONAL

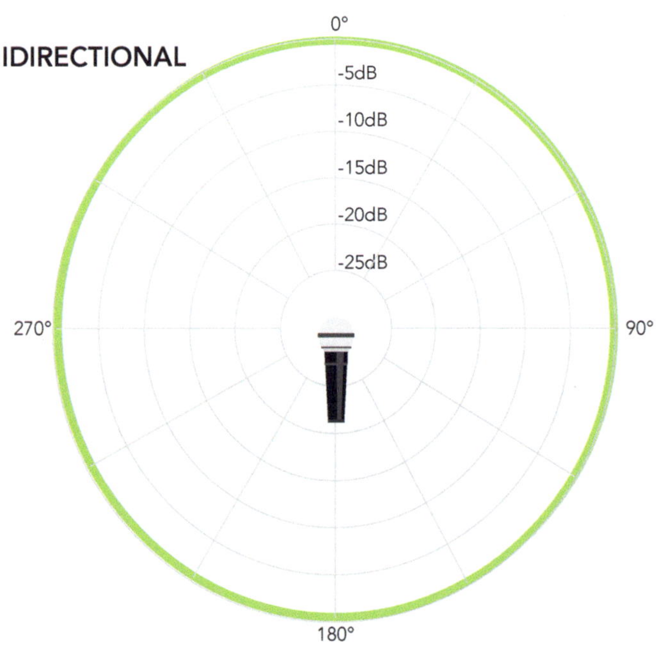

With **omnidirectional** patterns, the microphone has uniform sensitivity for sounds coming from all directions. It is not recommended on stages because it may pick up too much unwanted sound. However, it is essential for lavalier microphones used for TV announcers, for example. It would be inconvenient to clip directional microphones onto the announcers, as the direction of the microphone constantly changes depending on the movements of the announcer. Instead, we use omnidirectional microphones that ensure a constant sound even if we move the announcer's head or the position of the microphone itself. We also can use omnidirectional microphones as room microphones, capturing the reverberant field of a space.

BIDIRECTIONAL (FIGURE of 8)

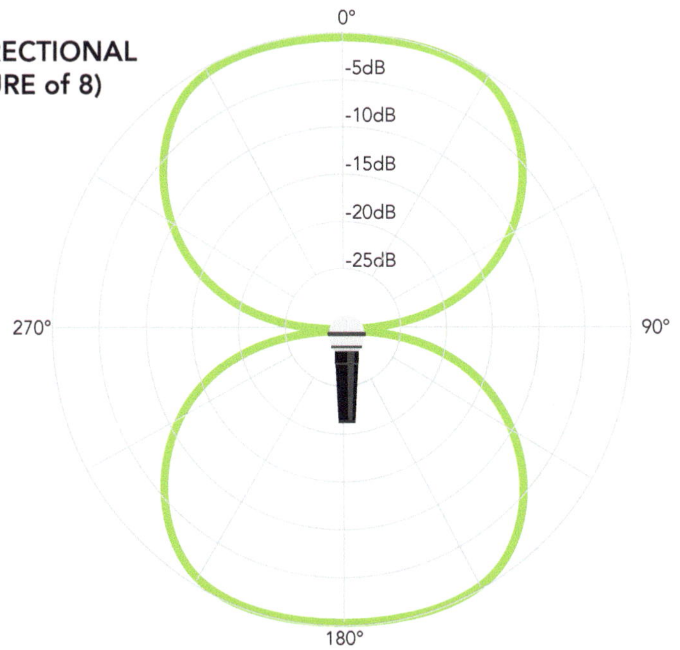

As the name suggests, this **bidirectional** or **figure-8** polar pattern indicates that the microphone receives sound equally from the front and the back. The exciting feature of these microphones is that the two main lobes, or pick-up angles, are quite narrow, making the microphones very selective. The null points for the bidirectional microphone are at 90° and 180°, allowing sounds from the sides to be significantly attenuated. In practice, bidirectional microphones are used in two types of stereo recording techniques: the ***Mid/Side (M/S)*** technique and the ***Blumlein pair technique***.

MICROPHONE ACCESSORIES

Shockmount Essential in the recording studio, particularly for condenser and ribbon microphones which are particularly sensitive to mechanical and vibrational noise, shockmounts are a system of elastic bands that suspends the microphone in the air that isolate the microphone from these vibrations. The shockmount absorbs the vibrations before they reach the microphone. It is intended to isolate the mechanical vibrations coming from the stand and the ground from the microphone itself.

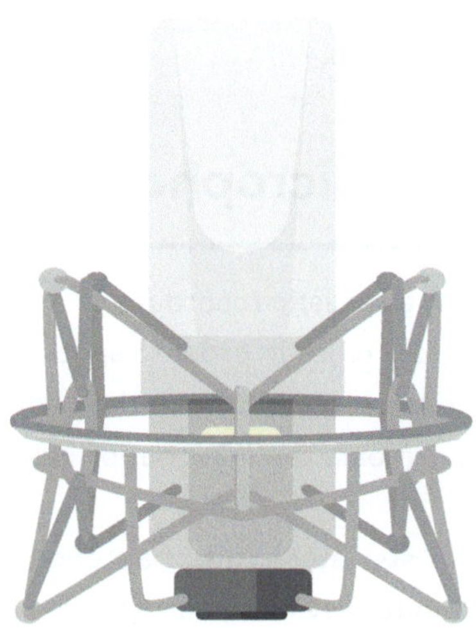

Pop filter These are physical mesh screens that are used in vocal recordings, especially in the studio, to reduce or eliminate artifacts caused by plosive sounds. Plosive sounds come from certain consonants, such as "p," "b", "k," "g," "t," and "d," which release a sudden burst of air pressure that impacts the microphone's diaphragm. The pop filter takes this burst of air pressure and diffuses it, thereby preventing the microphone from clipping. Pop filters are usually placed in front of the microphone, between the diaphragm and the vocalist. A secondary function of the pop filter is that it can protect the microphone from dust and saliva, which over time, could compromise the performance of the microphone.

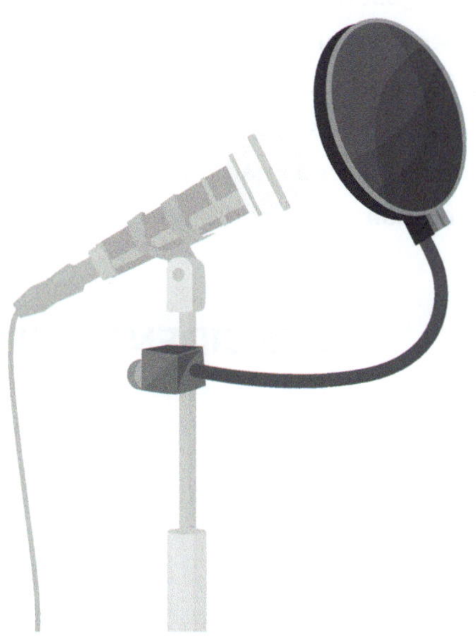

Windscreen A spongy or furry casing mounted over the microphone capsule, a windscreen, as the name suggests, helps to reduce the disturbance caused by wind and sibilant consonants. They become essential when we record outdoors, particularly in the recording practice called **field recording**. When our recording studio is essentially outside "in the field," wind noise can cause distortion in the recordings. Windscreens, though, can affect the frequency response of the microphone.

Parabolic reflector This accessory is also often used in field recording to pick up specific sounds within an environment, usually at a distance. The parabolic reflector is a concave structure made of usually plastic material that is attached so that it surrounds the microphone capsule. With this device attached, we can point the microphone toward a sound source, such as a bird tweeting. The parabolic reflector physically collects the sounds that are funneled into it and direct it to the capsule, usually sitting at or near the focal point of the reflector. This makes the microphone very directional, allowing us to point to specific sources while at a distance. We also often see these parabolic reflectors used in sporting events to capture the sounds on the field from microphones many meters away on the sidelines.

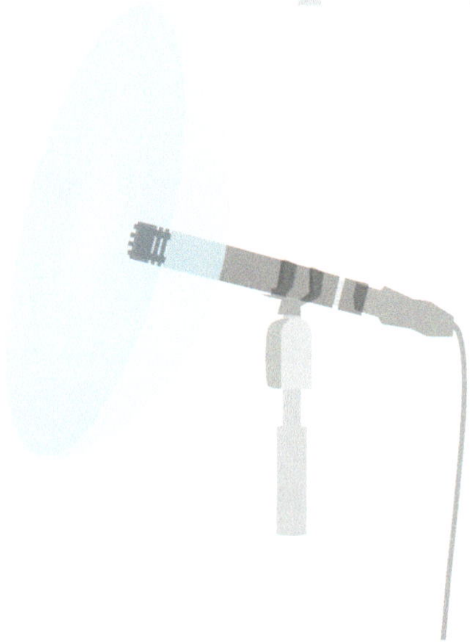

Stereo microphone techniques

To obtain a realistic recording of a single instrument or ensemble, we need a microphone technique that gives us the auditory clues in order to spatialize.
In order to recreate the spatial width of a single instrument or ensemble, we need at least two microphones to provide our ears the information needed to interpret the sound.

As we will see later in the chapter on spatialization, the way we locate a source is deeply connected to the physiology of our auditory system, particularly how the two pinnae of our ears collect sound. The fact that we possess two ears, and not just one, makes it possible for us to place, or localize, the sounds we hear in space. For this reason, to record in a way that allows us to listen back and recreate this space realistically, we need to utilize stereophonic imaging. This requires at least two microphones in order to provide the depth, spatial information, and localization cues of the instruments in our recording. While we can use more than two microphones, there are three general categories to achieve stereo imaging with just two microphones. These categories, **coincident pair**, **near-coincident pair**, and **spaced pair**, are based on the distance between the two microphones themselves.

COINCIDENT PAIR

In these techniques, two microphones are placed, theoretically, in the same location in space. Thus, both microphones receive signals at the same time and are in sync with respect to phase. However, because the capsules are pointed in different directions, there will be amplitude differences between the microphones. This is great if, for practical reasons (due to the playback device), the signals need to be summed to form a mono signal. Because the microphones are in phase, we will not have phase cancellation problems due to frequencies not in phase. This characteristic is called **mono-compatibility** and stereo recordings made with coincident pairs excel at this characteristic.

X/Y technique

Microphones: two cardioids, usually condenser

The microphones are placed with the capsules positioned in very close proximity with each other (coincident). The capsules are oriented such that the axes along their length are 90° - 135° apart, depending on the size of the sound source and the desired width of the stereo image. The pair is positioned so that the center of the angle between the capsules is pointed at the sound source. In other words, neither mic is pointed toward the center of the source but rather the center line separating the microphones is pointed at the source.

When mixing, all that needs to be done is to pan the two microphones, one totally to the left and the other to the right. Because of the proximity of the two microphones, the sound arrives at the two capsules at the same time, reducing phase-shifting problems. The X/Y technique has excellent mono-compatibility.

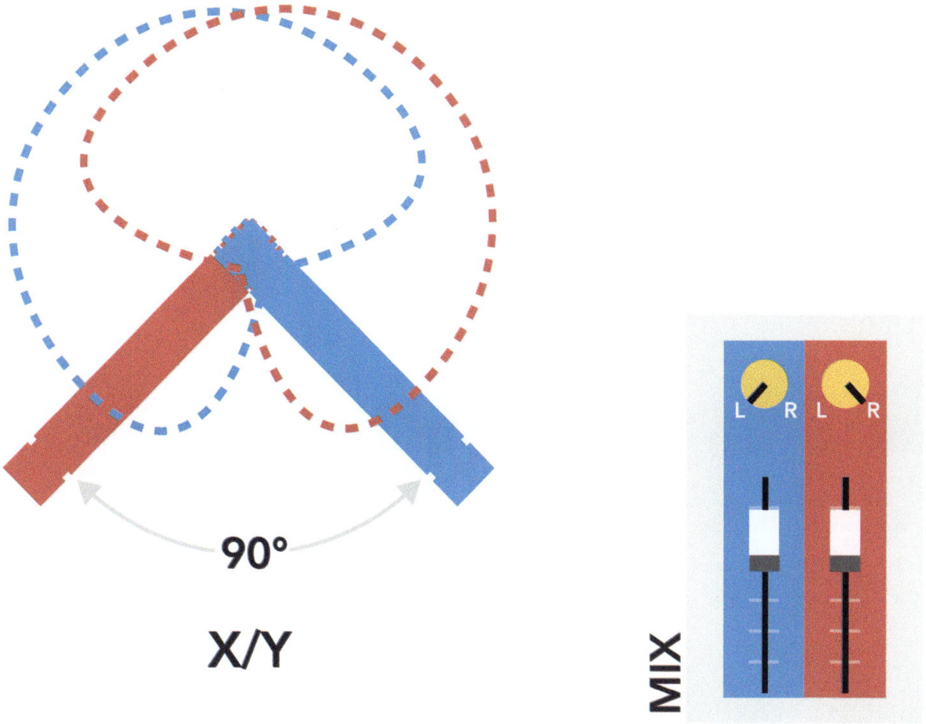

Mid/Side (M/S) technique

Microphones: one cardiod and one bidirectional, usually both condensers

The two microphones are placed coincidentally, sometimes even housed in the same unit that allow for some position variability. The cardioid capsule (the mid microphone) is aimed directly at the sound source, picking up mainly the on-axis sound, while the bidirectional capsule (side) is pointing left and right, picking up the cardioid capsule's left and right off-axis sounds and having a null point pointing toward the on-axis sound.

When mixing, the cardioid is positioned at the center of the mix, while the bidirectional signal is duplicated, with one of these bidirectional signals being inverted in polarity. One of these signals is panned to the left and the other signal is panned to the right. This operation recreates our sound's "side" part and keeps it separate from the center or "mid" part. One considerable advantage is that we can adjust the level of the mid signal relative to the side signal, resulting in a wider and narrower stereo image without having to move any microphones. Moreover, this technique is perfectly mono-compatible precisely because the separation between the mid and side is distinct. By selecting only the mid signal, there will be perfectly mono sound with no phase cancellation. This makes the M/S technique quite useful in television and radio applications.

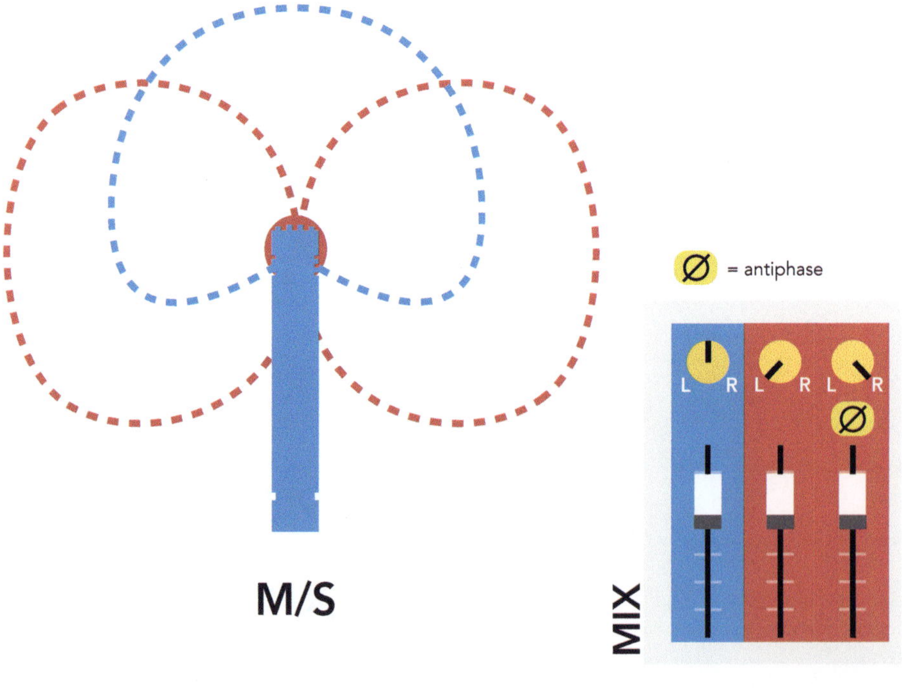

NEAR-COINCIDENT PAIR

These techniques involve using two microphones placed 15-30 cm apart. This distance is approximately related to the average distance between the ears on a human head. With this configuration, because the microphone capsules occupy different locations in space, in addition to amplitude differences, there will also be phase differences between the two signals. This, on the one hand, improves the width and quality of the stereo effect, but affects this technique's mono-compatibility.

ORTF technique (Office de Radiodiffusion Télévision Française)

Microphones: two cardioids, usually condenser

This technique, developed in France, sets the two cardioid microphones capsules at a distance of 17 cm and an angle of exactly 110° apart. The two signals are panned to the left and right. This stereo technique usually results in a wide stereo field and is often used for mid to large sized ensemble recordings.

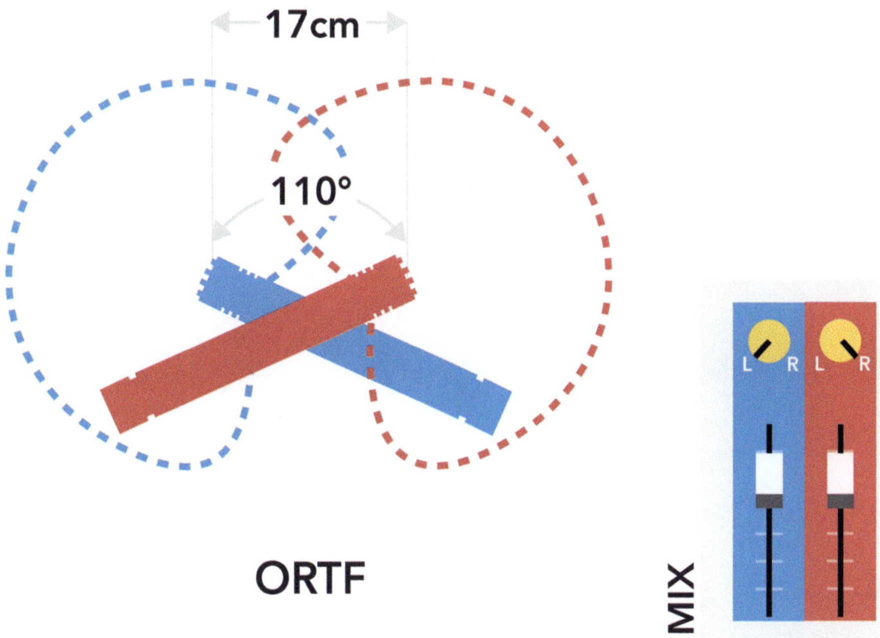

NOS technique (Nederlandse Omroep Stitchting)

Microphones: two cardioids, usually condenser

Developed in the Netherlands, this technique involves placing two cardioid microphone capsules 30 cm apart and at a 90° angle from each other. The two signals are panned to the left and right. While this stereo technique creates a wide stereo field, it is not generally as wide as the ORTF technique. This technique is also used for mid to large sized ensemble recordings.

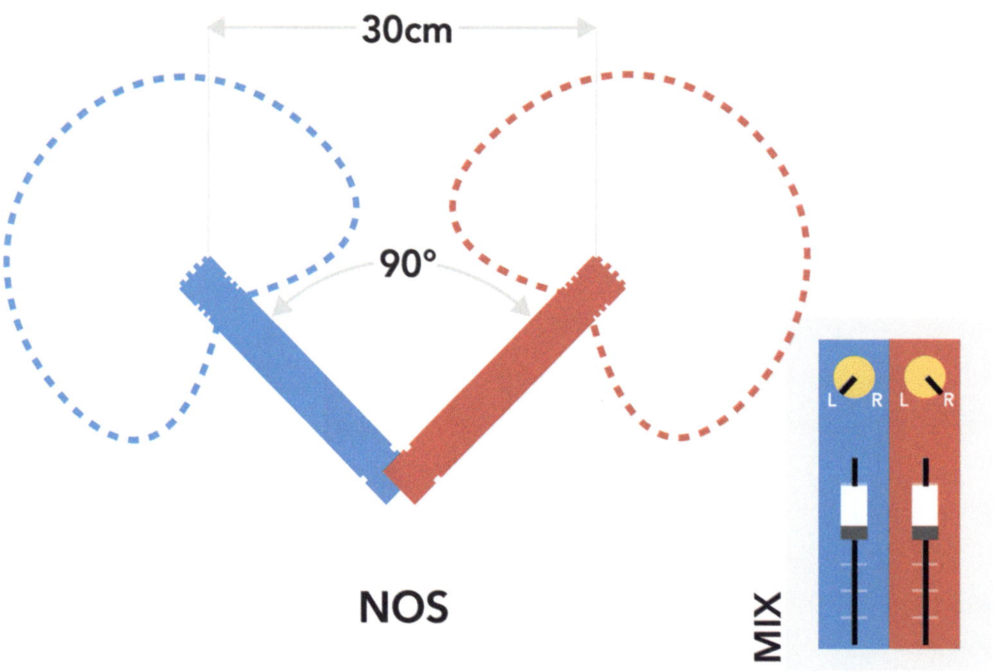

SPACED PAIR

These techniques require microphones to be placed at somewhat larger distances from each other, depending on the size of the sound source. Because of concerns with phase cancellation, we can apply the 3:1 ratio rule. This rule states that the distance of the second microphone to the first microphone should be at least three times the distance between the sound source and the first microphone. For example, if I am recording a chamber music group and I place the microphones six feet away from the musicians, I have to separate the two microphones by at least 18 ft. These techniques are generally not mono-compatible because of the significant phase differences between the sounds picked up by the microphone that are placed so far from one another. Thus, this technique is generally exclusively used in non-broadcast contexts.

A/B and spaced pair technique

Microphones: two cardioids or omnidirectional, usually condenser

The distance between the microphones, in this case, can be vast. Usually for the A/B technique, the cardioid or omnidirectional microphones are spaced 12"-48" inches apart. For the spaced pair, the two microphones are separated by a distance of at least 1-3 meters (3-10 ft) and the signals are panned hard left and hard right in the mix. In both these cases, the microphones face forward with no angle difference between the two. Because of the relatively large distance between the two microphones and the resultant difference in the arrival time of the sound at the microphones, phase interference (cancellations or summing at specific frequencies) may result in poor mono-compatibility.

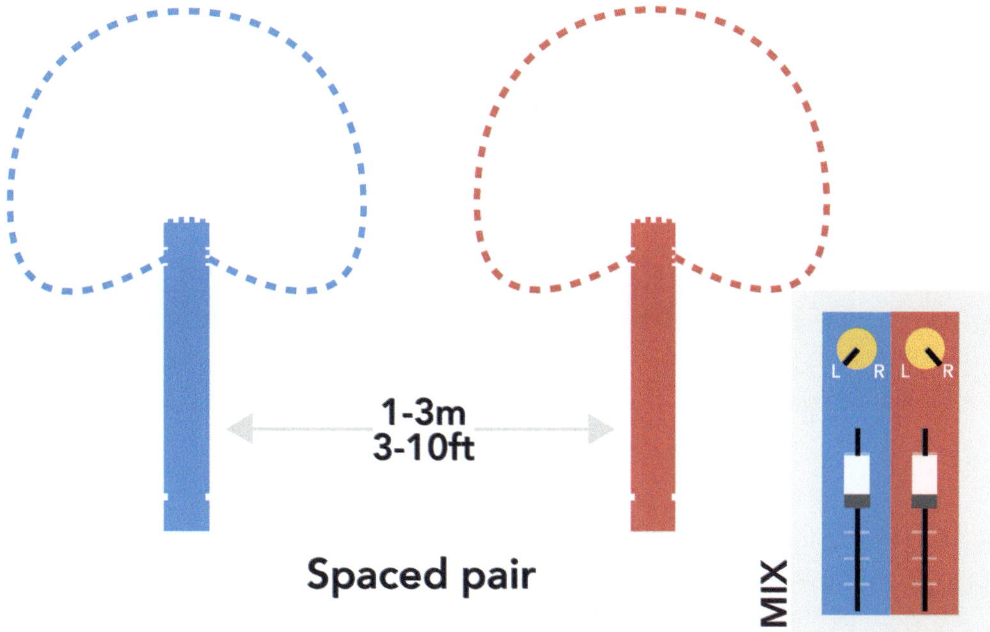

.choose one or more continuous sound sources in your home, e.g., a rather noisy refrigerator, a washing machine, a dishwasher, or even a sound caused by an app on your phone. Take a microphone and make a recording of the sound by moving the microphone. First increase the distance of the microphone from the source, then turn the microphone to different angles from the sound source. Record and experiment, then devise a performance in which these gestures and the corresponding sounds give life to a song of about 2:00. ***Theme: "My magic wand"***

Understanding Mic Specs - Shure ~ Karlheinz Stockhausen - Mikrophonie ~ Diego Stocco - Music from nature ~ GRM Parigi ~ Pierre Schaeffer ~ "Studio di Fonologia della RAI Milano ~ Luciano Berio

Magnetic pickups

The microphone technologies we have seen above are not the only types of transducers that convert mechanical motion into electrical energy. In fact, there is an entire family of instruments, introduced in 1932, that use **magnetic pickups**. This family includes electric guitars, electric basses, and electric pianos and is centered around a device called the pickup.

The pickup consists of a series of cylindrical magnetic poles placed in close proximity to an instrument's string, around which thin conducting wires are wound to form the coil. These pickups can be passive or active, the latter requiring energy to amplify its signal. A battery inside the instrument provides the voltage to power these active pickups.

Operation Taking advantage of the ***Faraday effect*** again (see page 54), the vibration of a metal string or a tiny metal cylinder (in the case of the electric piano) produces a change in electromagnetic field around the magnetic pole, thus creating an alternating electric current in the coils. This alternating current, derived from the motion of the strings, is the analog electric signal that the instrument produces.

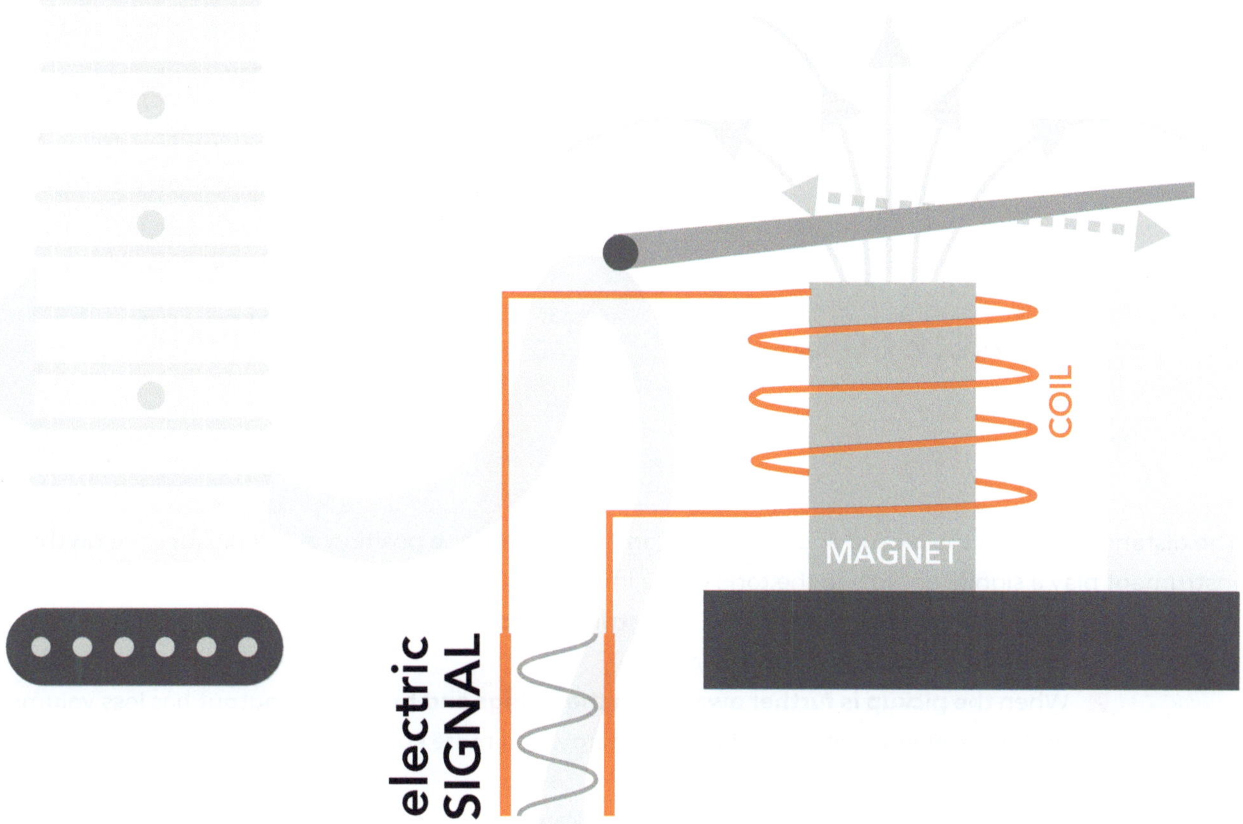

Several types of pickups have been developed over time, the two most important of which are the single coil pickup and the Humbucker pickup.

Single coil This style of pickup consists of a single coil of very thin wire wrapped around the magnetic poles. As stated earlier, the vibrating string, through the Faraday effect, causes the creation of a relatively weak signal that is subject to noise. The single coil pickup generates a bright sound with a rapid attack, with richness in the low and high frequencies and less presence of the middle frequencies. Because this output is already quite harmonically rich, the signal is often ready for use even without too much further processing. Historically, single coil pickups were used with a clean signal (no distortion) or with gentle overdrive distortion in genres such as blues and funk.

Humbucker Consisting of dual coils that are wound in opposite directions and magnets oriented in opposite directions to each other, Humbucker pickups generally generate a much more robust signal with lower noise when compared to a single coil pickup. The result is a fuller sound that is richer in sustained sounds and present in the midrange frequencies.

In a stringed instrument, **the bridge** is the point where the strings are anchored to the resonating part of the instrument's body.

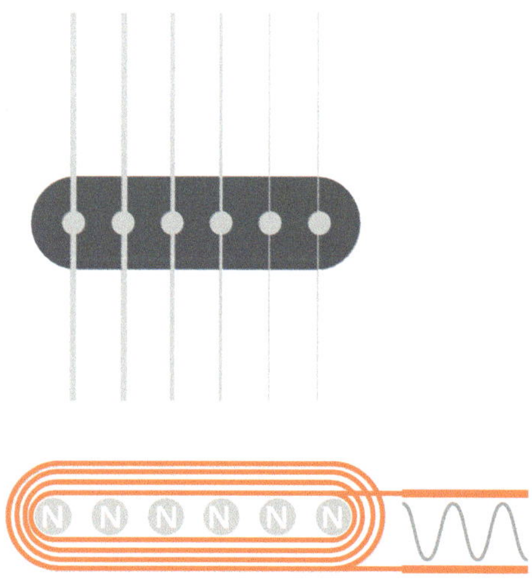

SINGLE COIL

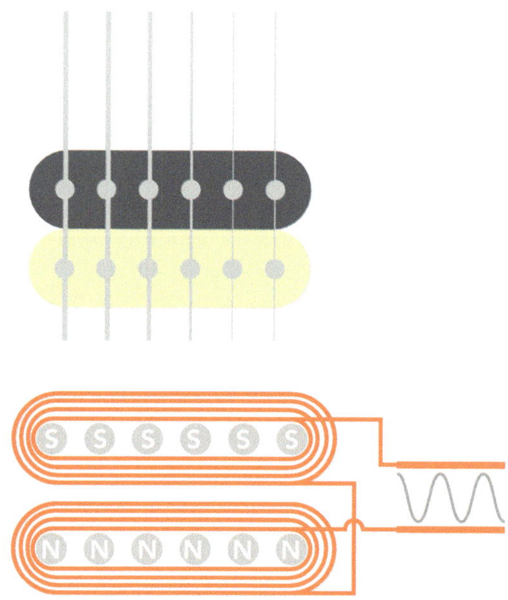

HUMBUCKER

The distance between the pickup and the strings and also where the position of the pickups are on the body of the instrument play a significant role in the tone of the instrument.

- When the **pickup is closer to the strings and bridge**, the output has more volume, more high frequency energy, and less sustain
- When the **pickup is further away from the strings and bridge**, the output has less volume, has more midrange energy with less high end energy, and more sustain

Intimately familiar with these characteristics, guitar makers usually mount several sets of pickups for the guitarist to choose from, to expand the tonal possibilities of the instrument. Usually, a selector switch allows the guitarist to decide which pickups to use, thus changing the timbre of the instrument.

Electric piano

In a **Fender Rhodes-type electric piano**, the keyboard action is similar to that of a traditional piano. On a traditional piano, when a key is pressed with sufficient pressure, a felt-covered hammer strikes some metal strings. On a Fender Rhodes piano, the hammers instead strike small metal cylinders (of different lengths depending on the note) called tines to create a metallic sound. As the tines vibrate, they also resonate corresponding tuned bars (resonators) placed above each tine, enriching the final timbre, especially in the low-mid frequencies.

Now that a note is created with the vibrating tines and resonators, a magnetic pickup transforms the note into an electrical signal, just like the electric guitar. The pickup's output is sent to the input of an amplifier, which can be adjusted to the desired amplitude. This amplifier, in addition to volume, also can enrich the timbre through distortion, increasing the number of harmonics in the output sound.

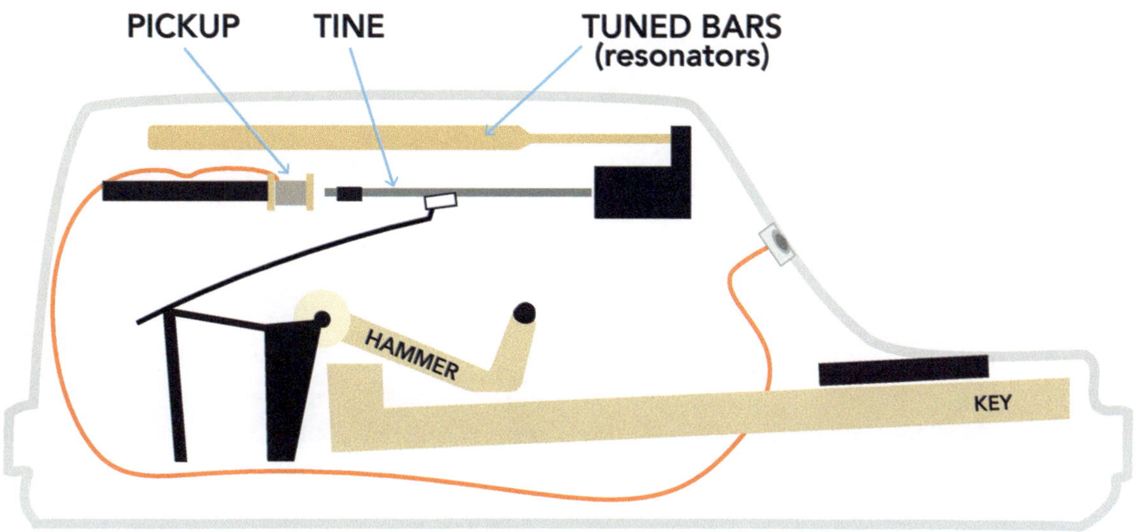

We need to include one last thought regarding instruments with magnetic pickups and electric instruments. Their timbre, unlike acoustic instruments, does not depend as much on the construction or on the materials that make the instrument itself. Instead, for electric instruments, one must consider the entire signal chain, from string vibration to the speaker output. This signal chain can include the pickup itself, a variety of audio effects, and the amplification and speaker system. Every element in this chain that handles the electric signal plays a fundamental role in the final timbre. These elements color, distort, and enrich the sound. Thus, when talking about the sound of an electric guitar, we need to consider this entire signal chain, and not just the guitar itself.

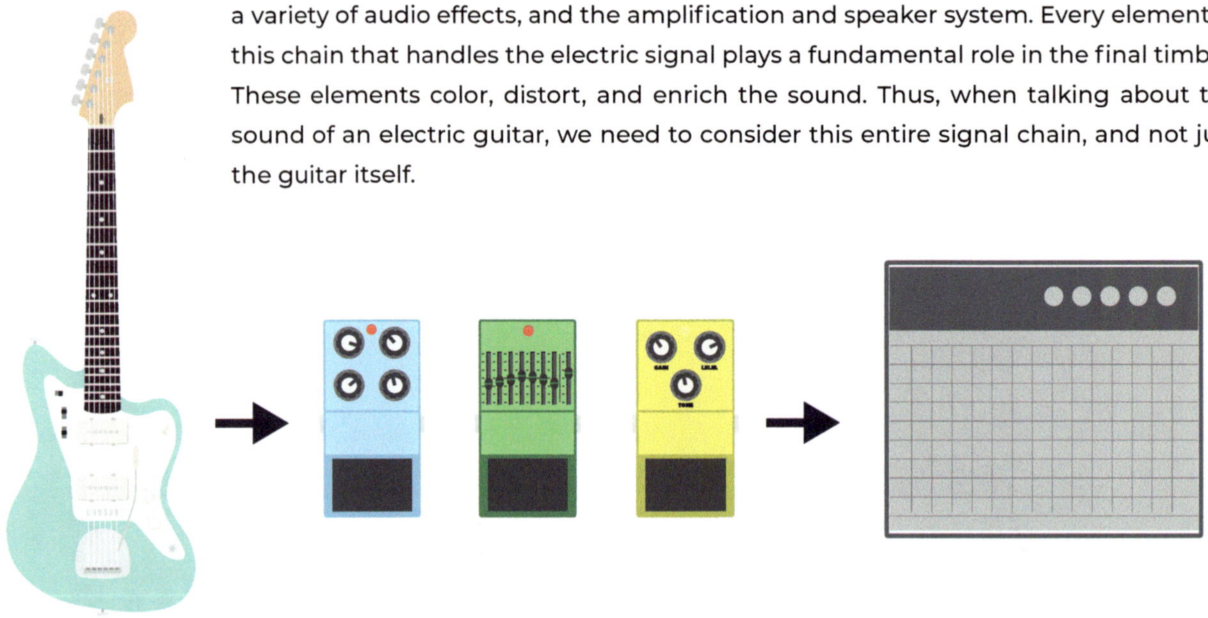

.take a metal tool (a screwdriver, a metal spatula, etc.) and create an improvised performance by touching the guitar or electric bass with your fingers and the chosen tool. Explore the various sounds you can achieve by plucking, rubbing, or even directly touching the pickup magnets with the tool. You can also use an effects chain between the instrument and the amplifier. Imagine telling a musical story, use a timer to so you can better manage the story as it unfolds. ***Theme: "The discovery of dynamite"***

Gilmour guitar sound ~ Fausto Romitelli trash tv trance ~ guitar pedalboard ~ fender rhodes inside ~ fender rhodes Herbie Hancock ~ fender rhodes Robert Glasper

Processing

We've created an analog signal. What can we do with it now? How can we creatively express our musical ideas? We can carry this signal over long distances and use effects to modify some of its characteristics because the sound is in the form of electrical voltage. We modify these sounds by turning potentiometers, moving faders, or interacting with other sensors that alter the signal inside an analog circuit. We reshape these sounds for either "corrective" or "artistic" purposes. In the first case, for example, we use devices to "clean up" the sound from unwanted frequencies or audio errors or we can amplify the waveform to have a higher volume. In the second case, we can, for example, change the filter's settings over time to create a rhythmic pattern or move the position of the guitar's sound around the listener during the song's chorus.

Mixer

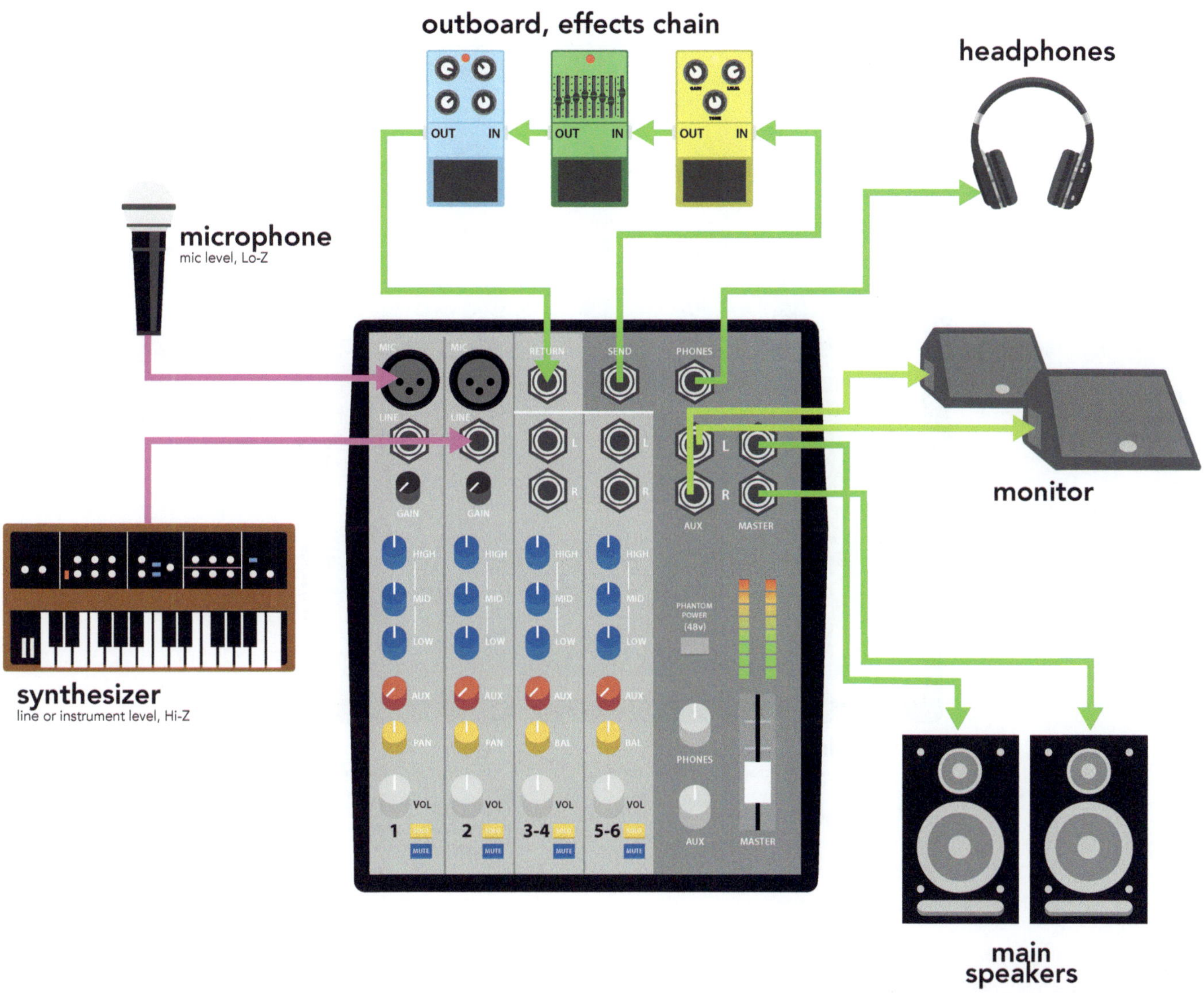

A **mixer** is a versatile device that encapsulates multiple audio devices, allowing us to perform various operations on our sounds. Its primary function is, as the word implies, to combine (or mix) several sounds together and return a single sound, often in the form of stereo output (i.e., distinct Left and Right channels) which is called the Master output. Meanwhile, a mixer consists of inputs and outputs. The input portion, such as the jacks and all the knobs and faders that correspond to each individual channel, sit on the left side of the mixer generally. The output and the components that deal with the master track, sit on the right side of the mixer. The inputs collect the various sounds into individual channels, ranging from two to several dozen channels. The outputs are divided into main outputs, and auxiliary outputs (AUX out). While there are countless brands and models of mixers with individual unique characteristics, audio quality levels, and price points, the essential functions are common to all mixers and can be explained in a few keywords.

The main functions of a mixer, and their respective general locations, are represented and explained in the following illustration.

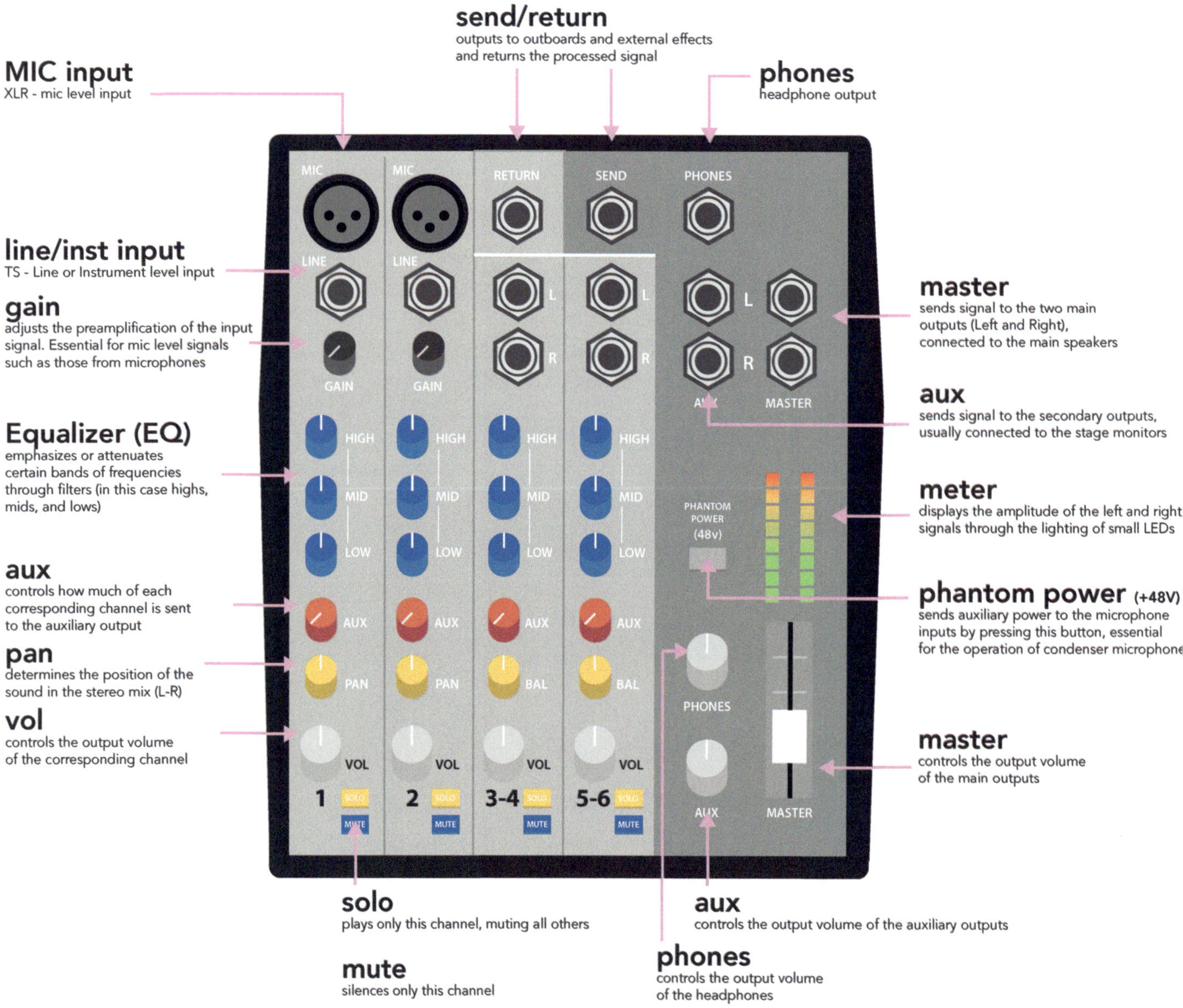

.involve your friends in a performance. Ask each person to make their smartphone produce a note or a chord (with an app or by playing a recorded sound). With a microphone connected to a mixer, change the microphone position by moving around the room. Another person, from the mixer, will operate the EQ-pan-volume parameters of the microphone channel. Together you will form a duet, creating short performances. Switch roles after each performance. ***Theme: "Inside the body"***

Digital Mixers

Digital mixers have a digital processor that manages their entire process. With digital mixers, users route and process sound in many versatile ways, save scenes or presets that can be recalled instantly, and rely on the advantages of digital signal processing. Similar to typical work or school computers, digital mixers have a screen on which you can view the parameters and processing being done to the sound, such as equalization or various effects such as reverbs, distortions, chorus, thus making operations more visually precise. Another key feature of these mixers is the ability to "virtually" route signals, i.e., routing, summing, and processing them computationally in the digital domain, then passing the sound to specific physical outputs that are chosen by the user. The advantage is that these processes can be done with a few clicks without disconnecting and relocating physical cables. This can be an enormous time saver while cutting back potentially on the human error that comes from cable management and physical connections of wires.

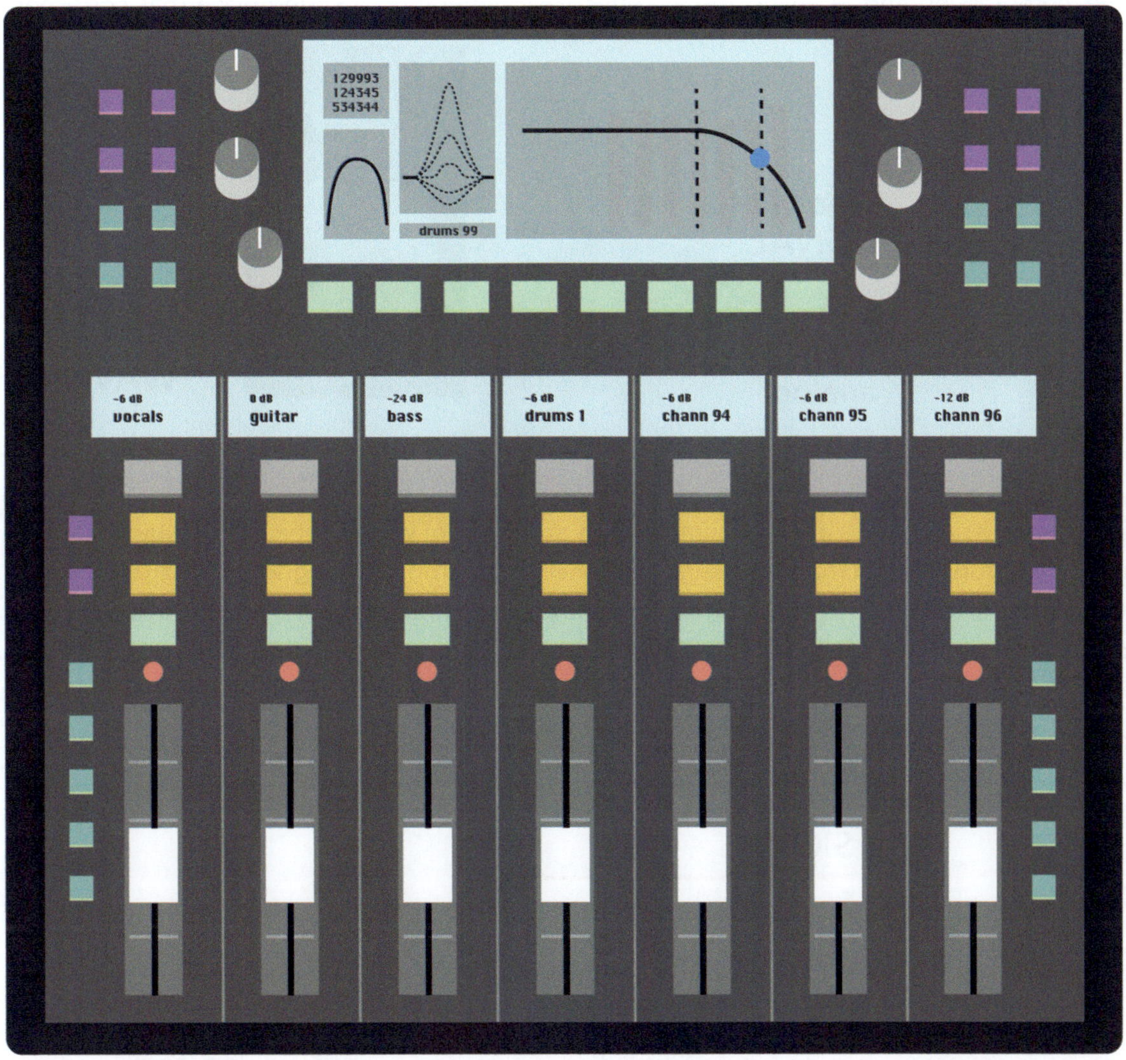

.get a mixer, choose four continuous sound sources (synthesizers, tuning apps...), input them into the mixer, and create a 2:00 performance by using only the mixer. Within the mixer, you should explore EQ, volume/amplitude, and left/right pan

.watch a tutorial on the "no input mixer" and build a short piece using only a mixer and cables.
Theme: "Big cats"

Output

Once the various sounds have been processed and combined, the mixer sends the signal out to the outside world. At this point, specific audio devices are used to re-transform the analog electrical signal back into an audible acoustic sound wave. This is the main function of headphones and loudspeakers.

Monitors

Dynamic loudspeakers, the most common type of loudspeakers, work in reverse to the dynamic microphones. Here, the drivers (the speaker component itself without the enclosure or other parts) receive an electrical signal that moves a cone, compressing and rarefying the air, effectively generating a sound wave that corresponds to the received signal.

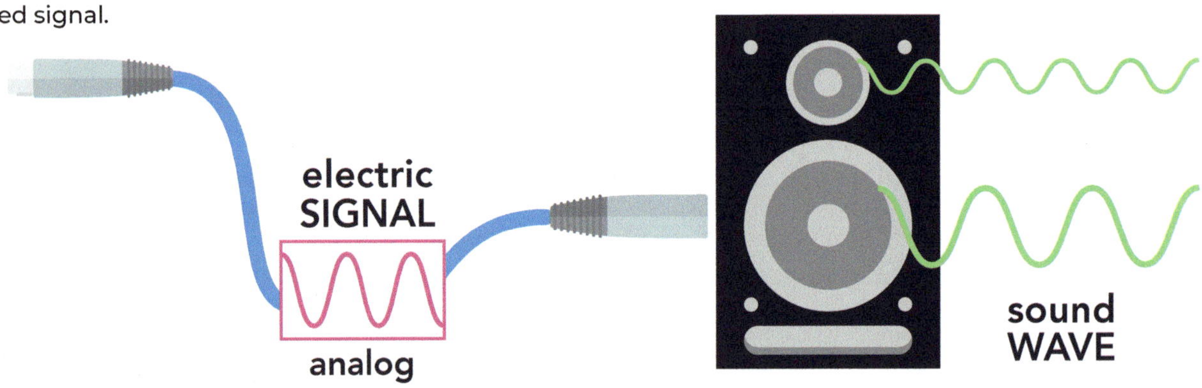

Operation The speaker driver has a permanent magnet and a coil of wire to which the voltage from the mixer is applied, usually after amplification from a built-in or external power amp. The magnetic field that is created with the magnet and coil is disturbed when a signal is applied to the coil. Again, because of the ***Faraday effect*** (see page 54), this signal causes the coil to move within the magnetic field, corresponding to the positive and negative portions of the audio signal. The cone is directly connected to the coil, so as the coil oscillates, the cone creates air compressions and rarefactions that ultimately generate acoustic sound waves.

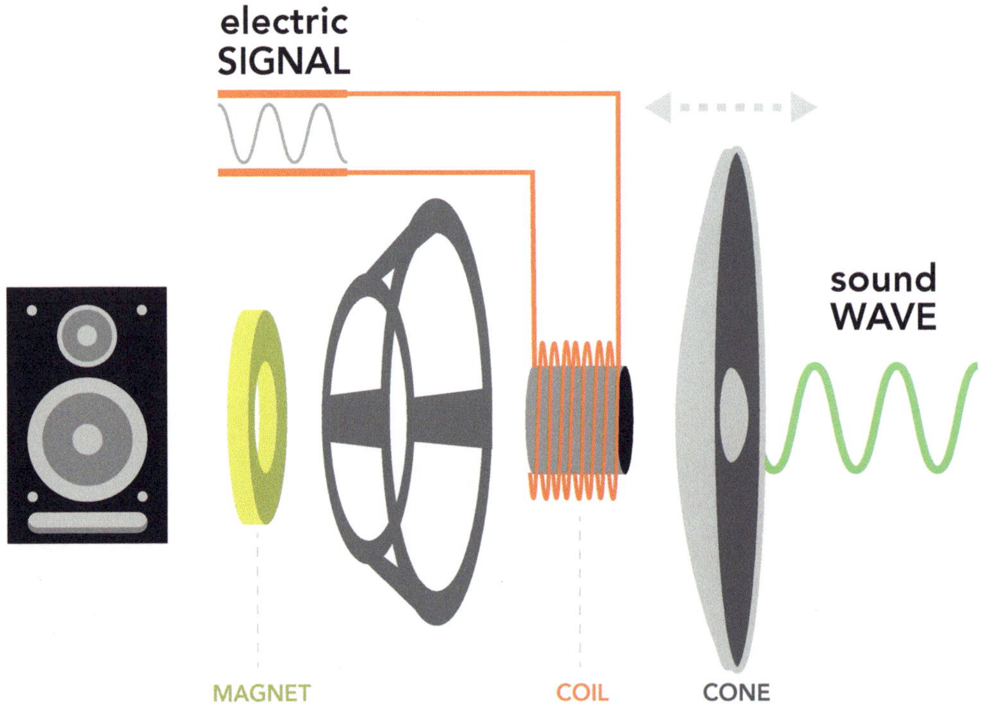

The amount of electrical voltage and current from the mixer is not sufficient to move the cone of a driver to make sound of a loud enough volume. Thus, the sound output from the mixer undergoes power amplification, which always occurs in a power amplifier before the signal reaches the speaker drivers. If the loudspeaker box contains the speaker drivers and a **power amplifier,** all integrated in one enclosure, it is an active speaker. If the enclosure contains all the components except the power amplifier, then we have a passive speaker.

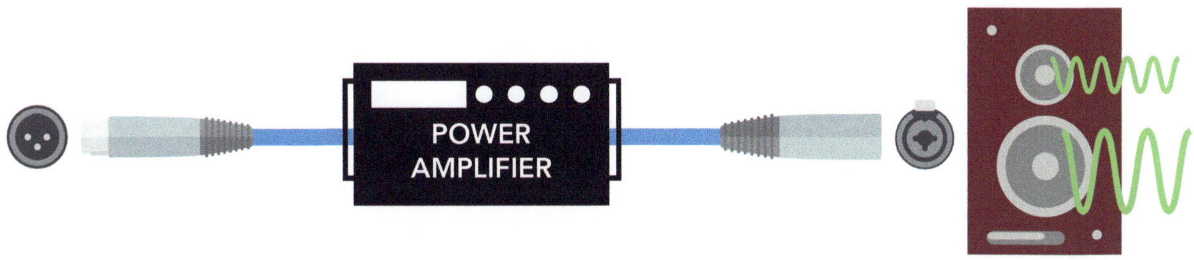

Cones

Different size cones are better equipped to recreate some frequencies over other frequencies. We can think of this like musical instruments, where large instruments excel at playing lower notes, and smaller instruments are optimized for higher notes. This is also the case for cone sizes, often characterized by the diameter (in inches) of the cone. For the lowest frequencies, the largest cones are known as **subwoofers**. The next largest cone, also optimized for low frequencies, is the **woofer**. Continuing to get smaller in size and higher in optimized frequency range, there are **mid-range cones** for the middle frequencies, and **tweeters** for the high frequency range. Tweeters often differ in that they are dome-shaped rather than cone-shaped. The cones, or speaker drivers as a whole, often coexist within the same box or enclosure. A two-way loudspeaker contains two drivers, while a three-way loudspeaker contains three drivers and so on. In these cases, crossover filters, containing multiple filters, divide the incoming signal, according to their frequency range, and send the corresponding filtered signals to the cones best suited for their reproduction.

Frequency response

When buying a loudspeaker, we need to evaluate its frequency response, which tells us about how the loudspeaker creates each frequency in the audible range. In all loudspeakers, some frequencies have louder amplitudes as compared to other frequencies, so we must know each loudspeaker's frequency response so we can be informed as to which loudspeaker to buy according to the sounds we want to reproduce. Some loudspeakers are mainly dedicated, for example, to bass frequencies. These loudspeakers would not be suitable for reproducing an entire musical ensemble. Loudspeakers that cover the whole frequency range are called full-range loudspeakers. Full-range loudspeakers are often used as "monitors," or loudspeakers intended for a musician or a studio sound engineer to hear the full range of sounds in a piece being produced in a recording studio or played live through loudspeakers.

Headphones

We can have a similar discussion for headphones, which in theory, behave like small speakers. One major difference is that headphones generate sounds with much less sound pressure, they do not require power amplification. Headphones are often used in studios when an alternative listening device is needed to compare sonic details when mixing or mastering a track. Commonly, musicians will produce music with headphones to avoid disturbing their neighbors in an apartment building or waking up their family members when working at night. Loudspeakers can create a more realistic sound with better stereo imaging, which is recommended for most production work, because headphones acoustically separate the left and right channels into the left and right ears, respectively, resulting in somewhat artificial perceived stereo soundscapes during standard listening practices.

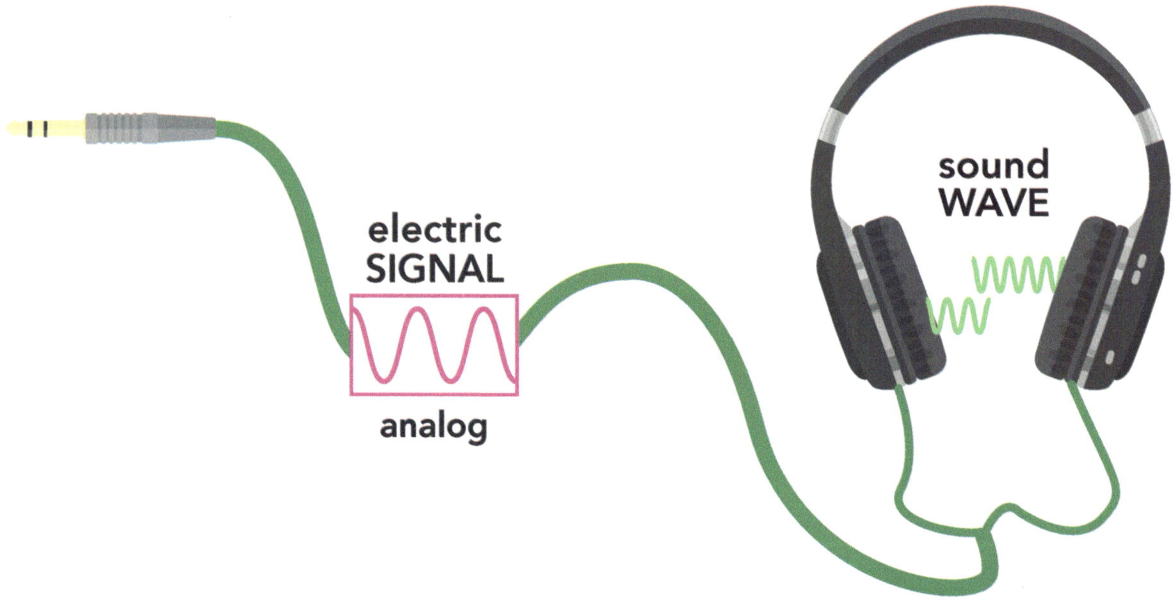

DIGITAL

We have talked about analog systems, but most of the work we do in music today interacts with digital systems. This is due to the enormous versatility that a computer makes available to us. With modern computational processing, we find near infinite possibilities for sound processing and synthesis tools without resorting to expensive, cumbersome, and sometimes unavailable analog electrical circuits. To access this world of digital possibilities, it is necessary to translate an analog signal into the digital domain at the beginning of the chain, and to translate a digital signal back into an analog signal to listen to through speakers or headphones. As we will discuss, this task is performed by the analog-to-digital convertors (ADC) and digital-to-analog convertors (DAC) within **audio interfaces** that act as a bridge between the analog and digital worlds. Let's start by talking about how the **computers** we use daily can be used to create and manipulate music in the digital domain.

Computer

The digital world is composed of hardware and software. Hardware is defined as physical devices that perform computational operations, and software consists of the programs, apps, and plugins that carry out a set of computational instructions, stored on a digital medium, to perform a particular task, such as playing a song or creating a video.

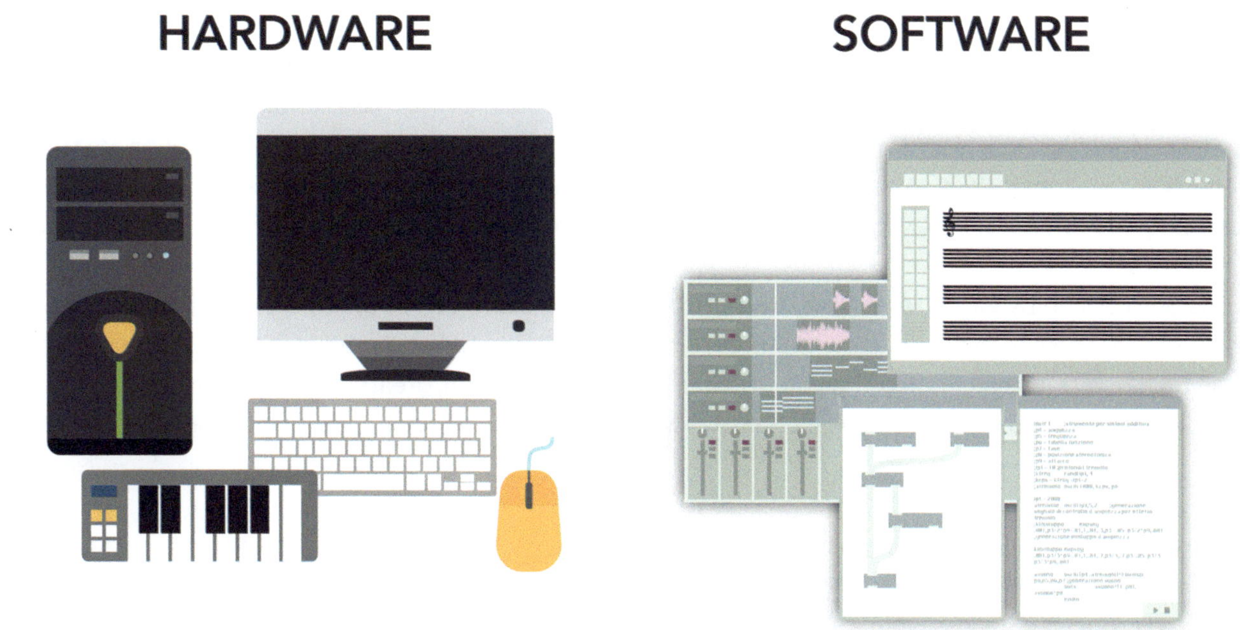

In hardware, the computer plays the role of the brain of the digital system, because its job is to collect and process the data coming from all of the input devices and then deliver the results to the output devices. We can place the keyboard, the music controller, the microphone, the mouse, and even the touch screen of our smartphone in the category of input devices. As for output devices, the computer screen, printers, headphones, and acoustic speakers all receive information from the computer. Both input and output devices communicate with the "brain," or main computer processor, through small pieces of code called drivers. Sometimes these drivers are self-installing (in peripherals called Plug and Play (PnP) devices), while at other times, we need to download them manually from the Internet and install them. If a device's drivers are incompatible with the computer's operating system, the device will not be able to communicate with the computer.

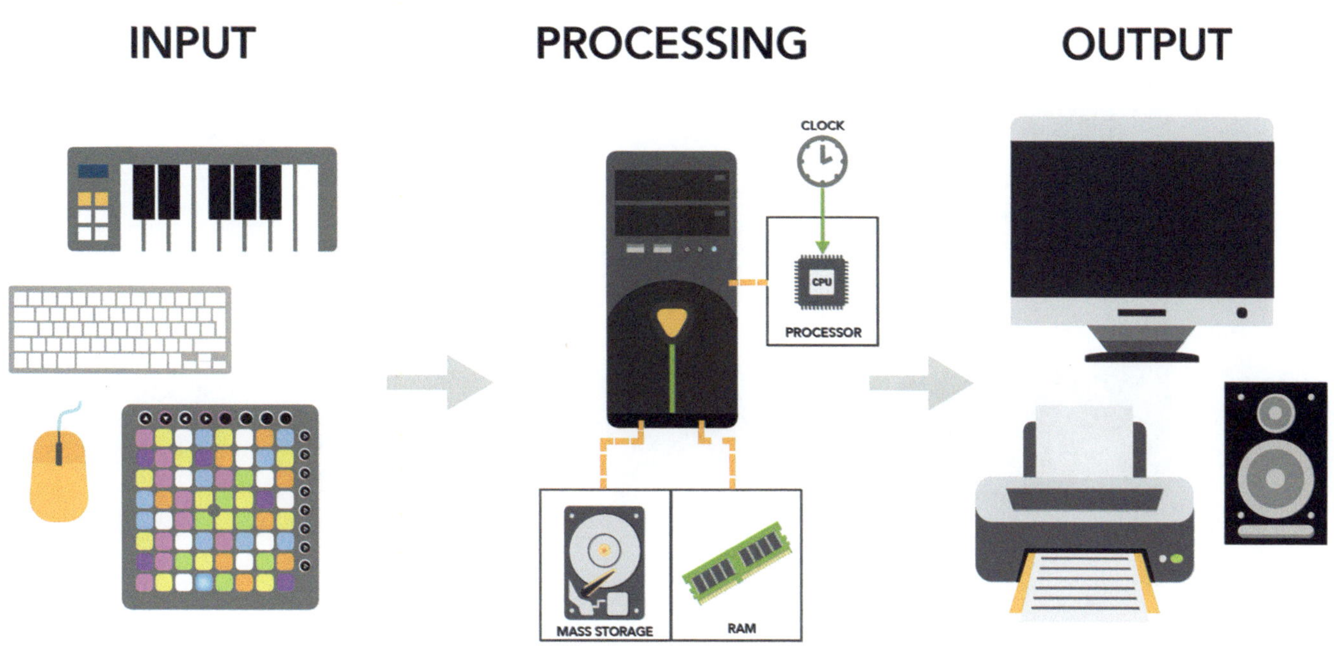

The **microprocessor** is responsible for handling all the computations required by the software, performing millions of operations per second as determined by the clock speed. Once the operations are completed, the processed data needs to be stored in the computer's memory in order to either use it again or display it. The type of memory that stores this processed data is the **RAM (Random Access Memory)** and is volatile. RAM, in handling the computer's most current computational needs, is continuously erased and written over by the computer itself, and therefore, it does not need to be of large capacity. RAM, however, needs to work at high speeds in writing and reading in order to keep up with real-time processing demands. A low-capacity RAM affects the computer's overall speed when it is full, by forcing excess memory needs onto slower memory locations, such as the mass storage device generally used to store conventional files. This is known as **swap memory**. This can occur when too many applications are running simultaneously for example. Thus, to speed up our computers, we need to minimize the use of swap memory by either increasing our computer's RAM capacity or by decreasing the number of software working simultaneously.

Mass storage devices can be either **Hard Disk Drives (HDD)** or **Solid State Drives (SDD)**. Hard disk drives, generally considered older technology, store data in a magnetized disk that is rotated and read by a head. Because of these mechanical movements, this technology has significant power consumption, greater fragility than SSD devices, and slower read and write speeds. The advantage of hard disk drives though are lower manufacturing costs and larger capacities.

SSDs, on the other hand, have no rotating parts, resulting in faster read and write speeds, lower fragility, and reduced power consumption. The latter two features are critical for laptops, tablets, and smartphones, because of the longer battery lives and reduced data loss when devices are dropped. SD cards in cameras and USB drives share the same technology as SSD drives.

Mass storage can be either **internal**, where it is plugged directly into the computer's motherboard, or **external**, where a cable is needed to connect the storage to the computer.

External hard drives are part of the endless galaxy of external peripherals that supplement a computer's abilities by extending the ways we input data (through input devices) or receive and display data (through output devices).

HARD DISK DRIVE
HDD

SOLD STATE DISK
SSD

Peripherals can connect to the computer through ports dedicated to specific devices or general ports where we can connect various types of devices. For example, the HDMI port is a dedicated port that allows us to connect our computer to screens or projectors by transmitting digital video signals (sometimes alongside audio signals). Both dedicated and generic ports usually continuously evolve due to market demands, standardization, and pressures to create smaller ports that take up less space on our shrinking laptops and mobile devices. At the time of this book's publication, the most widely used generic ports are USBs, which exist in different variations and forms. The most commonly used USB connector has been the Type A connector. The Type C connector is the most recent USB connector which, among its advantages, can carry large amounts of data alongside the power needed to power a computer. The Type C connector is also the first USB connector that is symmetric, allowing us to plug them in without worrying which side is facing up.

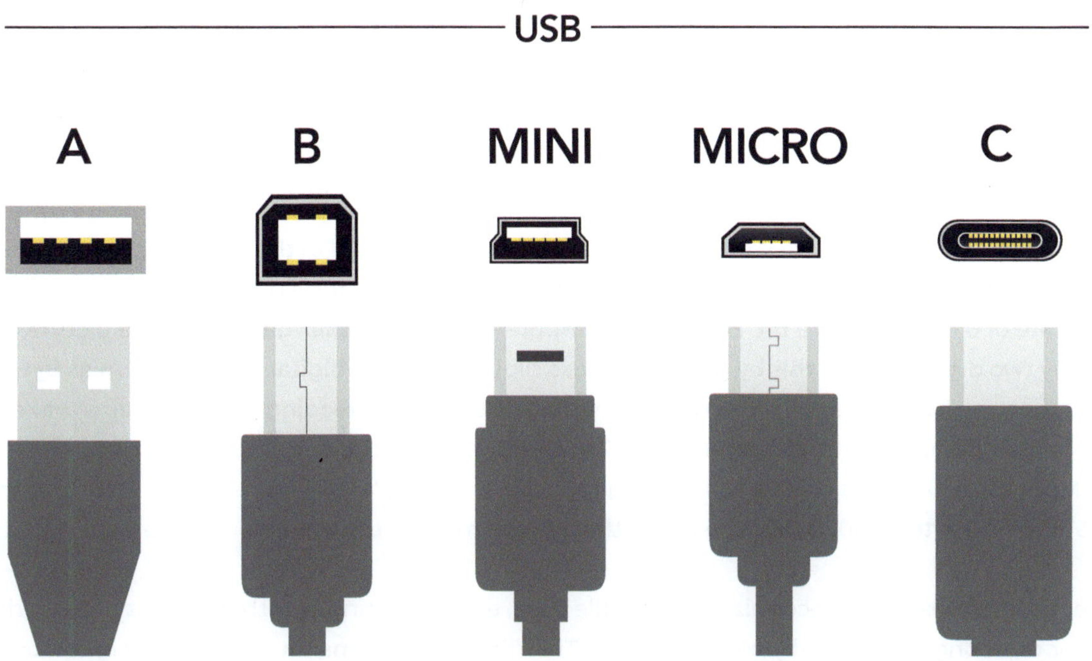

Software

Software is divided into two categories: operating systems and application software. Operating systems are large programs that manage the machine's hardware and software resources and provide essential services to the application software that is installed on the computer. The most common operating systems are *Windows*, *macOS*, and *Linux*. The first two are proprietary, i.e., the software license is not free, while Linux is a free and open operating system, allowing it to be used, modified, and installed free of charge on any computer. Linux is the recommended choice when, for example, we want to build hardware dedicated to a specific purpose, such as a "do-it-yourself" synthesizer.

On the other hand, application software consists of all the applications we install on our computers, smartphones, or tablets that we interact with to do a particular task. This software, which can be either free or have a licensing cost, enables us to perform various operations such as write a book, produce a song, edit a movie, and surf the Internet. The application software must be compatible with the computer's operating system in order to work.

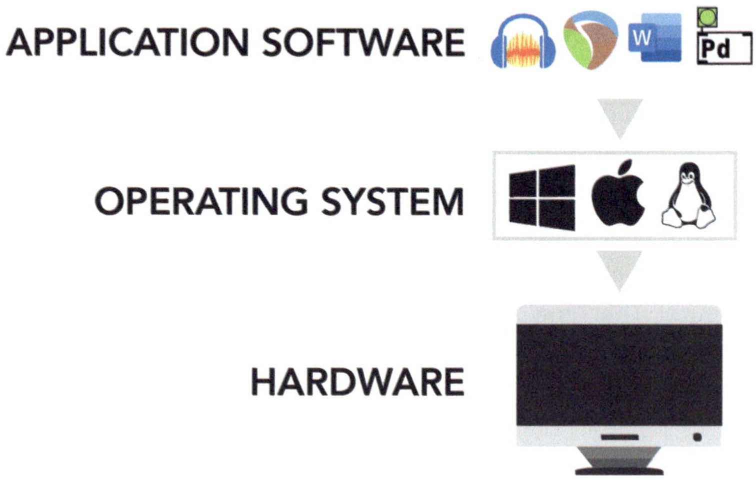

Files

The data handled by the computer are contained in **files**. These are encoded in the only language digital machines know: the **binary code**. This language uses only two digits (0 and 1) to encode all of its information. One digit, which can have the state of 0 or 1, is called a **bit**. How can a computer handle complex data, such as a picture or a piece of music, with only two digits? It does this by grouping these digits into small digital words, known as **bytes**, made up of 8 bits. Bytes then can be grouped into even larger chains. The successive reading of these chains makes it possible to store and handle complex data and operations. Typical file size units are the kilobyte (1 kB =1024 bytes), the megabyte (1 MB = 1,048,576 bytes or 1024 kB), the gigabyte (1 GB = 1,073,741,824 bytes or 1024 MB), and the terabyte (1 TB = 1,099,511,627,776 bytes or 1024 GB). The larger the file, the more bytes are used to store it.

The computer uses extensions to recognize specific file type, e.g., indicating whether a file is a text written with a word processor or a song to be read by a music player. The **file name extension** is a suffix assigned by the person or application that creates the file. This extension tells someone what kind of software application is needed to properly open a file. It is usually three characters, but can also be two or four. For example, if we find ".doc" after the file name, we know that we are dealing with a formatted text document. If we see ".wav," then we know we need to open the file with a music player.

Audio files fall into two categories: **uncompressed** or **compressed**. Uncompressed audio files preserve all the information of the original digital file and, for this reason, have a larger file size. Compressed files, on the other hand, undergo data compression and are smaller. Compressed audio can be either **lossless**, where no information is lost in the data compression system, or **lossy**, where the data compressions permanently alters the sound of the original file. The tradeoff with lossy data compression is that significant data compression comes at the cost of significantly degrading the original file's sound.
The most important types of uncompressed audio files are WAV and AIFF. Lossless compressed file type includes the FLAC format, and lossy compressed file formats include WMAs and MP3s, in particular.

The MP3, appearing first in 1997, created a real revolution in music because it significantly accelerated free, legal, and sometimes even illegal distribution of music. For the first time, files with good (or good enough) audio quality with small file sizes could be easily exchanged over the Internet or stored within portable playback devices. An important property of MP3s is that the amount of data compression and resultant audio quality are directly related. The user can decide how much data to store and, thus, how much audio quality to retain. This decision is made during compression by setting the **bitrate**, the amount of data stored per second of music. The higher it is, the higher the sound quality.

I can also choose whether this amount should be constant throughout the song **(CBR or Constant Bitrate)** or vary depending on the second-by-second complexity of the stored waveform **(VBR, Variable Bitrate)**.
To understand VBR, we can imagine the example that a second of silence will require less data storage than a second of a forty-instrument orchestra playing a forty-note chord.
It is recommended that the minimum sufficient bitrate used for music is 128 Kbps. It is better, for the sake of audio quality, to choose 192 Kbps, or optimally 320 Kbps, for the bitrate. For reference, CDs have a bitrate equivalent of 1411 Kbps.

Another exciting feature of MP3s are ID3 tags, allowing us to store not just the audio content, but also some data about the song itself (metadata). You can store, for example, the title, author, record, genre, track number, and much more. This feature comes in handy during playback where the software can read and display this data on a screen.

.download a song you like in .wav format, and compress it to MP3 with very low bitrates like 8 or 16 Kbps. You might need to use an online converter that allows you to select such low bitrates. Once you have the "super compressed and super degraded" file, sample sounds from the degraded song and compose your song with these sounds you have extrapolated. ***Theme: "The first thought as soon as I open my eyes"***

mp3 bit rate comparison ~ free mp3 converter ~ history of the mp3 player

Audio Interface

The **audio interface** is an essential device for music production and performances, because it is responsible for turning analog signals into digital signals, and transferring the signal to the computer. It is also responsible for the reverse process where it takes the signal from the computer and converts the digital signal back into an analog signal that our headphones or studio monitors turn into acoustic waves. As we have seen, binary code is the only language that a computer processes, so these conversions are critical. Because music happens in real time, the audio interface needs to be accurate and fast.

Audio interfaces can be internal or external. Internal sounds cards, designed primarily for the general audio needs of a computer such as listening to music or making conferencing calls, have lower quality and few inputs and outputs. On the other hand, the external audio interface can be specifically designed for musical uses and therefore have higher quality for preamplifiers, and analog-to-digital (ADC) and digital-to-analog (DAC) converters. They also can have more input and output ports. For these reasons, we will refer specifically to external audio interfaces in the following descriptions.

Before digitalizing an input sound, the audio interface uses **preamplifiers** to increase the amplitude of the input signal, making it suitable for further processing and listening. Similarly to a mixer, this amplification must be as clean as possible, needing to amplify without distorting or "coloring" the original sound. This is one reason why the price of an audio interface can be quite pricey because having good preamplifiers allows your computer to import a sound that is very faithful to the original sound. Other important features to evaluate in an audio interface are the amount and types of inputs and outputs, the sampling rate (from 44.1 kHz to 192 kHz in professional interfaces), and the bit depth that is necessary to handle more dynamic range (16-bit or 24-bit).

A good quality audio interface has a microphone, an instrument, and line inputs as input ports. Often these inputs are in the form of combo inputs, giving a single input the ability to accept both XLR and TS connectors. A button allows us to select either a low-impedance (Lo-Z) microphone, instrument, or high-impedance (Hi-Z) line signal.

The outputs of an interface usually are headphone outputs, followed by a series of primary (main) and secondary outputs, just as we have seen in mixers. The main, and sometimes the secondary outputs, are usually balanced and use a TRS output (balanced).

As far as the connection with the computer, audio interfaces behave like the other digital peripherals we have seen. They generally use traditional USB (Type-A and Type-B) or USB Type-C connectors.

The main functions of an audio interface are represented and explained in the following illustration:

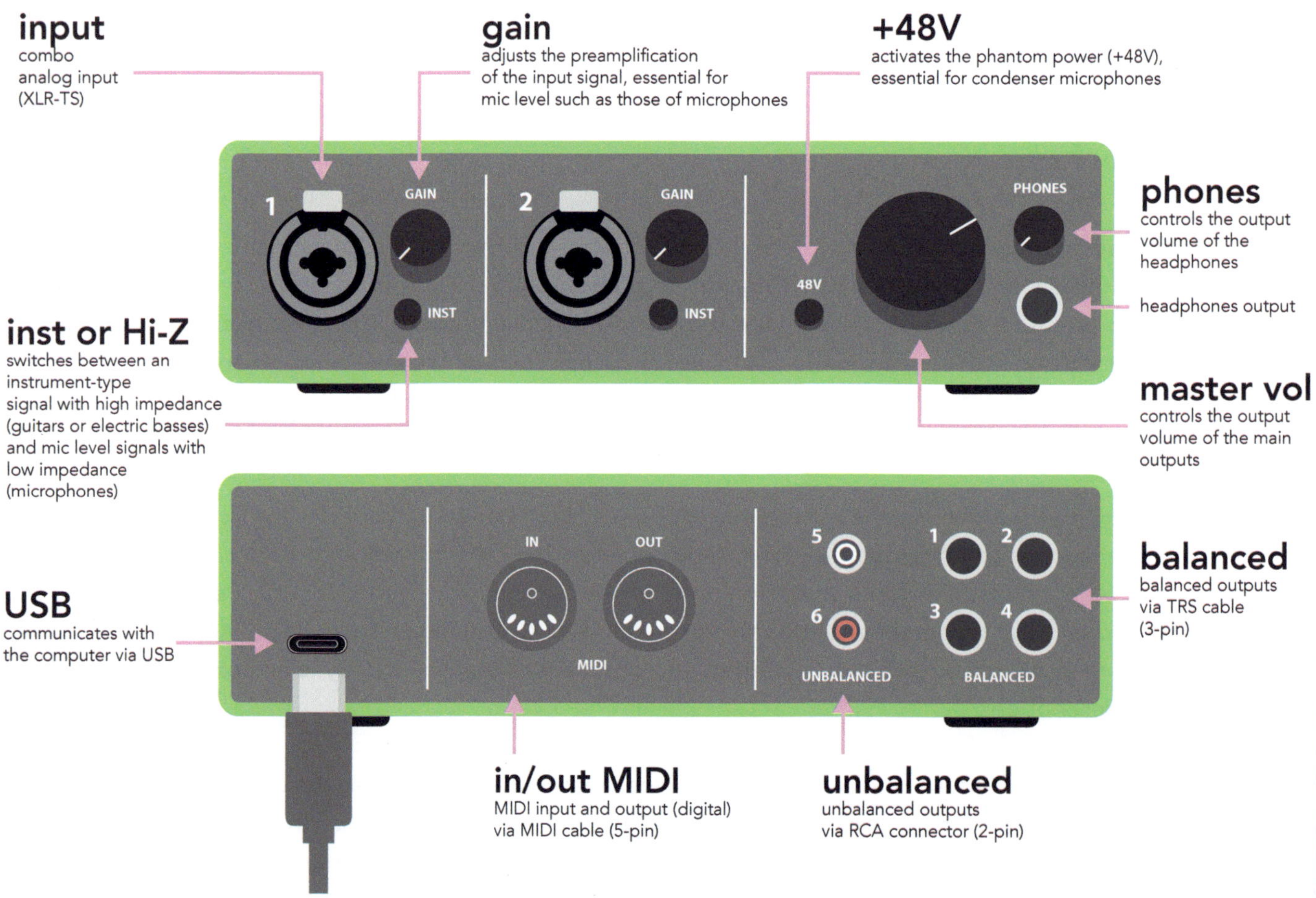

Monitors and Headphones

As the output signal leaves the audio interface, we are now back to an analog signal for the last part of our chain. Here, we find studio monitors and headphones, just as we saw in the analog chain section. For information on how these devices work, see the previous chapter. As a point of clarification, we use monitors here to refer to high quality full range loudspeakers that play detailed sound.

Here we will specify that monitors we use in studios are usually active and are positioned facing the listener to form an equilateral triangle. The two speaker cones and the head of the listener make up the three vertices of this equilateral triangle. It is important also to note that the room's acoustic design plays a significant role in creating a proper listening environment. Careful consideration should be made with the room size, the shape of the walls, the materials used in the room, and the overall reverberation time.

There are some general recommendations for monitor type, according to the distance the listening position is from the monitors.

- ***near-field*** monitors for short-distance listening (about 150 cm or 3-5 feet)
- ***mid-field*** monitors for medium distances (150-250 cm or 5-10 feet)
- ***far-field*** monitors for spaced listening (more than 250 cm or 10 feet)

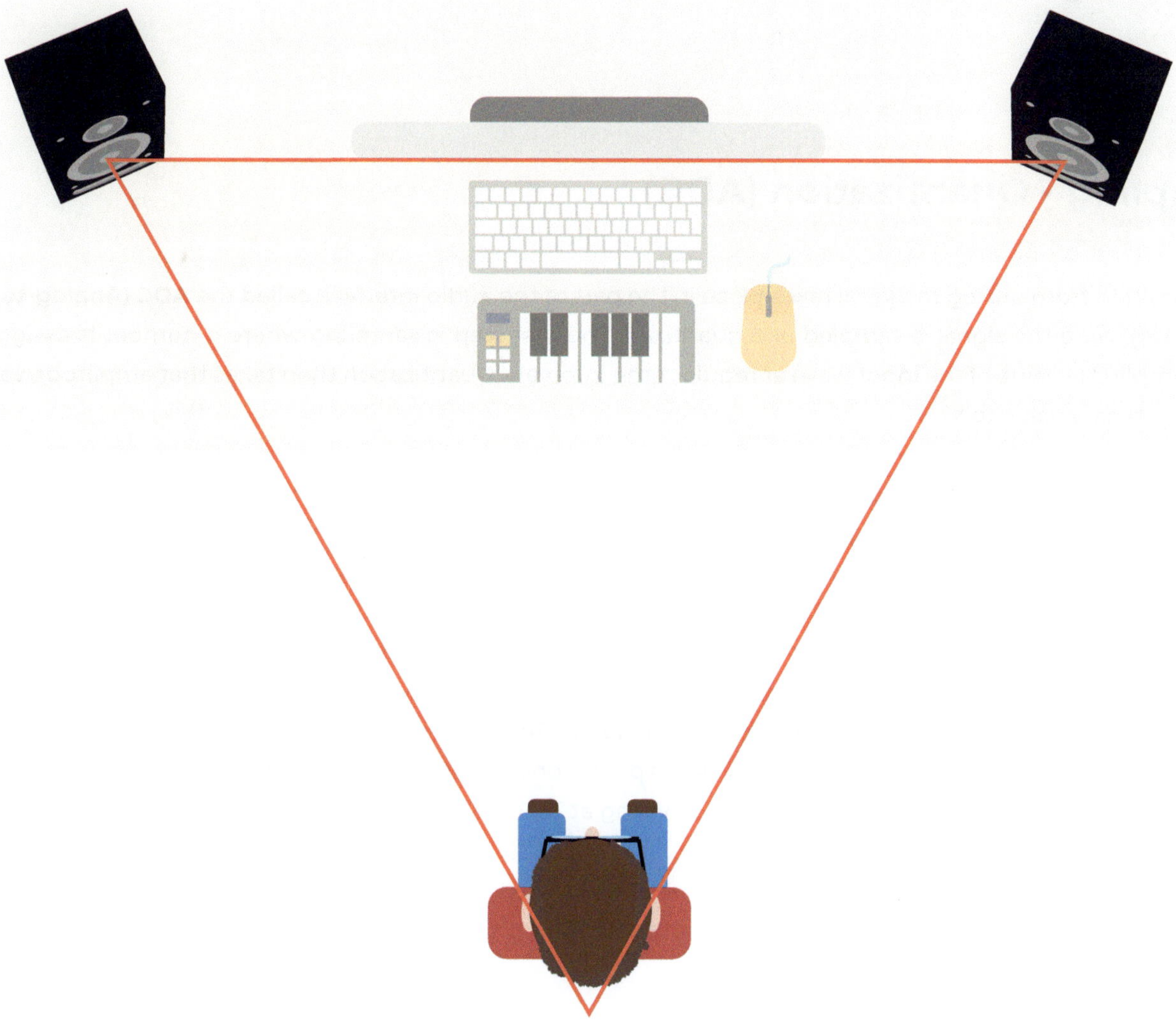

SAMPLING AND QUANTIZATION

Every time we record a guitar track for a new piece or even listen to a song from our favorite streaming service with headphones while riding our bike, signal conversions must happen to make analog voltages into digital signals and digital signals back to analog waves. In the case of the digital processors in our audio chain, like the ones we find in computers, smartphones, and tablets, we need our sound to be in the form of binary code since that is the only language a computer can speak. It's the language that the computer uses to generate, edit, process, and distort any sound to our liking.

Sampling - Quantization (ADC)

The transition from analog to digital takes place in the part of the audio interface called the **ADC (Analog-to-Digital Converter)**. Here the signal is sampled and quantized. The first step is sampling where a number is assigned to a given amplitude value of the input wave at regular time intervals. Quantization then takes that amplitude value and assigns a binary value to it.

Imagine that you are overlooking an auto racetrack following a single car. You stand at your window and decide to mark the position of this car at regular intervals, e.g. every 10 seconds. You are essentially taking a "sample" of the car's location at a frequency of 0.1 Hz. You can easily then reconstruct the car's trajectory on the racetrack with this information. What happens though, if this car is so fast that it takes only one second to complete an entire lap? As you take the position data every 10 seconds, the racecar will have taken ten laps and be at the same position, and your data will not accurately describe what the car did. Your data will show that the car hasn't moved at all. So, in order for you to be able to accurately track the car's position on the track, you will need to take data much more often, increasing the number of readings. How many times per second will you have to take this data for you to reconstruct the car's trajectory on the racetrack if the car is traveling at 300 mph?

This is the first problem that an ADC faces. We, along with the engineers who invented these devices, need to overcome this issue. An analog wave has infinite points since it is a continuous signal, but must discretize, or reduce, the analog signal to a discrete, or a non-infinite and countable, number of numerical values (for each of my beloved samples). How many samples of the analog wave do I need to take, for each second, in order not to miss a single detail of the sound? With the auto racing example, I need to be sure I sample fast enough to capture the most extreme case (or worst case), i.e., the fastest car in this case. If I can represent the most extreme, yet relevant, scenario, then I am sampling fast enough to characterize all my other cases.

If we talk about sound waves, the “fastest car”, or the most extreme case, corresponds to the “fastest” sound wave, which is the wave with the highest audible frequency. From the theory of timbre, we know that all sounds can be broken down into simple sine wave components. We also know from psychoacoustics that humans are generally only able to hear up to 20,000 Hz. From this, we can conclude that 20,000 Hz is the highest frequency, or most extreme case, that we need to be able to capture with our sampling. So, if I can sample 20,000 Hz correctly, then I will know that any lower frequency will also be accurately represented.

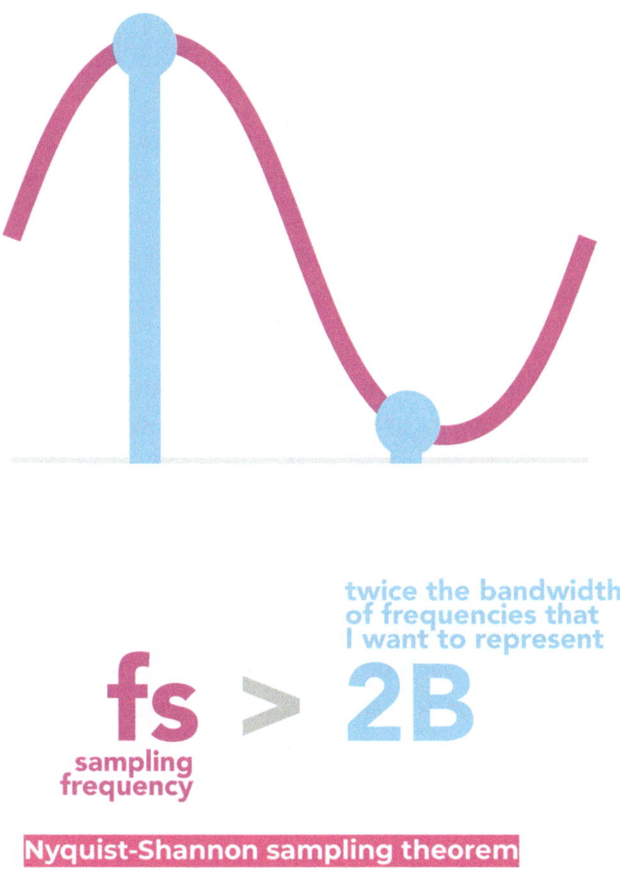

For each wave cycle, I will need at least two sample points, evenly spaced, to represent the wave in the digital domain: The **Nyquist-Shannon sampling theorem** states that my sampling rate needs to be at least two times the frequency of the highest frequency I wish to represent. In mathematical terms, this says that given a known upper frequency limit **B**, I must use a sampling frequency (**fs**) that is greater than **2B**. For example, if I want to accurately sample a 20 kHz sine wave, my sample rate needs at least 40 kHz. Thus, at any sampling rate at or above 40 kHz, I will be able to sample all audible sound. In other words, the **Nyquist frequency** is defined as half of the sample rate, and the highest frequency that we can accurately represent must be below the Nyquist frequency. This is one of the reasons why the standard sampling frequency for CDs is 44,100 Hz, slightly higher than the 40,000 Hz threshold we just stated.

Now that we know how often to take samples, we need to decide how many possible discrete amplitude values we need. In other words, how many amplitude steps do we need to sufficiently characterize audio waveform? Quantization is the process by which we convert these continuous amplitude values into discrete amplitude steps.

The answer, because we are headed toward a fully digital representation, cannot be "infinite values." In a fully digital representation, only discrete values that describe a finite number of points are allowed.

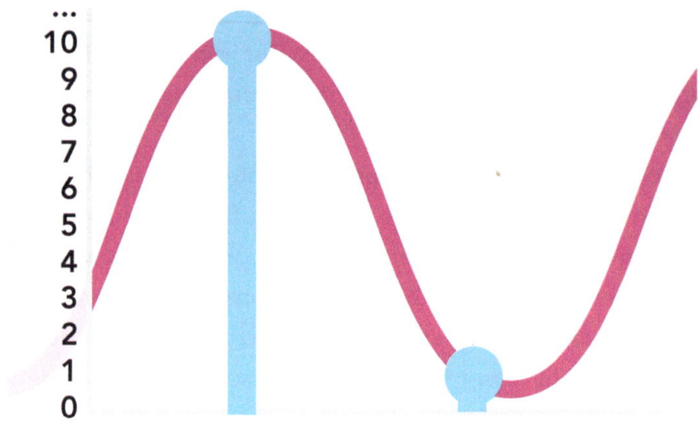

We begin by identifying the worst case here as well. In terms of our amplitude needs, we refer to what the Fletcher-Munson diagram teaches us, which is that 140 dB approximately spans the amplitude range we can hear, from the quietest audible sound to the threshold of pain. Thus, if we can correctly represent a dynamic range from 0 dB to 140 dB, we can be confident that we can describe all sound amplitudes.

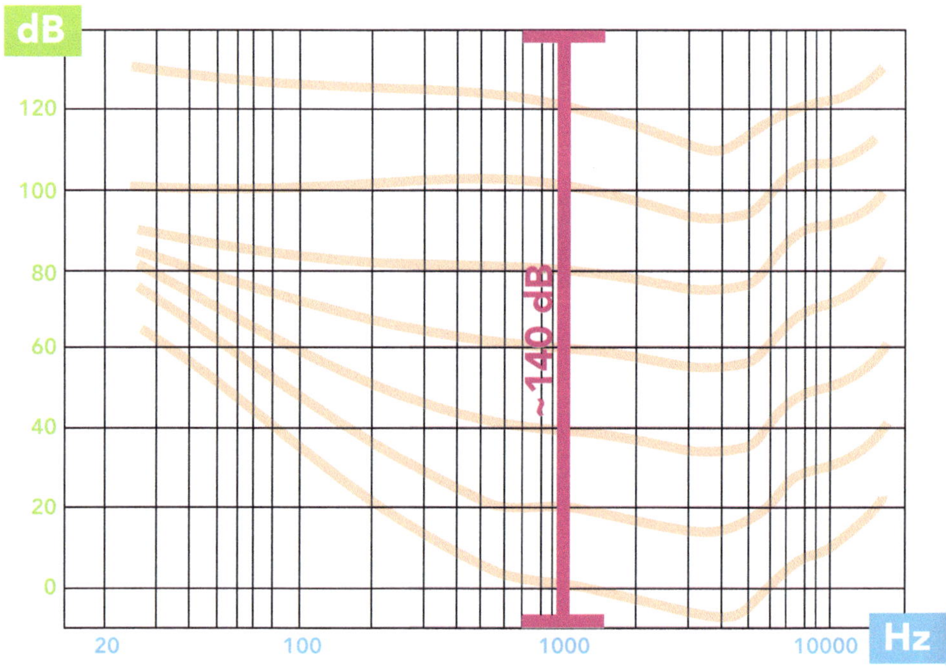

We go back to the concept of bits that we described earlier. We need to determine how many bits we need to correctly represent this dynamic range, considering that each individual bit has two possible states, 0 or 1. To calculate how many total states are possible with 2, 3, 5, 16, or N number of bits, we compute 2^N. In laypersons terms, we raise 2 (the number of possible states for each bit) to the number of bits we have in our system. N is also known as our quantization or bit depth. So, if my bit depth is 2, then I have a total of four possible amplitude states. Likewise, 5 bits equates to 32 states, 8 bits to 256 states, and 16 bits to 65,536 states.

Let us consider quantizing our previously sampled analog signal with only 1 bit, so with only two states. When we have 2 bits, our possibilities for our binary code are 00, 01, 10, and 11, totaling four states. When we double the number of possible states, we increase our dynamic range, above the noise floor, by 6 dB. Where does the noise come from? It comes from **quantization error**, the error that arises when we approximate a curve with steps. When we only have 2 states, this error is large. When we add steps, our approximation gets better, and our quantization error gets better. As this error gets better, our **signal to noise ratio** increases. A 16-bit quantization rate gives us ~96 dB of signal to noise ratio. Using this calculation, a 20-bit digital audio file will have a 24 dB lower quantization noise than a 16-bit digital audio file. While 96 dB signal to noise ratio is usually sufficient, we may need the increased signal-to-noise ratio of higher bit rates when we sum together many audio tracks in a large recording session, each having their own noise floor that accumulates as we add them together.

bit	states	signal-to-noise ratio (dB)
1	2	6
2	4	12
3	8	18
4	16	24
5	32	30
8	256	48
16	65,536	96
24	16,777,216	144

At this point, we look back at the 140 dB that deals with our range of hearing. If I want to represent this entire range, I need to divide 140 dB by 6 to get the optimal number of bits for a correct representation of my sound: a little over 23, which is rounded up to 24. It's a common bit depth when we quantize our sampled audio (24*6 = 144 dB range).

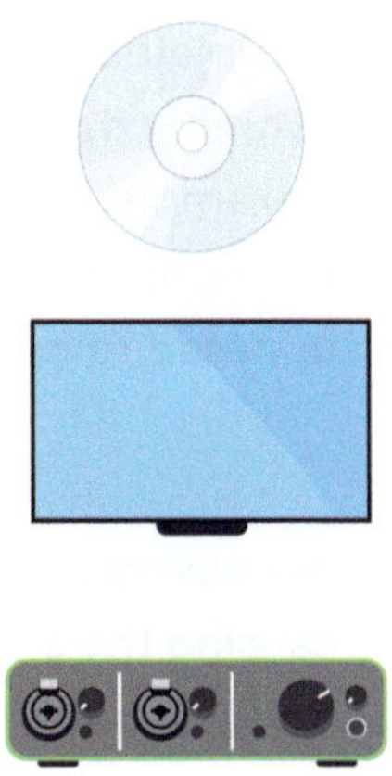

CD	44100 Hz	16 bit
VIDEO	48000 Hz	16/24 bit
AUDIO INTERFACE	96000 Hz	24 bit

The standard parameters for sample rate and quantization are 44,100 Hz and 16 bits for CDs. Otherwise, recording engineers and musicians use a variety of sample rates, including 44.1 kHz, 48 kHz, 96 kHz, and 192 kHz. Likewise, popular bit-depths also vary from 16 bit to 24 bits.

Reconstruction (DAC)

Once our digital signal has been processed and is ready to be heard, our sound must go back to the analog domain to be played through listening devices such as headphones or speakers. Therefore, **reconstructing the analog signal** from the digital binary code is necessary. To do this properly, engineers historically experimented with several methods before arriving at a mathematical method that now recreates an analog waveform that is quite faithful to the original. The **DAC (digital to analog converter)** ultimately must convert each digitally stored number to an electrical voltage. With discrete samples, we know the precise amplitude of each sample; however, the values between each sample are undefined and unknown. In other words, we only know the value of each sample and do not have any data to know what happens between these samples. Since analog is a continuous waveform, we need to fill in these data gaps somehow in order to reconstruct the wave. Initially, the sample and hold was used. This method takes the value of a sample and holds that value until we get to the next sample (using a rectangular-type pulse). However, these abrupt and sharp "steps" can create unwanted harsh timbres. The next method to fill in the gaps was linear interpolation using a triangular pulse. This method directly connects one sample's value to the next sample's value using a straight line with a constant slope. This method also creates sharp angles that can result in a harsh sound. The next type data interpolation method incorporates cubic splines, which significantly improves the result but is still not "perfect." The best result uses the sinc, or cardinal sine, function to interpolate between our points. This function reconstructs an analog signal that is virtually identical to the original wave.

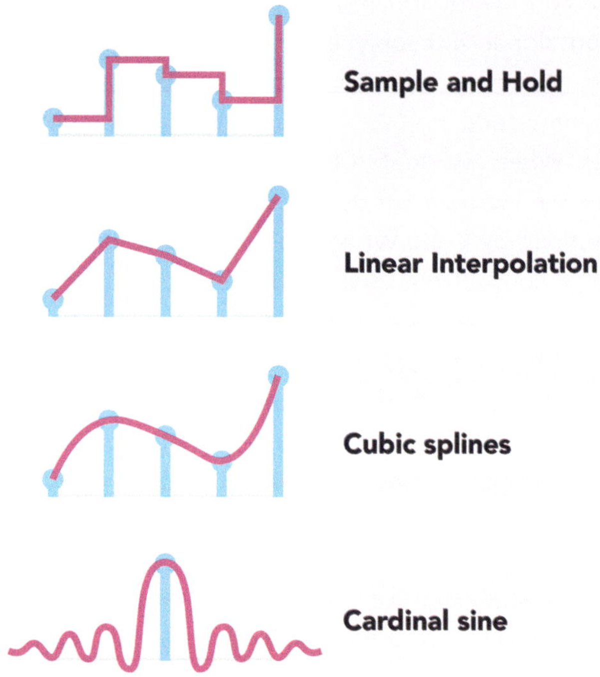

Issues in the sampling-reconstruction process

Let's go back to the initial example of observing a racecar from the window of your apartment. We said that if I sampled fast enough, I would not miss even the fastest car in the world. Let's say, however, that I re-analyze the data that I just tested and now I want to reconstruct the performance of the vehicle. Every time my data shows that the car has passed, I may start to wonder if someone has invented a super-fast car that could have completed two laps in the time that corresponded to what we thought was one lap. I essentially only "saw" one lap with my data while the car actually completed two laps. This can also happen when I sample an analog signal. For example, if I try to sample a 2 Hz wave with a 6 Hz sampling rate, I will have three samples per cycle. During reconstruction, all I see are these three samples per cycle. There is always some uncertainty if the reconstructed wave is supposed to be 2 Hz, 4 Hz, or potentially even higher.

However, from the other perspective, where I have three samples in a given time frame and do not know my original signal, how can I know that the original recording didn't have a sampling rate that was too low, causing the analog-to-digital conversion to miss an entire cycle (or more) of a higher frequency? In this case, an ambiguity arises: I can never be absolutely sure whether I am supposed to be reconstructing a 2 Hz wave or a 12 Hz wave (which would be the actual frequency multiplied by the sampling rate). The ambiguity can be seen in the spectral copies of the original signal that occur, as seen in the figure. These copies are called **aliases**. Generally, with an appropriate sampling rate, the ***aliases*** do not necessarily present too many problems as long as it occurs at very high frequencies that are out of the audible spectrum.

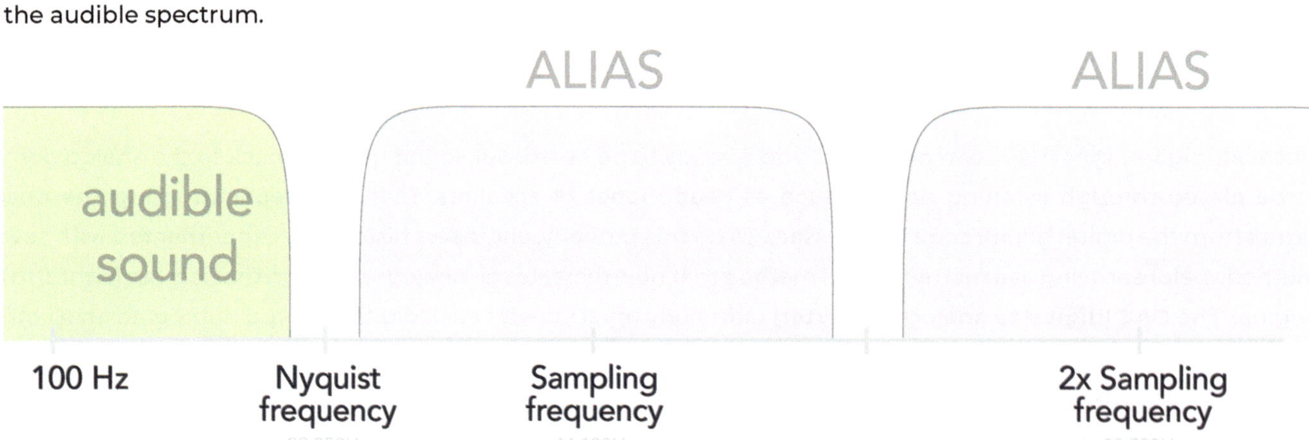

Importantly, the phenomenon of **aliasing** starts to happen when the ***aliases*** spill over into the audible spectrum and overlap one another. The reconstructed sound is then "enriched" with frequencies that are not supposed to be there. This effect is known as **foldover** distortion, or **aliasing**, and occurs when the sampling rate is too low, or if we try to sample sounds that exceed the Nyquist frequency. Low-pass filters are usually used to reduce the amplitude of any high frequency signals that arise from ***aliasing***. These are called **anti-aliasing filters**.

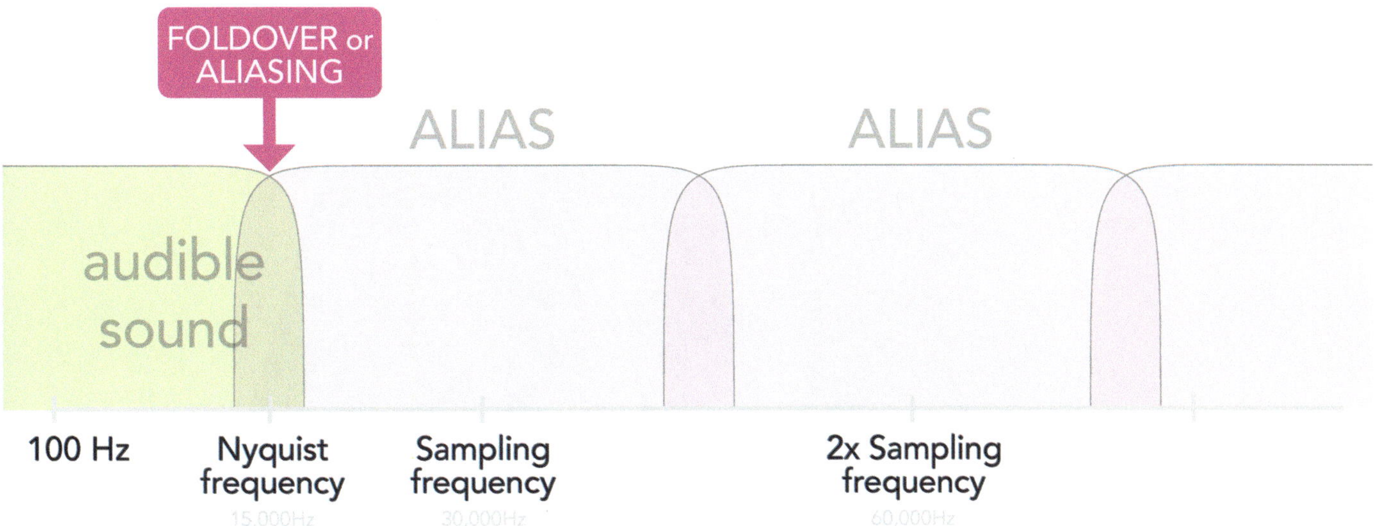

There are some methods during sampling or reconstruction that can help us avoid ***foldover distortion***.

- using **anti-aliasing filters**
  at the **input** to prevent the contribution of frequencies that are too high
  at the **output**, to attenuate any ***aliases*** occurring at very high frequencies

- increasing the sampling frequency

- using **oversampling**
  during reconstruction, adding one or more "artificial" samples between the "real" samples. It does not directly improve the sampling accuracy but results in a virtual doubling of the sampling rate, which helps us avoid ***foldover distortion***

.find the sampling and quantization parameters in the preference section of your audio software. Experiment with how to modify these parameters to suit your musical needs. If you want more creative exercises on this topic, look ahead toward the section on distortion

audio sampling

COMMU-NICATION PROTO-COLS

What happens when a pianist presses the middle C key on a synth keyboard? How can I control the cutoff frequency of my filter live to prepare the "drop" in my DJ set? How do the synthesizers or computers know what to do after the musician turns a knob?

When making music, whether acoustic, electronic, or a blend of the two, musicians essentially either generate a new sound with **sound synthesis**, as we see in the chapter at page 163, or take and modify an existing one with **sound processing**, as we can read about in the chapter at page 103. However, the whole thing would be rather complicated and clumsy without a way to control all these processes accurately. That is where communication protocols come in. These protocols are methods that enable communication between musicians, hardware instruments, and software instruments.

While every electronic musician can invent their own communication protocols, we can rely on a few commonly adopted protocols that have been established and standardized over the years: namely **MIDI** and **OSC**.

MIDI

MIDI, short for Musical Instrument Digital Interface, is a standardized protocol consisting of messages and rules for communication between musical instruments and other digital interfaces. It is important to note that MIDI is a series of messages that specify musical events, but it is not audio and does not contain any waveforms.

In 1981 *Dave Smith* and *Chet Wood*, designers of the American company ***Sequential Circuit*** that produced the ***Prophet*** synthesizers, began to define a communication protocol that could control polyphony and timbre.

During the ***NAMM (National Association of Music Merchants)*** trade show in Los Angeles in the summer of 1983, they introduced the first synthesizer with a MIDI protocol, the Prophet 600. This launched an era in which products that used MIDI proliferated and expanded musical creativity.
Since 2015, a more evolved variant has been made to complement the classic MIDI. It is called **MPE** or MIDI polyphonic expression. Even though it is built upon the original MIDI protocol, we will see that MPE allows more control precision, especially during performance.

Despite several attempts to modify the MIDI protocol, with MIDI 2.0 being the most recent significant update in 2023, its structure has remained conceptually the same, confirming that it is a valuable language that is easy to program and does not require complex, hard-to-find technology.

Connections

The **standard 5-pin MIDI connector** is the first type of cable connection developed to be used to connect MIDI devices. It passes MIDI signal only in one direction, so we need two cables if we need bidirectional communication between two machines. These cables are still used today, particularly on vintage hardware or, more generally, on standalone synthesizers and drum machines that do not require a computer to play. A 3.5 mm mini-TRS variant of this cable can be found on some synthesizers or small audio interfaces, usually requiring a special adapter to connect with the standard 5-pin cable.

USB cables are often used by controllers to interface with computers or smartphones. Using standard USB cables (type-B, mini, micro, or type-C), the MIDI messages can travel in both directions (both in and out) within the same cable. USB also has the advantage of being able to power a controller, allowing LEDs to shine, various indicators to display, and even small screens to turn on.

Virtual software connections are virtual connections that pass MIDI messages within a computer, allowing communication between programs. I can, for example, play a synthesizer in a DAW with MIDI notes generated algorithmically with Pure Data. At the time of the writing of this text, there are different methods for this for Apple macOS computers and Windows-based computers. While on Apple's macOS computers, there is a native solution (Driver IAC), a small software bridge (loopMIDI or MIDI yoke, for example) is needed for Windows-based computers. On both operating systems, the result is the creation of virtual MIDI in and out ports, which can then be used by all MIDI-compatible software.

Wi-Fi or Bluetooth are general wireless connections that can be used to transmit MIDI messages. This allows, for example, MIDI communication between a pedalboard and a smartphone or between a tablet and a computer. In the case of Wi-Fi, we use the same general Wi-Fi network that our devices are connected to in order to communicate. In the case of Bluetooth, on the other hand, we connect the devices directly to each other and thus activate a communication channel of MIDI packets. Bluetooth LE (low energy) is a particular type of Bluetooth that is popular because it consumes minimal power, making it appropriate for mobile devices. As with all wireless technology, distance between devices can be a limiting factor. Wi-Fi allows much greater distances because it is possible to extend the range through the amplification of signal or through mesh networks. For Bluetooth LE, on the other hand, we usually have a maximum of about 50 meters in an open field.

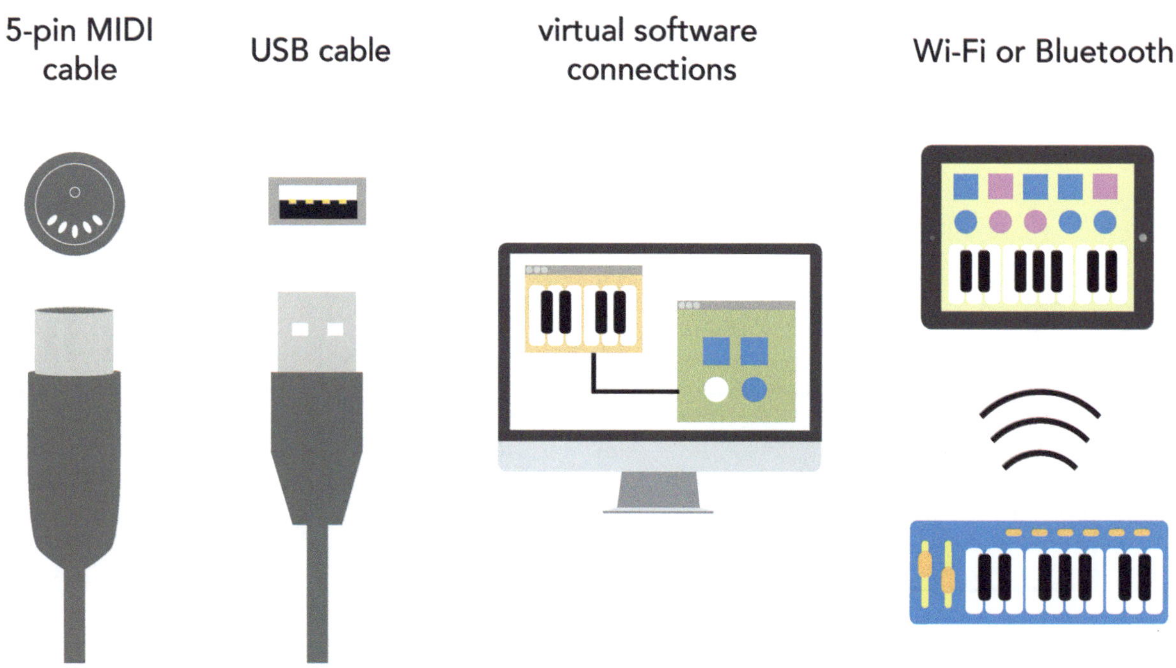

No matter the type of MIDI connection that is used, a hierarchy of devices is necessary. The main device (the master*) controls one or more secondary devices (the slaves*). MIDI connections with standard 5-pin cables have IN, OUT, and THRU ports. The OUT port sends MIDI messages out of the main device, for example. The IN port receives MIDI messages from other external devices and the THRU port passes the MIDI signal from the IN port to the OUT port without applying variations. The THRU port is most commonly used to connect multiple secondary devices.

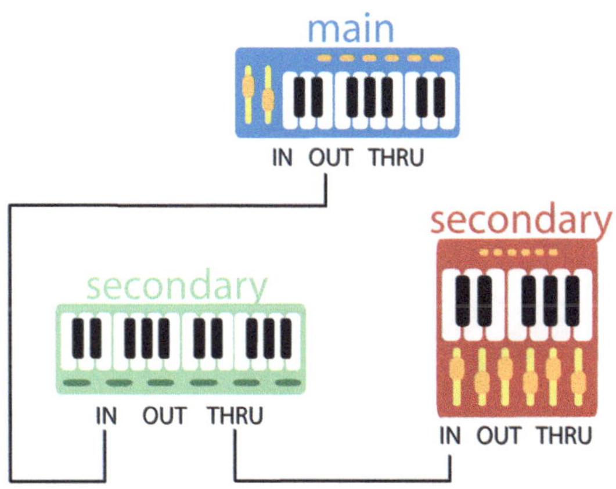

*Historically, the terms "master" and "slave" have been used to describe this type of computing network hierarchy since 1904. While the authors choose to use the terms main and secondary, you may see the historical terms used in devices, in the industry, and elsewhere in the field.

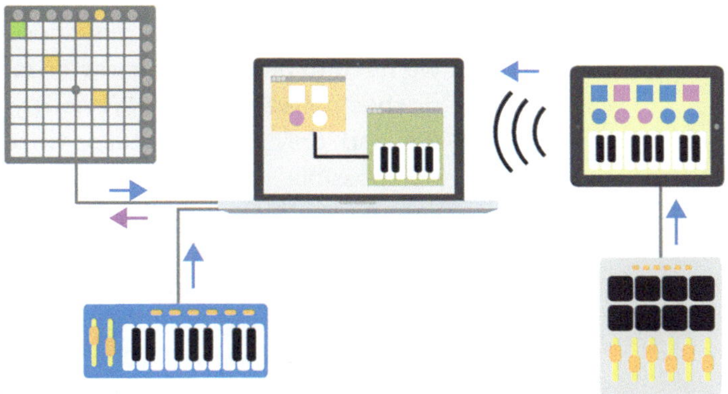

In systems that are comprised of entirely digital devices, the concept of main and secondary loses some relevance due to the flexibility offered by digital systems. Essentially, the hierarchy is customizable and adaptable. I can create infinite main and secondary relationships, or I can specify that a device act simultaneously as a main for one device and as a secondary for some other device. Even in this case, it is still important to be mindful of relationships, because the signal flow of our system requires us to recognize which devices are sending messages and which devices are receiving messages, a recurring theme in musical devices.

Types of messages

There are two macro-categories of MIDI messages: the **Channel Voice Message** and the **System Message**. Channel Voice Messages are the most commonly used messages because they cover all performance messages, such as information about notes, dynamics, modulations, etc. In contrast, System Messages are messages addressed globally to the system.

Channel Voice Message

Channel Voice Messages control the parameters that are needed to convert musical events into MIDI. These messages can be routed to one of the 16 channels available in MIDI. The channels in MIDI are like individual separate roads that carry my messages through the system. Each road, for example, can go to a different synthesizer. This means I can send a C4 note to one of the 16 synthesizers I have connected to my system without all the connected synthesizers playing it. For the sake of completeness, we should say that the routing of the messages into 16 channels is more important when working with vintage machines or standalone synthesizers. It is less important in the case of digital systems, where I can usually have the flexibility to route my signals with more than 16 connection possibilities.

0-127 is the numerical range of many MIDI messages. There are 128 discrete steps consisting of only integer values. To be clear, there is no value between the numbers 29 and 30 because fractional, non-integer values are not recognized. This is for two main reasons: 1) MIDI data is digital, i.e., formed by sequences of 0's and 1's, and 2) MIDI is a serial language, i.e., the data travels in a row one after the other. To avoid too much time passing between messages, it uses small data packets. To achieve this, MIDI uses packets of only seven digits or bits, leading to 128 steps ($2^7 = 128$).

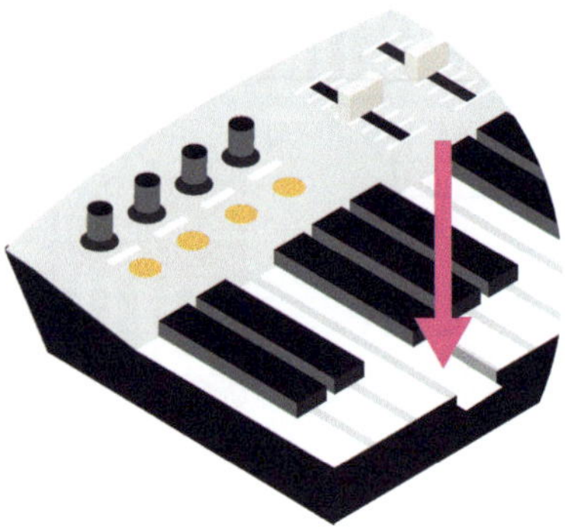

Note ON When a key is pressed on the keyboard, a Note ON (note pressed) message is sent, consisting of two numbers. The first number determines the pitch of the note (**pitch 0-127**), and the second number relates the amplitude of the pressed note to a velocity value (**velocity 0-127**).

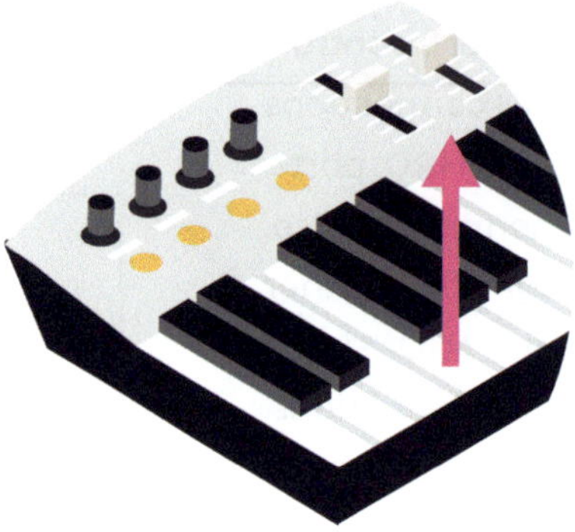

Note OFF When the key that was previously pressed is now released, a Note OFF message is generated that also consists of two numbers. Similarly, first number specifies which note is released (**pitch 0-127**), the second number dictates at what velocity the key is released (**velocity 0-127**).

Pitch bend MIDI keyboards have sliders, wheels, or joysticks which can be moved to vary the pitch during the sustain of a note. In order to have pitch variations needed for vibrato or to slide between notes with a glissando, we need to be able to characterize pitches between notes. Previously we had only integer steps, with no possible values in between semitones. We achieve greater pitch resolution by incorporating two pitch numbers instead of one number, resulting in 128^2 or 16,384 steps that define the MIDI pitches. The pitch bender is able to utilize all the steps to create the small pitch changes needed for vibrato and glissando.

Aftertouch or Channel Pressure This parameter takes the value of a sensor and transmits any changes in the pressure exerted on a previously pressed note in real time. This pressure, applied to the entire keyboard, is generically called Aftertouch and is usually mapped to change or control a specific sound characteristic (e.g., modulation, pitch, volume, etc.).

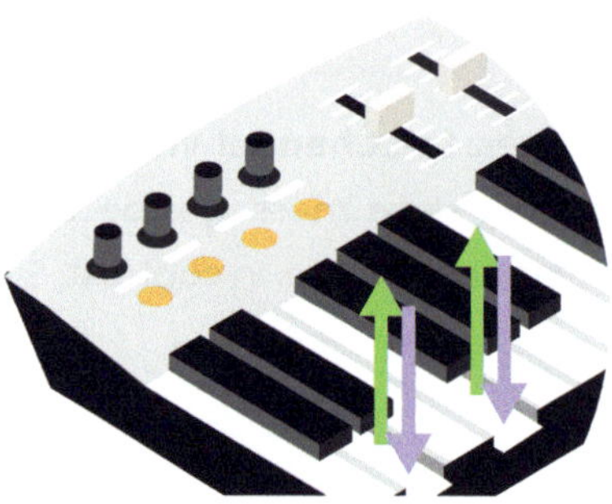

Polyphonic Aftertouch or Polyphonic Key Pressure It is similar to the Aftertouch but refers to independent pressure sensors for each note. It consists of two numbers: the first refers to the **note**, and the second to the **aftertouch value**.

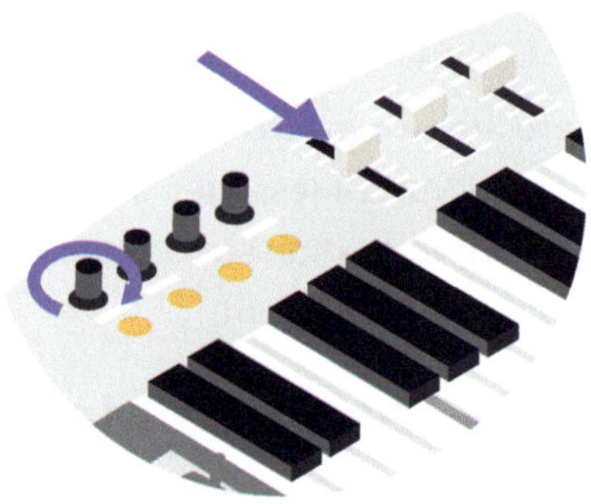

Control Change This message, consisting of two numbers, allows control values (up to 128 controllers for each channel) to be transmitted. The first number identifies the controller (**CC 0-127**), while the second specifies the value (**VALUE 0-127**). These messages are widely used in live electronics to control, for example, the effects parameters. They are also found in non-musical fields, where these values can control the rotation and color of a directional light.

Program Change We use it to change a preset, or program. A new preset or program can change what instrument is being played, the timbre of that instrument, or any other configuration within that effect chain.

System Message

These are the messages that apply **globally** within the system and not to a specific device. Therefore, they are not applicable to a single channel but rather to all connected devices.

MIDI Time Code Quarter Frame This message synchronizes multiple streams of audio and video in the format hours:minutes:seconds:frames. It is used, for example, to synchronize video with its associated audio and is based on SMPTE (Society of Motion Picture and Television Engineers) time code. MIDI Time Code Quarter Frame precisely indicates the SMPTE position with a MIDI signal.

Song Position Pointer This indicates the playback or cursor's position when playing a MIDI file. It's mainly used in Karaoke machines or with hardware MIDI track players.

Song Select This message allows you to select a song within a sequencer. It's primarily used by those doing Karaoke.

Tune Request This value is used to send the tuning value of an instrument. It allows a MIDI device to tune itself.

MIDI Clock The clock is used to synchronize the BPM (beats per minute) of multiple connected MIDI instruments. The main machine sends 24 signals for each quarter note value to all devices connected as secondary. It is widely used to synchronize hardware instruments such as drum machines, sequencers, and synthesizer arpeggiators.

Start This value is used to bring all instruments to the same starting position of the song or sequence in order to start them together in playback or recording.

Stop This stops the recording or playback of instruments connected to the sequencer.

Active Sensing This value is sent every 300 milliseconds to keep the connection between main and secondary devices active.

System Reset This command resets the secondary devices to the default conditions.

System Exclusive (SysEx) These messages control each instrument's global functionality and are used according to the manufacturer's requirements. Since they are specific to a particular device, they can only be interpreted by compatible devices. If the instrument cannot interpret one or more System Exclusive messages, it will return an error message.

MIDI controllers (connection and mapping)

MIDI controllers are devices that send and sometimes receive MIDI messages. They come in many shapes and sizes, and can vary in functionality. They can, for example, send MIDI signals upon pressing piano-like keys, mashing bright square keys, blowing into a tube, or even by moving a bracelet or ring worn by the musician. Unlike devices with standalone synthesizers, MIDI controllers do not produce a sound independently. They need to be connected to a computer to control a software synthesizer, to adjust the effect parameters, or even to manage lights. This is all because, as we said at the beginning of the chapter, MIDI is just a language for making multiple devices talk to each other. What you do with this language can drive your creativity.

A controller must be connected to the computer and be recognized by the MIDI compatible software. You may need to visit your software's MIDI preferences to ensure connectivity. To play **notes**, the only thing you usually have to do is assign a synthesizer to your controller. When you press C4 on your keyboard, the software will receive the C4 message, it will generate the sound of the note C4. Knob-type controllers, on the other hand, send **Control Change (CC)** messages, so we need to map or assign these CC messages to the parameters we are interested in adjusting. For example, we can customize our mapping so that potentiometer X controls a filter cutoff frequency and the Y button activates reverb. With modern controllers and software,we may encounter auto-mapping, where controls are automatically associated with specific standard parameters. From there, we can change those auto-mappings and get a customized control for our performance.

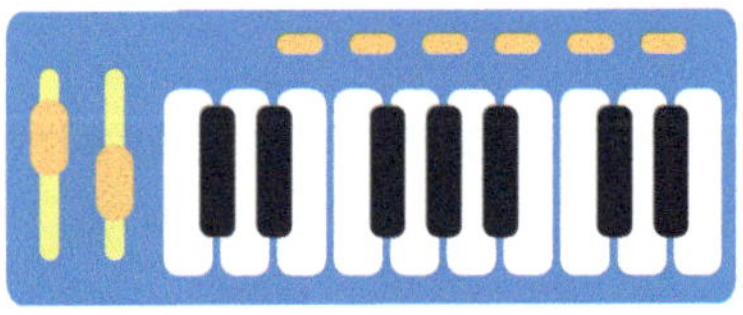

Keyboard MIDI Controllers They are the most common controller type with numerous companies manufacturing varying models. They may incorporate a piano-like keyboard that can consist of more or fewer octaves and subsequently send note messages to software or hardware devices that interpret them and generate sound.

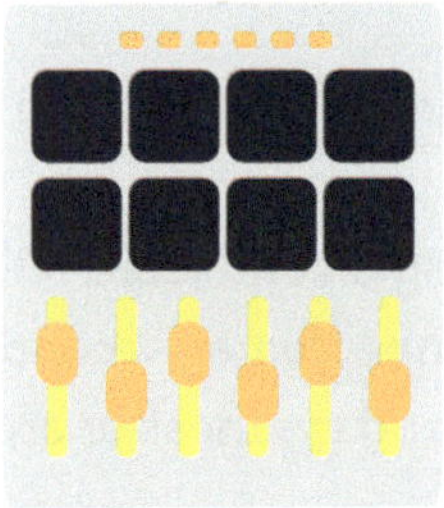

Mixer-like MIDI Controllers These controllers contain rotary potentiometers (knobs) or linear faders and are commonly used to manage effect parameters within software or hardware synthesizers. Generally, these knobs and faders send Control Change (CC) messages.

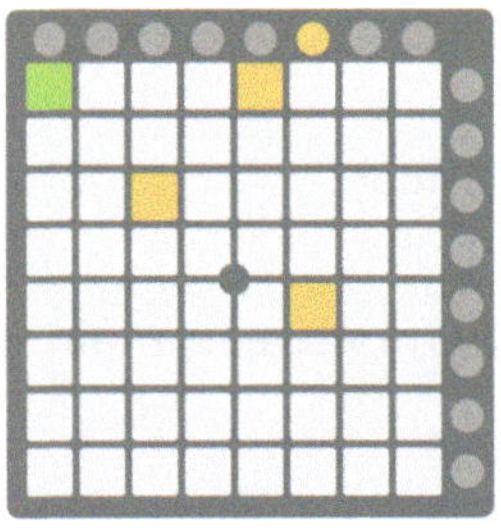

Matrix Style MIDI Controllers These controllers are based on a square matrix of buttons that are mapped to trigger notes or samples or are used to launch loops. The buttons can have LED lights within them and the lit colors can generally indicate whether the particular loop is in a play or a stop state. The buttons send MIDI note or control change information and can receive MIDI messages back to determine LED colors. A prominent example of this kind of controller is the ***Novation launchpad***, but there are many other types and sizes.

MIDI arpeggiator ~ MIDI chord ~ new MIDI controllers

Use your MIDI controller for these exercises. If you do not have one, find an app for your smartphone that sends MIDI to your computer (search for "MIDI" or "MIDI controller" in the AppStore or GooglePlay).

.set up three tracks in your DAW, each with a virtual instrument, that will receive messages from your MIDI controller. Apply a MIDI transposer for each track. Working only with the transposers and the controller, compose a track. ***Theme: "An orchestra in your jacket pocket"***

.download and import a song of your choice into a DAW and perform an extreme time stretch using Audacity's Paulstretch with a stretch factor of 20-30. Put a low-pass filter and pitch shifter on the track. Map the filter's cutoff frequency and pitch shifter's pitch to two potentiometers on your controller, each of which will send CC messages. Create a performance. ***Theme: "Inhale, exhale"***

.put a MIDI arpeggiator that drives a synthesizer of your choice in your DAW. Map the speed of the arpeggiator with a potentiometer on your controller (which sends CC messages). Create a song by playing a live chord sequence of your choice and varying the arpeggiator's speed. If you want, you can automate the movement of the arpeggiator speed instead of handling it live. ***Theme: "The takeoff"***

.with a DAW or programming software, create a system that, upon receiving a note from the controller, plays a randomly chosen instrument from a set of four that you choose

.mid files

A **MIDI file, .mid,** is a file format that contains a sequence of MIDI data, consisting of several messages distributed in various channels, capable of being interpreted by any MIDI compatible hardware device or software instrument. A MIDI file can represent an entire song, containing all the messages for the notes of various instruments. With a MIDI-playback software program, a MIDI file can be read and played back, reconstructing the various notes to different virtual instruments. Beware that a MIDI file is, therefore, not an audio file because it does not store the recording, or audio waveforms, of the instruments' sounds. MIDI files only store messages that specify pitch, duration, and note velocity data. It can be thought of like sheet music. The sheet music is just black markings on a page, needing a musician to turn the instructions into audible sound. MIDI messages are just instructions that need software to turn messages into audible sound.

Some standards, like ***General MIDI***, handle the way instruments are identified, allowing us to quickly assign tracks to various instruments of our choice.

.download a free MIDI file of a multi-track piece of classical music (for example, search for "free MIDI Bach"), import it into your DAW in separate tracks, assign a different synthesizer to each track, and create a new orchestration of the chosen piece. Also, experiment with the song's tempo by creating areas of accelerando and ritardando

Wendy Carlos ~ Wendy Carlos Switched-On ~ Pietro Grossi Mixed Paganini

MPE

Instead of using the 16 channels separately, **MPE** merges multiple channels to give each note more gestural possibilities. It is based upon and evolved from MIDI, creating different ways of using standard MIDI messages to achieve more performative possibilities. For example, in MIDI controllers using MPE, it is possible to send the values corresponding to horizontal and vertical finger position and finger pressure in addition to the standard note and velocity values.

So, with one finger, I can potentially control the note, its intensity, variations of its timbre, and even the amount of reverb I am applying to it. To perform this, I will also need software that receives the controller signals and interprets them into sound.

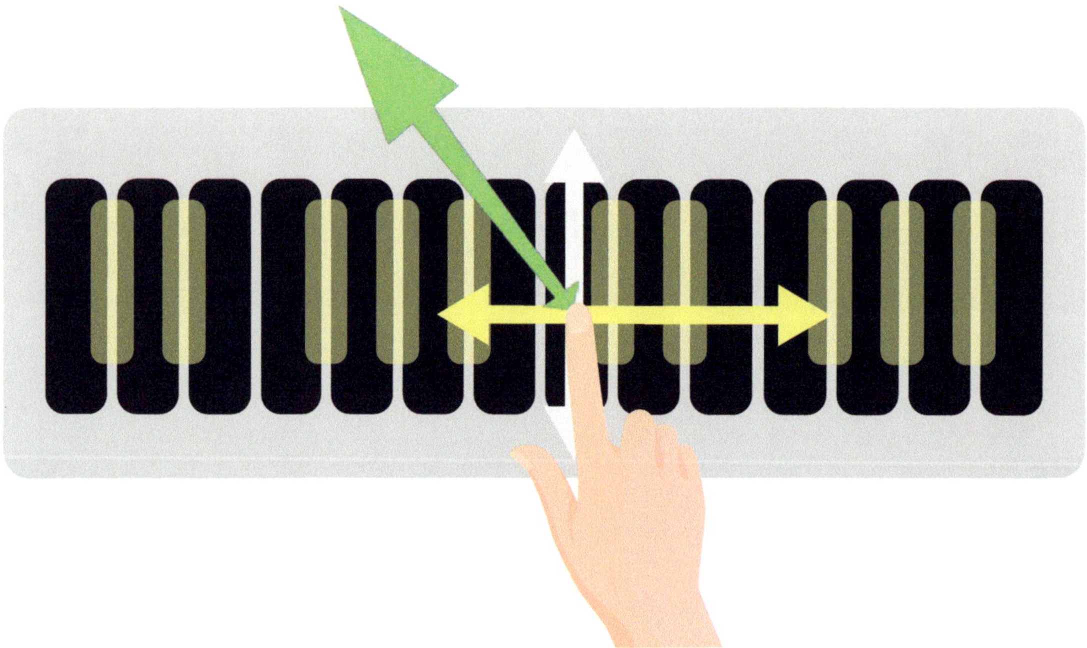

.orchestrate a video clip from a film of your choice using a single instrument that receives and plays MPE. To do this, use an AI chatbot to write a chord sequence and melody, focusing on the relevance between the visuals and the feelings you want to stimulate. Once you have the notes, play them on a virtual instrument using an MPE controller. As you play, pay attention to the various ways you can vary the details of the sound when using the numerous type of controls that MPE provides

MIDI polyphonic expression ~ Roli seaboard ~ Haken Continuum Fingerboard ~ Sensel Morph ~ Keith McMillen K-Board Pro ~ Expressive E Osmose

OSC

Open Sound Control (OSC) was created by the ***UC Berkeley Center for New Music and Audio Technologies (CNMAT)*** in 1997 and is an open-source protocol for communication between computers, audio synthesizers, and other multimedia devices over a network (either wireless or wired) or the Internet. When using a network, OSC-type messages can be passed back and forth using the classic network architecture type: client/server. Typically, in both hardware or software OSC devices, clients send messages to the server and servers receive and execute OSC messages.

OSC messages are composed of three parts:

ADDRESS PATTERN	**TYPE TAG STRING**	**ARGUMENTS**
is a string that specifies the address relative to the data that is transmitted	specifies the data type of each argument	are the parameter values contained in the message
example: *|squarewave/partial/one*	example: *float (number with a decimal place)*	example: *440.5*

For clients to send OSC messages, they need to set the destination/server **IP addresses** (unique addresses of a computer on a network). Both clients and servers should also be configured with a **send** and a **receive port**. In the figure below, for example, the server is "listening" on port 3000 and the client sends on port 3000 to the server IP. The server (IP address 127.0.0.4) essentially "hears" the messages.

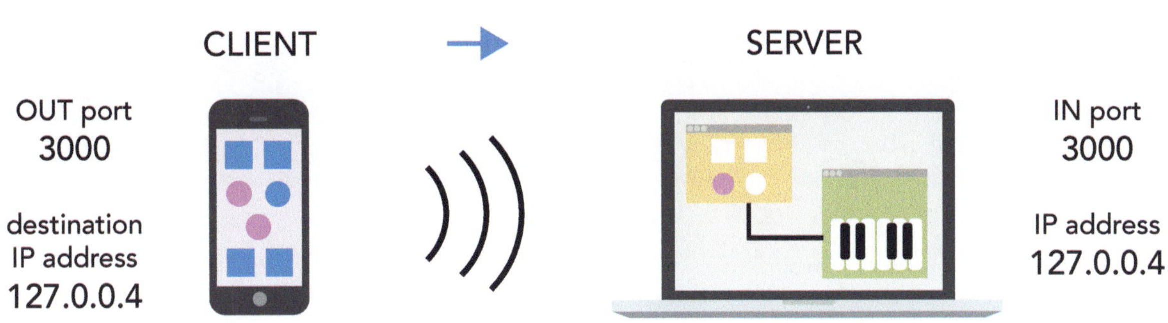

OSC has become popular due to its common implementation on smartphones and tablets, where OSC can be passed from device to device via Wi-Fi. On these devices, OSC-compatible apps allow almost limitless control by allowing the user to create customized control interfaces by choosing where to place sliders, knobs, and buttons. These apps can also transmit OSC parameters based on the acceleration and rotation sensors within smartphones or tablets for live electronics performance.

OSC works as fast as the network can handle, needing to communicate more data in comparison with MIDI. OSC also has higher resolution than MIDI as it is not bound to the 128 "steps," but rather it is based on 32-bit processing, allowing a much higher resolution and more flexibility than MIDI. The downside is that it is not currently as ubiquitous as MIDI and can be a bit cumbersome when connecting devices as we need to specify the address and port of both the client and server.

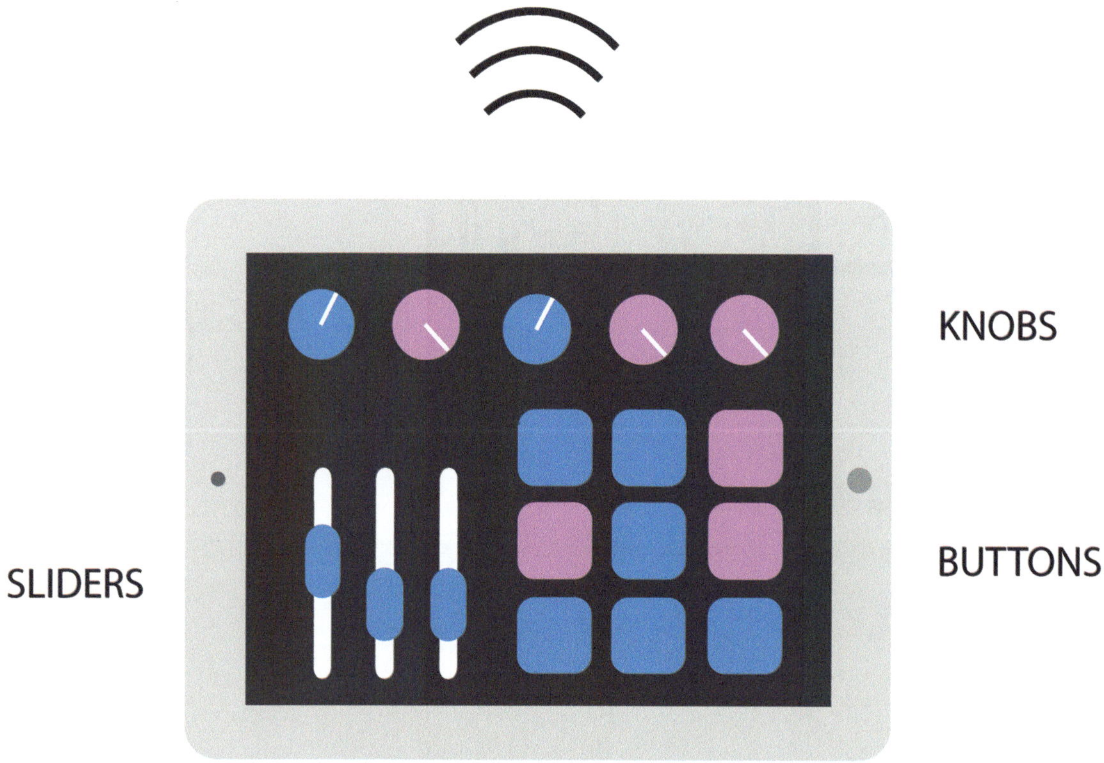

.install a smartphone app that allows you to send OSC (search for "OSC" on AppStore or PlayStore). Connect your computer and smartphone to the same Wi-Fi network and try controlling the PAN parameter of a track in your DAW or a Pure Data / Max patch with your smartphone. Play a loop of your choice and adjust the PAN while also physically moving around the room

.record separate video clips of eight close-up facial expressions using your smartphone. Import them into VJ software (touchdesigner, resolume, or even Max/jitter). With an app that sends OSC messages, create a system that uses your phone to control the crossfades between the video clips. Compose a musical soundtrack and then "perform" the clips as the music is playing. ***Theme: "8 variations of me"***

SOUND PROCESS-ING

Sound processing is a set of real time or non-real time processes used to modify a captured sound or pre-existing audio.
Devices intended for sound processing are sometimes called effects.

Sound processing can take place in three modes:

Pre-existing sound with processing and playback occurring at different times In this case, a sound is recorded, processed at some later time, and finally, performed or played back at yet another later time. For example, this is the case with acousmatic music in which the composer records sound materials, processes them later, creates the composition, and finally performs the piece live.

Pre-existing sound at an earlier time with real time processing during playback The sound is recorded or produced digitally at a point in time where later, it is performed live with real time processing. This is the case with a live set in which a musician processes live compositions that they have previously produced. Imagine a scenario where a live musician takes existing cello recordings and performs a live composition using those cello recordings with real time processing, giving the recordings new form and content.

Real time recording, processing, and playback This is essentially the field of ***live electronics***, which we mentioned earlier and involves recording, processing and playback in real time.

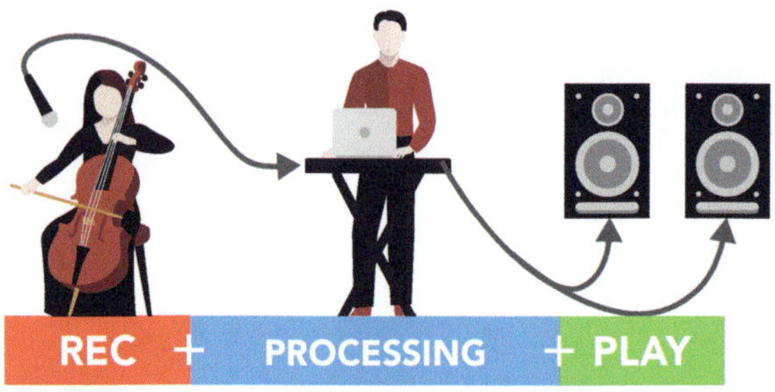

FILTERS, EQ, AND RELATED EFFECTS

A **filter** is a device that **attenuates** the amplitude and alters the phase of certain frequencies in a sound. With amplification and gain incorporated with filters, it is also possible to **emphasize** or boost certain frequencies. In most of the filters we will see in this chapter, our focus is on how the amplitude is altered at various frequency bands. We will also discuss all-pass filters, where the phase response is the critical output parameter.

While filters are generally devices or algorithms that manipulate or distort the spectral properties of audio, we use equalizers, or EQ, to generate the filter parameters to meet our sonic goals. We can think of EQ as consisting of banks of filters, and EQ settings as controlling the parameters of these filters to accomplish a more complex spectral task.

In the illustration below, we can see the spectrum of an input sound passing through a low-pass filter and the resulting output spectrum. The spectrum is shown here in frequency bands, where each band represents a range of frequencies. The X-axis represents the center frequency of each frequency range, and the Y-axis represents the total energy contained within that frequency range. The filter or EQ response, or generally the **frequency response**, shows the spectral change that is applied to the original spectrum. In this case, the flat part of the black line shows the part of the frequency response that does not affect the original spectrum. However, at the higher frequencies, this black line curves downward, showing that above a certain frequency, there is greater attenuation as frequency increases. Like with all the effects mentioned in this book, filters have parameters that control the frequency response, giving us, the user, opportunities to achieve our desired sonic result.

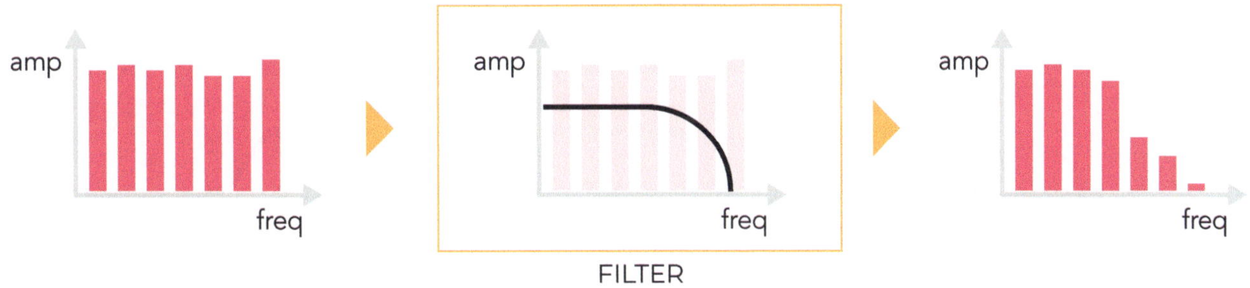

Low-pass and High-pass

Low-pass and **High-pass** filters are devices that, as their names imply, pass low and high frequencies, respectively, present in the spectrum of a sound while cutting off, or attenuating, the others. If we focus on our auditory response, low-pass filters make a sound more muffled, less "acidic," and "darker." A high-pass filter, on the contrary, removes the "deep" part of the sound while keeping the brightest and more "acidic" part.

Both are rather invasive effects and can significantly modify the sound. This makes filters suitable to use in subtractive sound synthesis, where the filter is used to "sculpt" the sound. Filters are also used to correct errors or isolate frequencies from the recording process. For example, I can filter out frequencies of an audio track that are not part of the timbre of the instrument I have recorded. In the case of the piccolo, I can cut out many low frequencies with a high-pass filter because it is an instrument with most of its spectral energy in the high frequencies.

Settings

Cutoff is the frequency threshold, in hertz, where the filter essentially activates. In the case of low-pass filters, frequencies above this cutoff are attenuated. Conversely, for high-pass filters, frequencies below this cutoff are attenuated. An important property for simpler filters is that the cutoff represents the frequency where the filter has a -3 dB response.

Q is the parameter used in resonant filters that determines how much amplitude boost there is at the cutoff frequency. **Resonance**, a concept that originated from analysis of audio circuits that contain capacitors and inductors, can be thought of as an emphasis of a certain frequency range. In most common filters, values from 0 to 0.7 do not create an amplitude boost; however, higher Qs can cause a boost.

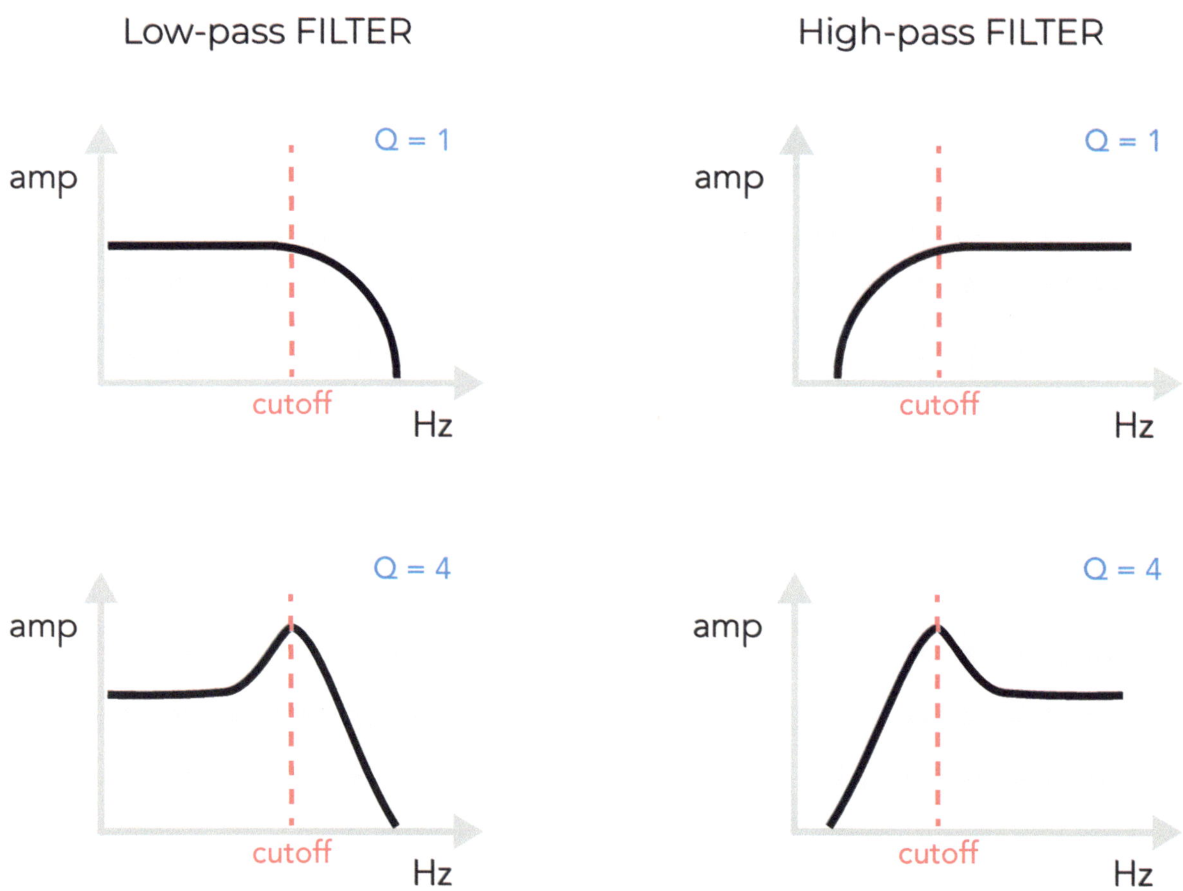

.generate a 30-second white noise track (with your DAW or by importing from a third-party), apply a low-pass filter to the noise, and create a composition where you dynamically control the cutoff frequency. As an example, you can try to recreate the sound of the waves of a calm sea that you hear while resting on the beach on a summer evening

Band-pass and Notch

These two filters have opposite responses to each other. The **Band-pass** filter selects a band of frequencies and lets audio in that frequency range pass while cutting out energy outside that range. Contrarily, a **Notch** (or **Band-reject**) filter blocks the audio energy within a certain band of frequencies, while passing all audio outside that band. The band-pass filter is widely used in sound synthesis or in substantial audio treatments where you want to keep only a small part of the spectrum. On the other hand, the notch filter is often use to precisely make corrections in a recording, such as eliminating the background noise of a tonal fan in the room during a recording session.

Settings

Cutoff or center frequency is the center frequency of the band that either passes (in band-pass filters) or attenuates (in notch filters) the audio.

Bandwidth is defined as the width of the notch band or band-pass filter's response. Both notch and band-pass filters have upper and lower cutoff frequencies, extending the concept of cutoff frequencies from before. Thus, the bandwidth is the frequency difference between the upper frequency and the lower frequency. Bandwidth is used in conjunction with Q to express the width of a filter.

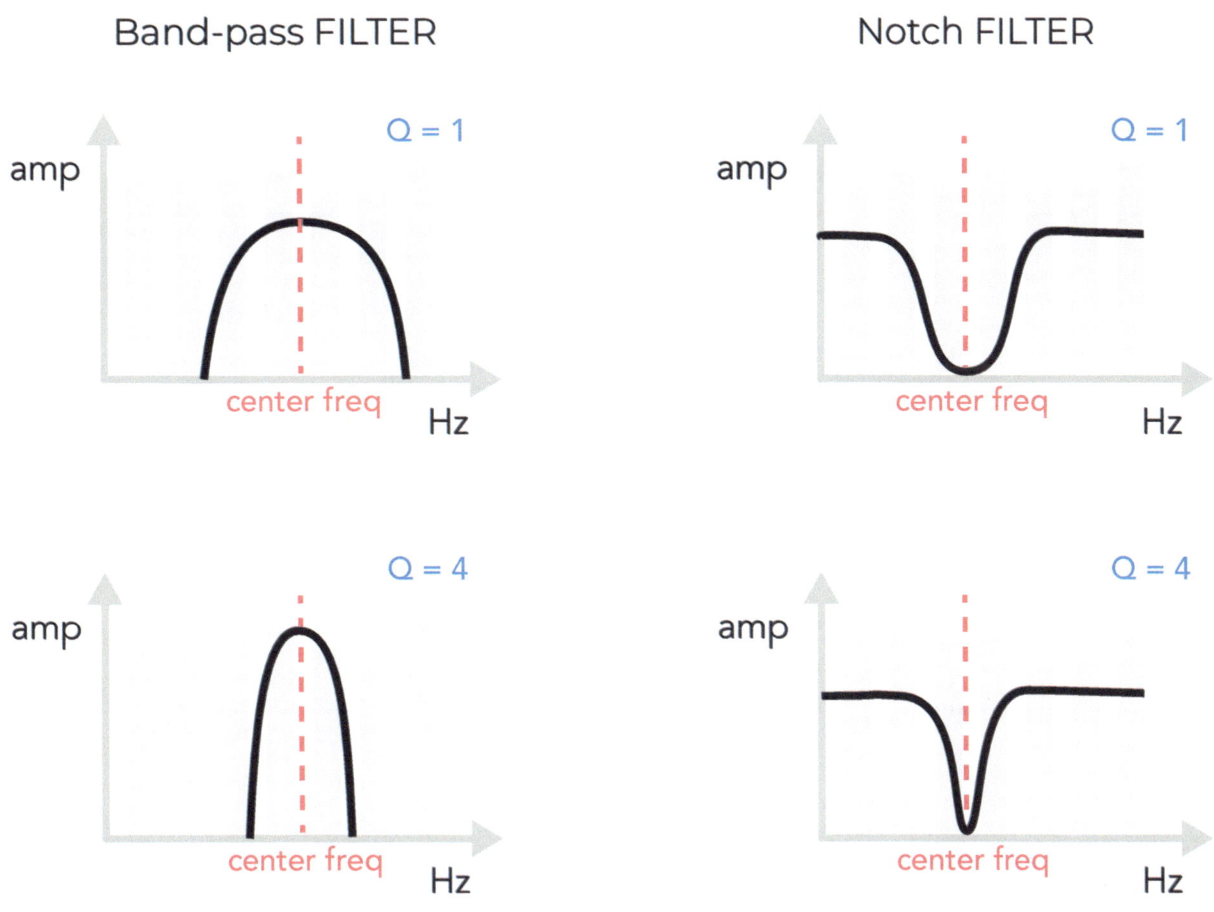

Q determines how narrow or wide the band-pass or notch filter is. High Q values create narrow bands and lower Q values make wider bands. This is because **Q is the ratio of the center frequency to bandwidth**. If I keep the center frequency value constant and raise the value of Q, I will be making my filter narrower. If I lower the value of Q instead, I will have a wider filter. In mathematical terms, Q and bandwidth are inversely proportional.

As we saw in the earlier chapter about frequency characteristics, musical notes do not have a linear frequency relationship but have a logarithmic relationship instead. Likewise, bandwidths also relate logarithmically to pitch. For example, a bandwidth of 200 Hz might span many musical notes in the lower frequencies but may only represent a fraction of a semitone in higher frequencies. To better preserve the musical relationships, we like to use Q instead of bandwidth. If I use a fixed Q filter, changing my center frequency requires the bandwidth to change to keep Q constant, allowing us to maintain the width of a musical octave or other chosen musical interval for example.

Low-shelf, High-shelf, and Bell EQ filters

These are a set of equalizers, consisting of a bank of filters, that we use to attenuate or boost particular ranges of frequencies. In the previous filters discussed here, the response beyond the cutoff gradually increased attenuation as it got further from the cutoff frequency. In **shelf filters** (within an equalizer), there is a transition band where the attenuation or boost gradually increases, but beyond the transition band, the response is flat across frequency. This is a key difference between a high and low-pass filter and a high and low-shelf filter. The **Low-shelf** filter focuses on frequencies below a certain threshold, also called the cutoff. The **High-shelf** filter affects the high frequencies above the set cutoff. Finally, the **Bell** filter works on a band of frequencies.

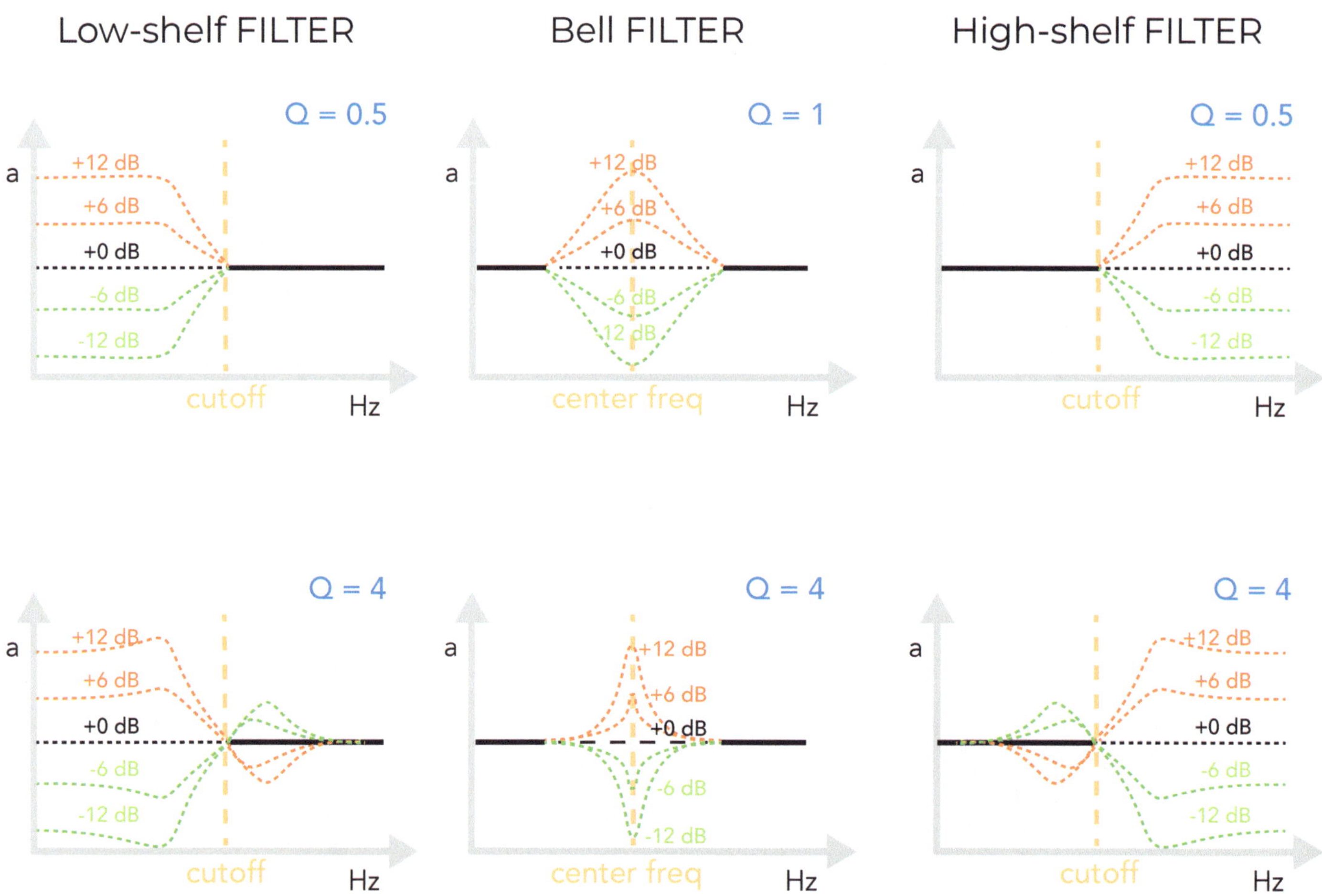

Settings

Cutoff indicates the characteristic frequency at which each filter of the EQ operates. In the case of the low-shelf, the frequencies below the cutoff are affected. For the high-shelf, the sounds above the cutoff are affected. Finally, for the bell, the characteristic frequency is the bell's center frequency.

Gain is the amplitude scaling factor that controls how much the shelf filters emphasize or attenuate the signal within the EQ's response. It is measured in dB and can have positive values in the case of emphasis and negative values in the case of attenuation. For example, a low-shelf with a cutoff of 150 Hz and gain of +6 dB essentially doubles the amplitudes of frequencies below 150 Hz.

Q sets the slope of the frequency response curve in low-shelf and high-shelf filters or it determines the amount of resonance around the cutoff frequency in bell filter. For example, high values create steeper slopes. In the bell filter, Q indicates how narrow the EQ's frequency band is, where higher values correspond to a narrower band, and lower values indicate a wider band.

Filter order

The filter order determines the slope of high and low-pass filters. The higher the order, the steeper the slope. Higher orders have traditionally required more analog components; whereas, now, higher order filters use more computational power.

A **First Order** filter attenuates **6 dB** for every octave beyond the cutoff frequency. You will often see this written as 6 dB per octave or 6 dB/octave. We have seen 6 dB before, as it corresponds to the halving of the sound amplitude. A **Second Order** filter attenuates our sound by **12 dB** for every octave above or below the cutoff frequency.

For example, as you can see in the figure for a 1st order filter, the amplitude at 880 Hz is 6 dB less than the amplitude at 440. Likewise, for the 2nd order filter, the change is 12 dB.

To get higher orders, place these filters in series. If you want a 6th order filter, place six first-order filters in series. Generally, for n-order filters, the slope is always n x 6 dB / octave. Additionally, sometimes these slopes are expressed in terms of decades instead of octaves. A decade, in this case, refers to a factor of ten (e.g, 100 Hz) is one decade higher than 10 Hz, 10,000 Hz is three decades higher than 10 Hz. The slope of an n-order filter can also be expressed as n x 20 dB/decade.

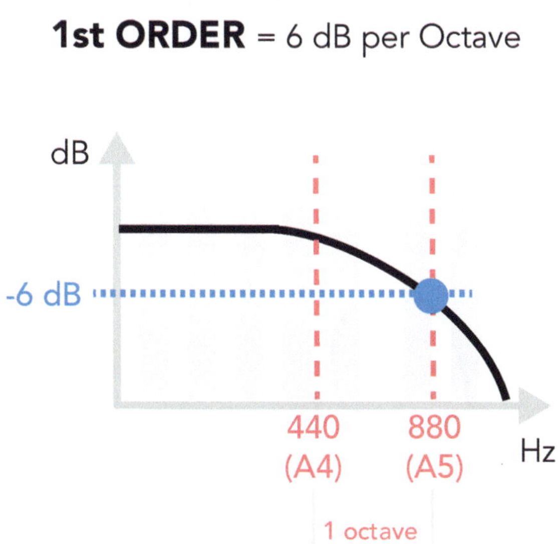

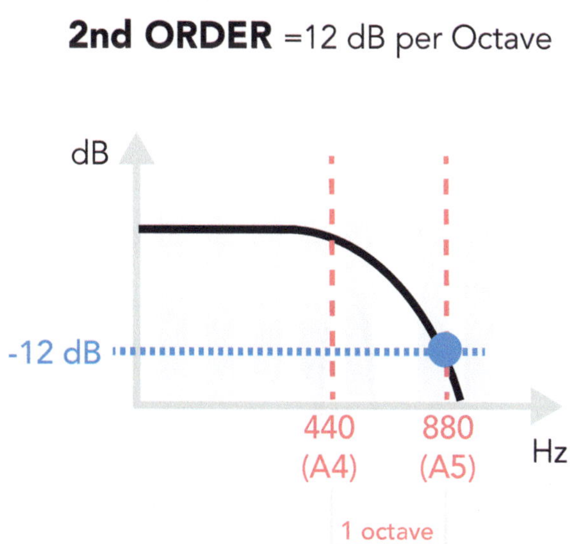

As a point of clarification, depending on device, you will sometimes see the slope at 6 dB/octave or -6 dB/octave. In this context, they refer to the same slope, just from different perspectives. In the former, it indicates that the signal is attenuated 6 dB per octave. In the latter, it shows that there is a -6 dB change per octave. Additionally, in some hardware and software devices, we will see the slope instead of the order indicated. For example, if we find that our plugin indicates a slope of -12 dB/octave, it means that we are looking at a second-order filter.

.using only ***band-pass***, ***notch***, or ***shelf filters***, create five versions of two sounds of your choice. Using only these 10 sounds, create a small composition of at least 90 seconds in length. Imagine telling a small story in which sounds are layered, sometimes acting as the protagonist and sometimes acting as background sounds. ***Theme: "The fabulous story of Petra and Ada"***

Q

Let's take a deeper dive into Q. We have seen a little about it already while discussing the filters above. Quality factor, or Q, is the value that describes the resonance of a system. We usually consider the Q of a filter for 2nd order or higher filters.

To review, for low-pass and high-pass filters (2nd order or higher), the Q shapes the **resonance bump at the cutoff frequency**, where a higher Q has more boost and steeper slope. In the case where Q is less than 0.707, there is no resonance bump anymore. This is due to the damping factor of the circuit, which indicates how much a given oscillation is attenuated over time. Practically, our selection of Q will be related to how noticeable we want the resonance peak around the cutoff frequency to be.

With band-pass, notch, and bell filters, we can revisit the definition of Q as the **ratio of the center frequency to bandwidth**. As we have seen, Q is a parameter that is used to control how narrow or broad the filter is. If we keep our Q constant and change the center frequency, then the bandwidth must change accordingly. In this case with a constant Q, a high center frequency corresponds to a bandwidth covering many frequencies, and a low center frequency corresponds to a bandwidth covering fewer frequencies. Let's translate this to a more interesting musical context, since the frequencies of our musical notes are distributed exponentially and not in equal steps. This works to our advantage in the case of the constant Q filters here. By keeping the Q constant, the filter will adapt, as if by magic, to the range of frequencies it is considering. For example, with a fixed Q filter covering one octave, all I have to do is adjust the center frequency to create a bass or treble filter, each covering exactly one octave.

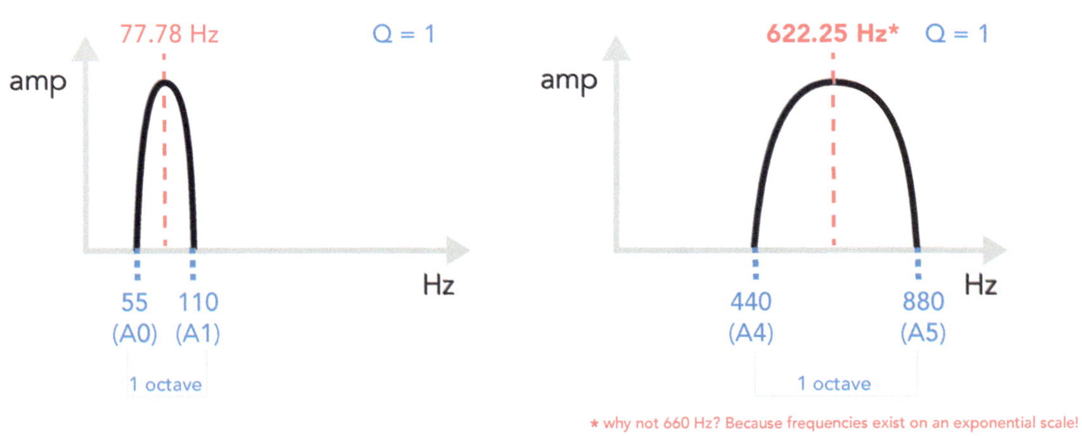

.record a white noise-like sound with your voice and apply a band-pass filter to it. Create rhythms by moving the Q and cutoff parameters randomly. For example, you can do this manually or with LFOs with random waveforms. On a second track, insert a drum beat that "talks" to it. Create two different beats, four measures each, using this technique

All-pass

The **All-pass** filter is a filter that passes all frequencies. On the surface, it would seem like the most useless filter in the world, but only because we often forget that a filter also significantly disturbs the phase of the input signal. That is the case with the all-pass filter, a special type of filter that is a phase "modifier" of a sound. This comes in handy when all-pass filters are used in conjunction with other copies of the same sound, causing boosts, attenuations, or even cancellations of certain frequencies of our sound. As we saw when we talked about phase properties in acoustic waves (page 34), we are not generally sensitive to a phase change of a simple wave. However, when we start modifying phase in complex waves or with multiple waves happening at once, we start to very audibly notice how these phase changes interact with one another, causing potentially dramatic effects like total phase cancellation.

Settings

Critical frequency can be set to control phase. An all-pass filter does not change all the phases of the spectrum that make up our sound in the same way. The phase of the frequencies surrounding the critical frequencies are most affected by the all-pass filter. As we move further away from the critical frequency, the phase response shifts less.

The all-pass filter gradually shifts the phase from 0 degree to -360 degrees with increasing frequency. Many graphs will wrap the phase around and show the response going from 0 to -180 degrees, then jumping to +180 degrees, and gradually decreasing back to 0. This jump happens at the critical frequency.

Q is the parameter that controls the steepness of the phase response curve around the critical frequency. For high Qs, the phase response passes more quickly from -180 degrees to +180 degrees at the critical frequency than the low Q phase response. High Qs make our all-pass more selective.

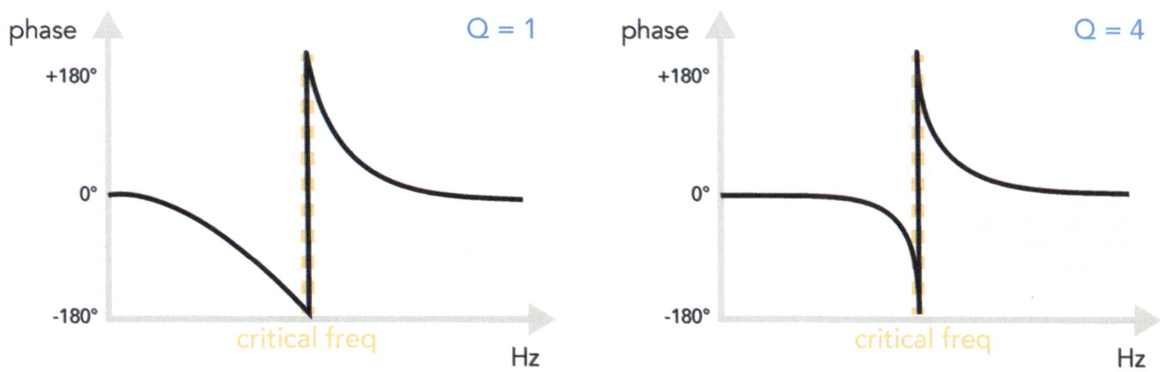

.program a function with your favorite programming language to take a noise signal input, apply an all-pass filter to it, and then sum the output with the original sound. Map the critical frequency and Q of your all-pass filter to the movement of a mouse, trackpad, or joystick. Additionally, map the amplitude of the filtered sound to a fader or knob of a MIDI controller. Using this setup, create a small performance. ***Theme: "Life under the fallen leaves"***

Wah-wah

Electric guitarists, from Jimi Hendrix onward, have loved to use the **Wah-wah** effect, a popular sound that is achieved by rhythmically varying the center frequency of a band-pass filter. Changing the resulting center frequency causes a kind of "mewing" of our input sound, precisely achieving the onomatopoeic name, wah-wah. The change in center frequency can be done manually by a pedal or another controller, or it can depend on an **LFO** (Low-Frequency Oscillator). This latter case refers to the **Auto-Wah**, because the oscillator acts as an automatic "assistant" to the musician. In some cases, we can now also find wah-wah effects that use a low-pass filter instead of a band-pass singular filters. Here we can vary the cutoff frequency and the Q of a low-pass filter to achieve the wah-wah effect.

Settings

Range or Width tells us how deep the action of the pedal is. In the case of the auto-wah, the width controls the frequency range of the highest and lowest center frequency.

Speed or Rate is the frequency of the LFO (in hertz), which determines the speed at which the center frequency oscillates. We find this parameter only in the auto-wah.

Q, seen in some wah-wah effects, can control the width or peakiness of the band-pass filter, or the resonance of the low-pass filter.

Wet refers to the amount of modified sound that is mixed in with the original. The greater this value, the more the wah-wah effect will be perceived.

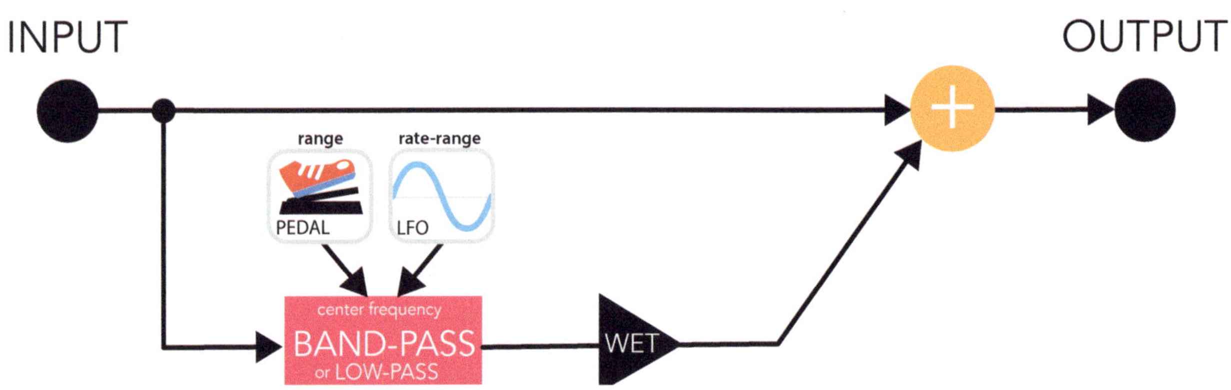

.build an auto-wah with the rate that is controlled by a potentiometer with a DAW and/or a programming language of your choice. Apply the effect to a sawtooth wave tuned to a fixed bass note (like A1). Create a song by controlling and exploiting different varieties of rate trajectories in a live setting. ***Theme: "Moths"***

wah wah songs ~ Cry Baby ~ Jimi Hendrix wah

Phaser

I can control the critical frequency of an all-pass filter continuously with an **LFO**. As this critical frequency sweeps up and down with a copied signal, phase cancellations will occur at particular frequencies. Because the LFO controls the sweep, the effect is a sort of "negative" glissando, where an absence of energy in a frequency band glisses higher and lower. This effect is known as the **Phaser**. This principle can be utilized with simple waves as we have discussed, or with complex settings for interesting sonic results. We see phasers in hundreds of digital and analog effects (e.g., guitar, bass, and electric piano pedals).

Settings

Speed or Rate refers to the frequency of the LFO, in hertz. It is essentially the rate at which the critical frequency oscillates up and down.

Range or Width of the LFO determines the range of critical frequencies, or the bandwidth of possible critical frequencies.

Feedback indicates how much sound is returned to the input after passing through the all-pass. At the effect level, the amount of feedback determines how long it takes for the output sound to decay. When we use negative feedback, we essentially subtract the all-pass signal from the input sound instead of summing them. The subtraction is equivalent to flipping the polarity of the signal and then summing it with the input. This polarity shift, or negative feedback, changes the phase cancellations in the process.

Wet is the amount of processed sound that is added back to the original, unprocessed sound. The higher this value, the more substantial the phase cancellations/attenuation are.

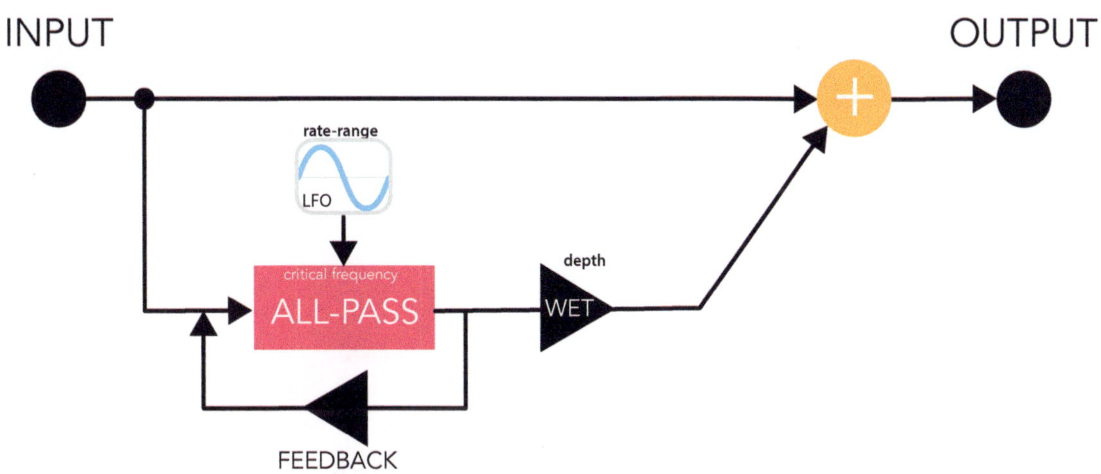

.create a micro composition for solo voice and phaser. Use only your own recorded voice. Record (using a microphone or your smartphone): four notes at least two seconds each,four short notes each lasting at most one second, two sounds of your choice (made with your voice).
Create the composition by applying a phaser or multiple phasers of your choice to the various parts. ***Theme: "Inhabitants of the enchanted forest"***

Phaser songs ~ Given to fly Pearl Jam ~ David Gilmour Phaser

DELAY AND RELATED EFFECTS

A **delay** is the time lag that is applied to an incoming sound.

Take, for example, a snare drum strike. If I apply a two second delay to the sound, I will hear an exact copy of it two seconds after the original sound. Although this may seem like we can only create echo effects with delay, in actuality, many audio effects use delay at the core of their operation. Often these effects only differ from each other in their delay time. In the illustration below, we see how these rather common effects, such as **Flanger**, **Chorus**, **Echo**, and even **Filters**, incorporate delay times that range from very small values, such as in filters (from as little as 1 sample or 1/44100 of a second) to very large values (in seconds) with echo effects.

The effects we can create are divided into two categories: **fixed delay times** and **varying delay times**.

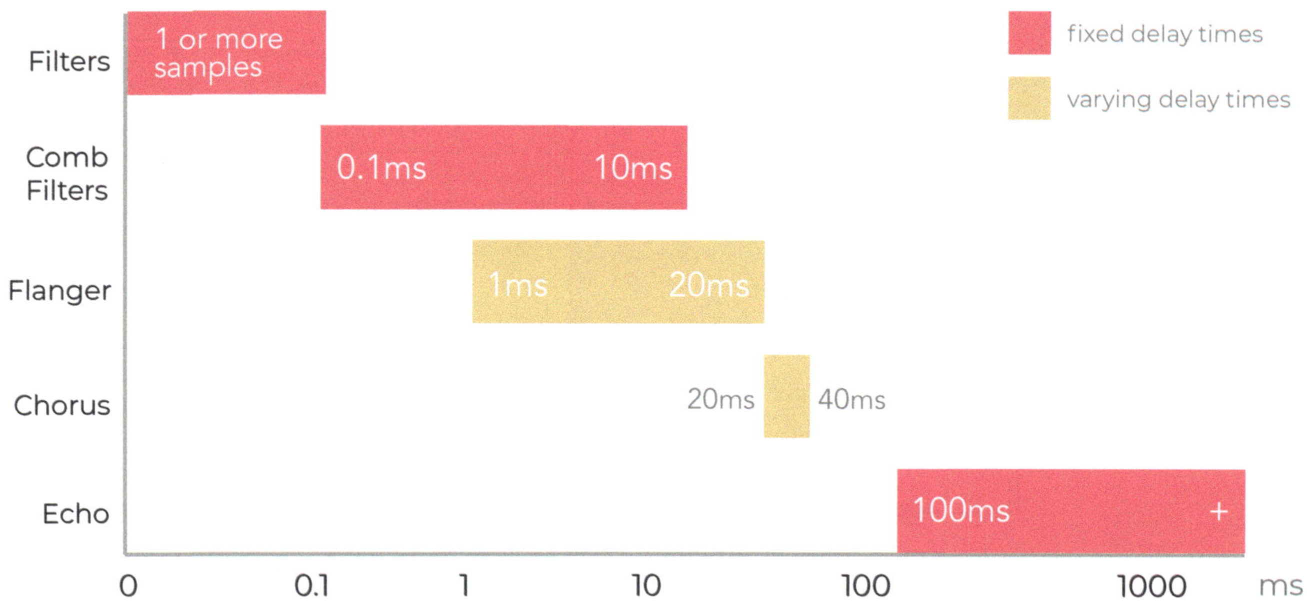

Fixed delay times

Echo

An **Echo** is the repetition of a sound and is a phenomenon we experience in nature. When, for example, we shout loudly toward a mountain, we will hear our voice again after a small amount of time. Our voice has "bounced" off the mountain in front of us and has traveled back to our ears.

This effect also applies to smaller spaces. In a large room, if the wall in front of us is far away enough, our voice will bounce off the wall and travel back to us, creating an echo, just like in the mountain example. In most rooms though, we do not experience a distinct echo. This is because, in order for echoes to sound distinctly as a separate sound, the delay time has to exceed a certain value. Generally, if the second sound arrives less than 35-50 ms* after the first sound, our ears fuse the sounds together and we hear only one sound, not two. Sounds greater than 100 ms apart are perceived as the classic echo effect.

We can artificially create this effect by passing our incoming sound into a memory buffer that holds it for a certain time and then lets it out. The time that it is held is called the **delay time**, and as we have said, it must exceed 35 ms if we want a distinct echo, related to ***Helmut Haas***' studies. Usually, these effects include both the original sound (**dry**) and the delayed sound (**wet**). The ratio of dry to wet is, as always, a very important parameter in achieving the desired sonic result.

* **PRECEDENCE EFFECT** is psychoacoustic phenomenon where two near-identical sound waves, reaching a listener within approximately 50ms of one another, are processed by the human auditory system as a fused single auditory event.

Settings

Delay time (or length) is how much delay I apply to the input sound. It can be expressed in units of time, such as milliseconds or seconds. When expressed in musical note types, such as quarter notes, eighth notes, or sixteenth notes, these delay times are dependent on the song's tempo. The advantage of using musical note types as our delay times is that, as the song's tempo (in BPM) changes, our delay times are automatically adjusted to the new tempos, since they are dependent on note type and not units of milliseconds or seconds. Lastly, delay times can also be expressed in number of samples. The number of samples gets converted to milliseconds or seconds by dividing the number by the digital audio's sampling rate.

Dry/wet is the amplitude ratio between the original and the delayed sound.

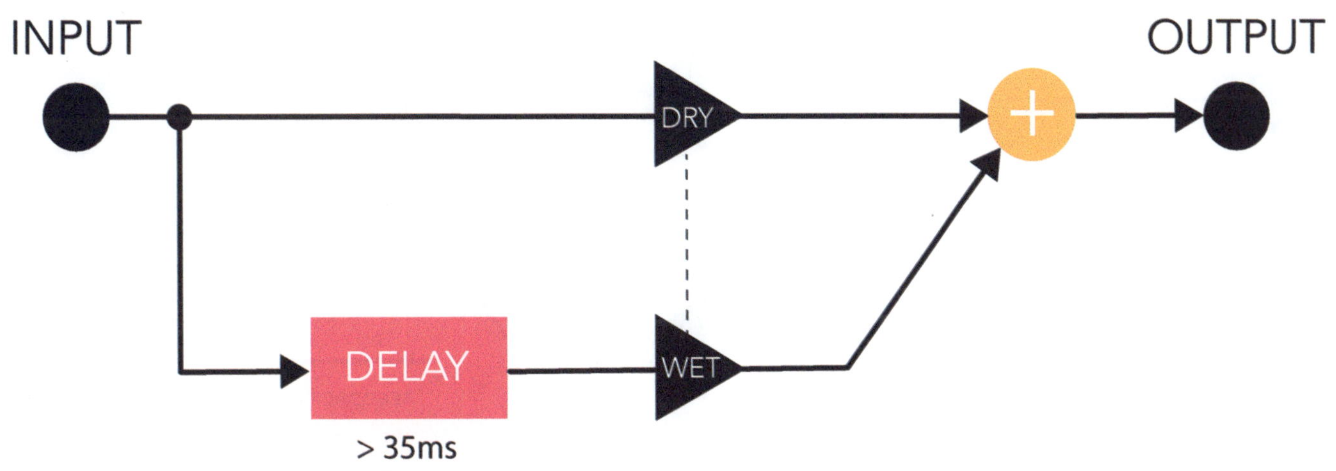

.create a rhythm with only three percussive sounds. Each sound should have its own delay that creates an echo that contributes to the overall rhythm. Experiment with different delay times, starting with musical metric units

delay pure data tutorial

Multiple echo

If we extend the delay concept explained above and loop the output of the delay back into the input of the delay, we will get a series of repetitions of the input sound at a time interval equal to the delay time. For example, if the time delay is 500 ms, I will get many copies of my input sound every 500 ms. If I do not reduce the volume of the sound sent back to the delay, I will get infinite copies. If, on the other hand, I lower the volume of the sound before going back to the delay, I will create a series of repetitions that continually get softer until the sound disappears. This mechanism is an example of **feedback**. In this case, an echo with feedback is called **Multiple echo**.

Settings

Delay time (or length) is the time increment between the incoming sound and the subsequent copies given by the feedback mechanism.

Feedback amount (commonly simplified to Feedback) is a value that indicates how much of the original amplitude of the sound I send back. Sometimes it can be expressed in dB (-6 dB means that every time it passes, the volume is halved). Frequently, feedback is expressed in percentages: 0% means that sound is fed back at 0% the input amplitude (meaning that no sound is being fed back), 50% means that the sound is halved each time it is fed back and will eventually fade away, and 100% means that the sound loops unattenuated and will result in infinite repetitions at constant volume. If the feedback is set at a value over 100%, the sound will theoretically reach infinite loudness unless I stop the process or decrease the feedback value to a number below 100%.

Dry/wet is the amplitude ratio between the original sound and the affected sound.

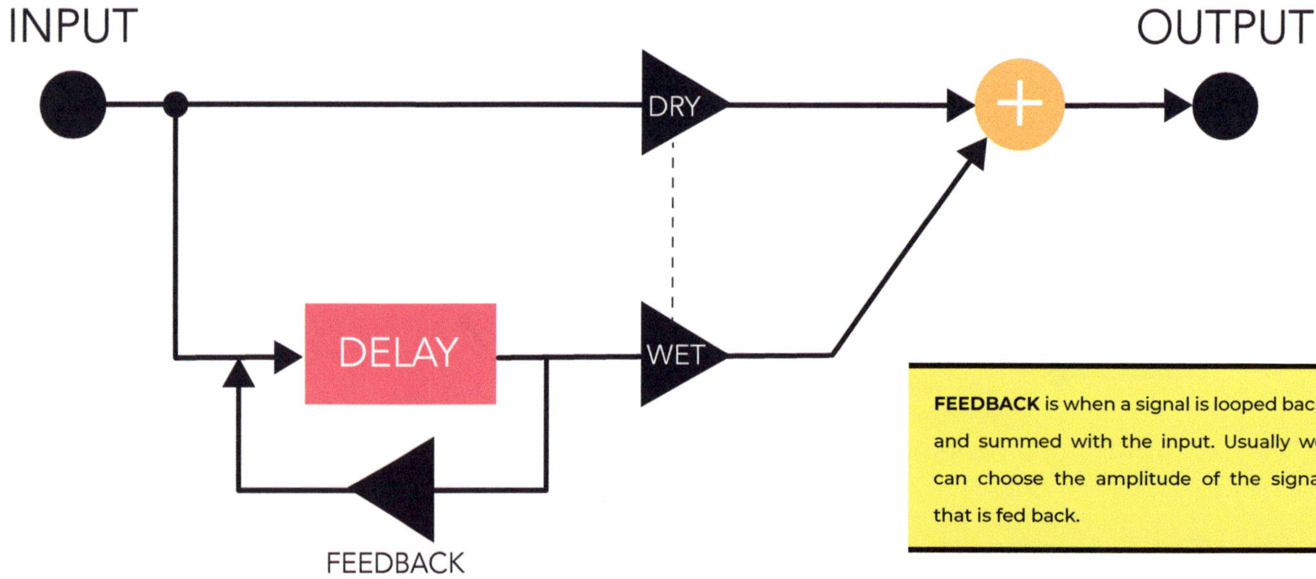

FEEDBACK is when a signal is looped back and summed with the input. Usually we can choose the amplitude of the signal that is fed back.

.create a looper with a multiple echo while listening with headphones. Set the feedback to 0 dB and block the input from your microphone. Set the delay time to one second. When you want to "record" in the looper, open the input and close it right away to avoid inputting "too much sound." Experiment with different delay times. What changes do you notice in your looper when you vary the delay time?

Comb filter

Using the echo with feedback effect, I can achieve a special effect called the **Comb Filter** if I use very small delay times, between about 0.1 and 10 milliseconds, and 95-99% feedback. The comb filter can **tune a sound** that would otherwise not be in tune, because it brings out several bands in the spectrum at integer multiples of a fundamental frequency. The comb filter works most effectively when we start with an input signal that is harmonically rich. As comb filters do not add any frequencies to the sound but rather highlight certain frequencies, the more complex the initial signal, the more sonically interesting the output signal will be. For example, white noise, containing all frequencies by definition, can be transformed into a clear pitch with a comb filter. The "comb" in the name comes from the visual representation of the spectrum, clearly resembling a comb.

To calculate the fundamental frequency, along with the subsequent harmonics of a comb filter, we calculate: fundamental frequency = 1/delay time. For example, if we have a 1 ms delay, we can calculate: fundamental frequency = 1/1 ms = 1000 Hz. The harmonics are then integer multiples of this fundamental frequency: 1000 x 2 = 2000 Hz, 1000 x 3 = 3000 Hz, 1000 x 4 = 4000 Hz, etc.

$$\text{fundamental Frequency} = \frac{\text{1 second}}{\text{delay time}} \qquad \text{delay time} = \frac{\text{1 second}}{\text{fundamental Frequency}}$$

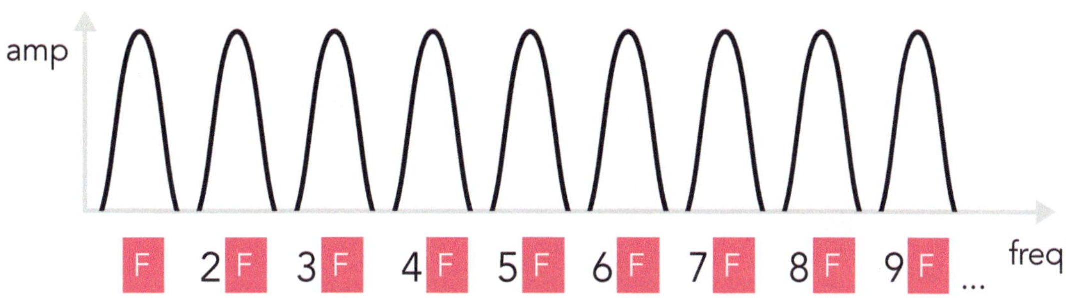

Settings

The settings are essentially the same as multiple echo, but they lead to different effects with comb filters.

Delay time (or length) is how much delay we apply to the input sound. It relates directly to the fundamental frequency or the note that the comb filter creates.

Feedback is how much of the original amplitude of the sound I send back. Specifically in the case of a comb filter, it controls the decay of the effect. The value for feedback should ideally not reach the value of 1 (100%) because then no decay will happen. This will result in an infinite loop of sound that would cause the dynamic range to max out in a very short time. If it exceeds 1, then an infinite loop of sound will cause the dynamic range to approach infinity very quickly.

Dry/wet is the amplitude ratio between the original sound and the affected sound.

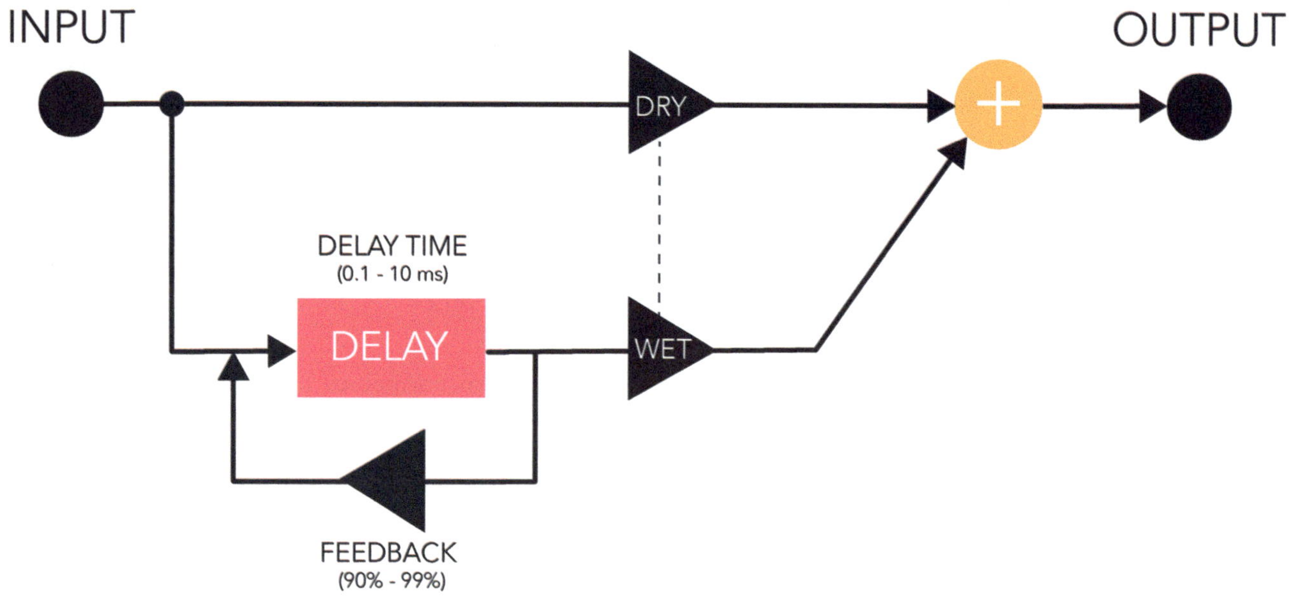

.create a rhythm with a snare drum sample and apply a comb filter, accomplished with a simple delay. Set the delay times so that each snare note changes pitch, arpeggiating between the notes C, E, B in the octave most friendly to you

.create 10 sound objects by recording footstep noise and tuning each of the footsteps to A4 with a comb filter. Then, apply a different feedback level, within a range of 85% to 99%, to each footstep. When you have all 10 sound objects, design an audio scene where someone initially walks and then gradually starts to run. You can freely decide on the sequence of the 10 objects

Comb filter pure data tutorial

Multitap delay

If I want multiple copies of an input sound at different delay times (simulating different distances) from each other, thereby achieving a richer and more complex effect, I can set up multiple echoes in **series** or **parallel**. If I put several multiple echoes in series, each successive delay acts on the result of the previous one, so the growth in the number of repetitions is exponential. In this series approach, each delay depends on all the previous delays, and the delays act upon the output of the previous delay. If, on the contrary, I place the delays in parallel, I will get fewer but more controlled copies. In parallel, each delay is independent and it directly duplicates the original sound and not the echoed sound of the other delays.

Each delay device with feedback is called a **tap**, and the overall effect is called a **Multitap delay**.

In a multitap delay, I can control the **number of taps** along with the classic **delay time** and **feedback** parameters of each tap. In addition, as always, I can adjust the **dry/wet** control that handles mixing the original sound and altered sound.

In series

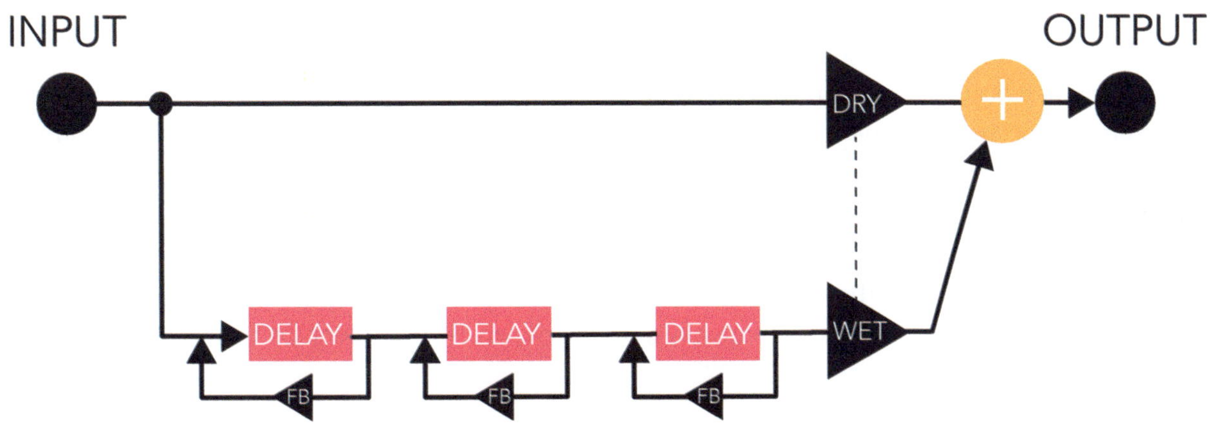

In parallel

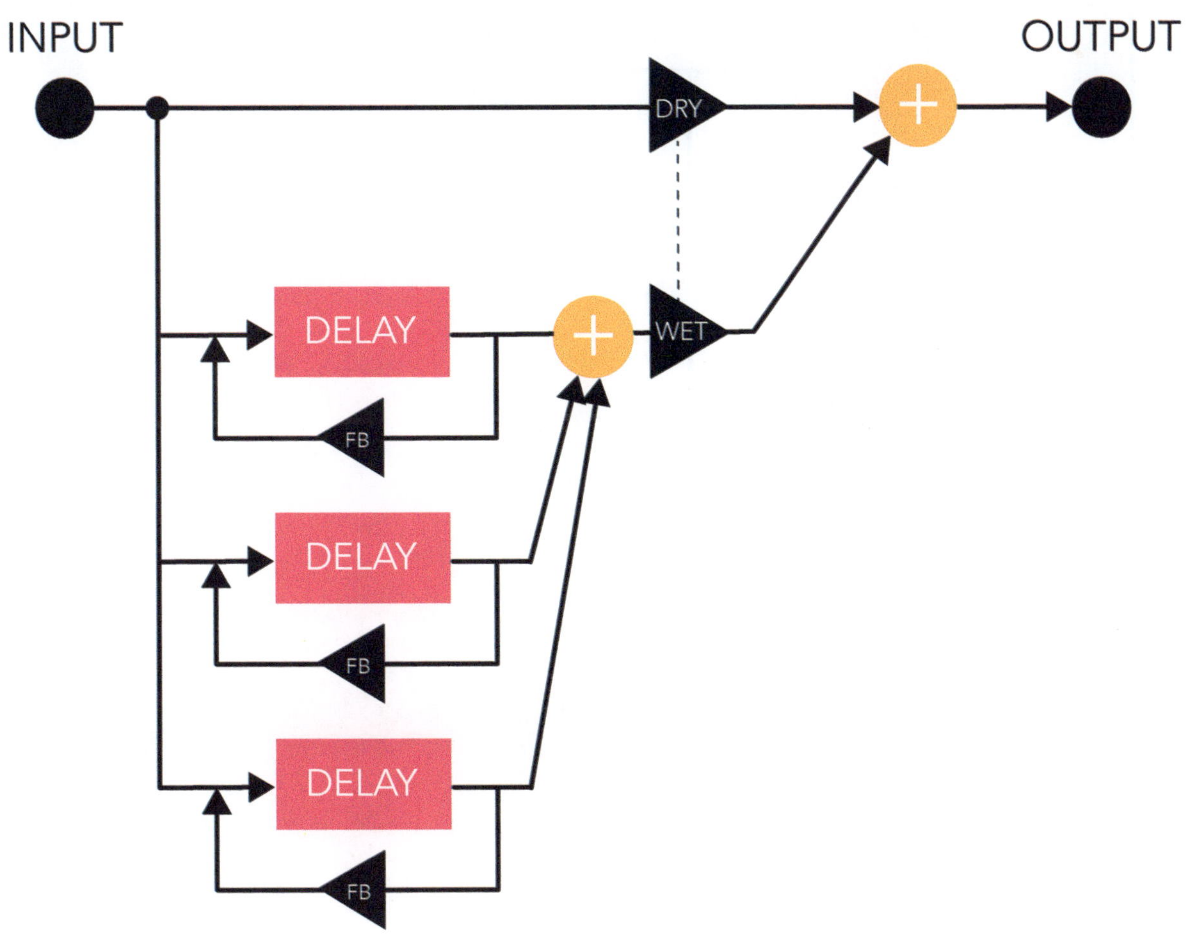

Multitap multiband delay

In simple parallel multitap delay, as we have seen, the processed sound is the same for all taps. If, on the other hand, I utilize filters and divide my sound into multiple frequency bands and send each band to a different tap, I get **Multitap Multiband delay**, also sometimes called **Filter delay**.

The simplest version of multitap multiband delay involves dividing our sound into a high frequency band and a low frequency band using a **crossover filter**. A crossover filter is a network of filters that separates an input audio signal into highs and lows, used prominently in speakers to send high frequencies to the tweeter and low frequencies to the woofer. Here, the outputs of the low-pass filter and the high-pass filter go into two distinct taps. From there, I can incorporate the multitap delay as seen in the previous section. The control parameter here, besides the classic **number of taps**, **delay time** and **feedback** for each tap, and **dry/wet** for the overall effect, is the **frequency band** selection for each tap. In the case of a simple crossover, this is where we can set the crossover frequency, where sonic energy above the crossover frequency goes to one tap, and sonic energy below the crossover frequency will go to the other tap.

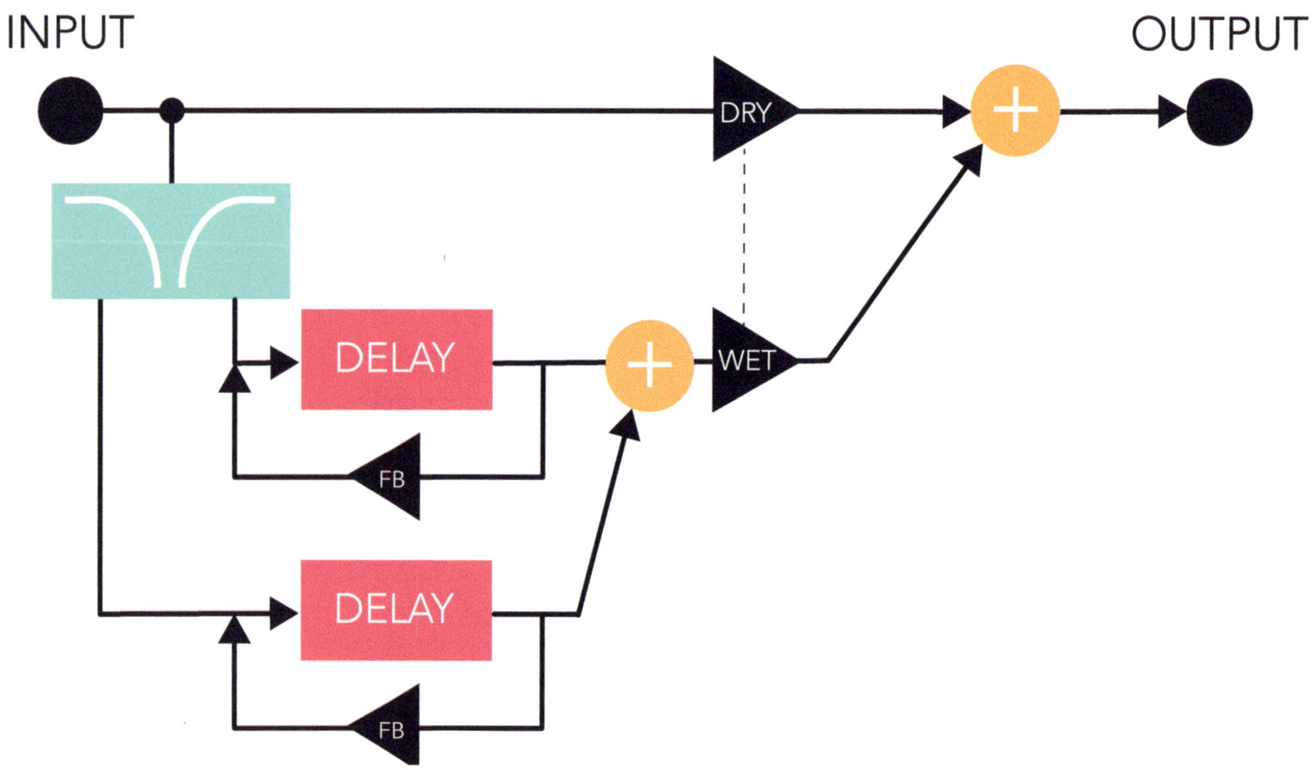

.choose three frequency bands of your voice and apply three different delay taps to them. The three taps should generate a rhythm that, in the 20 seconds of the exercise, becomes increasingly chaotic (use parameter automations!)

.create or download a drum loop consisting of two sounds, a kick drum and a treble sound. Apply a multitap multiband delay to divide the sounds into treble and bass components. The delay applied to the treble sound should imitate the rhythm of the kick drum sound, and vice versa

Ping pong delay

All the effects we have discussed so far are monophonic—not producing any output that uses the two stereo channels (left and right). Suppose I create two taps that deliberately cross feedback paths and then have their outputs sent to different channels. In other words, the feedback of one tap is fed into the input of the other tap and then the output of each tap is sent to different channels. The result is a **Ping Pong delay**, an effect that creates a series of delayed copies of my sound that are played back alternately between the left and right channels.

The parameters of a ping pong delay are **delay time**, **feedback**, and **dry/wet**.
These parameters are usually linked, meaning the left and right channels share the same values.

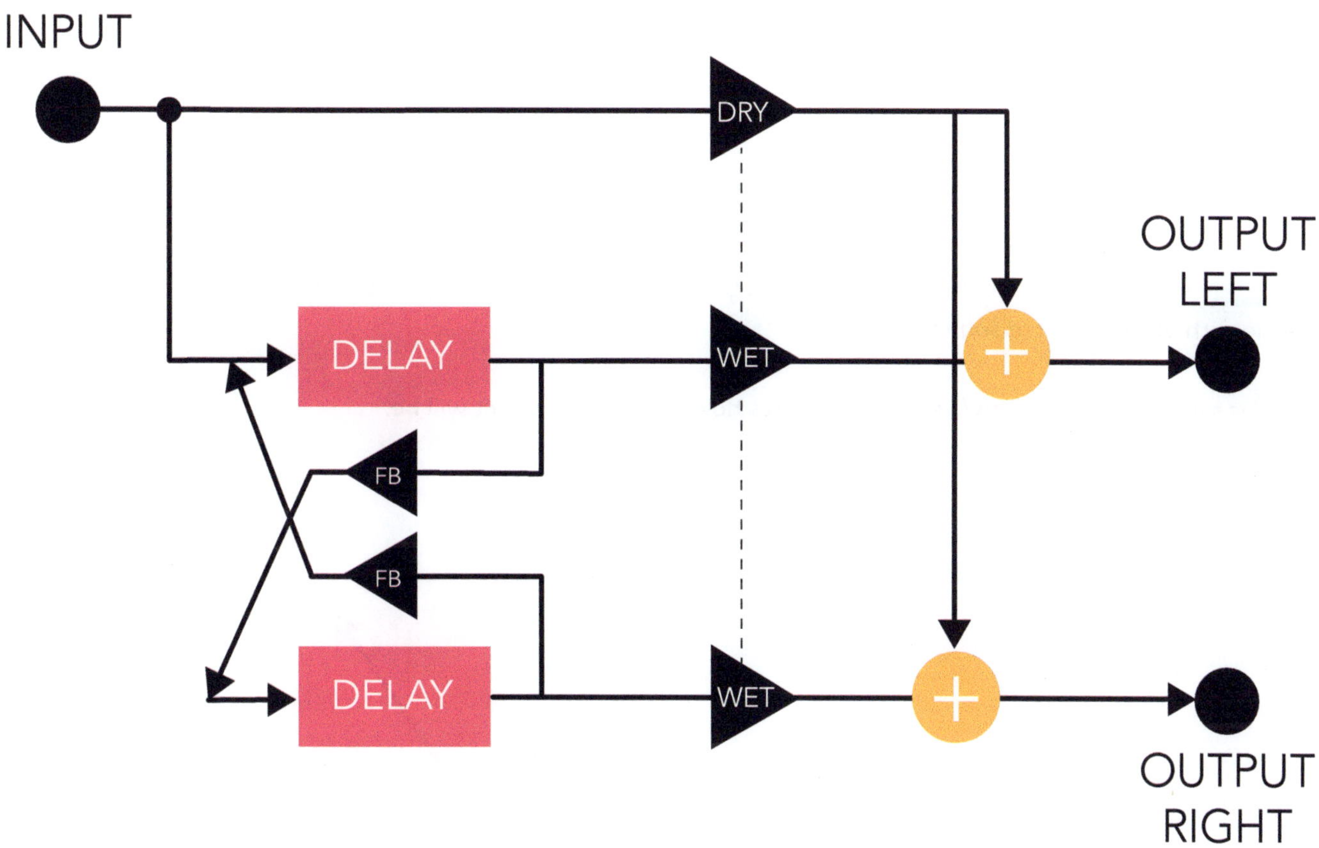

.create three tracks with a single note on each. The three notes should be three percussive notes of your choice, made and recorded with one of your instruments. The three notes should also create a rhythm through appropriately set delay times. The bounces of each note should "intertwine" with each other by bouncing between the left and right channels. The rhythm should change with each beat. Repeat the process for four bars

Varying delay times

Flanger

The **Flanger** is the first effect that we have discussed in which the delay time is not fixed but rather is periodically varying. To achieve this, the original sound is summed with a varying delayed copy of itself. This is made possible by using a delay that periodically changes. The delay times of classic flangers usually range from 1-20ms, where exaggerated delay times often can achieve less predictable results. Practically, to achieve a varying delay time, we can use the beloved **LFO (low-frequency oscillator)**, a device that comes in handy in many different contexts. The LFO's oscillations are not in the audible range (i.e., we hear between 20 and 20,000 Hz). Usually the LFO frequencies are set a slower rate, between 0 and 20 Hz, and this frequency automates the variation of a device parameter. In this case, the delay time parameter of our flanger is set to the output of the LFO. Doing this results in variable filtering of the original sound by utilizing variable delay.

Settings

Speed or Rate of the LFO is the frequency at which the delay time changes.

Width or Spread is width of the LFO, controlling the range of delay times. This sets the maximum and minimum delay times that the LFO oscillates between.

Delay is the minimum delay time that the LFO can reach at the trough of the oscillation.

Feedback indicates how much sound returns to the input after being delayed. Sonically, this dictates the overall decay length of the affected sound.

Depth is synonymous with dry/wet. It determines how punchy the effect will be.

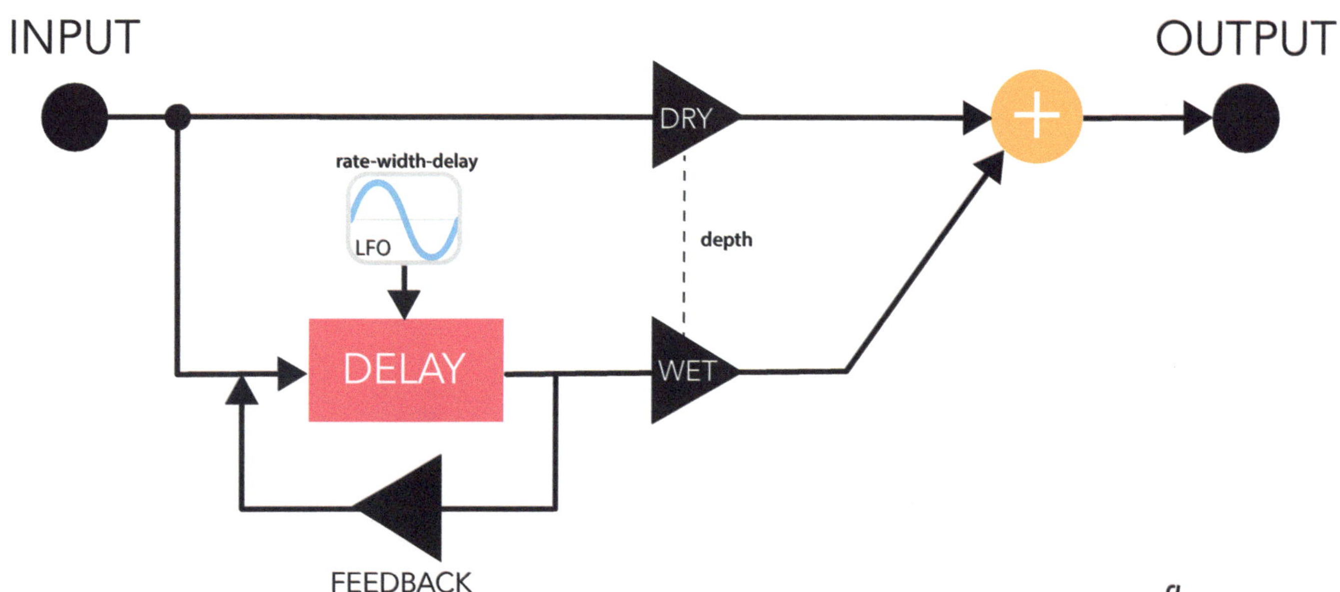

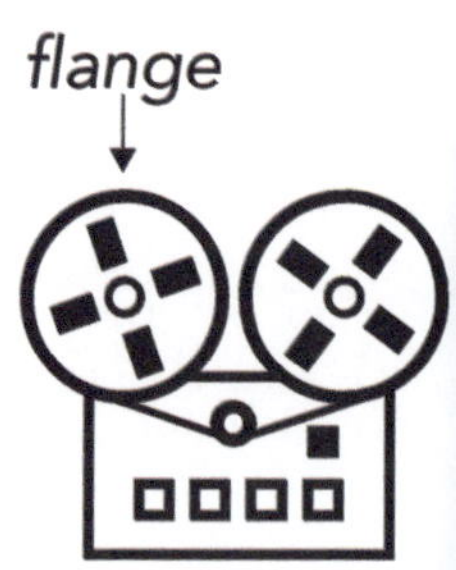

Fun fact: Flanger comes from "flange," the metal or plastic rim that holds the magnetic tape within a reel for an analog tape recorder or player. Early examples of flangers were created with two tape machines. With these two tape machines, identical tape was used for both machines, but on one machine, you would press your finger on the flange periodically, slowing down and speeding up one of the two playbacks. The sum of the two tape machines would then create a flanger effect. This is exactly what we simulate when we recreate this effect digitally. The tape machine that plays without intervention is the DRY signal, and the output of the machine that we tap our finger on is the WET signal. The frequency and force by which the finger taps the flange is recreated by the LFO.

.download or record a classical guitar arpeggio. Apply a flanger and try to get a guitar sound similar to what you hear in the song "Black Hole Sun" by Soundgarden

.create the sound of an ambulance siren by applying a flanger to any continuous sound that you choose

.create a composition using an acoustic drum kit and applying a flanger to each instrument in the kit. During the song, the flangers should create the effect of a general upward glissando that you will hear. To achieve this, set high feedback values and automate delay times. ***Theme: "Preparing for takeoff"***

flanger songs ~ Erica Fusion Delay/Flanger/Vintage ensemble ~ Synths and Modulation Pedals ~ flanger pure data tutorial

Chorus

Chorus is a multitap delay in which multiple taps have delay times controlled by individual LFOs. The delay time of the LFOs in a classic chorus is usually 20–30 ms, higher than what we saw in a flanger. The name of this effect is inspired by the vocal ensemble, the chorus where each tap is analogous to a voice, and like the voices in a chorus, each tap will generate a sound with slight time variations (delay) and with slight pitch variations (variability of delay values).

Settings

Speed or Rate refers to the frequency of the LFOs, dictating how fast the delay times oscillate.

Width corresponds to the amplitude of the LFOs, controlling the range of delay times. This sets the maximum and minimum delay times that the LFO oscillates between.

Waveform indicates the shape of the LFOs' output. Each waveform has unique oscillating parameters, causing different sonic output effects. For example, a square wave will create a strong rhythmic effect because of the abrupt transitions between low and high values. A random (noise) wave, on the other hand, will produce a less rhythmic and more "blended" effect, a result commonly used in traditional chorusing.

Delay is the minimum delay time that the LFO can reach at the trough of the oscillation.

Feedback indicates how much sound returns to the input after being delayed. Sonically, this dictates the overall decay length of the affected sound.

Depth is synonymous with dry/wet. It determines how punchy the effect will be.

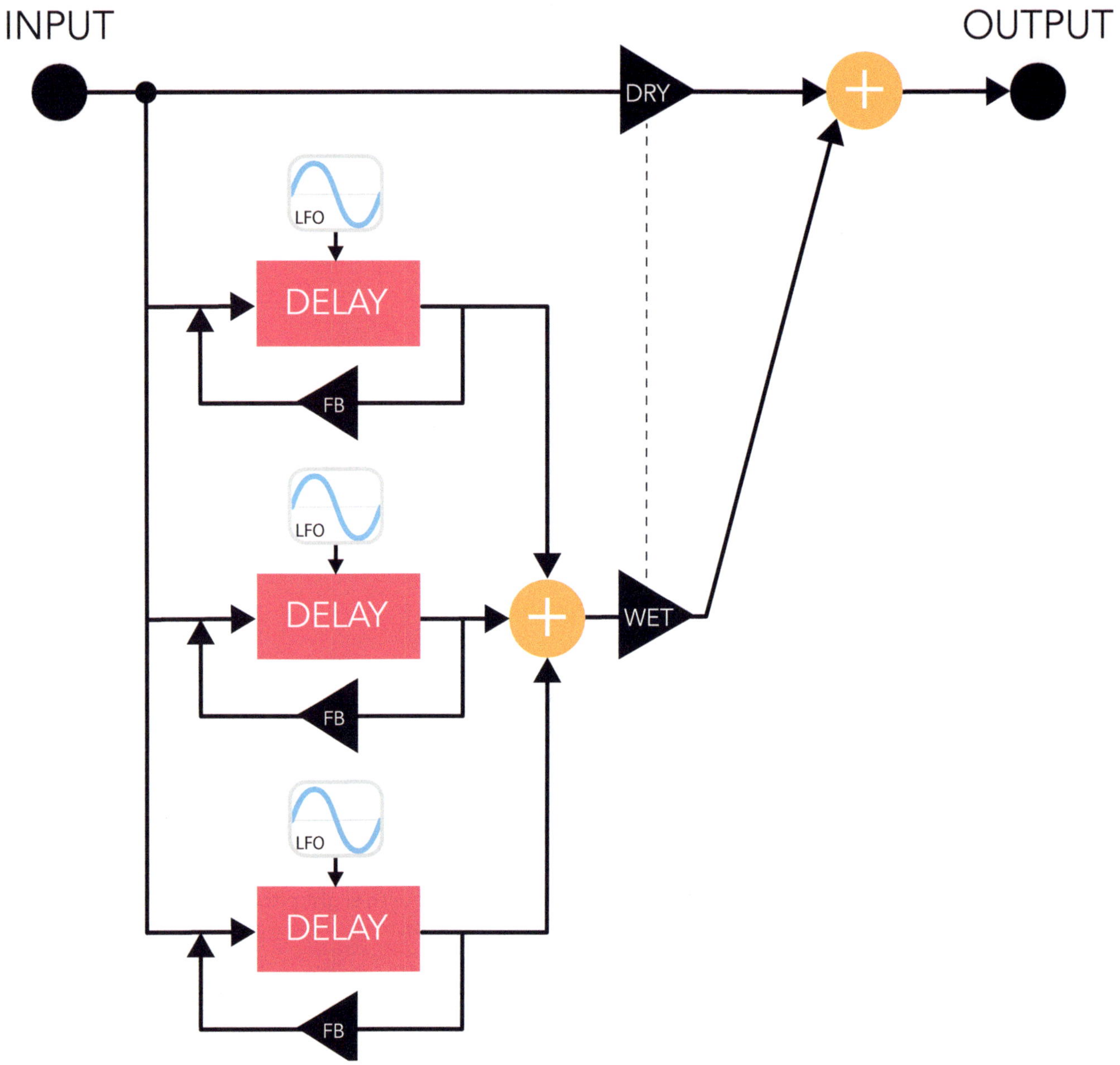

.record the three notes, C4 E4 B4, with your voice, sustained for about 10 seconds each. Apply three Chorus settings differently to the three notes. Using parameter automations, develop a song in which the Chorus settings take center stage, and the three notes appear and disappear several times. ***Theme: "Ghosts"***

.create a drum loop with surdo or floor toms. Apply a chorus effect with a low rate (between 0.1 and 1 Hz) and automate the feedback to create artificial glissando on just some of the notes in your rhythm. Try the same process on a melody of your choice and combine these two components into a micro composition. ***Theme: "Stones on the frozen lake"***

chorus songs ~ Nirvana come as you are ~ chorus pure data tutorial

REVERB

Reverberbation, or **reverb**, is the natural acoustic phenomenon that results from sound waves interacting with and bouncing off surfaces in a room. These reflections usually create overlapping echoes that ultimately reach the listener, giving the listener a sense of space.

Natural acoustic reverb

Different surfaces, different reverberations

Surfaces can be near or far, soft or hard, smooth or rough. They can be the floor, the ceiling, or any of the side walls of a room.

Reverberation is affected by the size of the room, the material of the surfaces, and the overall geometry of the room, all contributing to create the unique "sound" or "color" of the room.

When sound reaches a surface, some energy is **absorbed**, and some energy is **reflected**, depending on the material of the surface. In fact, how absorptive or reflective a surface is also depends on the frequency of the sound. For example, mid to high frequency sounds are often most easily attenuated because their shorter wavelengths interact more effectively with porous type of materials.

Dimensions

The room's size or volume greatly affects the reverberation type, length, and "color." If the materials are the same, the larger the room volume, the longer the reverberation.

A large stone cathedral will create a long reverberation time, with a very slow decay and little absorption by the walls. On the other hand, a small bedroom will produce a very short reverberation due to the small volume of the room.

Open spaces

If surfaces are absent, such as playing in the middle of a meadow in open air, we generally will not experience significant reverberation of our sound. We may receive a few echoes from some surfaces, but we will not experience the overlapping reflections that are characteristic of reverberation.

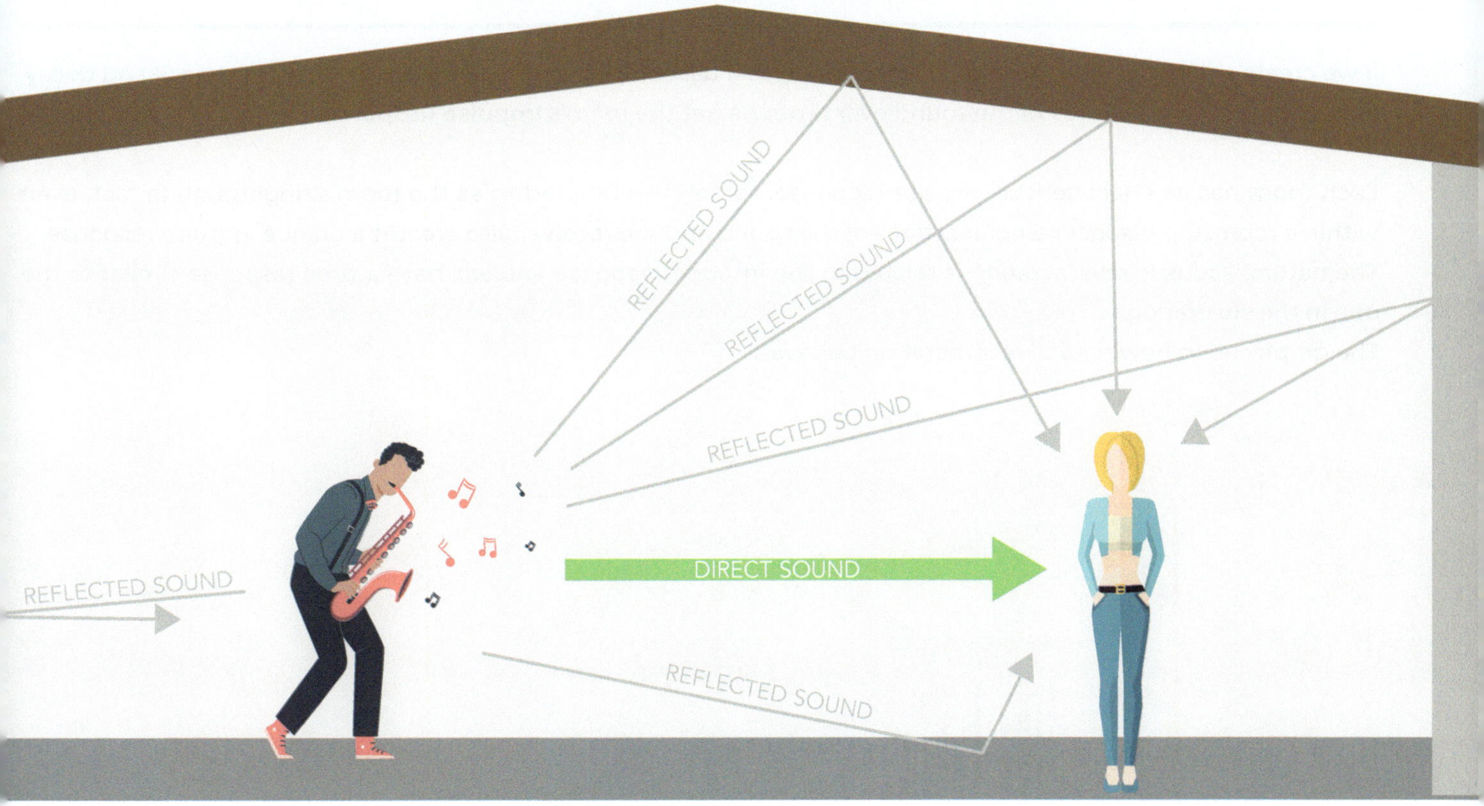

Direct sound, Reflected sound

In the case of enclosed spaces, the sound reaching the listener is of two types:

DIRECT SOUND

Direct sound is defined as the sound from a source that reaches the listener without encountering any obstacles or reflective surfaces of any kind.

This direct sound is, therefore, virtually identical to what might be heard in the near vicinity of a playing instrument. The only difference may be an amplitude reduction caused by the inverse square law*.

*

INVERSE SQUARE LAW

Inverse square law states that, in an open space without any reflections, the intensity of spherical waves attenuates at 6 dB per doubling of distance. Ideally, when converting to pressure, a trumpet at 100 meters will be 6 dB SPL less than the trumpet at 50 meters.

REFLECTED SOUND

Reflected sound is defined as all the sound waves that reach the listener after reflecting off the room surfaces. By definition, all the reflected sound occurs after the direct sound reaches the listener. As the waves travel around the room before reaching the listener, the sounds hit many surfaces where some of the sound energy may be partially absorbed and some may be partly reflected.
Reflected sound therefore is:

Filtered due to the fact that sounds of different frequencies are absorbed differently by room surfaces

Attenuated in amplitude due to the longer path the waves travel before reaching the listener* and because the room surfaces and the air absorb some sound energy

Time Delayed because the reflected wave has a lengthier path and travels at the speed of sound, it takes longer for the sound to reach the listener

Impulse response

If we create a rich, impulsive sound in a room, such as a balloon pop or a loud bang with very fast attack and decay, and measure the amplitude of the sound over time, we get the room's **Impulse Response**.

Each room has its characteristic impulse response, sometimes referred to as the room's fingerprint. In fact, even within a room, the distinct pair of locations of the sound and the receiver also creates a unique impulse response. The natural acoustic reverberation is related to the impulse response and will have a time response similar to the one in the illustration.
The graph shows how natural reverberation behaves:

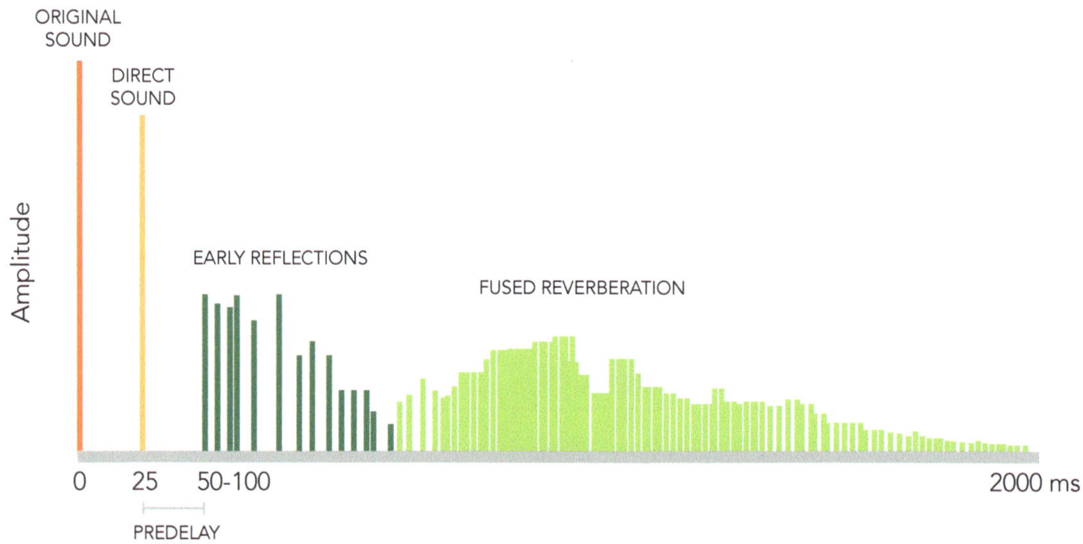

The original sound is created at the zero point in time. The sound travels through the air and the direct sound reaches the listener after some time. After the direct sound, the **early reflections** start reaching the listener. Of note, the time between the direct sound and the first reflected sound is known as the **predelay**. The early reflections have the characteristic that they happen distinctly in time, somewhat separately from one another. These early reflections will also have a lower amplitude than the direct sound due to the inverse square law and the energy absorbed by the room surfaces that they have encountered along the way. The number of reflections begins to increase because the sound continues to bounce off of the surfaces. In contrast to the early reflections, the reflections start reaching the listener from many different directions, overlapping in time as well. At this point, the listener's auditory system does not perceive directionality of the reflections and individual reflections start to fuse together. This is the definition of diffuse sound and **fused reverberation**.

Reverberation time: RT60

RT60 reverberation time is a measure of the length of reverberation. It's the amount of time it takes a sound to attenuate by 60 dB from its peak value in a room. Casually, RT60 can be thought of as how long it takes for sound to decay to silence. Larger, more reverberant spaces have longer RT60s; conversely, small rooms have short RT60s.

	(average values) **RT60**
Small bedroom	**0.1 - 0.5 s**
Recording studio	**0.3 - 0.7 s**
Concert hall	**1.5 - 3 s**
Cathedral	**3 - 10 s**

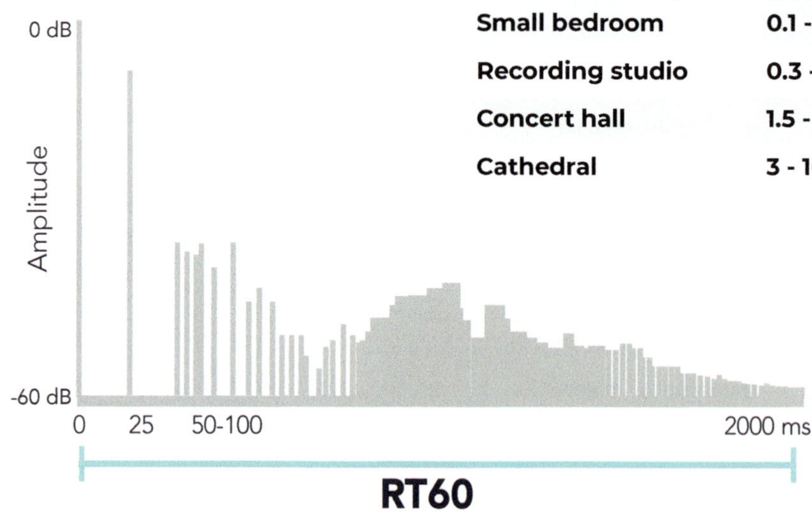

Generally, reverberation time is controlled by the volume of the space and by how sound absorptive the room materials are.

the Wikidrummer ~ reverb places ~ World's Longest Echo

To achieve artificial reverberation, we must recreate this natural sound phenomenon we analyzed in the previous pages. Various techniques and technologies have been used to do this throughout the history of music.

Artificial acoustic reverb

Acoustic echo chambers

Acoustic echo chambers are real rooms where sound is played back from a speaker into a room. The sound then propagates in the room where a microphone and a recording system (like shellac discs or tape) re-records the resultant sound, consisting of the direct sound from the speaker to the microphone and the reflections that bounce around in the room. Usually, the special echo chambers contain reflective panels or even movable reflective walls that allow the room's geometry to be changed and, consequently, the reverberation itself. These artificial echo chambers were used as early as in the 1950s *Studio for Electronic Music (WDR)* in Cologne and in the iconic *Capital Studios* with such artists as *Frank Sinatra*, *Nat King Cole*, and *Michael Jackson*. Other examples of artificial echo chambers include houses of worship, stair wells, bathrooms, and corridors.

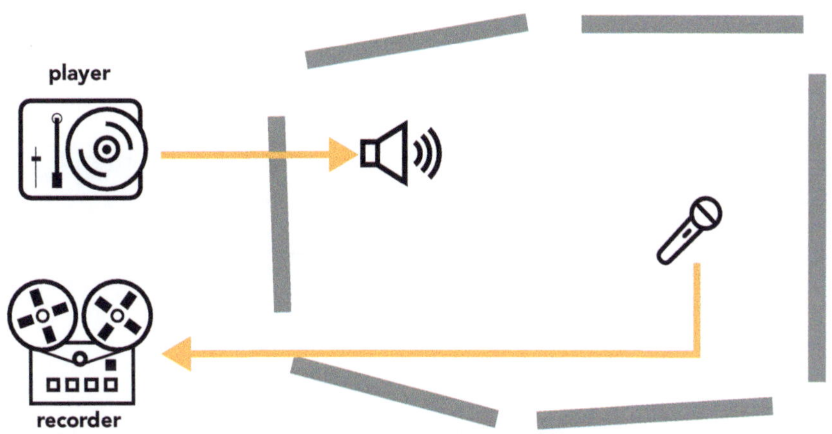

.record using the video recorder from your phone or device, a single note of your instrument in each room of your house, being careful to pick up the natural reverberation of the rooms by not standing too close to the microphone. Then compose a song by editing the recordings (cutting, duplicating, and assembling them as desired) so that a composition emerges. Do this using a DAW (if it supports video) or any video editing software. ***Theme: "Home sweet home"***

WDR Electronic Music Studio ~ Echo chambers ~ Karlheinz Stockhausen ~ echo chamber Capitol Records Studio

Electromechanical reverb

Electromechanical reverb uses the interaction between the electrical signal and mechanical parts to introduce a reverberation effect to a given sound. The principle of this kind of artificial reverb is based on putting a transducer that transforms an electrical signal into mechanical vibrations, passing the mechanical energy into a reverberating and vibrating medium that is then picked up by another transducer that converts the mechanical energy back to an electrical signal. The vibrating physical medium is responsible for creating the phase-shifted copies of the original sound that generates reverberation. Different mediums will create different reverberant signals. The most commonly used mediums are springs and plates, resulting in **Spring Reverb** and **Plate Reverb**, respectively.

Spring reverb is very common in guitar amplifiers because they are small and versatile. These electromechanical reverbs can also use larger metal plates; they were used historically in the studios in Cologne in the 1950s.

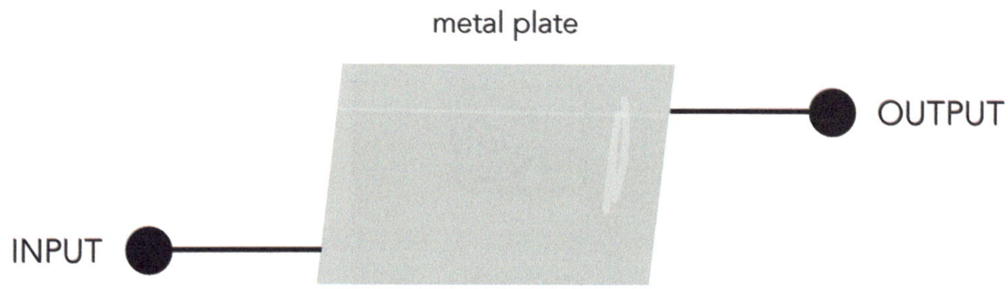

WDR Electronic Music Studio ~ Karlheinz Stockhausen ~ plate reverb furniture hack

Classic digital reverb

In **digital reverb**, an algorithm simulates the various components of natural acoustic reverberation. The algorithm is written with a programming language, and the computer processor executes it.

The first person to create digital reverberation algorithms was *Manfred Schroeder* at *Bell Telephone Laboratories* starting in 1961. His algorithms are still relevant today. While in Schroeder's day the calculation time for these algorithms would take hours to complete, the speed of the microprocessors inside computers today now allows for complex digital reverberation to be achieved in real time.

As we have seen, reverberation can be divided into three parts, the (1) direct sound, (2) the early reflections, and (3) the fused reverberation.

As before with natural reverberation, the delay between (1) direct sound and the (2) first reflections is the **predelay**.

The ratio between the amplitude of direct sound (1) and reflected sounds (2-3) is called dry/wet, similar in function to other audio effects that we are familiar with.

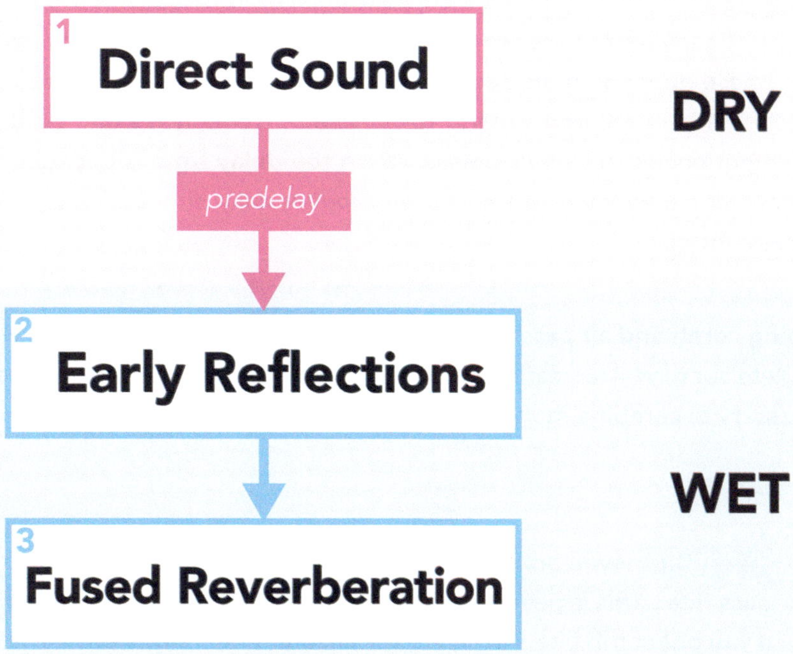

Now, we deconstruct these various parts and create an algorithm to simulate their characteristics.

Multitap delays are used to simulate the first early reflections. As we saw in the delays chapter (page 114), these are a set of devices that create delayed copies of the incoming sound. Each device has its independent delay and is called a "tap."
To simulate the complex geometry of real spaces, the various taps must have different delays from each other to simulate reflections from different points of the walls of a room.

The diffuse reverberant field is a vastly different and more complex problem because there are several hundred or thousands of reflections to be created from the initial sound. To achieve this, we need to utilize, connect, and duplicate two processes: **Comb filters** and **All-pass filters**.

Comb filters

As we have already seen in the Delays chapter, the comb filter is a delay with feedback that has a very short delay time. If the delay time is under 10ms, the output will exhibit a series of frequency bands at a constant difference in hertz, creating a harmonic spectrum. It is used, for example, to add a tuned "tail" to a noise. If, on the other hand, we use longer delay times, we obtain a very dense series of repetitions of the sound, quite suitable for recreating the diffuse part of our desired reverb. We must be careful when we put several comb filters together. To avoid creating major resonances within our reverb, the delay times should not only be different, but also should not be integer multiples of each other.

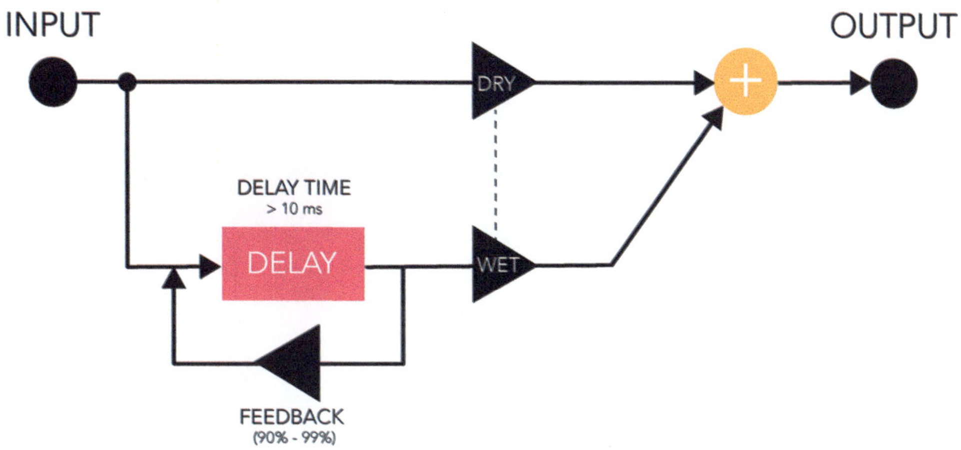

All-pass filters

As we have already seen in the chapter on delays, the all-pass filter will pass through amplitudes unchanged, but will alter the phase depending on frequency. The effect of this is the introduction of delays associated with particular frequencies. This is because varying the phase of frequencies can be thought to be like sending the energy of different frequencies to various delays. When the **delay time** is between 5 and 100 ms, a series of delayed copies of the input signal are created that decay exponentially, similar to what happens with comb filters with feedback amplitude control.

Combining comb and all-pass

To complete our digital recreation of diffuse reverb and achieve sufficient density to perceive a natural reverberation, it is necessary to combine multiple comb and all-pass filters together.

How it's done:

> **In parallel** fewer processes are needed because you will add up the reflections given by each comb or all-pass filter. This is generally good for comb filters because you minimize any spectral problems. However, if you put comb filters in series, the second filter might eliminate a frequency passing from the first comb filter.
>
> **In series** more density in processes occur because each reflection is multiplied by subsequent reflections. This is commonly used for all-pass filters because in parallel, these all-pass filters may result in having phase cancellations when adding them up.

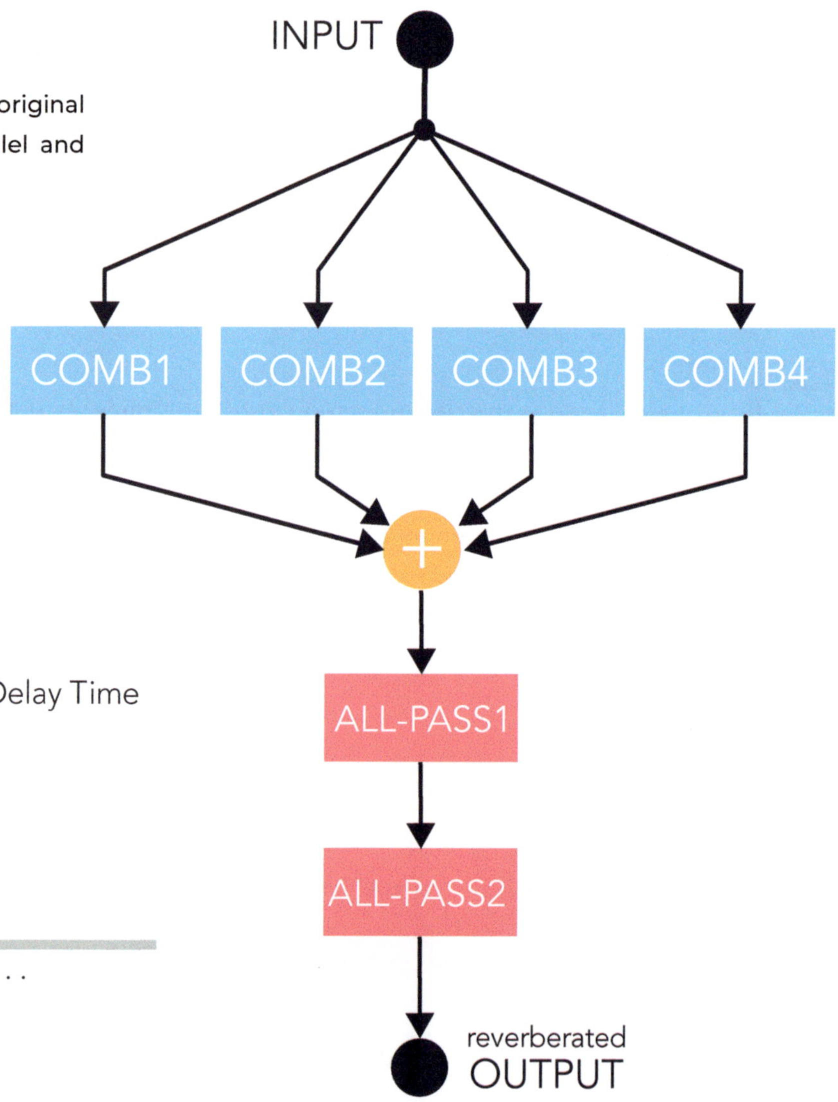

The illustration here portrays ***Schroeder***'s original reverberation algorithm, using both parallel and series processes.

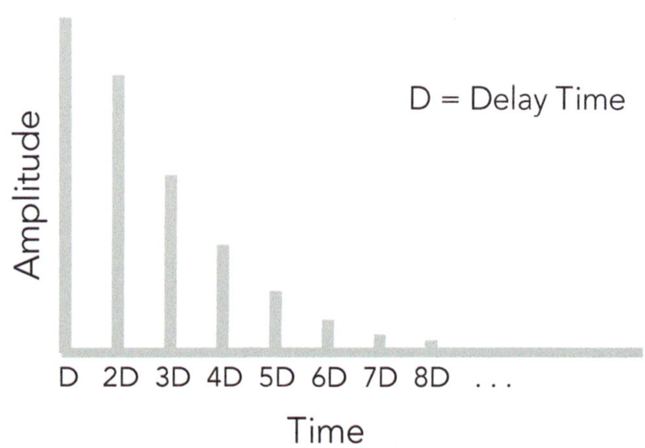

Filters

To further refine our digital reverberation, we can use low-pass or high-pass filters at the end of the algorithm to simulate the natural absorption that would be caused by the wall materials reflecting and **absorbing certain frequencies of sound**. With a low-pass filter, we will essentially absorb high frequencies, thus creating a more "muffled" middle frequency having a rich or even dark final sound. With a high-pass filter, we will get a less full sound in the low end and, therefore, experience a brighter and more "scratchy" final sound. Using a low-pass filter is an effective way to simulate a real room because most wall materials absorb and dampen high frequencies and reflect low and mid frequencies.

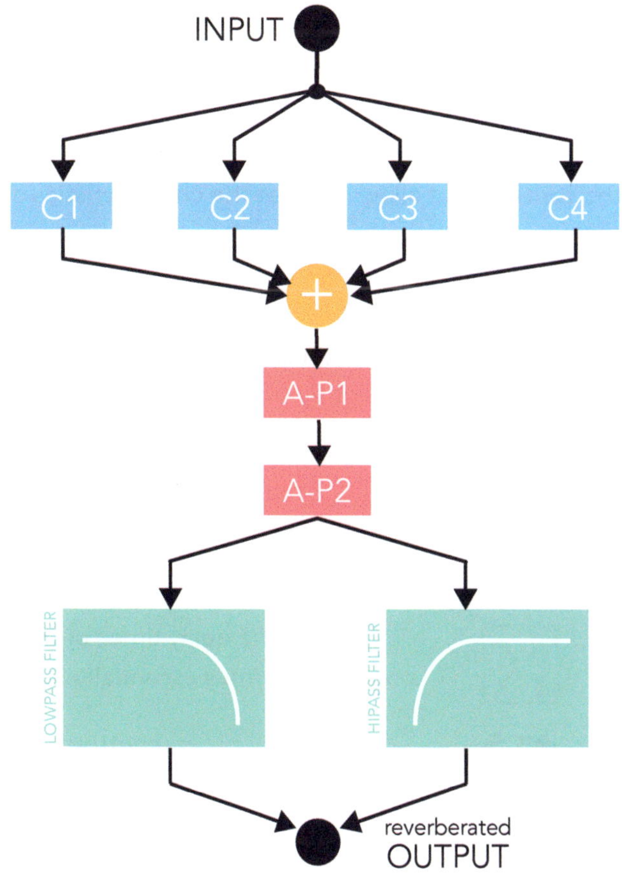

Stereo reverb

So far, we have discussed artificial reverbs in the context of only a single channel (mono). In reality, since our listening occurs in "2 channels" due to our auditory system being equipped with two transducers (our ears), placed in different locations in our head, we should strive to create our digital reverb in two channels, or stereo reverb, as well. In a natural space, the reflections that bounce around and reach the listener will arrive differently between one ear and the other. The time it takes for a sound to reach each ear is different, resulting in phase differences. Likewise, the amplitude of sound experienced by each ear varies as well, due to an acoustic shadow cast by the head, and by the inverse square law accounting for amplitude differences related to slightly different distances traveled. Stereo, or 2-channel reverbs, must account for both these phase and amplitude differences. We can extend this concept beyond two channels to "multichannel reverbs," so that digital reverb can be applied to multiphonic systems (quadraphony, hexaphony...). For more on the sound spatialization, please refer to the chapter on page 153.

In stereo reverb, it is necessary to account for the phase and amplitude differences between the left and right channels. The easiest way to ensure that the left and right channels are slightly unique is to apply a different all-pass filter to the each channel. One all-pass filter per channel in the final process is sufficient to create a perceptually acceptable stereo reverb. If, however, we need more than one filter per channel, then we will increase the required calculations exponentially.

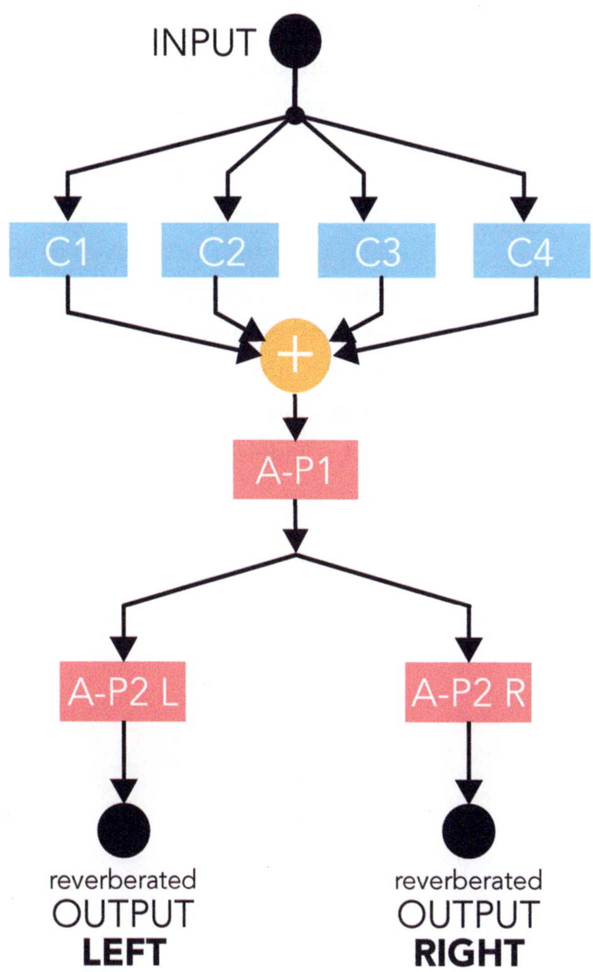

Settings

The parameters we see in reverb whether we are talking about analog circuits or software (plugins or standalone), are the controls that allow us to set the characteristics of our desired reverb. In most cases, these are macro-parameters (delay, comb filter parameters, all-pass filter parameters, etc.), settings that work on multiple parameters within the reverb units.

Here is a quick summation of the most commonly seen parameters. Keep in mind that, like with other effects, the names may change slightly from one effect to another, but the general function will often stay the same.

Predelay sets the delay time between the original sound and the first reflections. A very large predelay simulates the feeling of a very large room. In essence, for very large rooms, it can take a long time for the initial sound to reach the nearest wall and bounce toward the listener, creating the first reflections.

Size creates the delay times of the various reverberating units, simulating the feeling of room size. Longer delay times essentially replicate the greater distances of reflective walls.

Reverberation Time controls the overall duration of the reverberation, that is, how long the sound decay lasts (RT60). It is often related to the size parameter.

Diffusion determines the density of reflections that our reverberation creates. It emulates the complexity of the space caused by the geometry of the room and the acoustic properties of the wall materials.

Filter or Damping simulates the absorption of certain frequencies caused by absorptive properties of the walls. Often in digital reverb, we can choose which bands of frequencies to pass and which to attenuate by precisely managing these parameters. Sometimes the term damping is used where the larger the damping, the greater the absorption of the high frequencies in the tail of the reverb.

Reverb type allows for presets that simulate particular types of analog reverbs by setting various parameters to specific values.
Plate: emulates the behavior of an analog plate reverb
Spring: emulates the behavior of an analog spring reverb
Chamber: emulates the behavior of the natural reverberation of a small room
Hall: emulates the behavior of a natural reverb of a generic concert hall
Gated: sharply cuts the decay of the reverb when it falls below a certain amplitude threshold. This effect is widely used in 80s style pop drums.

Mix or Dry/Wet controls the ratio between the amplitude of original sound to amplitude of the reverberated sound.

.record two sounds on your own and compose a song using only the two sounds, reverberating them artificially in different ways (you can cut and duplicate them at will). ***Theme: "Sound is sacred"***

Schroeder reverberator ~ plate spring hall comparison

Digital convolution reverb

A more recent approach in creating artificial reverberation uses **physical models**. This technique involves creating mathematical models that describe how sound waves propagate, reflect, absorb, and diffuse in physical spaces. Using these mathematical models results in very realistic reverberant fields that almost perfectly simulate real spaces. However, the calculations require a considerable computational "cost," needing very fast processors and powerful computers to achieve in real time. While there are several types of physical models that we can discuss, we will focus on the most widely used and high-performing method: **convolution reverb**.

Convolution reverb uses a mathematical operation called convolution to transform the original sound to reverberate as if it were in a simulated room.

To perform convolution, we need the impulse response of the room that we want to simulate and the original musical sound that we want to apply reverb to.

The **impulse response** is a recording of a frequency-rich impulsive sound, such as a loud bang, inside a room or other physical location. Essentially, it measures how the room responds to a sudden impulsive sound, carrying within it the acoustic information of the room. When analyzed, the impulse response shows how each audible frequency within the space behaves over time. This happens because this impulsive sound that we recorded is composed of a broad band of frequencies. Alternatively, sometimes we can use a frequency sweep instead of an impulsive sound. This sweep is essentially a glissé sound from the lowest to the highest audible frequency. How the room responds to each frequency in the sweep is another way to determine how each audible frequency behaves over time in a space. Practically, impulse responses can be synthesized by yourself or can be found in audio software programs and databases. This option potentially gives us access to reverberations from distant or inaccessible places.

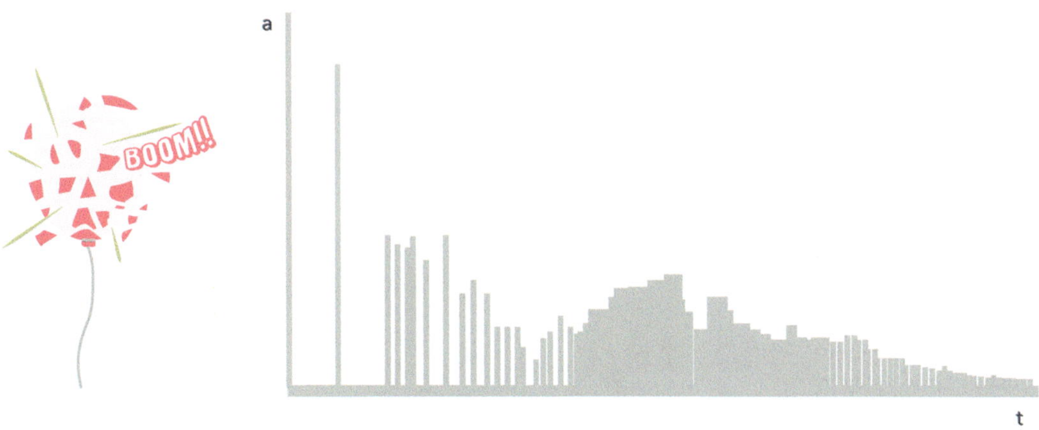

Once the impulse response of a given place is made, it is then convolved with the musical sounds that reverberation is applied to. Classical convolution (direct convolution) is an operation in the time domain.

In theory, convolution involves a process where signals are flipped, shifted, and added together. However, to simplify this process, a tabular method can be used to perform convolution.

If **h** is the room impulse response and **x** is the dry musical sound, I need to:

- **Multiply** $\mathbf{h_n}$ by $\mathbf{x_n}$
- **Place** each resultant in a table from the bottom up, offsetting each new row to the right by one column
- **Add** each column up vertically to get the output **y**

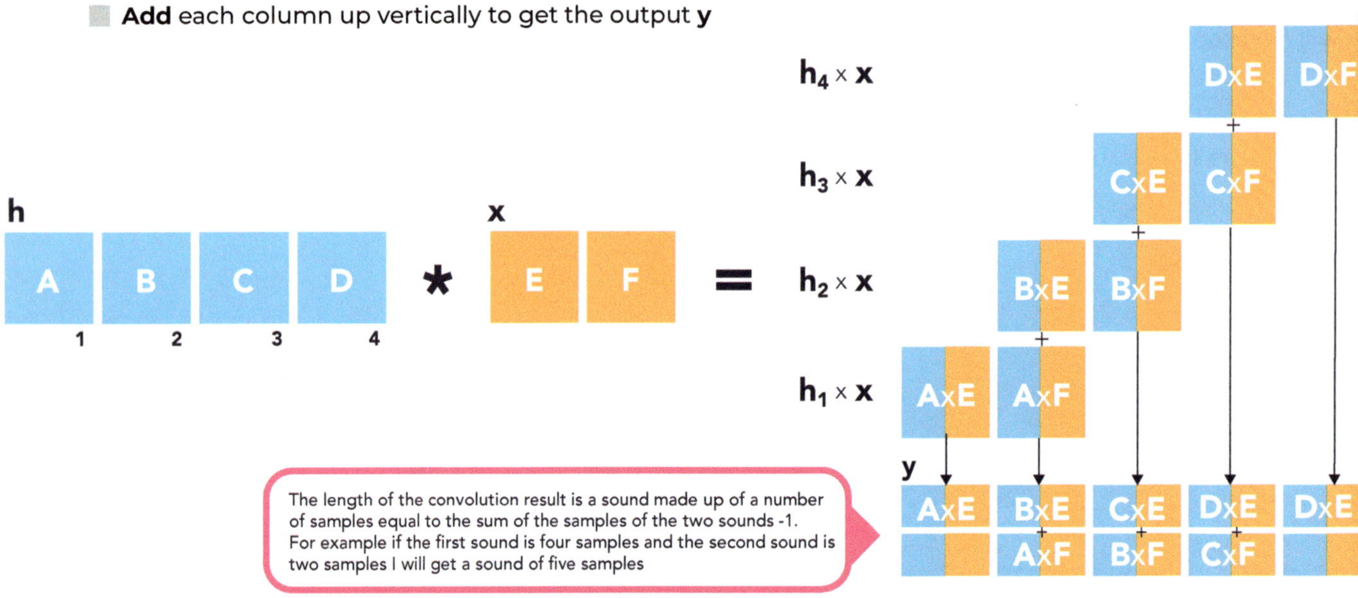

Let's take three simple cases to illustrate this mathematical operation better:

1. I convolve my sound with an impulse response that has a single sample with a value of 1. The result sounds identical to the original because, even after the time flip and overlapping operations, all its samples are multiplied by 1.

2. In this next example, the impulse response still has only one sample, but has a value of 0.5 instead. This in effect is a scaling factor for the amplitude of my original signal. In this case, the output is half the amplitude for all the original samples. It essentially lowers the volume.

3. The impulse response now consists of three samples, of which the first two have an amplitude of zero and the last has an amplitude of 1. This causes a time delay in our sound, starting two samples later in the output.

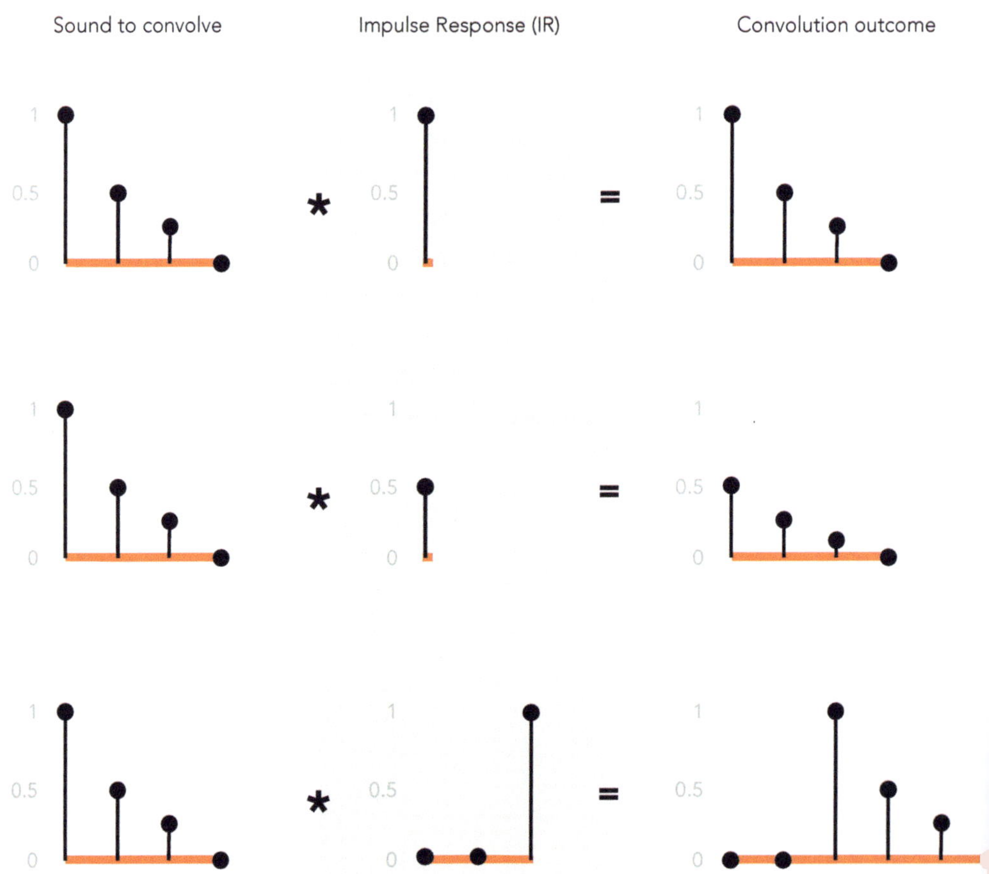

Let us now analyze a more complex example. The two sounds have four and two samples, respectively. In the upper part, we see the operations to be performed, and in the lower part, the results are displayed graphically. As we can tell from the graphical result, our final sound will be **a sound with characteristics of the first and second sounds**.

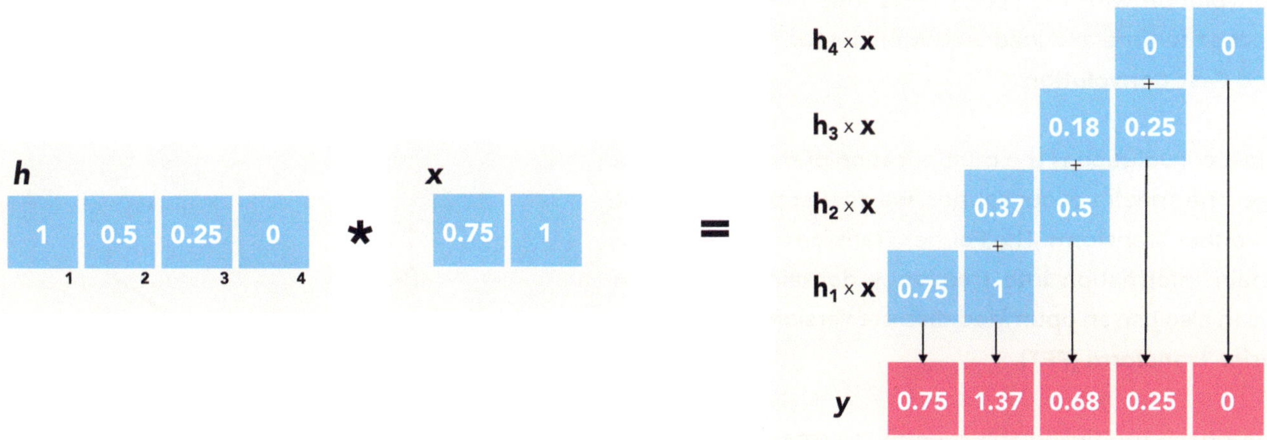

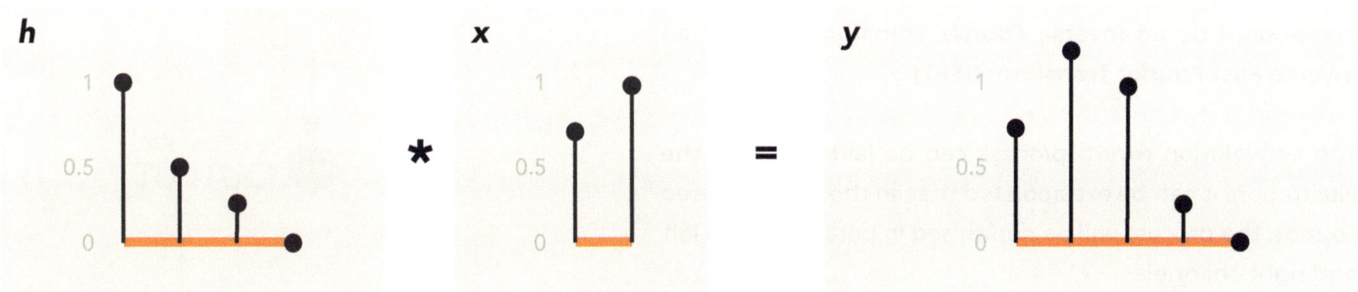

An interesting effect arises from the mathematical operation of convolution:

The direct convolution in the time domain of two sound signals is equivalent to the **multiplication of their relative spectra**!

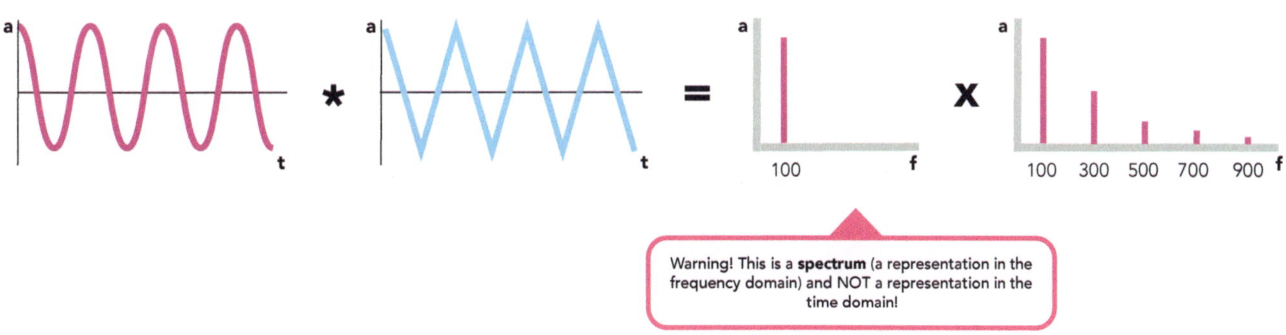

Going a little deeper, to perform convolution in the frequency domain, we multiply each band of the spectrum of the first sound with each band of the second sound. If we then convert the resultant spectrum back into the time domain, we will get the exact same result as if we had done the sample by sample direct convolution in the time domain.

Why is this important? Because doing convolution between two sounds in the time domain (**Direct Convolution**) by hand is very tiring and computationally expensive. Doing a convolution with the spectrum is much more agile and reduces the time and load on our processor. This process is called **Fast Convolution**.

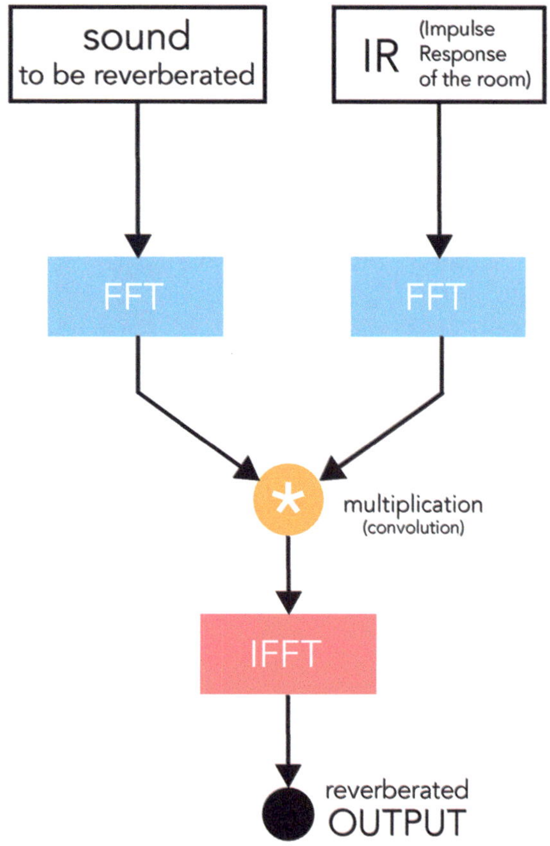

So, fast convolution is the multiplication of the two spectra. To get the spectra of our sounds, we do an operation called the Fourier Transform. The Fourier Transform converts time domain information into frequency domain information. We can also use an optimized discrete version of it, the **Fast Fourier Transform (FFT)**.

Once I have multiplied the spectra together, I have to go back to the time domain in order to get an audio signal made from samples that I can play. To do this inverse operation, I do an **Inverse Fourier Transform (IFT)** or an **Inverse Fast Fourier Transform (IFFT)**.

The convolution reverb process can be laid out as in the illustration. It can be extrapolated that, in the case of stereo sounds, the process will be performed in parallel for the left and right channels.

.create three recordings:
1) clap once in a large room (church, garage, ...), effectively creating an impulse response of the chosen space
2) generate a rhythmic sound of up to 5 seconds (can be the tapping of a pen on a wooden table, the snapping of fingers, or a rhythmic drumbeat)
3) produce a pitched sound (a single note from an instrument of your choice)
Make three micro compositions of about 40 seconds doing the following:
1) convolve sound 1 with a melody created with your instrument (it can also be a virtual instrument)
2) convolve sound 2 with the sound of your singing voice
3) convolve sound 3 with a drum or percussion part
Theme: "Three studies on states of matter: gas, liquid, solid"

free impulse response download ~ Rhythmic Convolutions - Diego Stocco ~ Convolution Reverb Ableton Live ~ Convolving a clarinet with a piano

DYNAMIC PROCESSORS

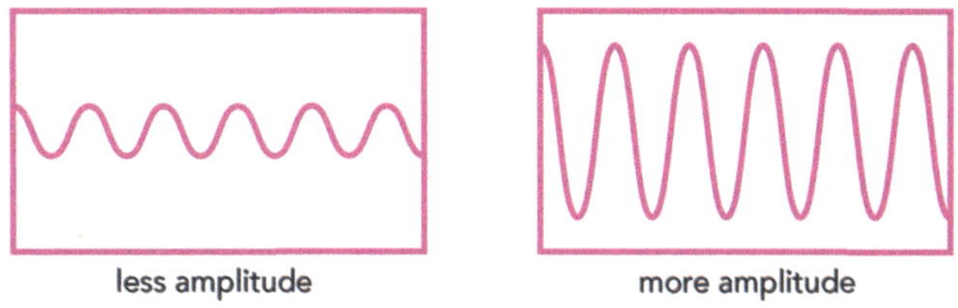

Do you want a powerful sound but are afraid that the large peaks may distort the sound? Do you want to open, or activate, a filter on strings only during the times when a bass drum is playing? If so, then you need dynamic processors to do the job.

Dynamic processors operate on and affect the "amplitude" parameter of an incoming sound by processing it for technical or creative purposes. In other words, the processing of the signal is based on the incoming sound's amplitude. One prominent use of dynamic processing is **mastering**, the last stage of production.

Envelope follower

The **envelope follower**, or envelope detector, extracts the envelope of an incoming sound by tracking and measuring the overall shape of the signal. Rather than looking at individual peaks and valleys of an audio signal, it follows the positive and negative peaks to create the positive and negative boundaries of the signal. With this envelope information, we can produce a control signal that can then be applied to a parameter of another device. The envelope follower can be used creatively and performatively to relate the sound of one instrument to the treatment done on the sound of another instrument. For example, I can turn on the filter on a pad when cello pizzicati are played. In this example, the audio signal of the pizzicati is analyzed, the amplitude envelope of the pizzicati is analyzed, a control signal is created that mirrors the shape of this envelope, and the degree of which the filter is activated is controlled by this envelope shape. This way, the filter's properties will precisely follow the dynamic pattern of the cello notes, thus turning on and turning off gradually, creating a strong interconnection between the two instruments.

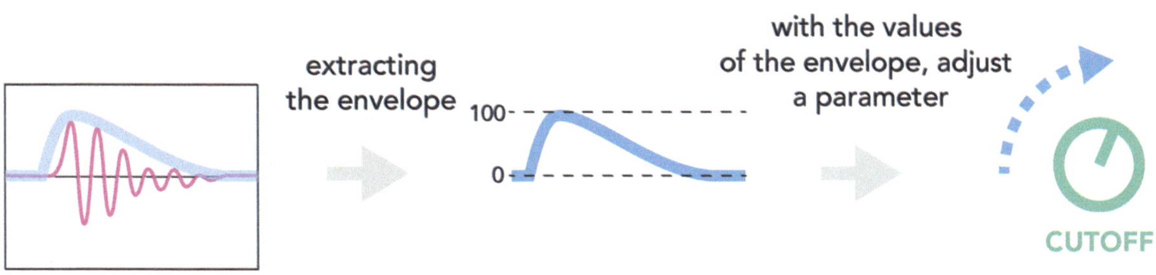

.download a track that has a well-defined beat and a BPM that you know. Import it into your DAW. Set up this track so that the volume is controlled by the envelope follower of a second track. For this second track, load kick drum samples and compose any rhythm of your choice. Using an envelope follower, set up the overall output so that the volume of the first track is controlled by the amplitude of the kick drums of the second track. In this scenario, you will hear the sound of the first track only during kick drum hits, and silence in between hits. You should never hear the drum track in your final output. ***Theme: "In the boxing ring"***

Compressor

A **compressor** is a device used to reduce the dynamic range of sound by attenuating the peaks and then amplifying the resultant waveform. It is widely used as one of the important tools to refine or correct the sound in the final stage of mixing or mastering a song. The latter is the last stage of production, which optimizes the waveform as we discussed in the foreword, on page 12.

There are two types of compression, both of which have the effect of "compacting" the sound wave but act differently to do so:

Downward compression In this type of compression, amplitudes above the threshold are acted upon, attenuating them.

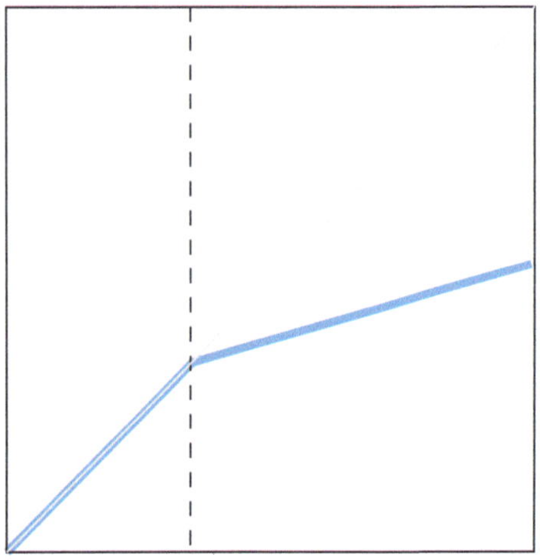

Upward compression In this type of compression, the amplitudes below the threshold are acted upon, amplifying them.

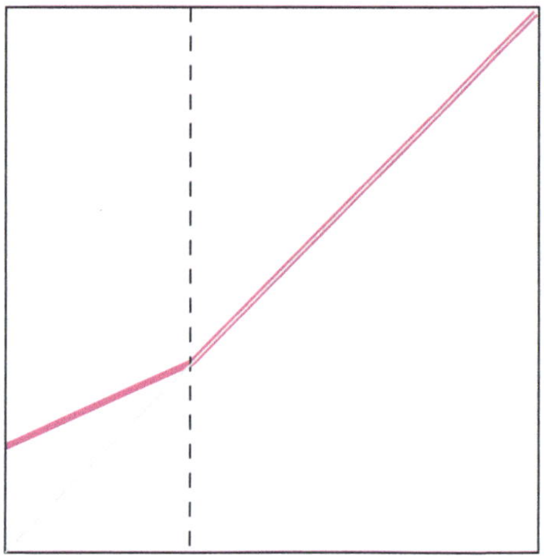

We will discuss downward compression first.
The (downward) compressor has two main stages:

1. **Measures** the amplitude of the incoming waveform
2. **Attenuates** the output amplitude when the waveform exceeds a specified threshold

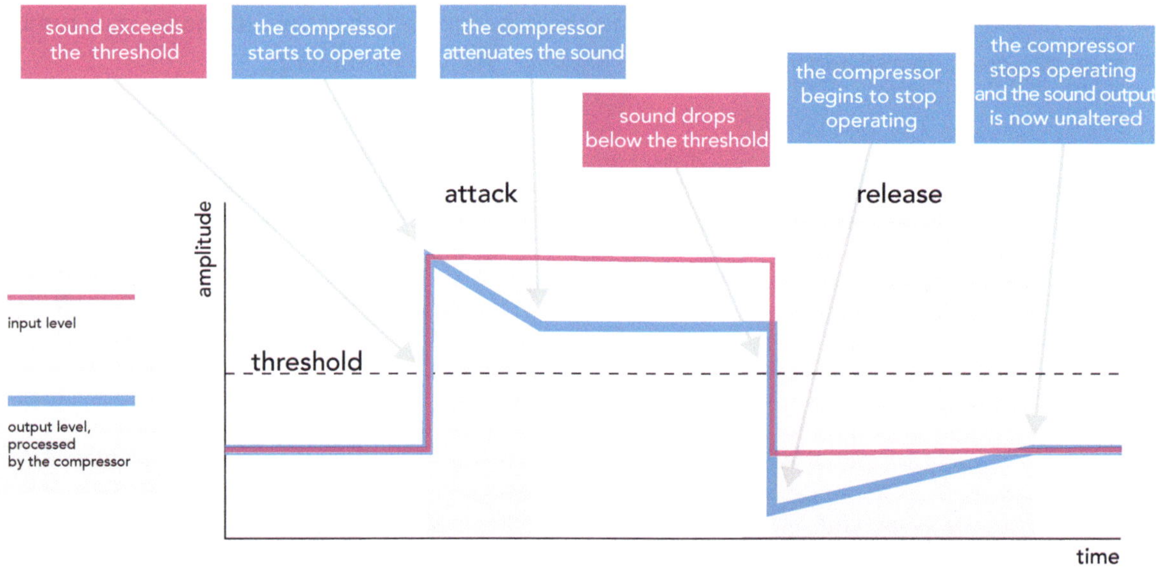

The actions of a compressor, belonging to the same family of devices such as ***limiters***, ***gate***, etc., can be schematized with the compressor response curve. This graph indicates what our compressor's task will be and what its main parameters are. First, let's work through how to read a compressor response curve (illustration below).

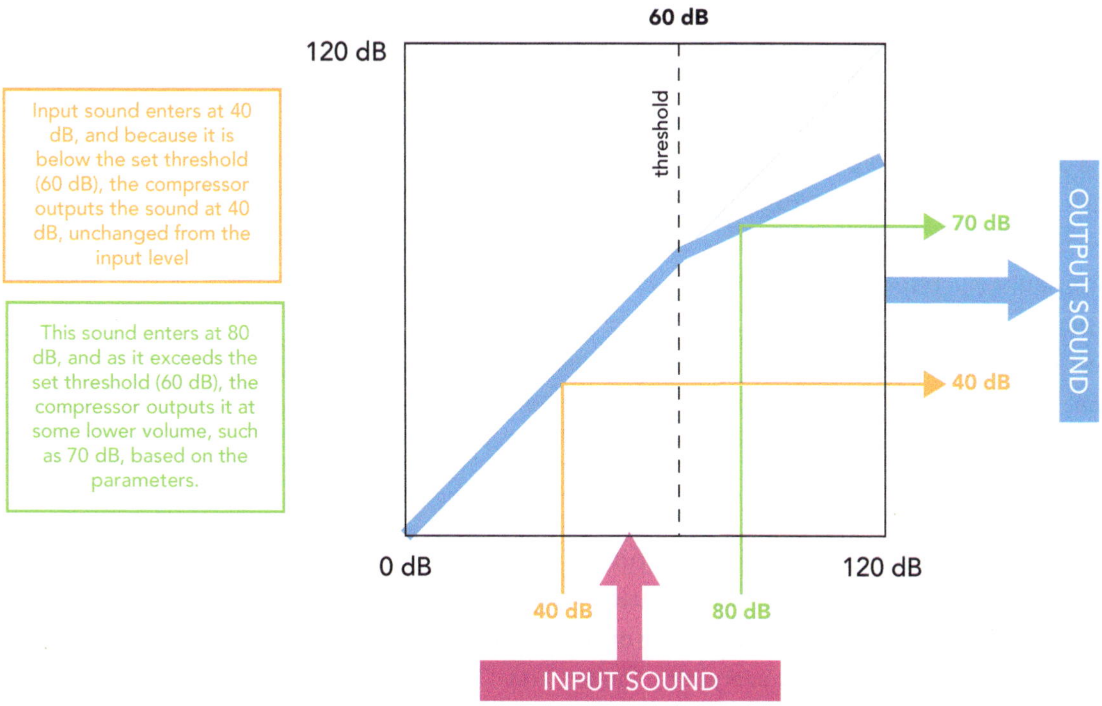

Settings

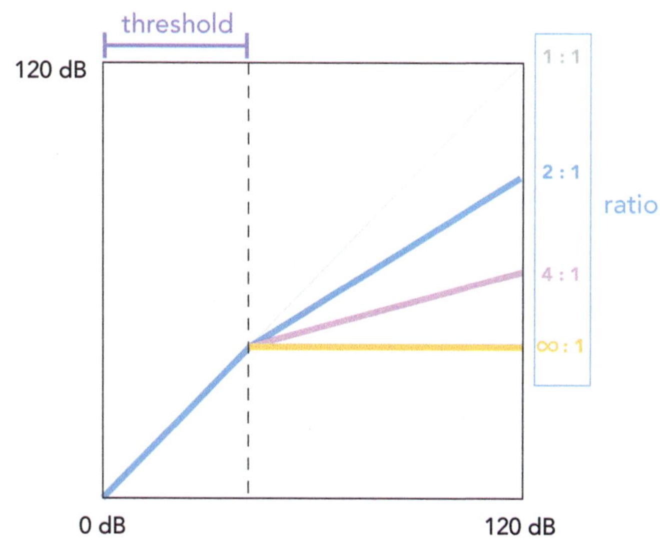

Threshold The amplitude level, or threshold, above which the compressor kicks in. This level is in the units of decibels.

Ratio (compression ratio) The ratio dictates how amplitudes above the threshold are rescaled. This ratio is unitless, as it is a ratio between two numbers, such as 3:1 or 5:1. For example, when an input sound of 90 dB is put into a compressor that has a 2:1 ratio and a 70 dB threshold, the output is 80 dB. This is because the input sound is 20 dB above the threshold, leading to only a 10 dB increase in the output.

Attack (attack time) This parameter determines the length of time it takes for the compressor to be fully engaged after the sound exceeds the threshold. This attack time is generally set in milliseconds (ms).

Release (release time) The length of time it takes the compressor to fully disengage after the sound falls below the threshold is the release time. Similarly to the attack time, it is also set in milliseconds (ms).

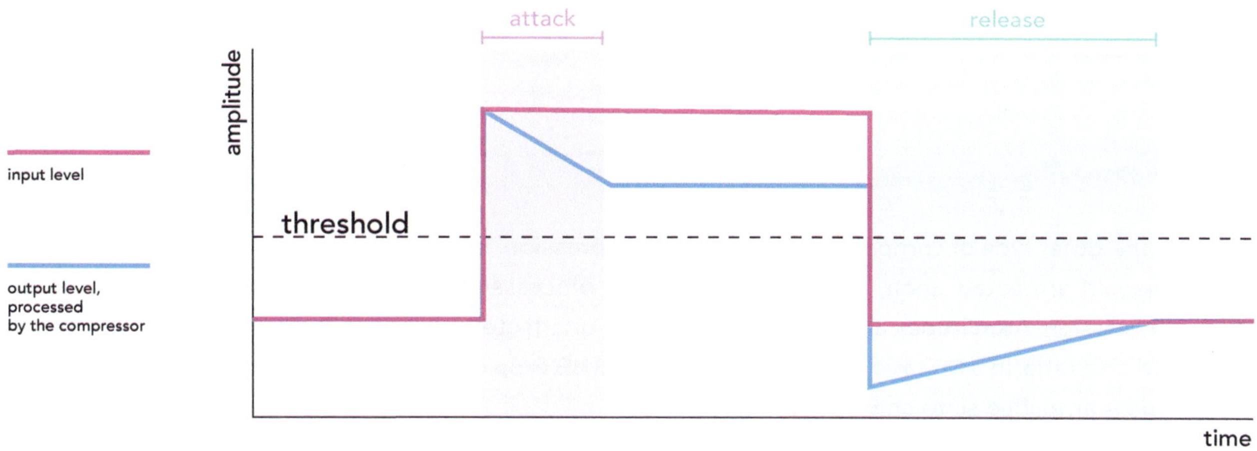

Knee (or curvature) The knee, in dB, dictates how sharp the angle of the compressor curve is at the threshold value. When the knee approaches 0 dB, the response curve indicates that right below the threshold, the compressor is off. Immediately after the threshold is crossed, the compressor is fully engaged. To create a smoother activation of the compressor, softer knees (with higher numerical dB values) can be selected. This, in effect, will create a **gradual activation** of the compressor around the threshold value.

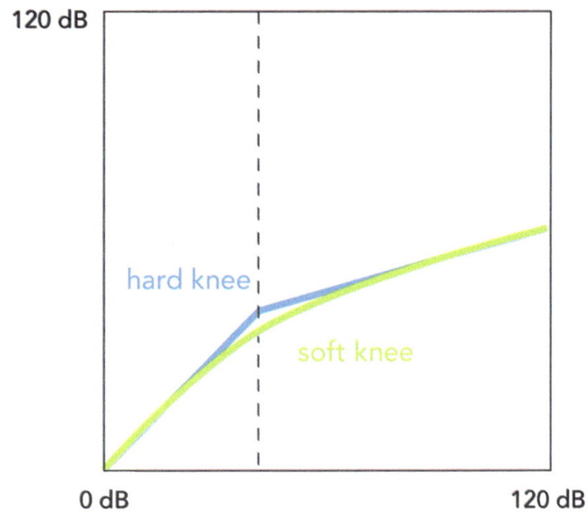

Output gain or makeup gain Compression on its own will effectively make everything sound quieter because the loud sounds have been attenuated. The output gain, or makeup gain, **amplifies the output**, making everything louder. This parameter's unit is the decibel. This gives us the opportunity to "make up" the volume that got attenuated through the act of compression. In other words, this parameter is important because it gives us the ability rebalance the output amplitude with output gain. If, by using our makeup gain, we match the amplitude of the peaks of the output to the peaks of the original input signal, there would be no change in the peak amplitudes. However, all the other lower amplitudes would be amplified, thereby "compacting" the dynamic range. Essentially, all amplitudes get louder at the expense of dynamic range.

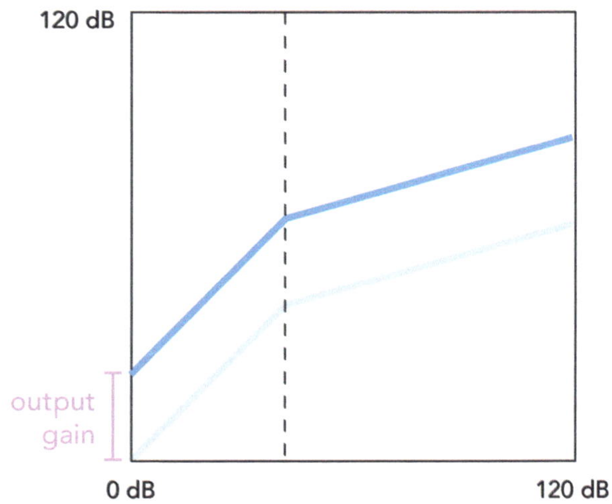

In compressors, there is often an **auto-makeup gain** feature that automatically sets the output amplification based on how much amplitude sound is lost during compression.

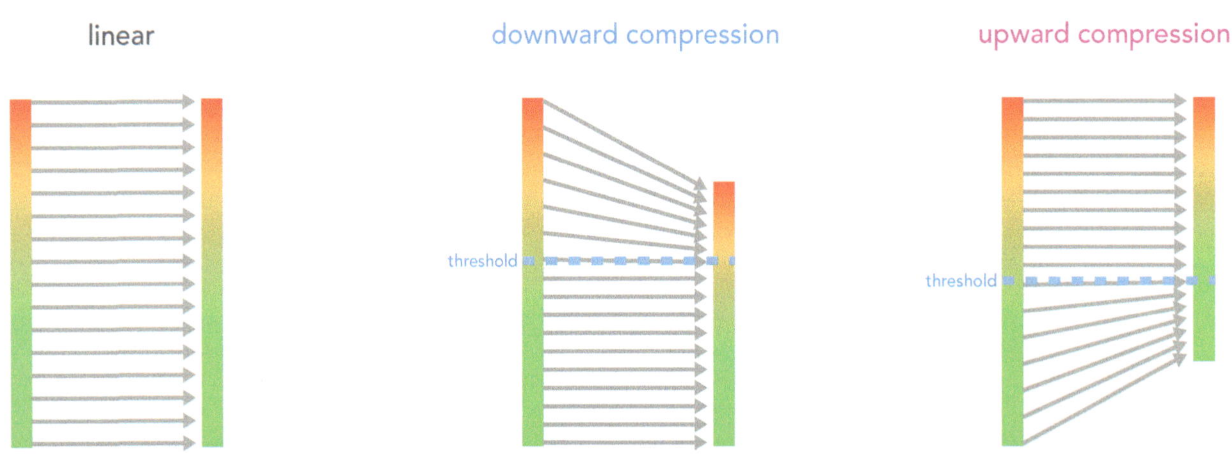

As a reminder, the other type of compression is **upward compression**. In this type of compression, the amplitudes below the threshold are acted upon, amplifying them. The processes for upward compression are opposite of downward compression. Amplitudes above the threshold are unaffected, and amplitudes below the threshold are amplified based on a ratio. In a 5:1 ratio for example, for every 5 dB drop in input amplitude below the threshold, the ouput amplitude is amplified so to only be reduced by 1 dB.

Multiple compressor

We can combine different compressors, each of which independently acts on different parts, or "zones," of the sound. The most used is the one that is based on frequency bands (Multiband compressor), but we can also select zones based on amplitude ranges or transients.

Frequencies Multiband Compressor

In this case, the different sub-compressors are applied to different frequency bands. I can accomplish this by using crossover or band-pass filters immediately before each sub-compressor. This, in effect, isolates one particular frequency band to each sub-compressor. This is similar to the process we saw earlier with multiband delays and delay lines. With this kind of schematic, I can set each individual sub-compressor up independently so I can have different compression parameters for each frequency band.

For example, I could have three frequency bands (0 – 300 Hz using a low-pass filter, 300 Hz – 2000 Hz using a bandpass filter, and 2000 + Hz using a high-pass filter) to control the compression for low, mid, and high frequencies in their own particular way.

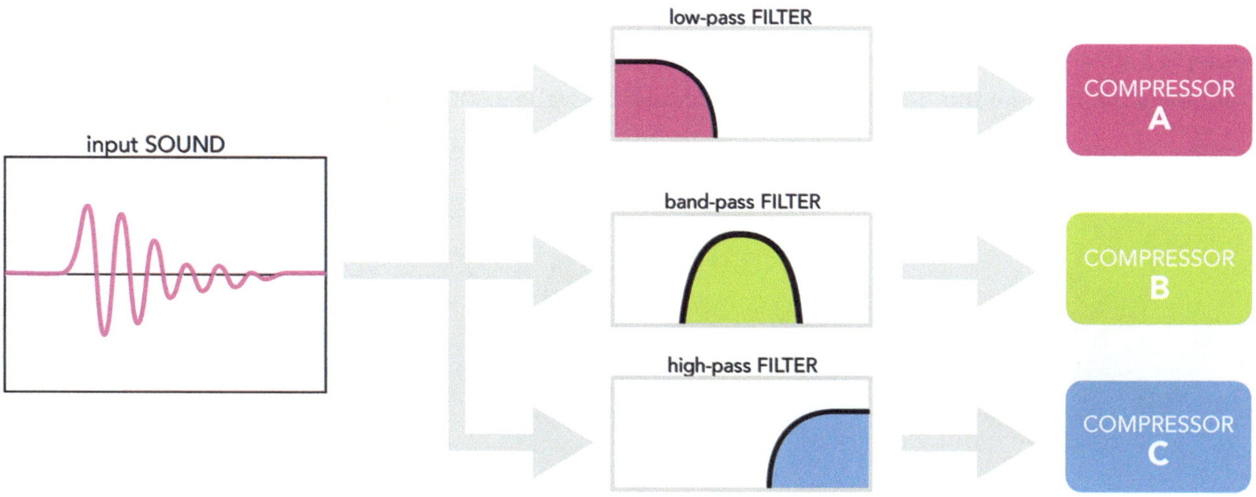

Amplitudes

In this case, the different sub-compressors work on specific amplitude ranges. For example, I can set up a 3-band compressor so that between 0 dB and 30 dB, 30 dB and 60 dB, and 60 dB and louder, Compressors A, B, and C and operate indepedently on these amplitude regimes.

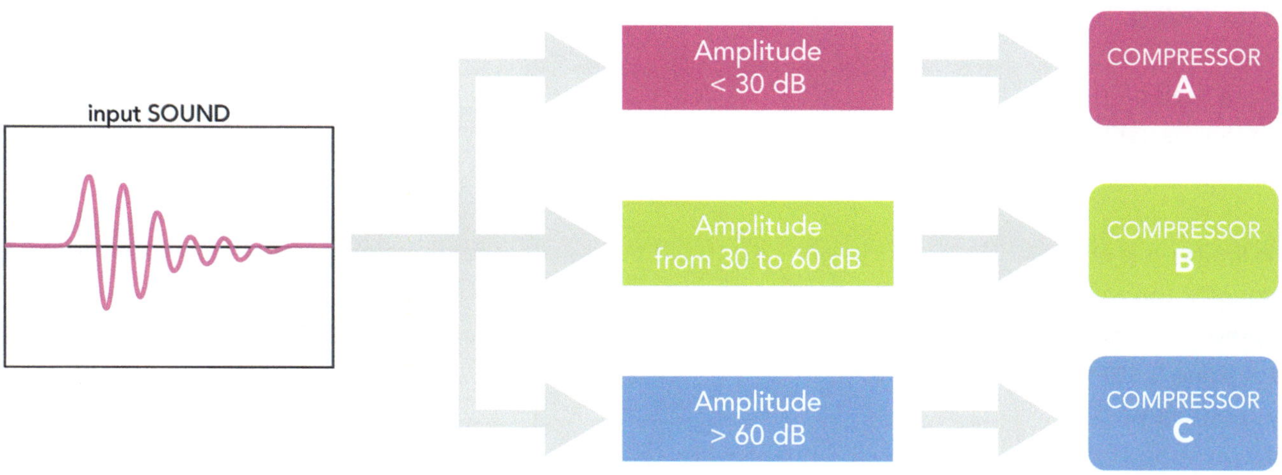

Transients

Different compressors are applied for different temporal bands of transients (attacks).

For example, for short transients, I use a compressor set a certain way; for long attacks, I use another setting.

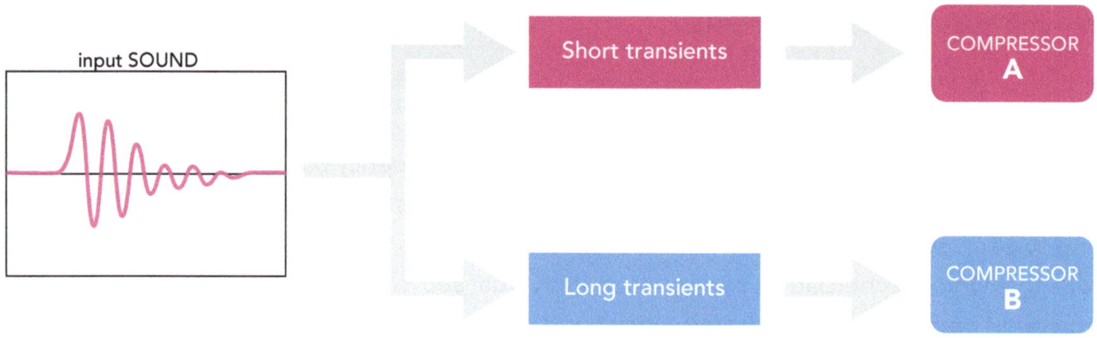

De-esser

The **De-esser** is a special type of multiband compressor that attenuates sibilant "S's" in recorded vocals. It acts ONLY on the frequency band where the "S's" are generally located: between 2,500 Hz - 9,000 Hz.

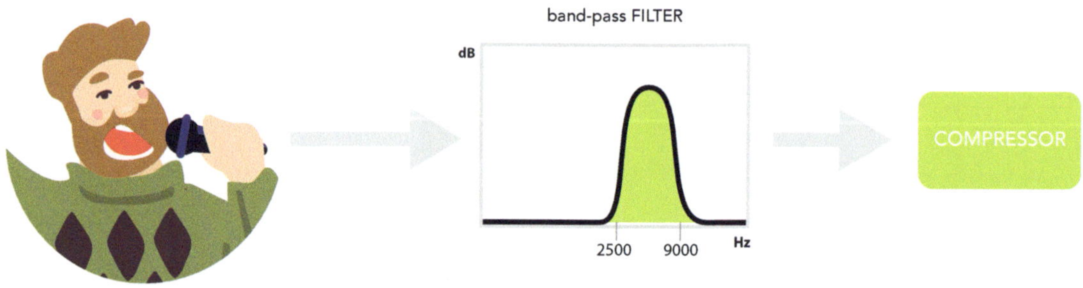

Limiter

A **Limiter** is a special compressor that prevents amplitudes above the threshold from passing through. To do this, the compressor ratio needs to be ∞:1 in theory. Practically though, limiter ratios are usually >20:1.

The threshold in a limiter is called the ***Ceiling***.

Limiters are used particularly in the mastering process.

With the limiter, it is possible to "squash" the waveform to prevent sounds from exceeding 0 dBFS, thereby suppressing digital distortion.

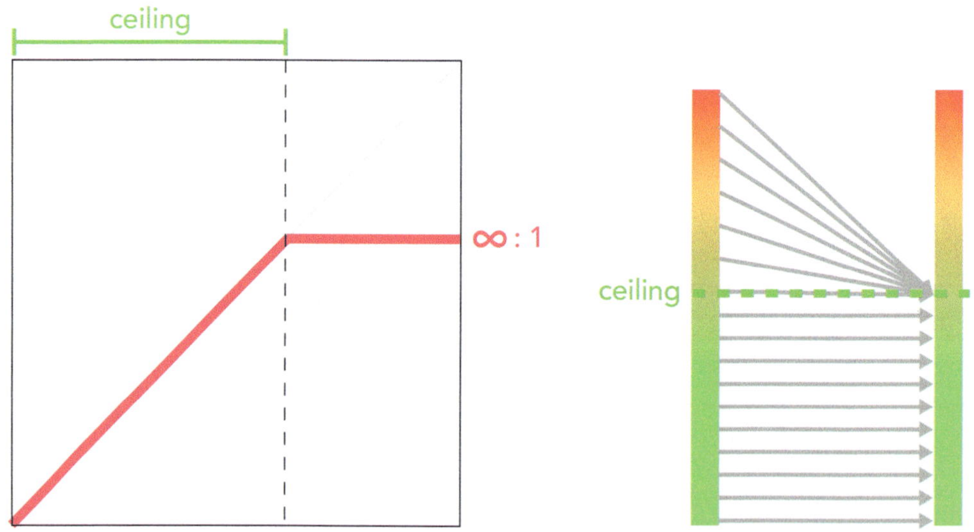

Expander

The **Expander** is a sort of reverse compressor because it increases the dynamic range of audio. Whereas in compression, sounds above the threshold are attenuated, with the expander, sounds below the threshold have a reduction in amplitude. In this case, the loud sounds above the threshold remain unchanged, but sounds with amplitudes less than the threshold will be reduced by a ratio. Again, in contrast to the compressor, a 2:1 ratio for an expander means that for every 1 dB in level below the threshold, the expander reduces that sound by 2 dB. This effectively widens the range between the dynamics of input sound, so there will be a larger range.

Downward expansion affects quieter sounds.

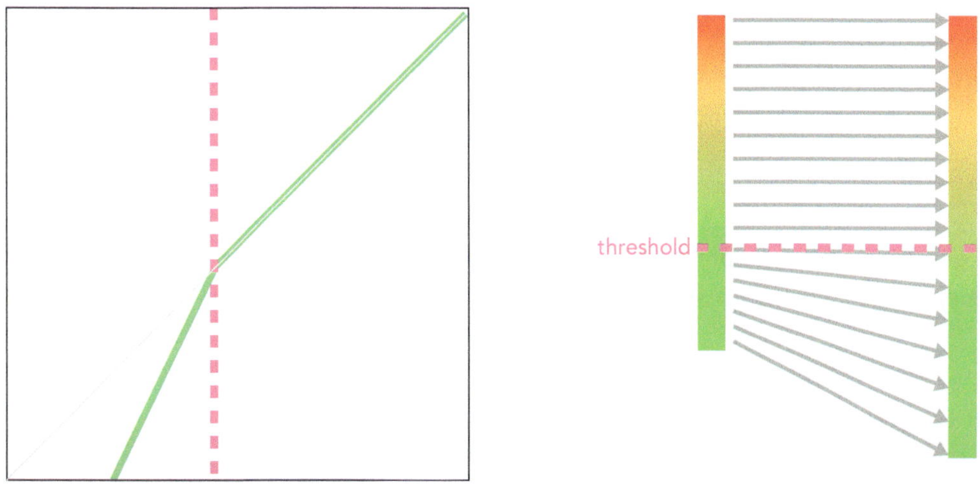

Although not as common, some expanders act on the louder sounds. This is **upward expansion**. For this kind of expander, sounds greater than the threshold are amplified with additional gain to make sounds above the threshold louder while keeping the sound below the threshold constant.

Gate

A **Gate** is a dynamic processor that eliminates sound below a user-selected threshold. A **noise gate**, as the name suggests, is used to eliminate background noise. For example, when putting a gate on a recorded vocal track, the gate will turn on during pauses in the singing, due to the amplitude dropping below the threshold. When the gate is on in these vocal pauses, the volume is lowered to reduce unwanted noise.

A limitation to a noise gate is that it can only remove noise when the vocalist is not singing. In the case where noise occurs during the singing, the gate cannot do magic and eliminate that unwanted noise since the singing voice and noise are summed. Here, the summed amplitude is above the gate's threshold and the gate will not turn on.

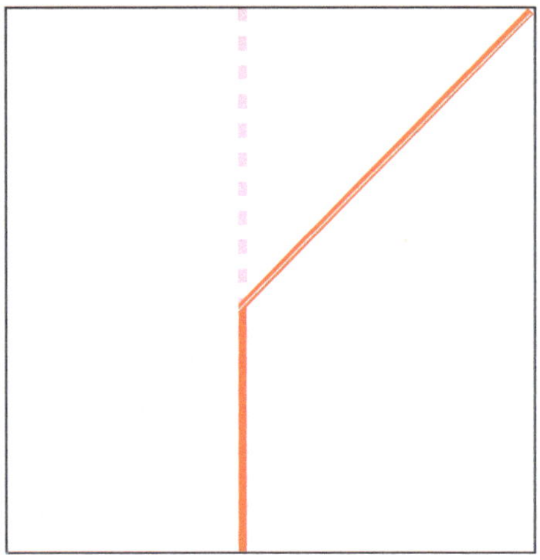

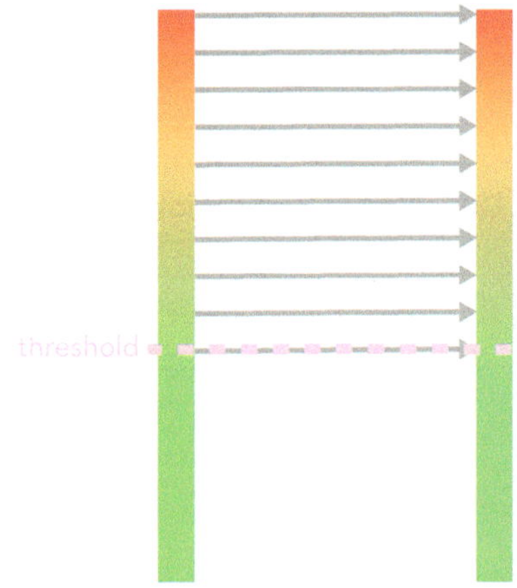

The following is a graphical summary of how the different types of compressors and expanders transform the input amplitudes into their respective output amplitudes.

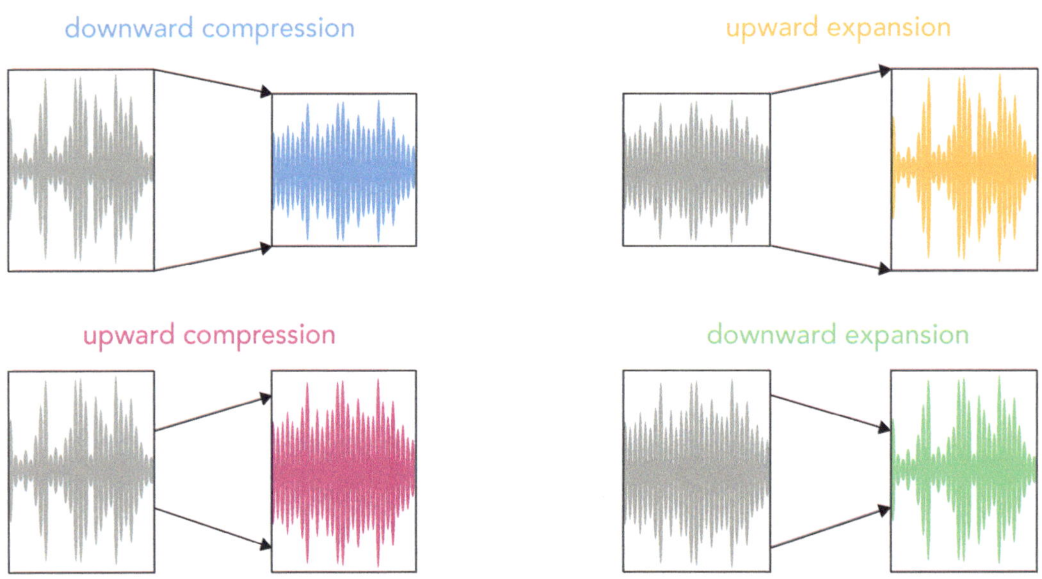

.download a set of multitrack stems from any free online multitrack library and use various types of dynamic processors needed to get a good mix. Do not use any other type of processing. In particular, use a gate to remove noise breaks and a compressor to make one track, like the lead vocals or a solo instrument, stand out

.take the same music as above but use no more than four tracks of your choice to create a completely new version of the music itself. Use loops and the effects that we have just studied together

.download a drum loop and apply a gate to it. Experiment with the gate so that the rhythm itself is changed. Create four different new versions of the drum loop by altering only the attack and decay parameters of the gate

DISTORTION

Distortion is the result of intentional or unintentional waveform modification. In particular, audio distortion is generated from an alteration in waveform that can come from analog circuit effects or special digital audio algorithmic treatments. This ultimately creates a "dirtier" and muddier sound that is more harmonically complex and scratchy in tone.

There are times when distortion of a signal can be considered an error and should be avoided. For example, when making an archival recording of a choral concert, the recording engineer will want clean audio without distortion. However, in many cases, distortion is intentional and used for creative purposes to "color" the timbre of instruments. This is the case of the electric guitar in rock music or in other instruments, including electronic ones, in ***noise***-related genres.

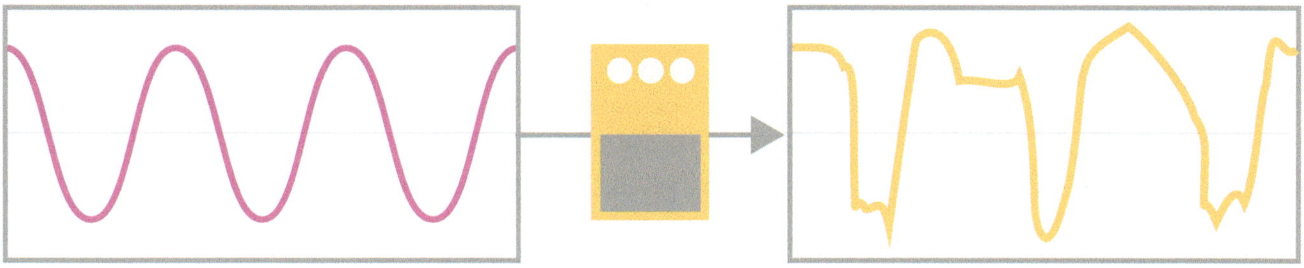

The original creative use was actually an unintended side effect. Musicians, particularly electric guitarists, have successfully used distortion ever since. This most fortunate accident revolutionized audio and changed the sound of music forever.

Overdrive

After the invention of the electric guitar and the first tube-based amplification systems, people realized that if they turned up the amplifier a lot, the sound would have a "color" to it, stemming from a type of distortion called **overdrive**. This happens when the tube transistor gets an input beyond the normal limits of operation. The result is a distorted output waveform. The fascinating thing is that distortion does not happen linearly, and the amount and quality of distortion can depend on several factors, such as the input sound level and the tube's timbral characteristics. This effect can occur either in the preamp part, at the beginning of the circuit, or in the final stages of an amplifier. Bluesmen began exploiting these sonic characteristics of tube amplifiers as early as the late 1940s. Perhaps unknowingly, they were inventing the rock sound as we know it today.

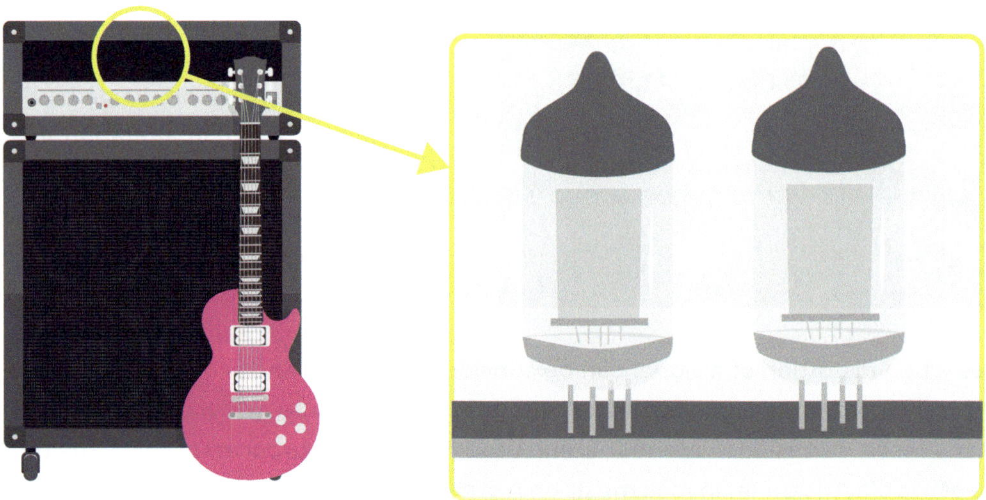

To see how overdrive distortion works, let's send a sine wave into an overdrive circuit. Internally, the sine wave is amplified and experiences clipping, causing a flattened waveform at the peaks. The outputted wave, instead of matching the sine wave shape of the input, begins to look closer to the shape of a square wave. This square-like wave, having an edgier sound because it is richer in high harmonics, is **"distorted"** by the overdrive circuit. By analyzing the new sound spectrum, we notice that it possesses many new harmonics placed at odd harmonic frequencies, exactly where we also find the harmonics that make up the classic square wave. The waveforms of electric guitar or other complex timbres are far from a pure sine wave; thus, overdrive distortion will form even more complex output waves that, at its limits, will ultimately approach the characteristics of the square wave.

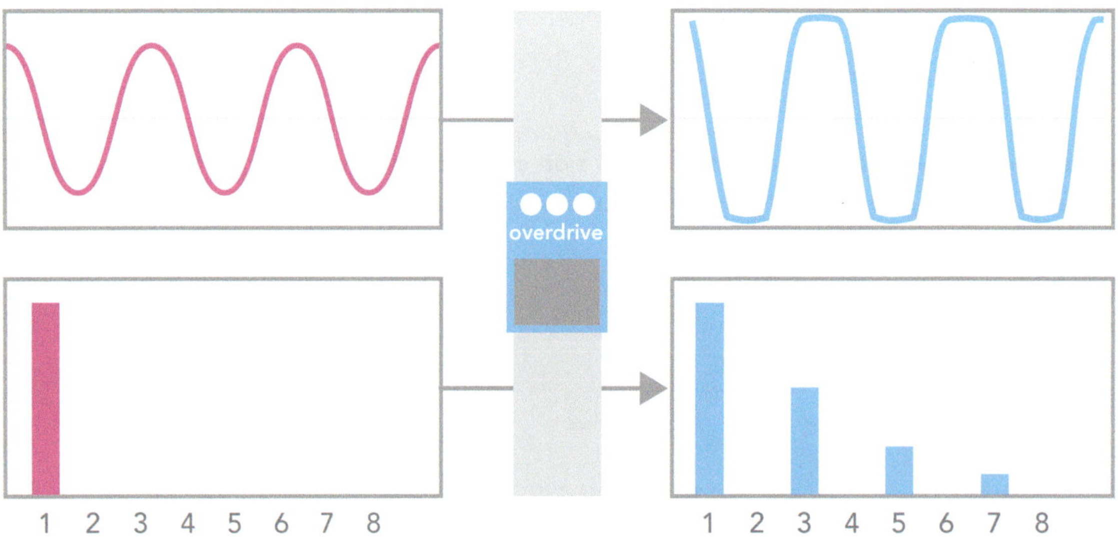

Fuzz

Fuzz also originated from a chance mistake in 1960 in a Nashville recording studio where *Marty Robbins* was recording the song *"Don't Worry."* At one point in the recording session, the transformer on the guitar amplifier broke, and the amplifier began to produce a distorted sound. Despite the artist and the sound engineer immediately noticing the sonic surprise, everyone enjoyed it so much that they decided to leave it in. The track was released with this effect, and it was a great success.

It didn't end there. The engineer *Glenn Snoddy* wanted to recreate this distorted sound; he reverse engineered it with the world's first fuzz pedal circuit. This was the birth of the **Maestro Fuzz Tone** in 1962.

When we take a simple sine wave into our fuzz circuit, we will find a distinctive distorted output that is more harsh. When compared to overdrive, the fuzz distortion exhibits peaks that are not only a bit squashed in amplitude, but also asymmetrical, with seemingly skewed triangles on top of a square wave. When analyzing the spectrum of this waveform, we will find the addition of even harmonics, even beyond the ninth harmonic. This is the primary reason why we hear fuzz sounds to be a bit invasive, scratchy, and sour.

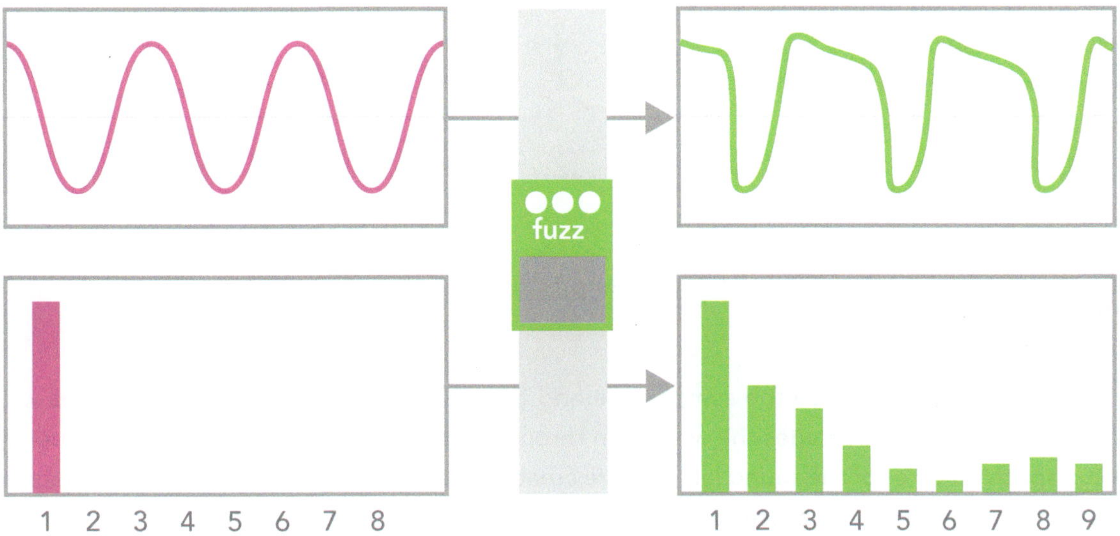

.generate a 9-chord sequence using an AI chatbox. Play the sequence with simple sine waves by setting very long attacks and releases. Use overdrive with automation to create distortion that has a crescendo-diminuendo effect. Organize them into a composition. ***Theme: "Brain waves movement"***

.write a 4-bar melody line for a trumpet. Using a clean classical or electric guitar sound, apply fuzz tuning to mimic a trumpet-like sound. Harmonize the initial trumpet melody with your "new" guitar sound

fuzz vs overdrive ~ Marty Robbins Don't worry ~ Maestro Fuzz Tone ~ A Brief History of Electric Guitar Distortion ~ Zvex Fuzz Factory

So far, we have discussed two distortions that originated primarily in the analog world, although we can reconstruct them with digital systems. Some distortions, however, are only possible through **digital signal or digital sound processing**.

Two of these types of distortion are **Resampling** and **Bit crushing**. If you need a more thorough refresher on digital sound, particularly sampling and quantization, see the chapter on page 86. To review here though: in an analog to digital convertor (ADC), the first major step is sampling, where we convert a signal from analog to digital by taking the continuous original signal (without any gaps) and turn it into a discrete one (with specific time steps). The rate at which these time steps occur is the **sample rate**. By only having a certain number of samples per second, we are, in effect, approximating the original analog signal. As for the amplitude, we convert, or quantize, the continuous amplitudes of the discretized signal into specific amplitude bins. The **bit depth** determines how many possible values of amplitude are possible. This, in effect, also approximates the amplitude. By manipulating the sample rates and the bit depths, we see the rise of resamplers and bit crushers, respectively.

In digital audio, we find some standard values for the ADC parameters. The sampling rate is generally at least 44,100 samples per second and the bit depth is at least 16 bits. For reference, quantizing at 16 bits leads to 2^{16} or 65,536 total possible amplitude steps. If I reduce one or both of these parameters, I get the type of distortion we will discuss next.

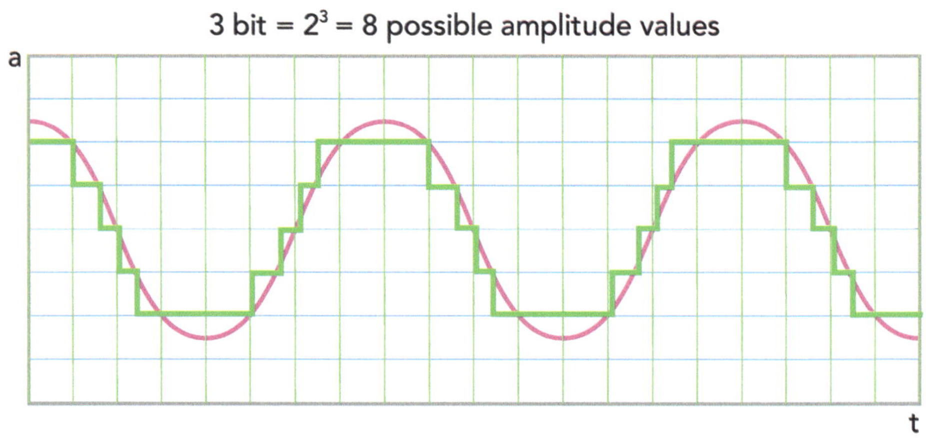

Resampling

In the case of **Resampling**, we reduce the sample rate and therefore lower the number of samples we take per second. This action distorts and degrades the waveform through ***aliasing***. When we look at the frequency domain when sampling, spectral copies of the sound (aliases) are created at integer multiples of the sample rate. When the sampling rate is sufficiently high, the aliases do not cause any issue because there is no significant audible overlap in these spectral copies. When the sampling rate drops below the Nyquist Frequency (half of the sample rate), the aliases begin to overlap in a substantial and audible way, creating a distorted waveform. This is aliasing. With ADC convertors, aliasing is generally undesirable. However, with resampling, we can creatively choose lower sample rates to create aliasing purposefully.

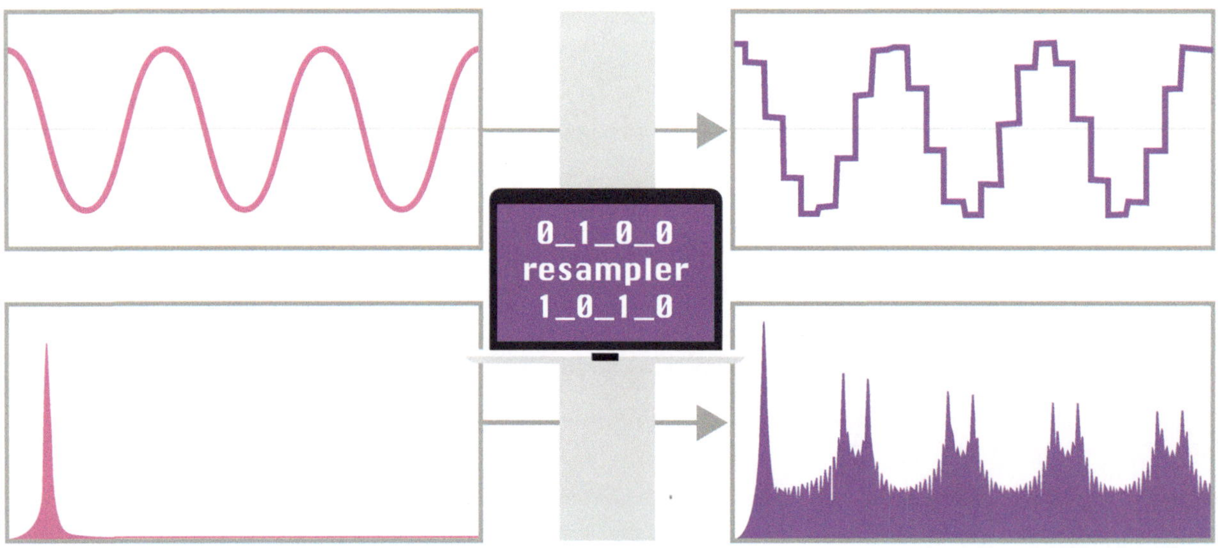

This resampling distortion exhibits well-defined harmonics when a deliberately low sampling rate creates noticeable overlap between the spectral copies. With a very low sampling rate, we will see many spectral copies overlapping one another. Unlike with bit crushing where the distorted sound has harmonics at regular frequency intervals, resampling distortion's harmonics are irregular, defined solely by the overlapping spectral copies. Unlike unintended aliasing that might occur with the severe data compression associated with an MP3 file, the aural effect of a resampler is that we have a kind of intentionally "random" harmonization of the input sound.

Bit crushing

Bit crushing decreases the bit depth of the original sound, thereby reducing the number of amplitude steps that are possible to describe the wave. It is like approximating a clay sculpture with *Lego* bricks. These possible amplitude steps are larger with a lower bit depth, leading to the shape of the wave becoming coarser and "dirtier" with larger "stair steps." The result is a sound that is richer in high frequencies, sometimes described as a sharp or acidic sound. At its limit, if the bit crusher is set to only 1 bit, we reduce the original input to only two possible states, a maximum value or a minimum value. This output wave resembles a wave with characteristic rectangular shapes. If we bit crush a perfect sine wave to just 1 bit, we will get a perfect square wave as our output.

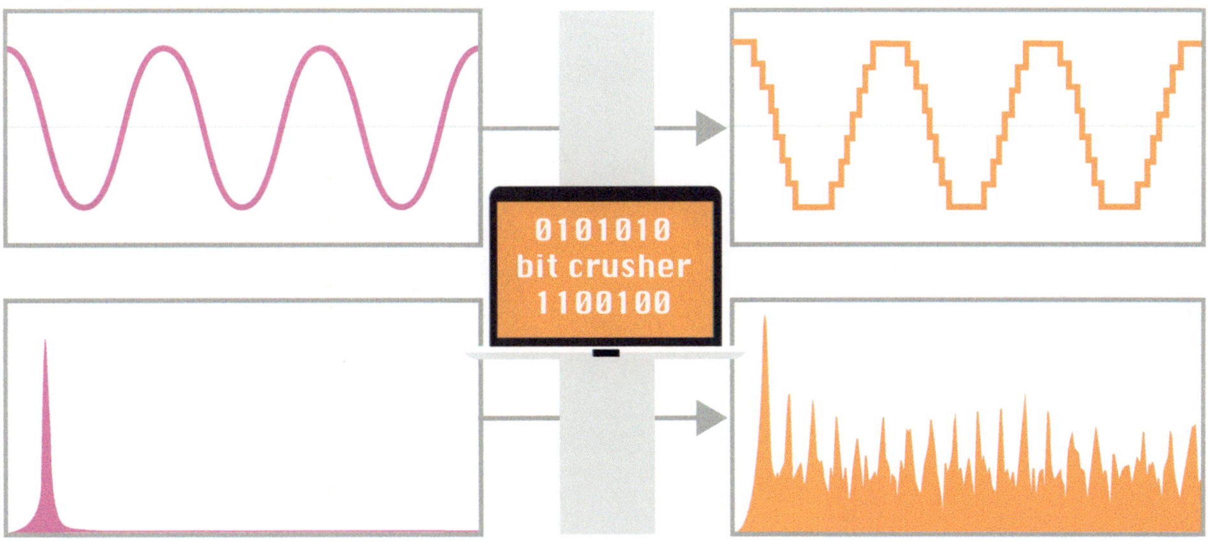

Nine Inch Nails – We're In This Together ~ Aphex Twin - Come To Daddy ~ Squarepusher – Do You Know Squarepusher

.create a composition of at least 50 seconds using only voices (sung or spoken) and bit crushing treatments. ***Theme: "We speak different"***

.download or record a note from any melodic instrument. With this recording, apply a resampler-type distortion to create four new harmonic sound objects, setting the sample rate each time to get four "different chords." Create a random arpeggio among the four sound objects with a total duration of 20 seconds

Waveshaping

Among digital systems, **Waveshaping** is primarily considered a sound synthesis technique (see sound synthesis chapter, page 179). While we may think of waveshaping in terms of sine waves, any sound can act as an input, and we can exploit waveshaping to create efficient distortion. This algorithm is based on inputing the audio signal into a transfer function that distorts its shape. The transfer function is a curve that I can customize, vary, and store in a table. The values of the transfer function range between -1 and 1. This function acts as a distorting "mirror" where I make an altered "image" of the original audio. From the illustration below, the original audio acts as the input, from below, to the transfer function where it "bounces" off the curve and exits as the modified distorted curve to the right. To visualize it, let's take a look at four examples here:

perfectly linear function: each input value equals the same output value, so I do not have any changes to the input wave

total polarity inversion: the negative transfer function flips the polarity of the input signal

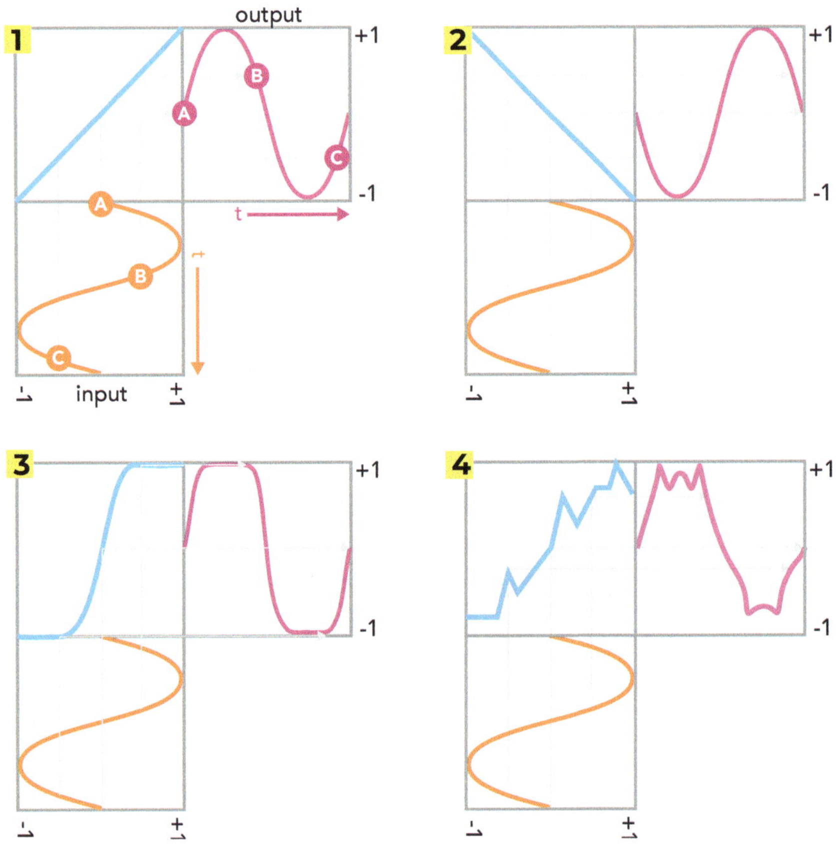

overdrive like: this distortion is similar to overdrive because the function tends to squash the peaks of the wave

complex distortion: arbitrary transfer functions can create much more complex distortion

One of the interesting features of this technique is the graphical possibilities of it. I can easily draw my transfer function by hand and hear how the new distorted output sounds. With many modern audio programs, we can even do this dynamically, in real time, during a live performance. Distortion with waveshaping is greatly affected by differences in the input amplitude because low amplitudes work only on the central part of the function and large amplitudes on the side parts. Because of this mathematical phenomenon, we often need to normalize the output amplitude from distortion to avoid overly large or annoying amplitude differences.

.choose a painting that you like by J. Miró or one by V. Kandinsky. Extrapolate five curve-like elements from these paintings and use them as your waveshaping distortion's transfer function. Apply the five curves to a single sound of your choice, thus creating five distorted versions of it. Create a beat with the five sounds generated

SPATIALIZATION

Spatialization is the compositional parameter allowing composers and producers to place and present sounds from positions surrounding the listener. Whether the composition is traditional, electroacoustic, or even a live electronics composition, these sounds can include acoustic, electric, electronic, and virtual instruments. Spatialization allows us to position these sounds statically, or even dynamically, relative to the listener. This chapter will show the many different theories and techniques of how this is made possible.

Psychoacoustics of spatial perception

We can localize sound, or perceive where sounds are coming from, due to the way sound interacts with and is processed by our ears and brain. Our auditory system can decipher whether a sound is coming from above or below, from in front or behind, or from the right or left with fairly high accuracy. The following concepts determine how we perceptually localize sounds.

Interaural Time Difference (ITD) This parameter is defined as the difference in arrival time for a sound to reach our left and right ears. As a sound travels to our head, the path length to our left and right ears may be slightly different. This path difference is the reason that it takes different lengths of time for a sound to reach our left and right ears. Essentially, this is the difference in time for which the sound reaches our two pinna (outer ear).

For example, imagine a sound coming to you from your left side. That sound will reach your left ear before reaching your right ear, since the sound has to travel an additional distance around your head to reach your right ear. This extra distance takes a certain amount of extra time. It is this difference in arrival time between the right and left ear that is the ITD.

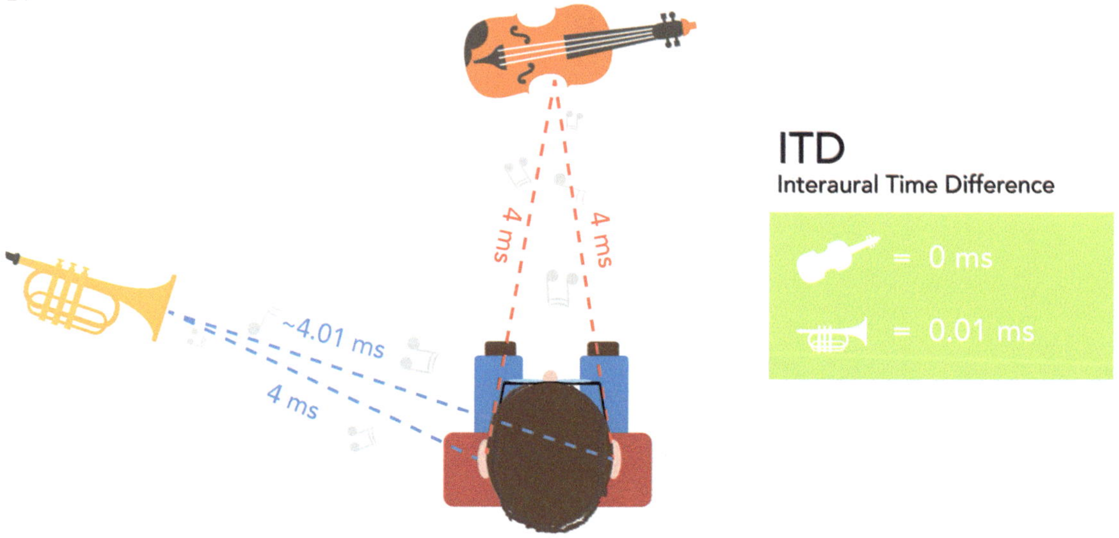

Interaural Level Difference (ILD) ILD is the phenomenon where the amplitude that each ear receives can be different due to the spatial positioning of the sound source. Most notably, our head can cast an acoustic shadow and prevent one of our ears from experiencing the full sound amplitude.

For example, a sound coming from the left will reach the left ear with greater sound intensity than the right ear because of our head's acoustic shadow. The difference between these two values is the ILD.

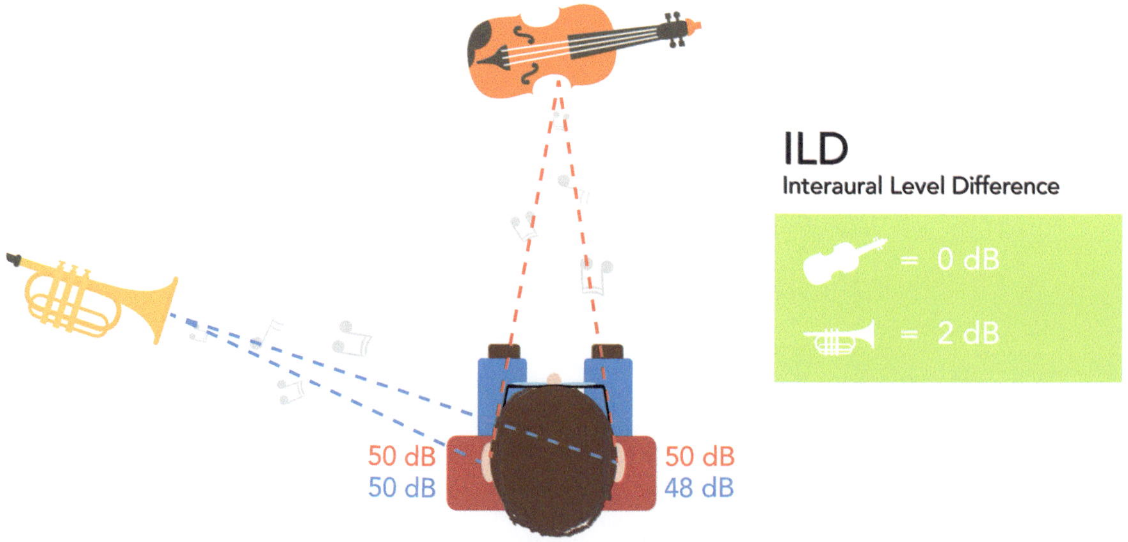

Head-related transfer function (HRTF) As sound reaches a listener, the human body itself creates a set of acoustic interactions that results in essentially a frequency filter. Filtering refers to the frequency dependent attenuation of a sound or timbre (see chapter on filters, page 105). In particular, the combination of the pinna (outer ear), the head, the shoulders, and the torso produces a filter that affects the frequency response of an incoming sound. This is sometimes known as the head-related transfer function. What is interesting is that the characteristics of the filter are dependent on the direction that the sound is coming from. That is, the filter that our body creates for a sound coming from the right side is different than the filter that is created for a sound coming to us from above.

The irregular shape of the pinna, with all of its folds and curves, produces unique reflections and refractions of incoming sound waves dependent on the incoming direction of the sound. The result is this direction dependent filter, or transfer function, that modifies the sound that is then processed by the brain, which interprets the content spatially. As everyone's ear, head, and general body shapes are unique, this transfer function is unique for everyone.

To put these three concepts together: if a sound reaches the right ear first, is attenuated by 10 dB at the left ear, and has a 5 dB cut at 6 kHz, due to the head-related transfer function, our brain will perceive that sound source to come from the upper right of the listener.

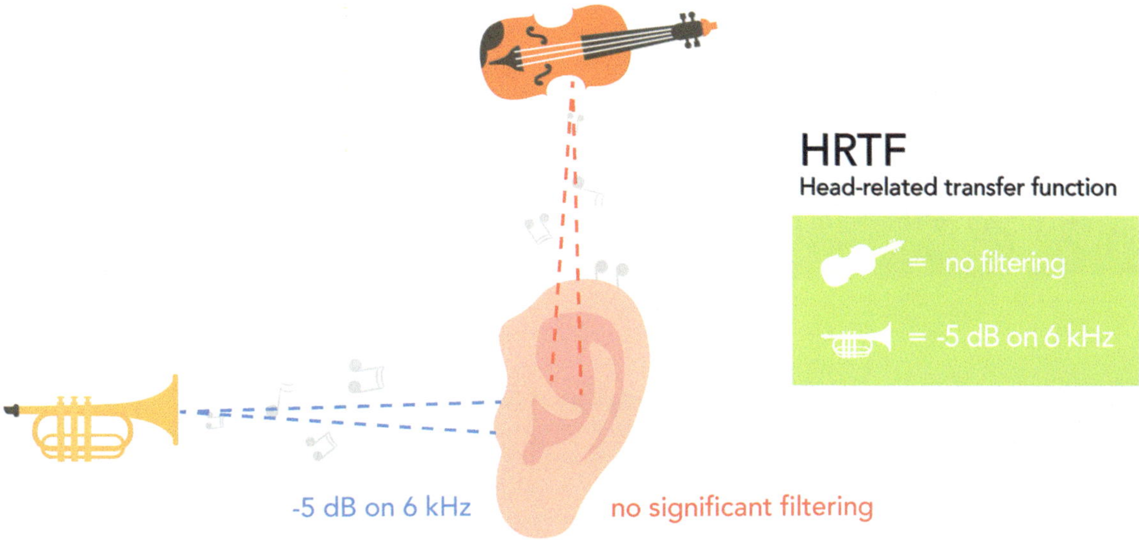

The environment The reverberant field of a space can play an important role in how we localize sound.

For example, a sound with a lot of reverberation can be perceived as distant because the ratio between the energy of the direct sound and all the sound that bounces off the walls before reaching the listener is small. When that ratio favors the direct sound, then we perceive the sound as closer. However, if that ratio favors the reverberant sound, then we will think that the source is farther away.

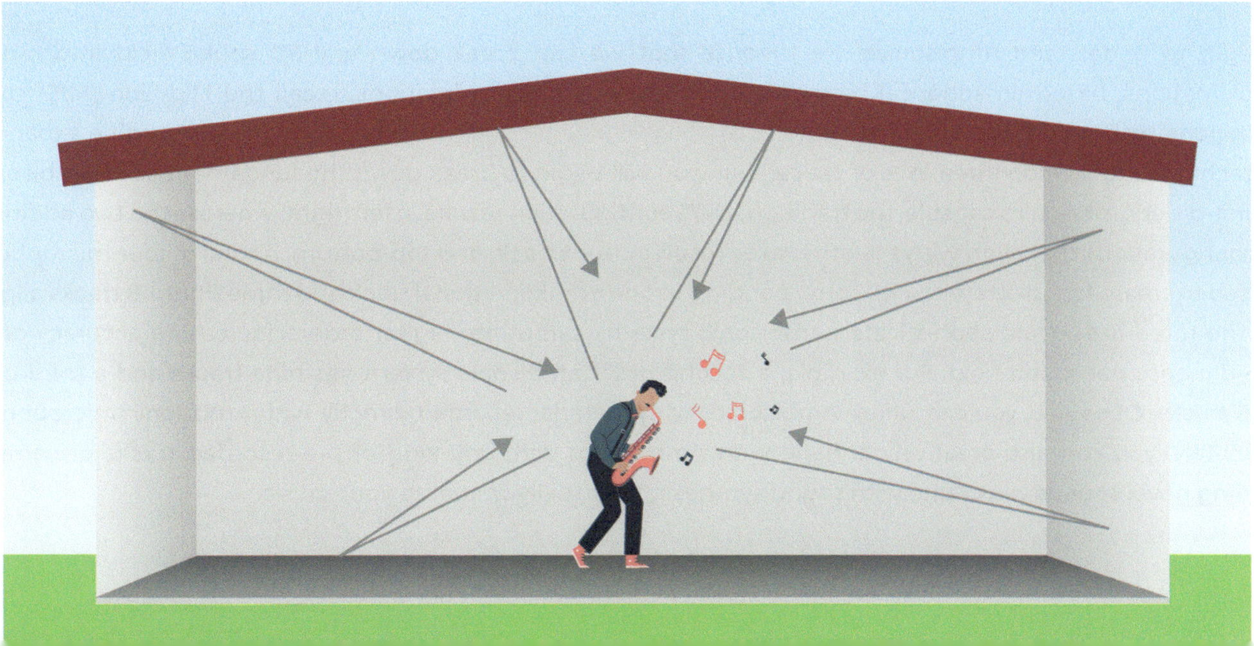

Spatialization systems

A spatialization system allows a user to virtually move a sound source through space.

There are many spatialization systems with varying degrees of complexity. The more realistic spatialization systems consider all the parameters described in the previous paragraphs: ITD, ILD, HRTF, and environment. With all of these parameters, the tradeoff is that for more accurate spatialization, there will be more calculations that the computer has to make.

There are both **hardware** spatialization systems, with external machines dedicated to spatializing audio, and **software** solutions, using computer software that does the calculations that result in spatialization. Due to the high cost and the powerful computers that we have today that can easily achieve spatialization with standalone software or DAW ***plugins***, dedicated hardware is much less common today.

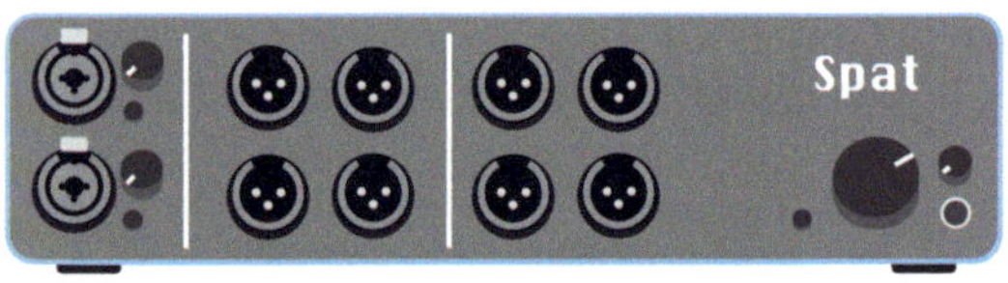

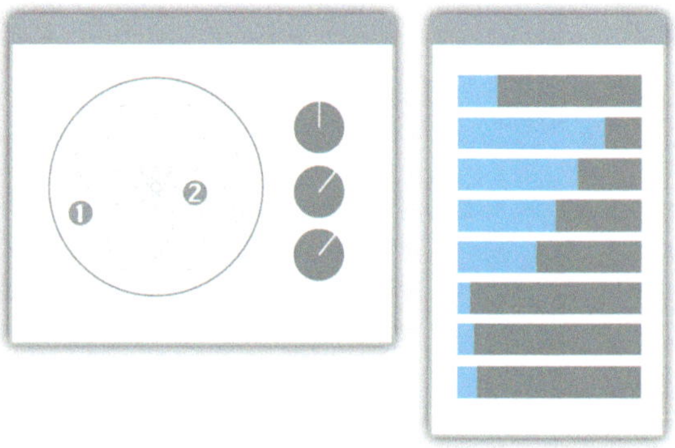

Ambisonics

A very interesting technology for virtual three-dimensional recording and spatialization is **Ambisonics**. This technology, based on spherical harmonics, originated in the 1970s and initially had little success due to the lack of widespread use of multi-channel playback systems, such as quadraphonic sound. In recent years, growing interest in this technology has been rekindled due to its increasing use in 360° Video, video games, virtual/augmented/mixed reality, and more recently, spatialized music.

To begin to understand Ambisonics, we theorize that we can break down any 3D sound field into n-order approximations, based on spherical harmonics. For first order approximations, recall the Mid-Side (M/S) stereo microphone techniques we discussed in the section on M/S techniques, page 64. Now, if you imagine expanding that technique to include three axes of space, then you will begin to break down the fundamentals of Ambisonics. In a first-order Ambisonics capsule, the traditional M/S configuration results in left-right, whereas the two additional M/S configurations that align with the other axes result in front-back, and top-bottom. A total of four microphones are used to create four discrete tracks, corresponding to one omnidirectional track and three figure-8 tracks aligned with the three axes. More sophisticated Ambisonic systems can utilize higher orders, increasing accuracy of the three-dimensional sound field. For example, a second order ambisonic system has nine tracks and a third order has 16 tracks. Of course, you can utilize Ambisonics with material recorded directly with Ambisonic microphones. Fortunately, you can also creatively engage with Ambisonics with any kind of pre-recorded tracks or samples, including novel sounds you create with sound synthesis, to virtually spatialize your music.

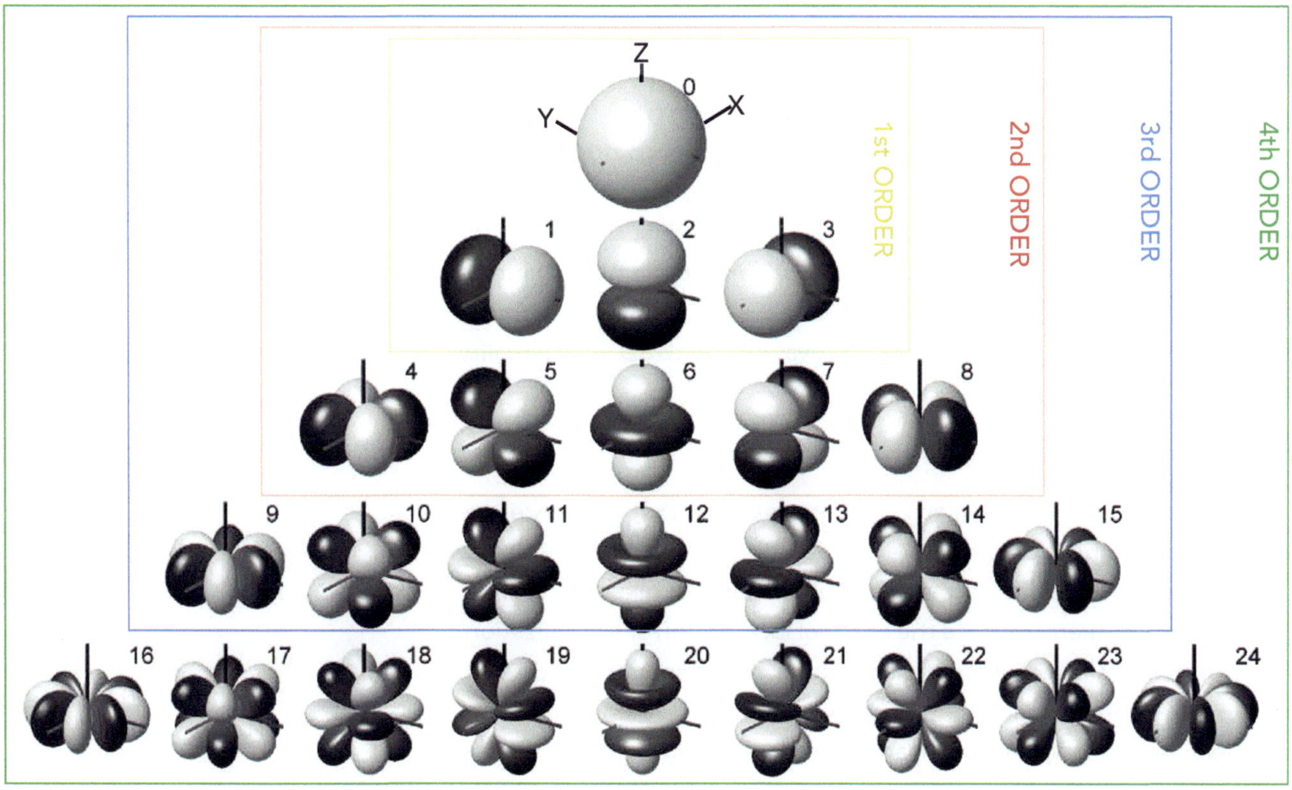

Let us consider the first order Ambisonics format again. The raw recording of the four microphones is called the **A-Format**. These raw tracks are pass through an **Ambisonics Encoder** and transformed into **B-Format**.

In the B-Format, there are four tracks: **W** (the omnidirectional one in the center), **X** (the figure-8 pattern that picks up front-back), **Y** (the figure-8 pattern for right-left), and **Z** (the figure-8 pattern for top-bottom). There are two main standard formats for B-Format: ***AmbiX*** and ***Fuma***. These two formats are similar but differ in the channel ordering. When doing the encoding, it is important to decide which of the two to use based on the playback decoder. This Ambisonics decoder is needed at the playback stage, where the magic happens. This B-Format is **adapted by our playback system** to different outputs. We can experience this 3D audio binaurally with headphones or within a space with multichannel speaker systems (quadraphonic or beyond). One of the great advantages of Ambisonics is that through "simple" decoding, the output audio can be adapted to many different scenarios.

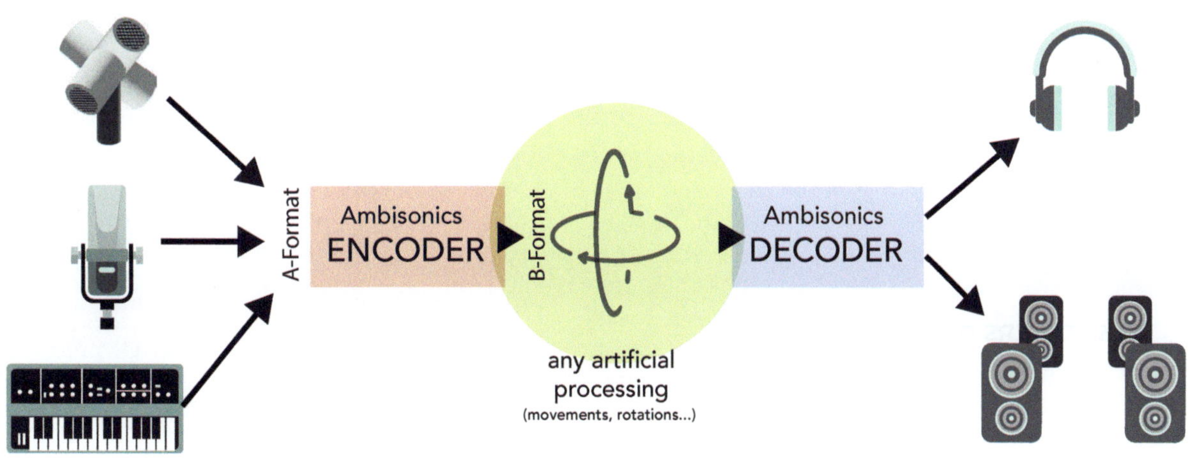

Spatialization playback systems

Binaural spatialization

When we spatialize sound directly with headphones into our ears, also known as binaural spatialization, we essentially trick our auditory system by making use of the perceptual parameters we have just seen: ILD, ITD, HRTF, and reverberation (the environment). With only two channels of audio, we can create the illusion that the audio represents three-dimensional space. This method is used prevalently with 3D virtual reality systems, and especially in gaming.

Spatialization through groups of speakers

In a studio or concert (except silent shows because, in that case, listeners are provided with headphones), it is possible to surround the audience with several speakers to achieve audio spatialization. While technically it only takes two speakers to create the effect of localization or spatialization, using four speakers (quad) or more will create more rich spatial sound fields. If you arrange speakers all in one plane, you can achieve one horizontal sound field. However, when you arrange speakers along multiple heights or orders, you can not only explore the vertical plane in sound, but you can also emphasize the perception of vertical shifts of sounds.

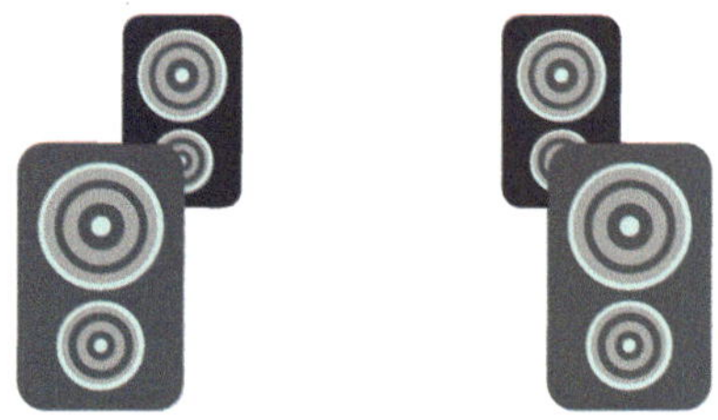

4 SPEAKERS

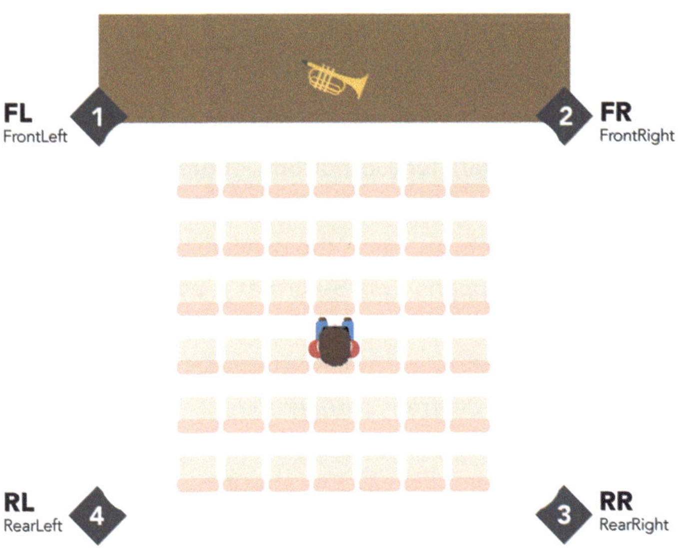

8 SPEAKERS

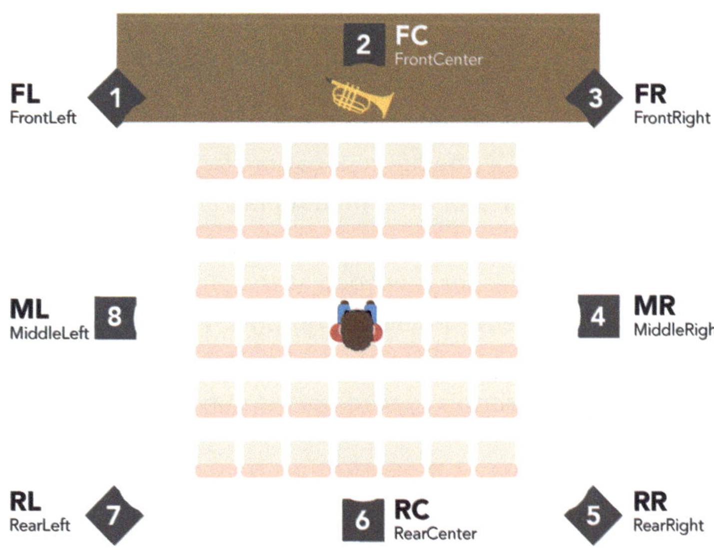

12 SPEAKERS ON 3 ORDERS

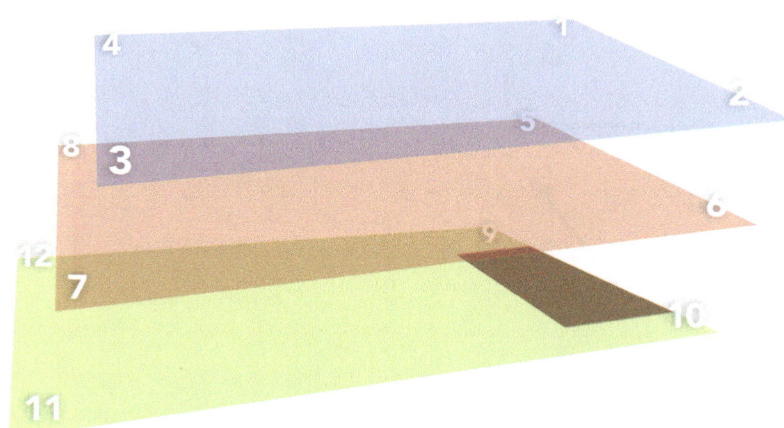

Low frequencies We need a separate discussion for the topic of low frequency spatialization. This is still an active area of current audio research. The limitation of spatializing low frequencies is that it is difficult for humans to localize low (20-100 Hz) frequencies. Because of this, it is usually sufficient to use a single speaker called a subwoofer that can be placed anywhere in the room. In some rooms and situations, multiple subwoofers can be used; however, we generally do not need as many subwoofers as mid-range speakers in a space.

Spatialization control

There are two main ways to control spatialization:

Non-Real time

You produce your work ahead of time in a DAW by creating separate tracks for each speaker or using a spatialization plugin that manages the various output channels. During concert performances, a multichannel playback device then distributes the audio to their respective speakers. This track player can be either a standalone hardware device or incorporated into computer software. This technique of pre-processing your spatialized audio is used to make electroacoustic tracks for concerts.

Real time

Real time spatialization gives the creator and performer the opportunity to move sounds through space virtually in the present moment. This technique makes use of a mixer or more sophisticated control surfaces such as multi-touch surfaces (tablets, smartphones), joysticks, or even sensors. With the computational power afforded to us by modern computing, the spatialization software can be relatively easily processed by the spatialization instructions given by the creator.

IRCAM spat ~ lemur app ~ live spatialization ~ 3D sound ~ anaglyph free vst ~ Gestural Control of Spatialization ~ binaural spat ~ spatial mixing

Panning

Panning is the angular placement of a sound in the stereo space of a playback system. Panning is achieved by controlling the ratio of amplitudes that a sound is sent to each speaker in a stereo system. If all the sound is being sent to the left speaker, the sound will appear to come from the far left of the playback system. If 2/3 of the sound comes from the right speaker, and 1/3 of the sound comes from the left speaker, then the sound will appear to come from somewhere mid-right. This is essentially a basic spatialization technique, limited to two speakers. By controlling the ratio of amplitudes, it essentially exploits only one of our perceptual parameters of sound localization: the ILD. It is adjusted by a potentiometer (a pan pot) found on all mixers, or with a virtual knob in DAWs.

There are two main algorithms for panning:

Linear

This is the most simple mathematical way to achieve panning, even if it does not necessarily realistically match our auditory apparatus. This is most noticed when I pan a sound source to the center, where 50% of the amplitude is sent to the left speaker, and 50% of the amplitude is sent to the right speaker. We will experience the "hole in the middle" effect, where there is a general lowering of volume. This is related to our perception of amplitude (see section about amplitude, page 30).

To achieve linear panning, we rescale the sound by multiplying it by values, corresponding to the potentiometer position, ranging from 0 to 1 on one speaker and the inverse (1 to 0) on the other.

For example, if I multiply the sound coming out of the left speaker by 0, I have to multiply the sound coming out of the right speaker by 1, to simulate a sound localized to the right.

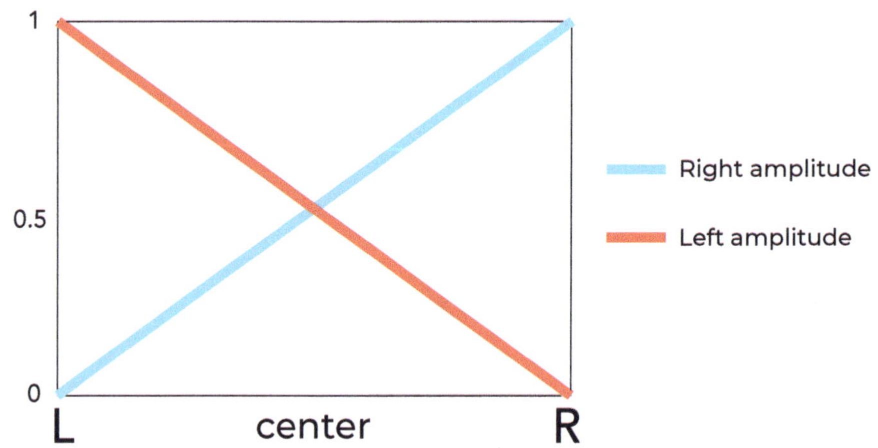

Constant Power Pan

This is an alternate panning algorithm that allows you to localize the sound to match our perceptions better. Instead of a linear relationship of position and amplitude, this technique follows a logarithmic curve instead. The most important effect of this is that I will not perceive having amplitude losses when I center my sound.

To implement this method, instead of using the 0 to 1 scale from before, I will simply take the square root of those same values as my new multiplication factor. This new method, based on the square root, causes the amplitudes to follow a logarithmic rather than a linear pattern with respect to panning position.

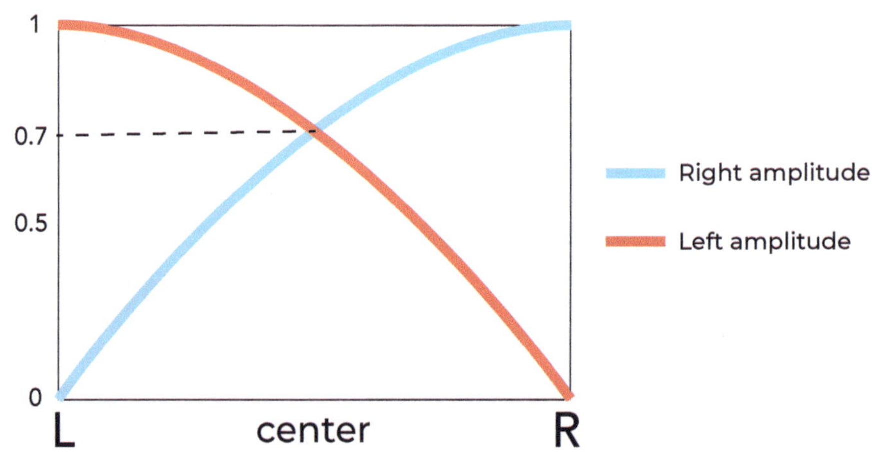

.using your favorite programming language, create a system that allows you to experiment with the two panning modes we have just covered. Evaluate and experience with your ears the differences between them

.create a 4-measure percussion loop. Pan each sound in this loop using extreme Left-Right panning. With an AI chatbot, generate a harmonic sequence and orchestrate these suggested chords with a virtual instrument of your choice with fixed center panning. ***Theme: "Romantic particle accelerator"***

Space as a compositional-performative parameter

Space can be used as a truly creative **compositional parameter**. For example, the composer can choose not only the position of the instruments in the composition, but also go further and assign unique spatial positions to the different notes of a single instrument, shaping the piece's evolution over time.

One of the most important decisions a producer makes is how to utilize panning to distribute the various instruments in a stereo space. This way, the listener will hear the track approximately as if they were in the room where the musicians were playing.

In the illustration, you can see a very typical or classic positioning of instruments in a mix of a Pop, Rock, or Jazz song. The vocals, bass, and kick drum are in the center, the guitars are slightly shifted to the sides, and any coloring sounds (non-structural sounds that act as rhythmic or timbral filler) are more decidedly panned to the left or right. It is possible to intervene creatively with this scheme, changing something or even radically upsetting it to suit artistic needs. All of this is made possible by the fact that, in this type of music, the instruments are generally recorded on separate tracks, allowing you to precisely manage each instrument's position, volume, and effects.

Even with classical music, we still must place the various instruments within a stereo field. Particularly with this style of music, we usually tend to preserve the physical arrangement of the musicians without seeking unusual or creative positions. Often we can obtain this by recording an orchestra with only two microphones (see section on stereo recording techniques, page 62). Therefore, unlike with the music discussed in the previous paragraph, it is not easy to alter the stereo placement of instruments in post-production for classical music.

Remember that spatialization, whether it involves simple stereo panning or a more complex spatialization system, is a compositional and production parameter. Spatialization requires a set of intentional artistic choices that the composer makes alongside the writing of notes, dynamics, rhythm, or timbre. These choices result in positions of sounds that can be static as well as dynamic. With the dynamic approach, I may choose to move the sound of a trombone so that it revolves around the listeners in certain sections or have the sound of a violin move closer to or further away from the listener in the coda of my piece.

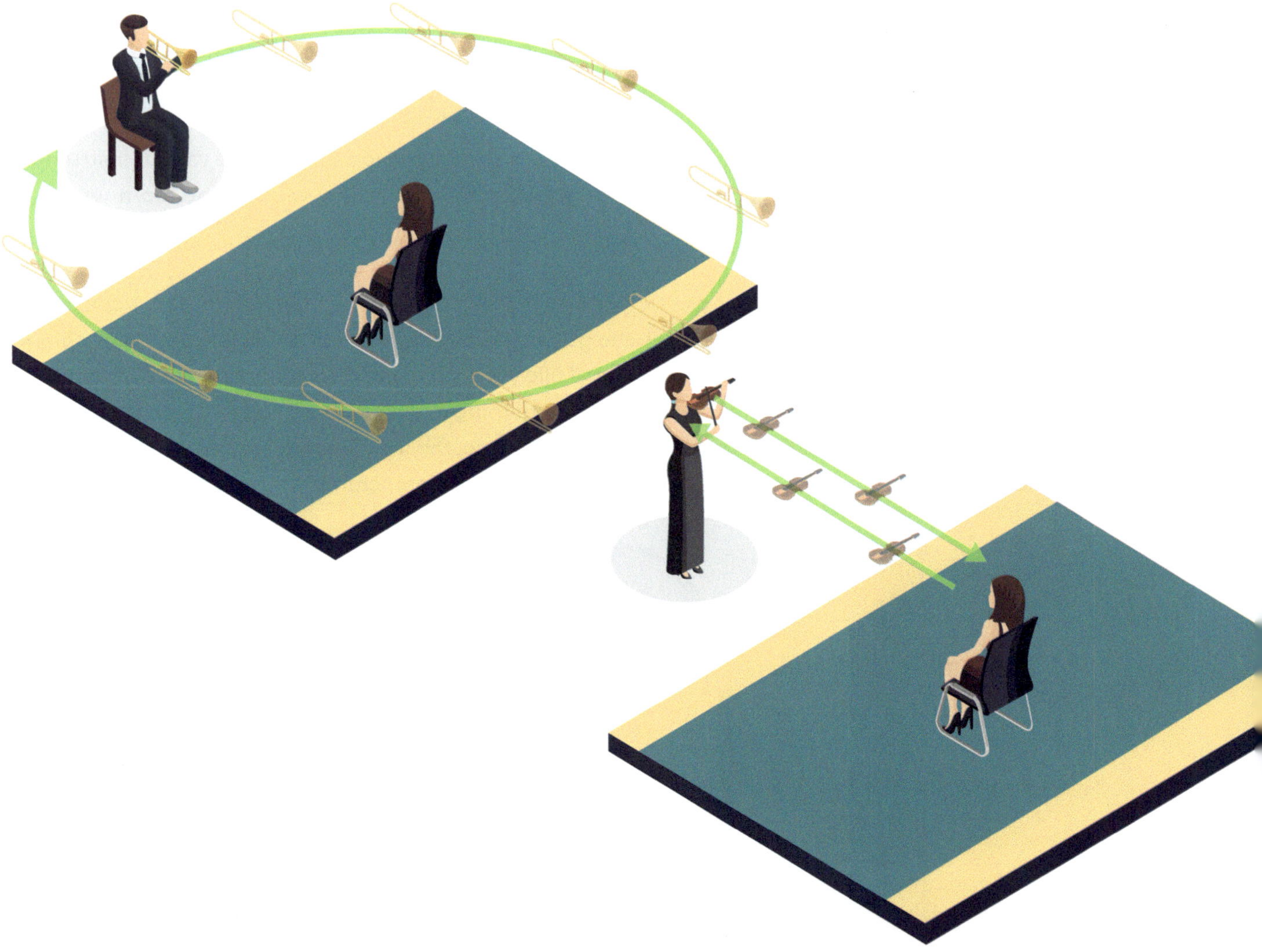

.record or download the sound of a bouncing ping pong ball and the birdsong of five different species of birds. Build an immersive soundscape in which sounds move around the listener. You can optionally also add other natural sounds of your choice

.record your voice reciting one of your favorite poems from literature and compose a piece for synthesizer and your speaking voice in which spatialization is the primary compositional parameter. Have each note of the synthesizer be placed at a different point in the spatial field

SOUND SYNTHE-SIS

INTRO-DUCTORY CONCEP-TS

Sound synthesis creates sounds from scratch, with a timbre of certain qualities based on the creative wishes of the musician. It is based on a series of sound synthesis techniques or algorithms. These techniques are driven by parameters that ultimately give the resulting sound its character and voice.

There are several dozen different techniques that are utilized in both software and hardware devices. Keyboard synthesizers, digital audio plugins, and a variety of other analog and digital devices are some examples of sound synthesizers.

Sound synthesis can take place in real time or non-real time applications. In the first case, the system plays the sound as it is generated, so there is no substantial delay in sound. For example, my keyboard synthesizer creates sounds in real time and acts like an acoustic musical instrument. In the case of non-real time synthesis, the system creates the sound, the sound is recorded or saved as a file, and later the recorded sound is played back.

Today, non-real time synthesis systems are less widely used because computers are very powerful and often allow us to work in real time. However, there are still some situations in which non-real time synthesis is required. For example, non-real time synthesis is commonly used with very complex algorithms and in text-based music programming software, where we program the step-by-step operations to be performed by the computer and then execute the program at some later time.

real time

non-real time

Filters

We have talked extensively about **Filters** in chapter page 105, so we return to them here only to highlight their important functions within synthesis algorithms. Many of these synthesis algorithms involve a stage of filtering because filters are simple and versatile devices that can help us refine or sculpt the sound to meet our sonic design goals.

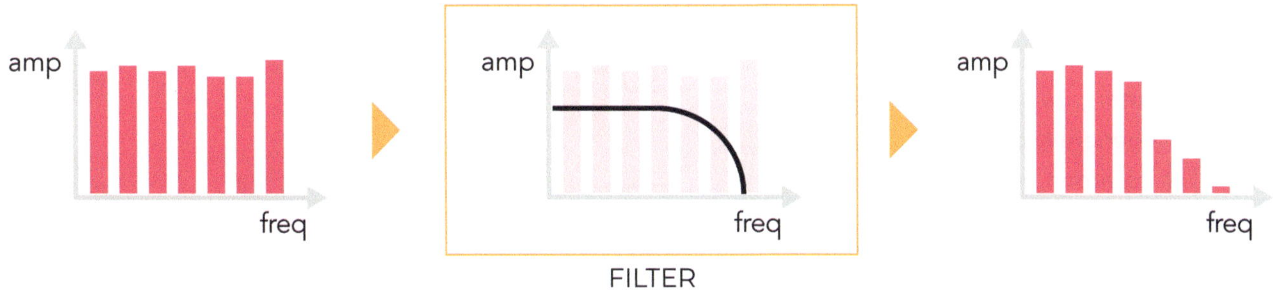

Envelopes

We have examined **Dynamic envelopes** previously in the section about timbre on page 37. As with filters, envelopes are worth discussing here because they directly affect the temporal aspect of our resultant timbre. The most common envelopes generated for sound synthesis follow the four-parameter ADSR model. Beyond just ADSR, there are synthesizers that use as few as three parameters to generate a dynamic envelope, while there are other envelopes that involve many more parameters, affording the designer many more complex amplitude changes.

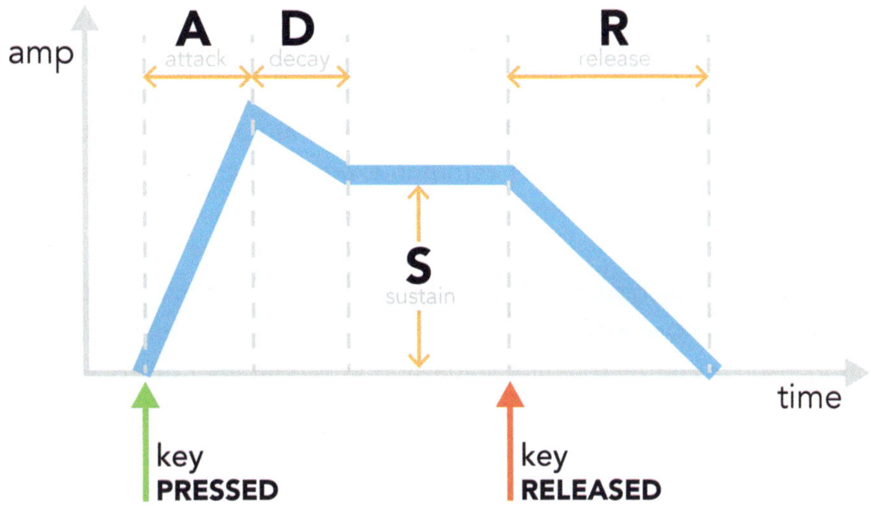

LFO

LFO (Low-Frequency Oscillator) is an oscillator that is not used to generate sound but to move certain parameters of the synthesis algorithm. Since the LFO output is not heard directly, the oscillation frequency can be lower than 20 Hz, the lowest perceivable frequency. Higher oscillation frequencies may end up being audible or they become modulating frequencies, leading to another types of synthesis, like frequency modulation for example. While LFOs are used in many other audio processes, they are important elements in synthesis techniques. A simple example of using an LFO in synthesis is to have the output of the LFO control, or drive, the volume of a sound. This is like a scenario where a "robot" cyclically raises and lowers the volume potentiometer of a sound, creating the effect known as tremolo.

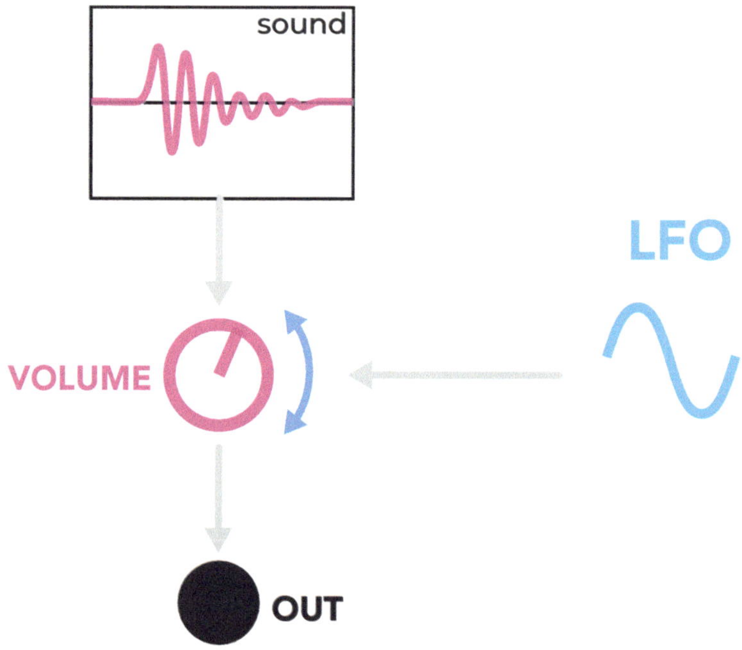

LFO are oscillators, as stated above, meaning that generally they can take the form of common wave shapes. Most typically, LFOs use one of five typical oscillator waveforms: sine, triangle, sawtooth, square waves, and random. The shape of these waves defines the path by which the LFO controls the changes of an external parameter. Sine, triangle, sawtooth, and square waves are periodic in nature and have a frequency associated with them. However, random, by definition, is not periodic as the shape of the waveform consists of random values.

CV (Control Voltage)

Control Voltage is the system by which the output voltage of analog synths are used to control various parameters of another synthesizer or algorithm that ultimately generates the sound. It is important to note that this control voltage is not an audio signal, but rather is a signal, or voltage, that is used as a control for something else. Change in this control voltage, as it flows into the control parameters a synthesizer, allows us to be intentional about the time-varying nature of our synthesizer controls. For example, when I press the middle C on my keyboard synthesizer, it sends out a precise electrical voltage that the synthesizer interprets as note C. It then tunes the oscillators to that precise frequency. The output of an LFO is another common example of a control voltage, where the oscillating voltage can control the volume of a sound, creating tremolo as we saw above.

In some synthesizers, particularly those in subtractive synthesis, there are distinct, yet standard, modules that take the names **VCO (Voltage Controlled Oscillator),** that is commonly used to control the pitch of the oscillators; **VCF (Voltage Controlled Filter),** used to control the filter stage; and **VCA (Voltage Control Amplitude)**, used to control a dynamic envelope such as ADSR). These names are also often found in software synthesizers, where there is no actual voltage control. While the "control voltage" for software solutions is virtual and does not involve actual voltage, these names are still used since they are so familiar and because of their "historical" origins.

Hardware or Software, Analog or Digital, Standalone, Modular or Semi-Modular

Sound synthesis techniques and algorithms can be implemented by **hardware** systems with dedicated physical machines, or **software** programs with code executed on a computer.

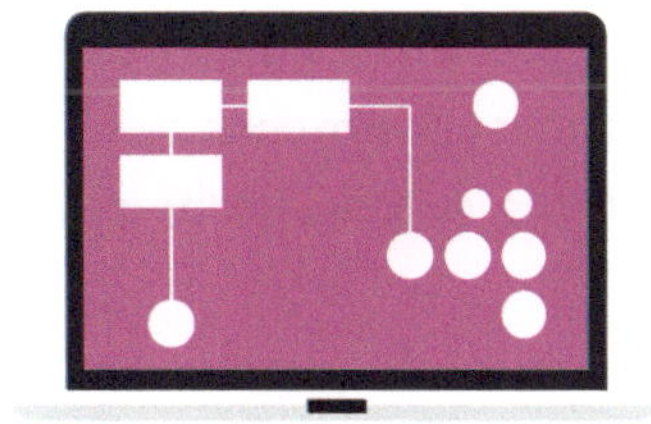

In the case of software, the synthesis will be **digital**. Of note, digital algorithms that simulate analog circuits are sometimes known as virtual analog synthesizers. In hardware synthesizers, we historically only found **analog** circuits. In modern hardware synths, we see a hybrid approach with both analog and digital circuitry inside. With these hybrid systems, the synthesis involves sampling and quantization, digital signal processing, and reconstruction of an analog wave form through a digital to analog conversion process.

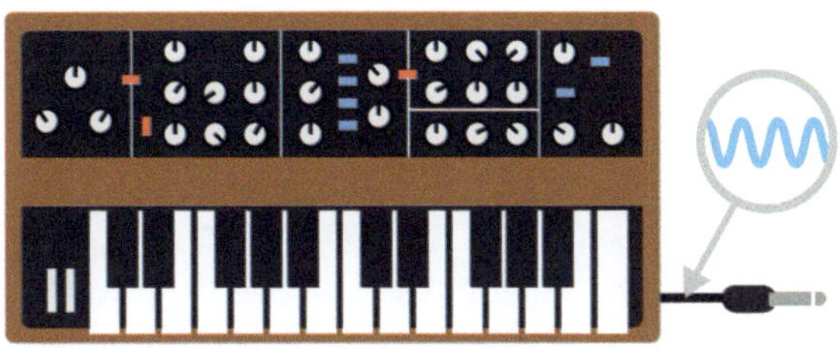

Another way to classify synthesizers is categorizing them as standalone, modular or semi-modular synthesizers. **Standalone** synthesizers have internal circuitry that cannot be changed, only allowing for the variation of parameters through potentiometers or other controls. The *Minimoog*, an analog synth, and the *Yamaha DX7*, a digital synth, are prime examples of integrated synthesizers.

Modular synthesizers, on the other hand, are made up of separate modules that can be connected as desired by the musician, thus creating many possibilities for configuration and sound. The connections are made through patch cords, and each configuration is called a patch. Modular synths are often hardware devices, such as in the case of *Eurorack* synths; however, they can also be software devices, like with the *VCV Rack*, a *Eurorack* simulator.

Semi-modular synthesizers combine aspects of standalone and modular synthesizers together into one unit. Semi-modular synthesizers have the ability to create sounds entirely on their own; however, they also have a patch bay, allowing users to send to and receive signal from external devices, such as sequencers, signal generators, and other processors. These semi-modular synthesizers are essentially standalone synthesizers that give us the freedom to combine aspects of modular synthesizers.

standalone

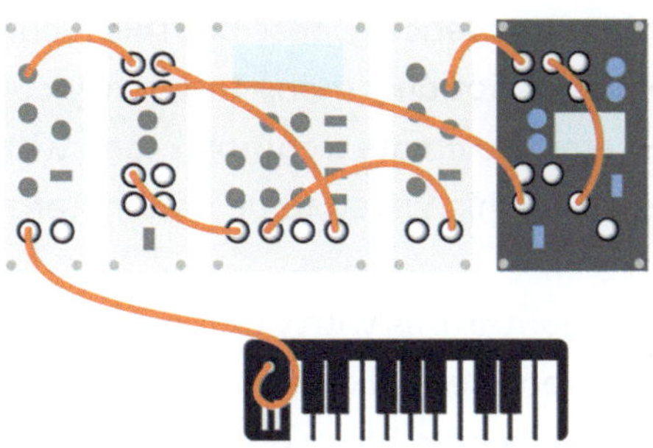

modular

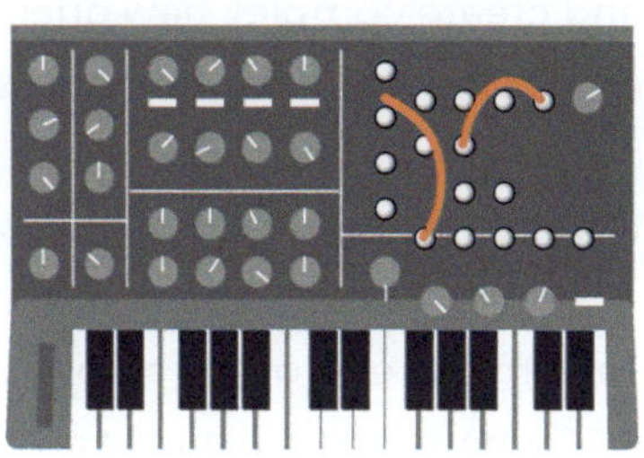

semi-modular

Linear and Nonlinear synthesis algorithms

Synthesis algorithms with **Linear Techniques** are based on adding and subtracting processes. Consequently, the degree of the algorithm's complexity is directly linked to the spectral complexity of the sound produced.

For example, if I superimpose five sine waves in classical additive synthesis (as we will see below), I will get a sound with five components; if I superimpose ten sine waves, I will get a sound with ten harmonics or partials. Types of linear synthesis algorithms include **additive**, **subtractive**, and **granular** synthesis.

Distortion of one signal by another signal often results in the category of **Nonlinear Synthesis Techniques**. They are nonlinear because the sonic result does not vary in proportion to the signals' complexity but rather, the complexity of the sonic result follows relationships of another nature. For example, if more than one modulator is added in FM, the number of components does not vary proportionally, but rather, it increases exponentially. Thus, while nonlinear synthesis techniques may be more difficult conceptually, we can generate signals with many harmonic or inharmonic components from just a few initial elements.

The category of nonlinear synthesis includes **AM** (Amplitude Modulation), **RM** (Ring Modulation), **FM** (Frequency Modulation), and **waveshaping**.

LINEAR	NONLINEAR
additive	RM
subtractive	AM
granular	FM
	waveshaping

ADDITIVE SYNTHESIS

A linear sound synthesis technique, **additive synthesis** operates on the summation of properly tuned sine waves. Each sine wave adds a spectral component to the sound; thus, the more sine waves there are, the more complex the overall sound will be. Additive synthesis can be thought of like a sculptor creating a statue using *Lego* bricks. The bricks here are the building blocks, like the sine waves in additive synthesis. The final sculpture is made up of many bricks, just as a final complex sound is made up of many sine waves

As we know from our discussion previously on timbre, every sound can be thought of being composed of an appropriate combination of pure waves (sine waves) with specific pitches, amplitudes, and phases. The frequency ratio between the various pure sine components allows us to obtain harmonic or inharmonic timbres, with infinite nuances between these two extremes. Potentially, with additive synthesis, it is possible to reconstruct any timbre and create complex new ones. While this is theoretically possible, this technique, in reality, is very computationally expensive. Complex timbres usually consist of not only many frequency components, but many components that also change continuously over time. Therefore, to create a complex tone with additive synthesis, we need individual temporal control over all the harmonics, all of which need to be parameterized individually as a function of time.

Toward the end of the additive synthesis algorithm, as with other sound synthesis techniques, we utilize a dynamic ADSR envelope which, thanks to its four parameters, allows us to create percussive, soft, long, or short sounds. The ADSR envelope is usually activated by turning a note on, or by pressing a key on a musical keyboard.

Additive synthesis is a simple, yet precise synthesis technique, which is excellent for reinforcing timbre theory. At the same time, its use is somewhat limited because it allows the creation of only simple timbres due to the computational demands of using many oscillators.

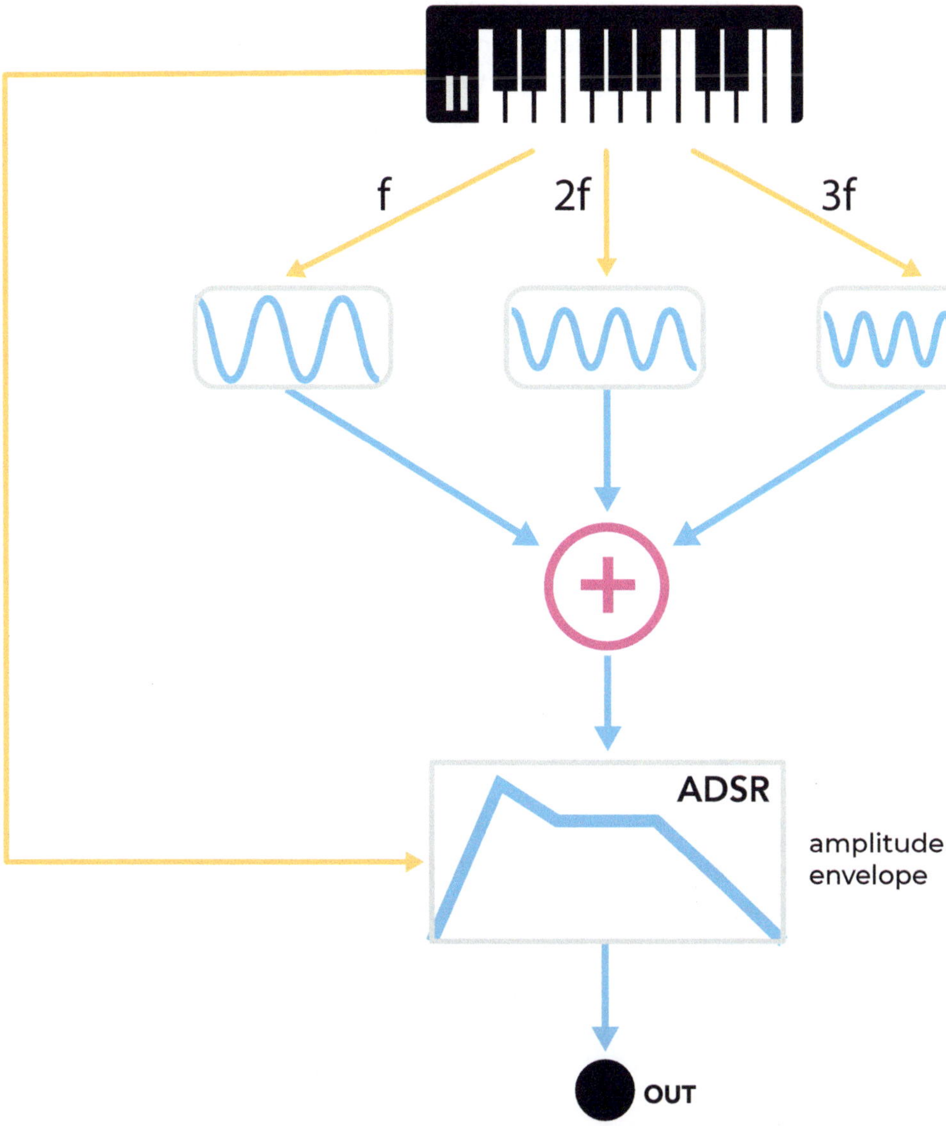

.generate eight sine waves: four with integer multiple frequencies of 100 Hz (i.e., 100 x 2, 100 x 3...) and four with non-integer multiple frequencies of 100 Hz (i.e., 100 x 2.3, 100 x 3.1...). Create a song in which the sine waves you generate undergo long crescendos and diminuendos of amplitude, overlapping each other, adding up on top of each other, and then disappearing. Duration two minutes. ***Theme: "Calm sea, moderate wind"***

.using your favorite programming language, create a five-part additive synthesizer with control over the volume and the harmonic ratio of each partial. Add a timing system that makes random, gradual changes in the harmonic ratios. Your system should arpeggiate the notes that make up a Gmaj7add9 chord

WDR Electronic Music Studio ~ Karlheinz Stockhausen Studie II ~ Additive synthesis max/msp ~ Additive synthesis Pure Data

SUBTRACTIVE SYNTHESIS

Subtractive synthesis, another type of linear synthesis, is one of the most widely used synthesis techniques today because of its simplicity in understanding and implementation, in both analog and digital domains. Subtractive synthesis is based on simplifying a complex timbre through filters. We take a complex sound with many frequency components, and then selectively use filters to shape the frequency of our resultant sound. If additive synthesis is when a sculptor creates works by building up brick-by-brick, then subtractive synthesis is when a sculptor who, starting from a block of marble, chisels away pieces of material to obtain a definite shape that will contain less material than the starting block.

The components that make up subtractive synthesis are present in almost all software or hardware synthesizers, regardless of the synthesis algorithm used. Most notably, **filters** are employed to shape, carve out, and create the final sound from our initial complex sound.

Subtractive synthesis consists of three stages:

VCO, the voltage-controlled oscillator, is a circuit that outputs an analog signal representing a sound wave at a frequency that is controlled by an input voltage. The piano keys on synthesizers trigger VCOs, with each key typically being able to trigger up to three VCOs, each tuned to a particular frequency. While VCOs can output sine waves, usually there are options to also output more complex waves such as sawtooth waves , triangle waves, square waves, and even noise. The one to three oscillators, per key, add up to create a rich complex wave.

VCF, the voltage-controlled filter, is a circuit that shapes a filter that alters the frequency content of a signal, based on some input voltage. In subtractive synthesis, the VCF takes this newly minted complex wave (from the VCOs) and selectively carves out frequency components through the VCF. If the popular ***low-pass*** filter is utilized by the VCF, then the higher overtones of the complex sound will be attenuated and thus create a carved-out version of the original rich signal.

VCA, the voltage-controlled amplifier, is an amplifier that acts upon a signal based on an input voltage. This is the last stage of the subtractive synthesis algorithm and is used primarily to implement the dynamic ADSR envelope to our newly created spectrum. This amplitude envelope makes our sound have temporal character. For example, we can achieve sounds resembling percussion, pads (sounds with a gentle attack and a simpler spectral timbre for longer sustained chords), or a lead sound (a sour and edgy sound, suitable for melodies).

Subtractive synthesis often includes an **ADSR envelope** that controls the filter cutoff frequency. Practically, the filter cutoff frequency follows the trajectory of an ADSR curve, varying the cutoff frequency in time as the note is being played. For example, the filter widely opens in the attack portion and gradually closes again in the decay and release portions. The same ADSR can control the filter and the amplitude envelope or be independent of each other. Clearly, in the second case, we have more timbral possibilities.

Finally, as with most other synthesizers, we can also incorporate an LFO into the subtractive synthesizer. The LFO in this case can modulate parameters such as pitch (to achieve a vibrato) or output volume (to create a tremolo). In general, the LFO provides an oscillating output voltage that is then input as a control voltage into the VCO, VCF, or VCA.

Commercially, subtractive synthesizers are widespread in both software and standalone instruments. Certainly, the best-known and historically pioneering subtractive synthesizer is the ***Minimoog Model D***, released in 1971. It is still a widely used and emulated instrument, heard in many musical genres ranging from pop to jazz to EDM (Electronic Dance Music).

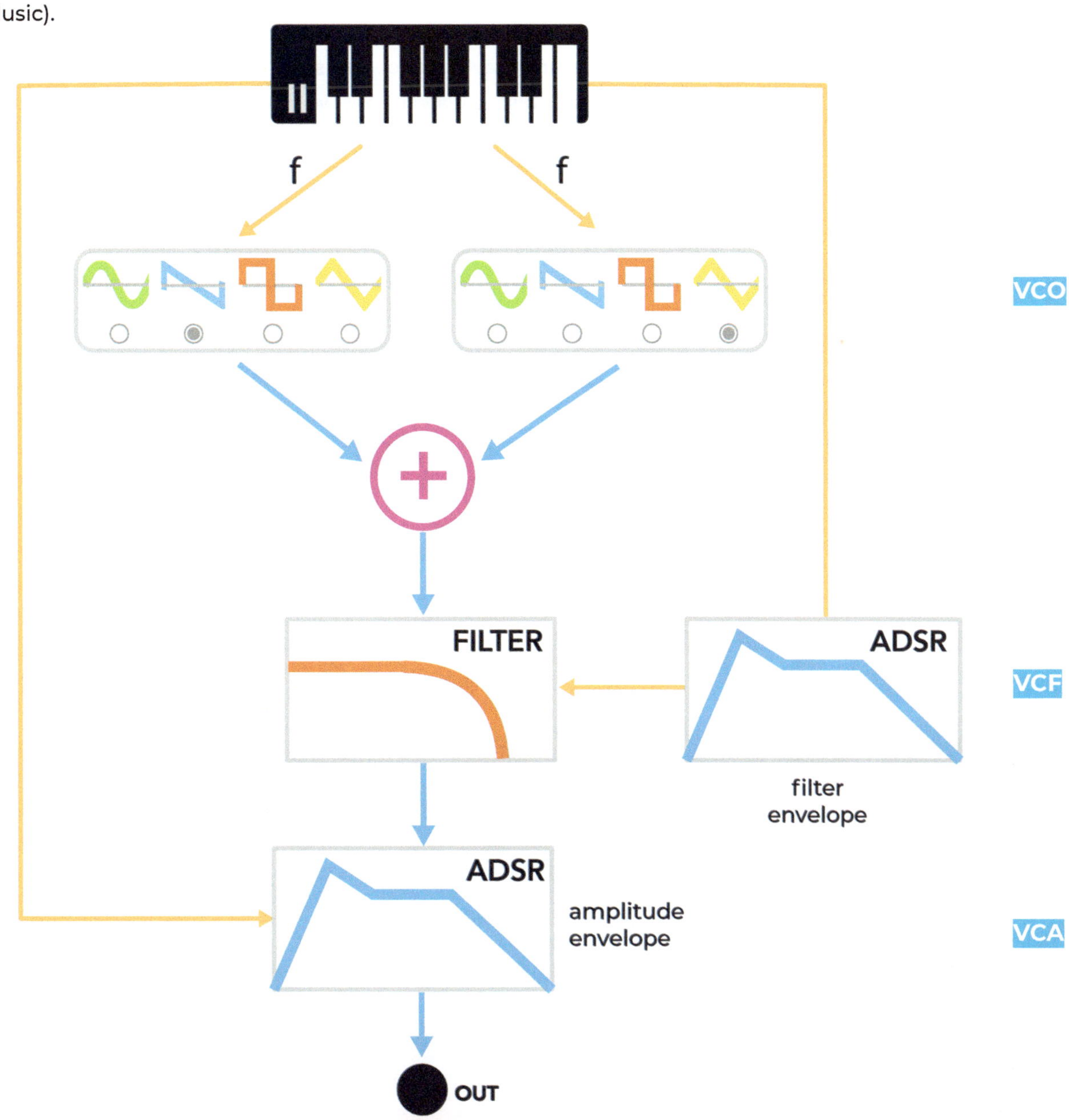

.write down the notes of the bass part of a song of your choice. Play them with a subtractive synthesizer, radically change the rhythm, and try to use only long notes (e.g., half notes at 80 BPM). Apply an LFO to the cutoff of the filter. Play the LFO by changing the frequency in real time. Create a song in which each repetition of the bass round has a different rhythmic character given by the frequency of oscillations of the LFO itself. ***Theme: "In the cave"***

.using your favorite programming language, create a subtractive synthesizer and have it arpeggiate the loop of the song "***On the Run***" by ***Pink Floyd***

Minimoog ~ Minimoog songs ~ Lokomotiv vst ~ Subtractive synthesis Pure Data

AM-RM SYNTHESIS

AM (Amplitude Modulation) and **RM (Ring Modulation)** belong to the category of amplitude modulation synthesis. For both AM and RM synthesis, the **modulator** is a sine wave that controls the amplitude of the **carrier**, which is another sound wave. If the frequency of the modulating sine wave is low, we have a simple tremolo (the oscillation of the volume of a sound), but if the modulating sine wave exceeds 15 Hz, a rich new timbre emerges.

In the algorithm, the only difference between AM and RM lies in the amplitude range of the modulating sine wave. For AM, the modulator is a unipolar wave, which means that the modulating wave's amplitude values oscillate between 0 and 1. For RM, the modulator is a bipolar wave, where the modulating wave's amplitude values range between -1 and 1.

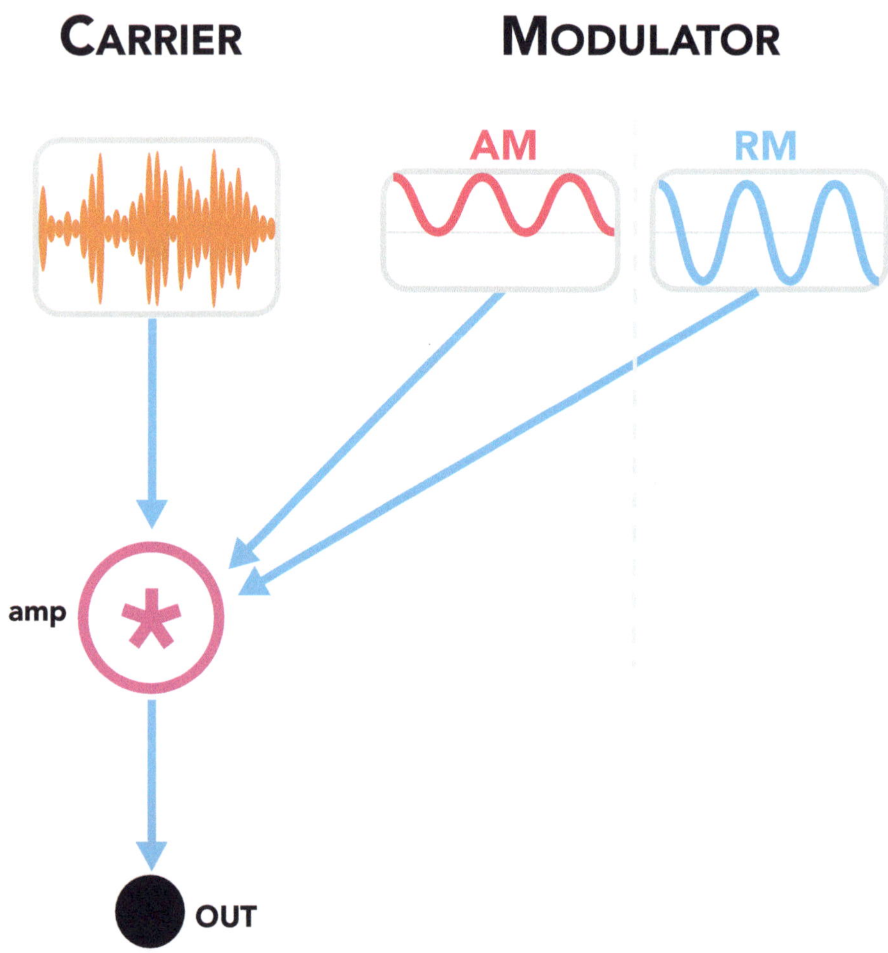

The new timbre creates two side frequency bands or components. One new frequency component is the carrier frequency plus the modulator frequency, and the other new frequency component is the carrier frequency minus the modulator frequency. In AM, the original carrier frequency is retained, while in RM, only the two new sidebands remain. Note that the sidebands are added to each incoming partial. Thus, for both simple and complex timbres, the number of frequency components doubles or triples. In addition, the total amplitude of all the frequency components always remains equal to the amplitude of the original carrier; this means that the energy of the original components of the carrier is distributed over the new spectral components.

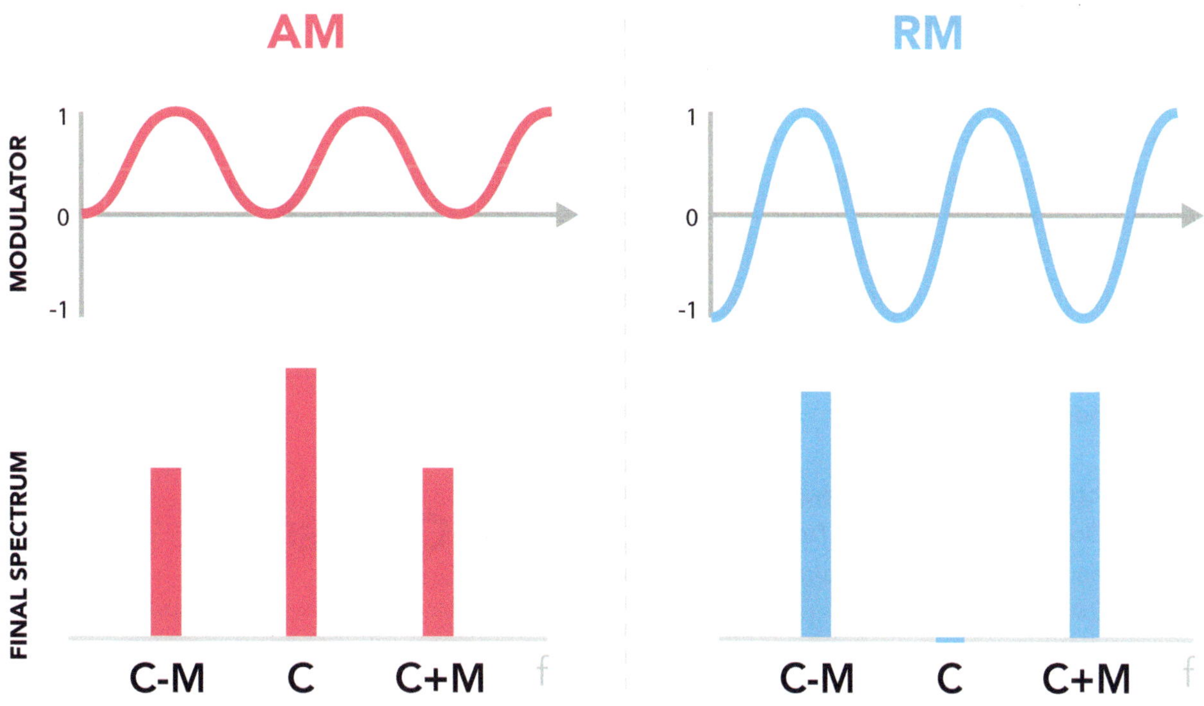

In AM and RM, the sidebands are formed at the frequencies given by the sum and difference between the carrier frequency and modulator frequency. So if, for example, I have a carrier at 1000 Hz and a modulator at 100 Hz, I will get sidebands at 900 and 1100 Hz. The only difference between the two, as we said, is that in RM, the carrier frequency is lost, while in AM, the carrier frequency component remains in the final timbre.

AM and RM synthesis are more commonly used to modify existing timbres than to generate tones from scratch. For example, they can easily enrich percussion or create robotic voices suitable for a science fiction film.

.create an arpeggio of the notes found in the Dm7 chord played by a sine wave in the rhythm of eighth notes at a speed of 90 BPM. Loop duration: four bars. Apply an AM synthesis to this arpeggio with a modulating frequency varying between 100 to 2000 Hz throughout four bars

.create a rock drum loop in 4/4 and apply RM synthesis to the snare drum. Vary the frequency of the modulator so that you get four variations for every two bars of the loop

.using your favorite programming language, reconstruct the first 30 seconds of Stockhausen's ***Studie II***

WDR Electronic Music Studio ~ Karlheinz Stockhausen Mixtur ~ paranoid android guitar solo ~ Forbidden planet Main Titles ~ Gesang Der Junglinge · Karlheinz Stockhausen

FM SYNTHESIS

The **Frequency Modulation**, or **FM**, algorithm was one of the first synthesis processes made possible by digital audio, and it was also one of the most commercially successful types of synthesis. Although the concept was theorized earlier, analog systems were not suitable for its implementation, or at least the potential analog circuit devices could not necessarily output perfectly harmonic and easily manageable sounds.

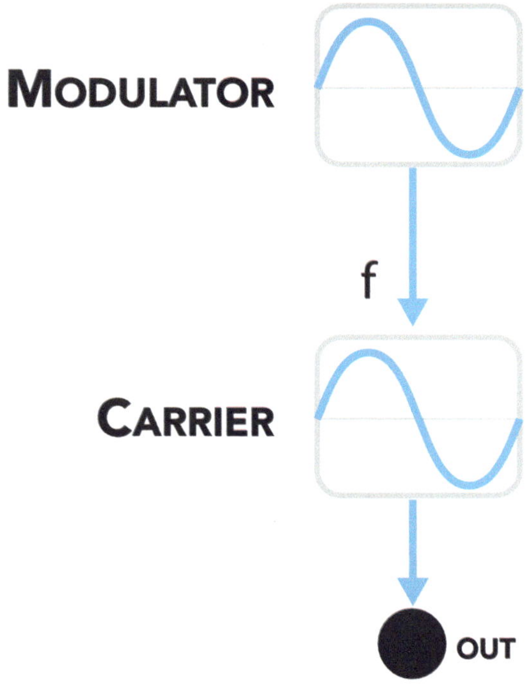

As for its practical application in music, we owe everything to John Chowning, who from 1973, put into practice many of the classic FM algorithms that we still use today. Yamaha eventually purchased his algorithms and built one of the most famous and revolutionary synthesizers: the ***DX-7*** (1983).

Frequency Modulation synthesis is based on an oscillator wave, called a ***Modulator***, that varies the frequency of another oscillator called the ***Carrier***. This process is nonlinear because it can create a complex spectrum with many frequencies, all while using just a few elements.

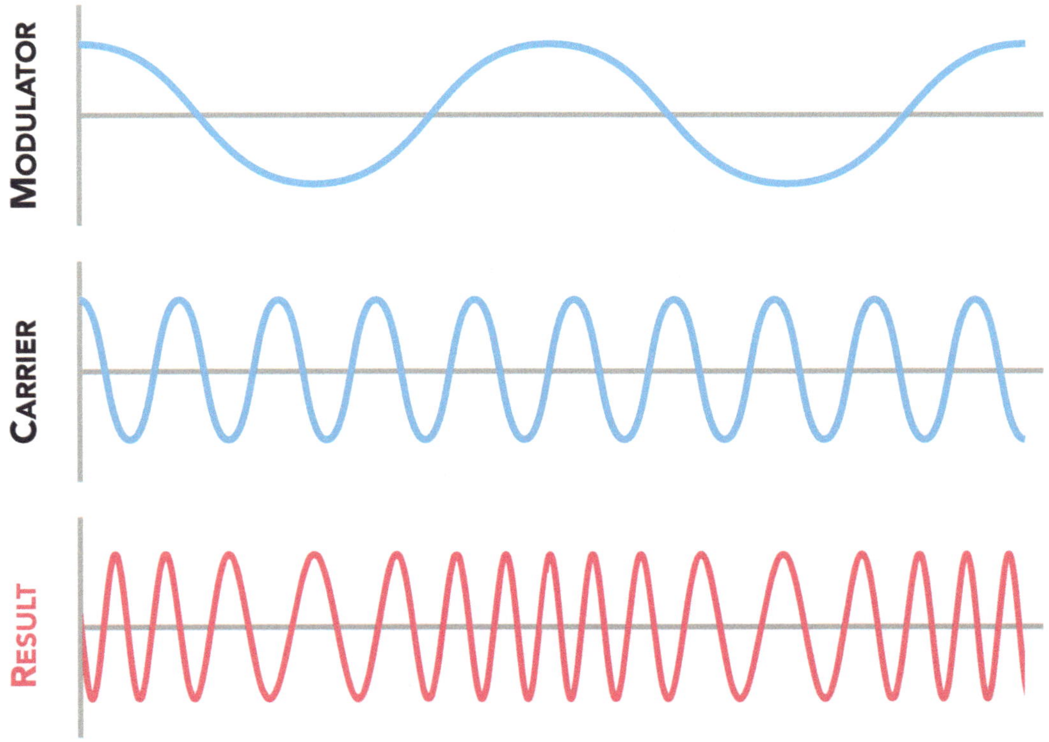

The result of FM synthesis is a timbre with a series of sidebands centered around the carrier frequency. If C and M are the carrier and modulator frequencies, the sideband frequencies are C+M, C+2M, C+3M, ... and C-M, C-2M, C-3M, etc.

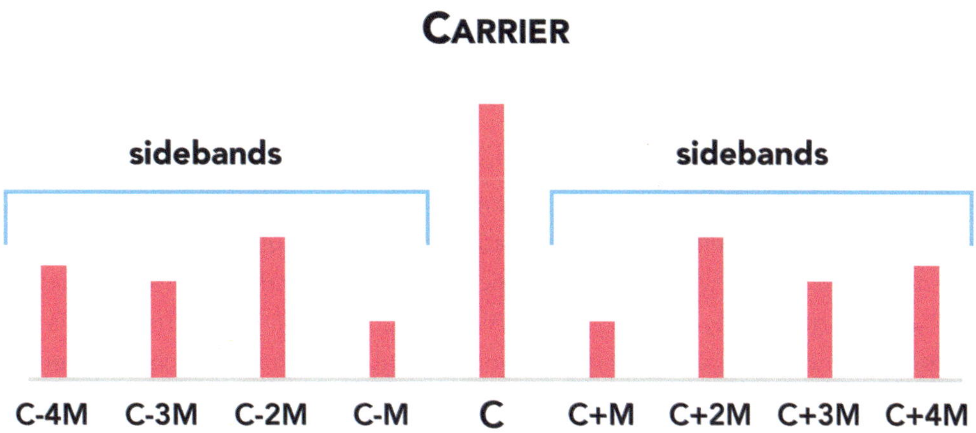

Therefore, the resultant frequency of the sidebands depends on the ratio between carrier and modulator, or the **C:M ratio**. The FM generates a harmonic spectrum when the C:M ratio can be reduced to an integer (e.g., 4:1).

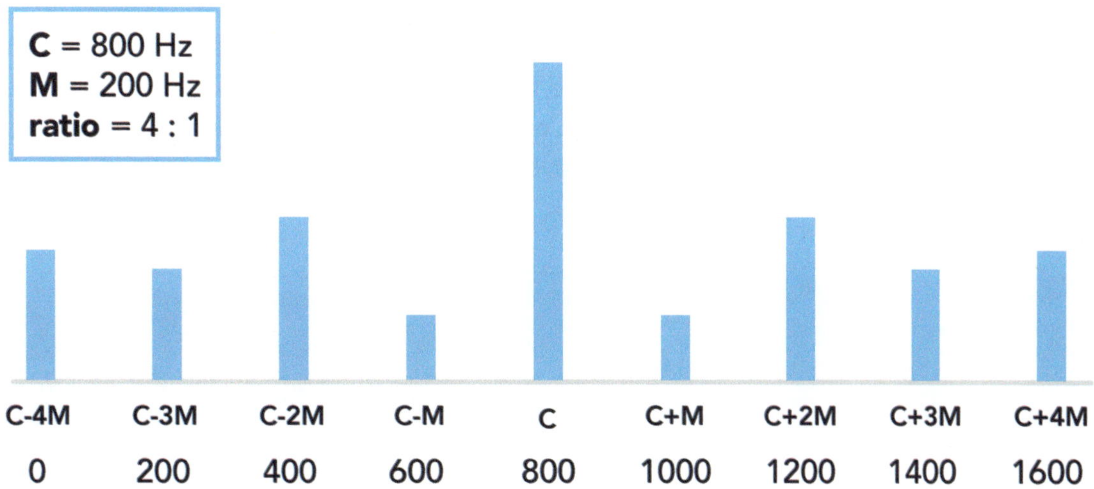

If the C:M ratio, on the other hand, is not an integer (e.g., 8:2.1), the resultant sound has an inharmonic spectrum. Note that when a sideband is calculated to have a negative frequency, it is "reflected" to the corresponding positive frequency value, creating a sideband with its polarity reversed. For example, -40 Hz becomes 40 Hz inverted in polarity. Similarly, a band is reflected with a polarity flip if it goes above the Nyquist frequency, or half the sampling frequency (see chapter on sampling, page 86).

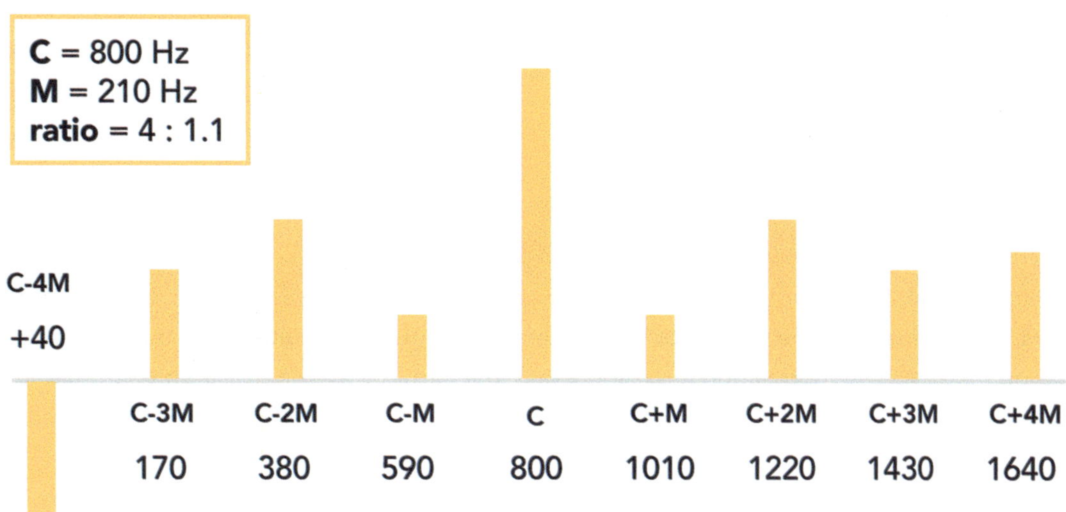

So far, we have talked about where the sidebands occur in the frequency domain, but we have yet to say what weight they have within the spectrum. How many of these sidebands will be heard and with what importance?

The **Modulation Index** gives us insight into answering these questions. As the modulation index increases, the timbre becomes more complicated with an increasing number of sidebands.

To understand why this happens, we note that the number of sidebands depends on the width of modulator. The modulator is dependent on the modulation index, the modulation frequency, and the C:M ratio. Since the modulator is integrated with the carrier frequency, the output frequency oscillates around the carrier frequency with a width defined by the **Deviation**. The deviation (amplitude of the modulator) determines how high or low the frequency 'deviates' from the carrier frequency. Similarly, modulation index is equal to the deviation divided by the modulating frequency; thus, deviation can also be thought to be the modulation index times the modulation frequency. The modulation index essentially acts as a regulator for the amount of deviation we want. Given a fixed modulation frequency, the higher the deviation, the higher the modulation index. Thus, if the deviation is large, I get many sidebands; conversely, if it is small, I get few bands.

If, for example, the modulation index is 0, then I have no deviation and no sidebands. If it is 1, I will have a deviation equal to the modulation frequency. If it is 2, then the deviation will be equal to twice the modulation frequency. As the modulation index gets bigger, there will progressively be more sidebands, creating a more complex timbre.

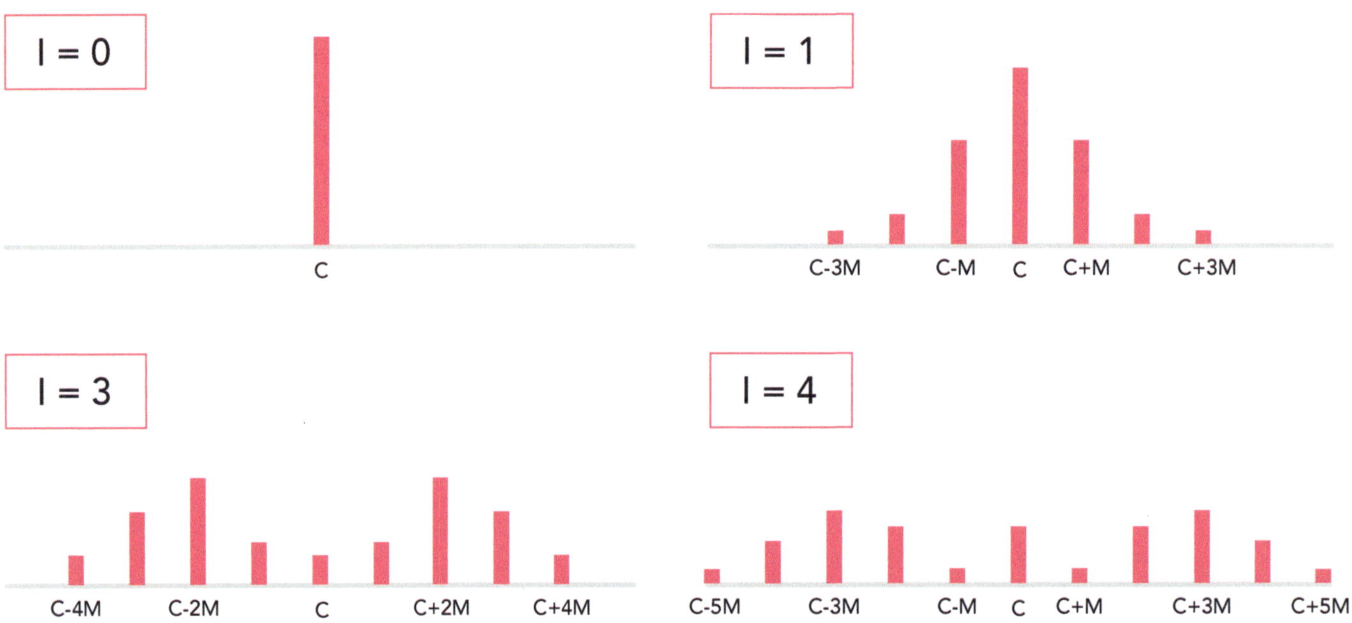

Similar to amplitude modulation synthesis where the energy of the carrier wave is distributed over the sidebands that are created, in FM synthesis, the energy of the carrier wave is also distributed over the sideband as a function of the modulation index. As the modulation index increases, the carrier wave energy is spread out and amplitude of the sidebands increases.

Let's now analyze a simple FM algorithm with only two operators: the carrier wave and the modulator wave. The pitch, in hertz, from a keyboard or other device, is multiplied by the harmonic ratio (C:M), establishing the frequency of the modulator wave. In parallel, we enter a modulation index, which we multiply by the frequency of the modulator wave and use it to set the amplitude of the modulator wave itself, thus defining its deviation. The deviation is also known as the range of frequencies that the modulator wave can oscillate. At this point, we add the obtained modulator with the initial frequency established by the keyboard and get the carrier frequency. Our FM synthesis is ready to go out.

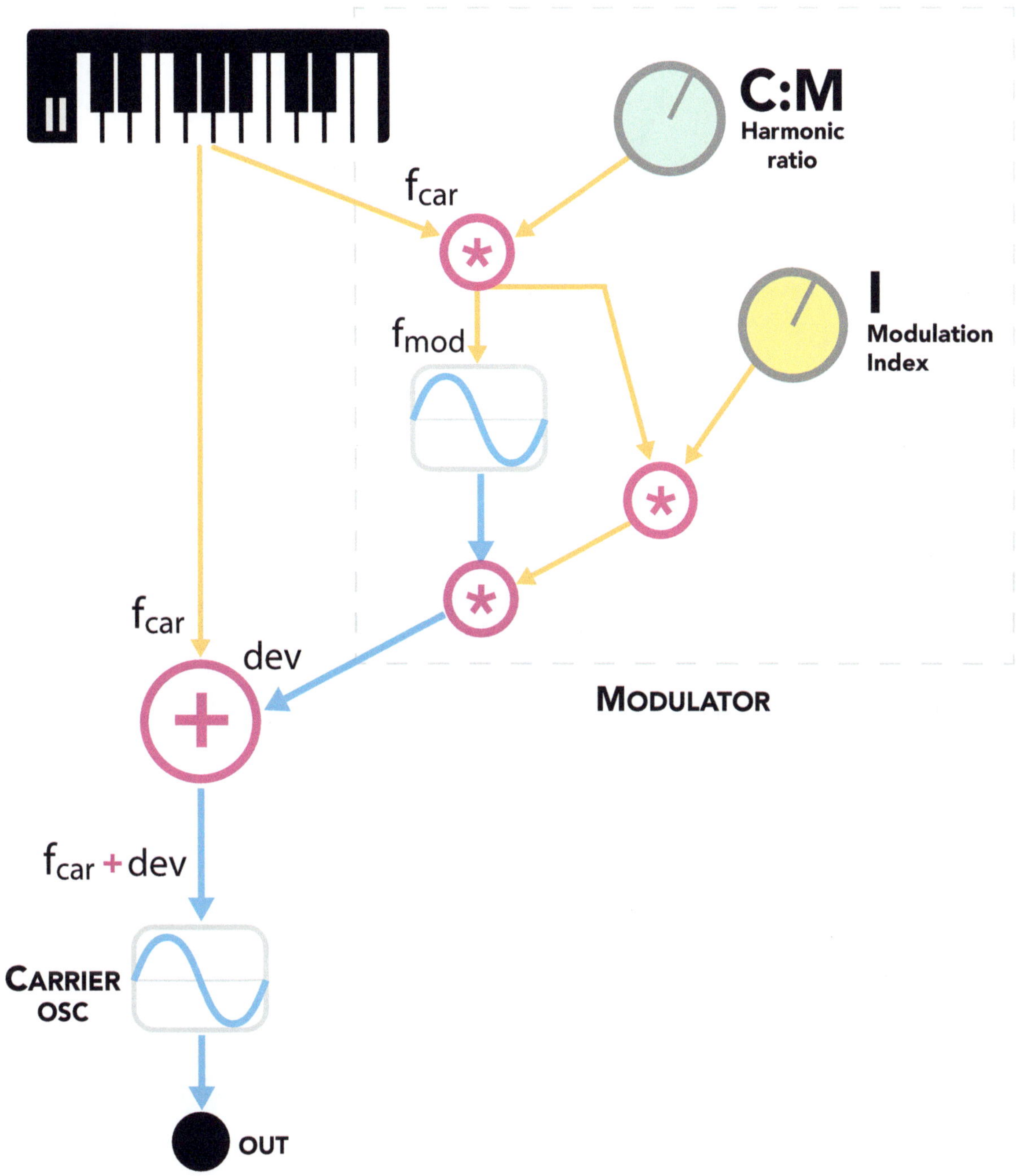

FM synthesis uses simple components and operations but allows us to obtain very complex timbres with little computational effort; however, it's a synthesis that leads to results that are not very intuitive. Once the parameters are set, it may not be easy to imagine the final spectral result. Some functions make it possible to predict the precise increase in sidebands as the Modulation Index increases. Bessel functions of the first kind and the nth order can help us predict the behavior of these sidebands.

In FM synthesis, each oscillator usually has its own envelope, which adjusts the amplitude, creating movement within the timbre that is less static. The **EG (envelope generator)** makes these movements possible and is composed of four amplitude levels and four rates that control the slope (and consequentially the time) of the envelope segments. In this case, the rate controls how long it takes for the amplitude to reach the next level. For example, with a low rate 2 (R2), the time it takes for the amplitude to change from level 1 (L1) to level 2 (L2) is longer than if we set a higher rate.

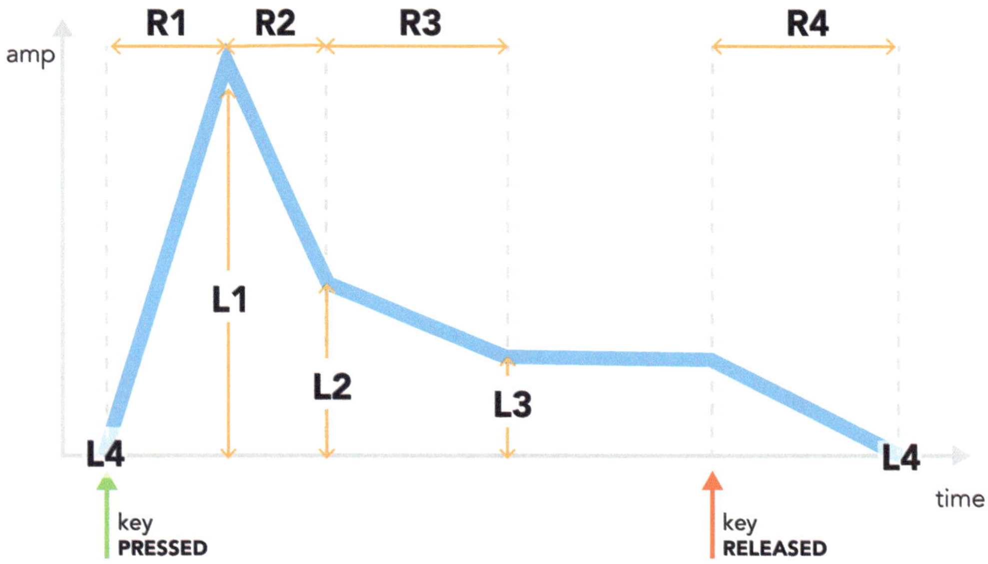

In the classic FM synthesis model, oscillators are called **operators** and an **algorithm** is defined by how we combine, organize, and configure multiple operators together. We arrange modulators and carriers in various algorithmic ways, creating more timbral possibilities. Thus, I can create algorithms with 3, 4, and 5 operators so long as they are properly arranged. For example, oscillator 1 modulates the frequency of oscillator 2, which in turn modulates the frequency of oscillator 3. This model is used, in particular, with popular synthesizers such as the Yamaha DX7 and its software clones and descendants. In the DX7, for example, there are six operators and 32 possible algorithms.

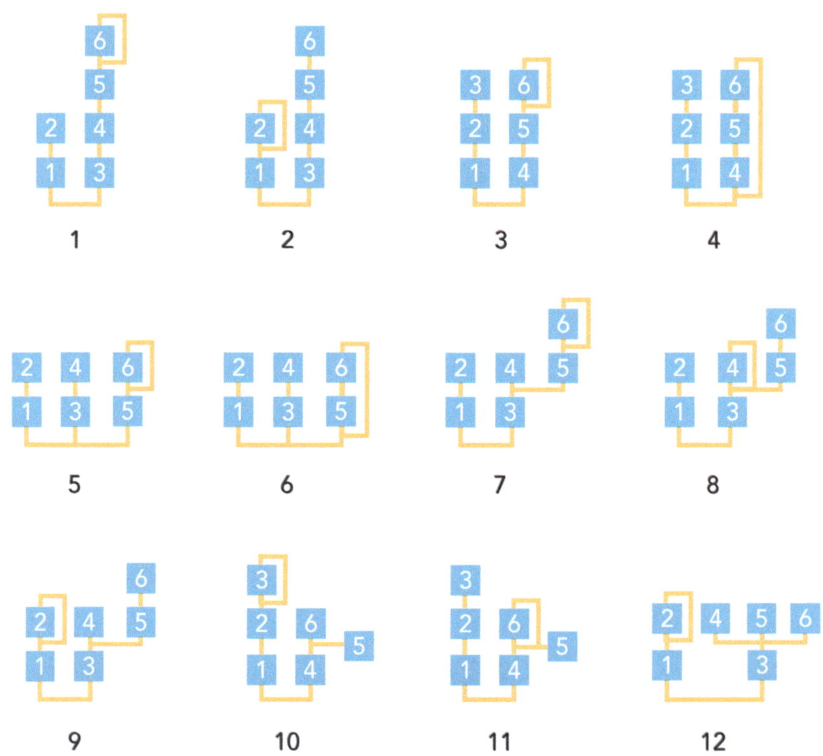

John Chowning ~ John Chowning Turenas ~ YAMAHA DX-7 ~ YAMAHA DX-7 songs ~ DEXED vst ~ Volca FM ~ Elektron Model cycles ~ Jean Claude Risset

.create three timbres from the initial settings of a VST for FM synthesis: one harmonic, similar to an electric piano; one inharmonic, similar to a bell; one other timbre that is similar to a snare drum

.create a song using only one VST with FM synthesis. This process should provide the complete set of timbres that you will use in this song. Focus on two opposite and complementary types of tones (e.g., percussion and pads). Create a track where these two opposite sounds have a dialogue with each other by experimenting with encounters and clashes. ***Theme: "Halfway around the world"***

.create a piece starting from an FM timbre in which you vary only the modulation index (or indexes in the case of multiple operators) of modulation. Essentially you are altering the harmonic content of the timbre itself. ***Theme: "Scratches"***

WAVESHAPING

Waveshaping is based on passing one period of an input wave, such as a sine wave, through a transfer function that alters its shape and results in one period of an output wave. As we saw in the previous chapter about distortion (page 152), the wave shaping transfer function is a curve that I can draw and store on a table and that maps the input values, between -1 and 1, to different output values, again between -1 and 1. This function acts as a distorting "mirror" where I make an altered "image" of the original audio. The transfer function takes the original input wave as the input to the function, similar to function composition, and creates a new output wave.

The transfer function is represented within a graph in which, from below, the sine wave enters. In other words, the input values from below slide up to transfer function graph. The input values then find their corresponding values in the transfer function curve and then exit to the output, modified to those found values. To visualize this process better, let us take four situations as examples:

perfectly linear function: each input value equals the same output value, so I do not have any change on the wave

total polarity inversion: negative values are turned into positive and vice versa

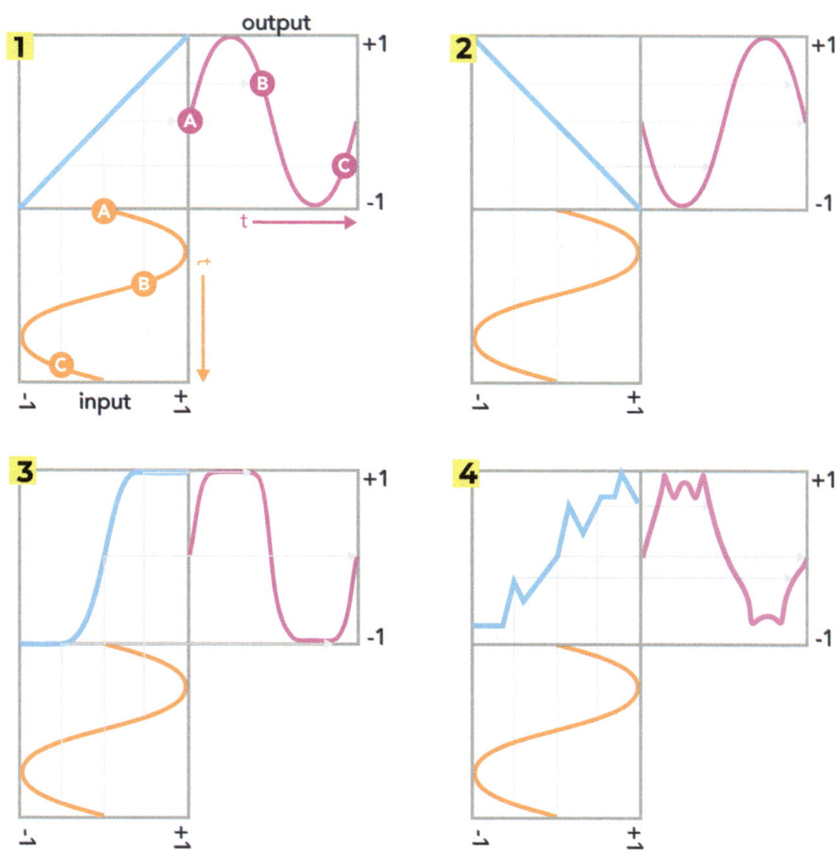

sine wave gains harmonics in a way similar to what happens in an overdrive distortion

with more complex transfer functions, the final timbre will also be rich

Waveshaping can also create distortion devices, sending in generic signals to be distorted, not just sine waves.

One of the interesting features of this technique is the graphical aspect: I can easily draw my transfer function by hand and hear how it "sounds." With the computational power of today's computers, I can even do it dynamically during a live performance.

The input amplitude range determines how much our input "reflects" off the transfer function. If we dynamically control the gain of the input, we can change, in real time, how much of the transfer function is used, thus changing the timbre of distortion of our output. This behavior mimics how instruments have different timbres when played at different amplitudes. In waveshaping synthesis, the amplitudes of the input signal closer to zero map to the parts of the transfer function at the middle of the graph. In order to reach the highest and lowest points of transfer function graph, the input signal's amplitude needs to be closer to the maximum value of +1 or minimum value of -1. By using transfer functions that create an output wave that is more angular and reaches the maximum and minimum values of +1 and -1, we can get richer timbres.

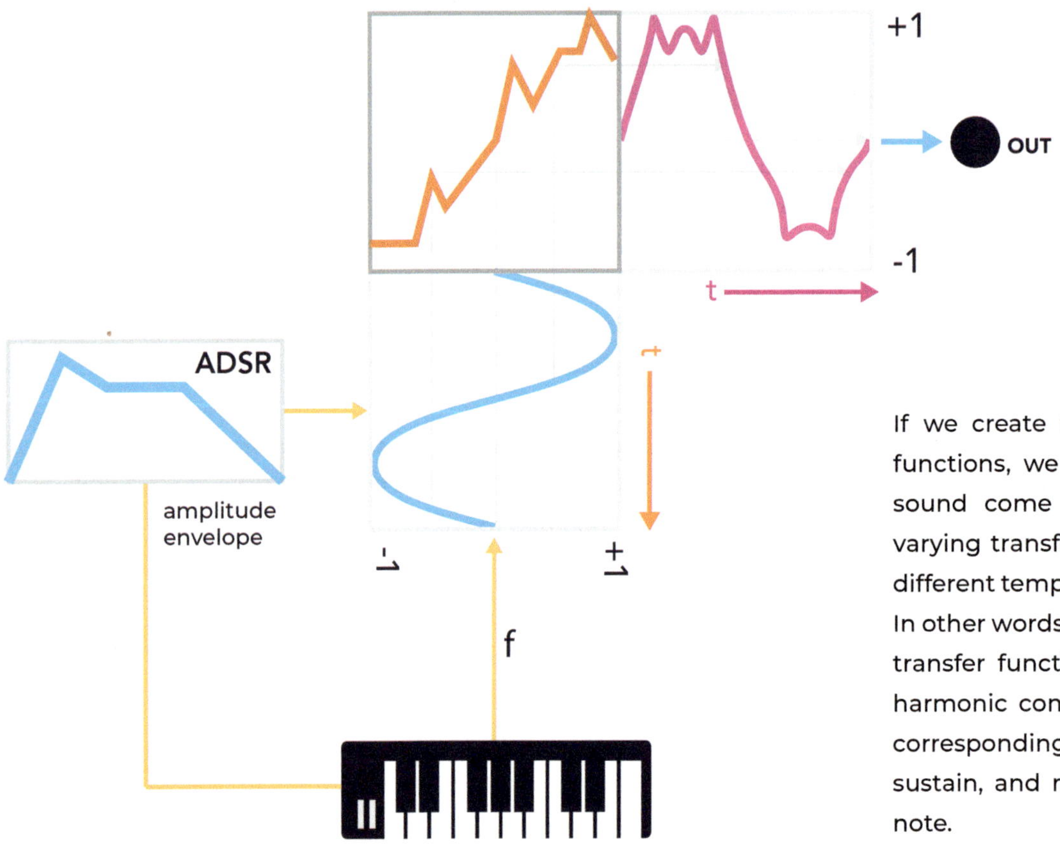

If we create time-varying transfer functions, we can have an output sound come "alive" if we match varying transfer function shapes to different temporal aspects of a note. In other words, by having a dynamic transfer function, we can vary the harmonic components of a sound, corresponding to the attack, decay, sustain, and release portion of the note.

.look for a hiking route whose elevation profile is also provided. You can choose any route you have taken or would like to take. Choose a segment of the elevation profile that is generally uphill and copy it as your waveshaping synthesizer transfer curve as closely as possible. Apply the entire elevation profile, this time both ascents and descents, to the dynamic form of the song while working freely with all the other parameters (pitch, rhythm, etc.) ***Theme: "Trails for experienced hikers"***

transfer function ~ distortion synthesis ~ Jean Claude Risset ~ microTERA app ~ wavefolding ~ wavewrapping ~ waveshaping eurorack module

PHASE DISTORTION

Casio synthesizers use **phase distortion** synthesis in their *CZ series*. In principle, phase distortion is based on reading the values of a sine wave stored in a table at a variable rate. Usually, with table lookup synthesis*, the table-lookup occurs at a constant rate, correlated to a desired pitch. The total duration of reading one complete wave cycle is defined as the period. For phase distortion synthesis, the duration of the period is preserved; however, as we progress through the various parts of the table, portions of the cycle can be read faster or slower, leading to variations of phase within the time frame of one period. One common phase distortion algorithm reads the wave faster from 0° to 180° (the first half of the full cycle), and then reads slower from 180° to 360° (the second half). The result is that the pitch remains constant on average, but the waveform varies leading to an embellishment of harmonics.

Let us help, as always, with illustrations:

A In a conventional table-lookup process for a sine wave, there is no change in the table lookup speed, leading to an undistorted sine wave

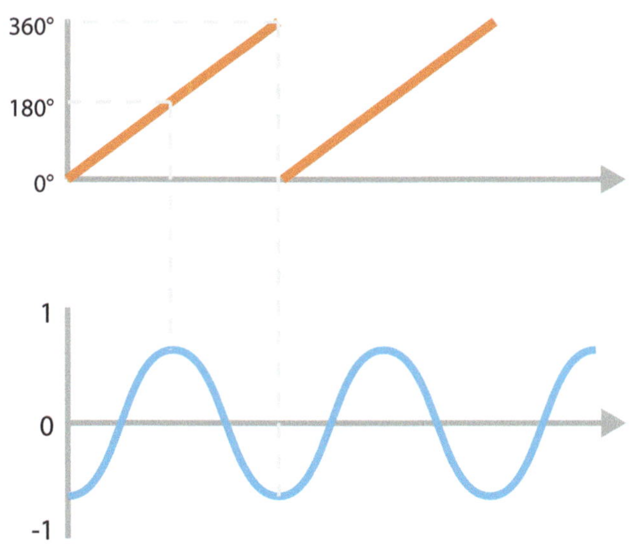

B The 180° phase has a faster lookup speed, leading to a compressed sine wave. For the 180° to 360° portion, the lookup speed is slower, leading to a stretched out sine wave. Note that the total time for one period matches that in Example A. Here, though, instead of a simple sine wave, we have a new waveform that looks more like a sawtooth waveform

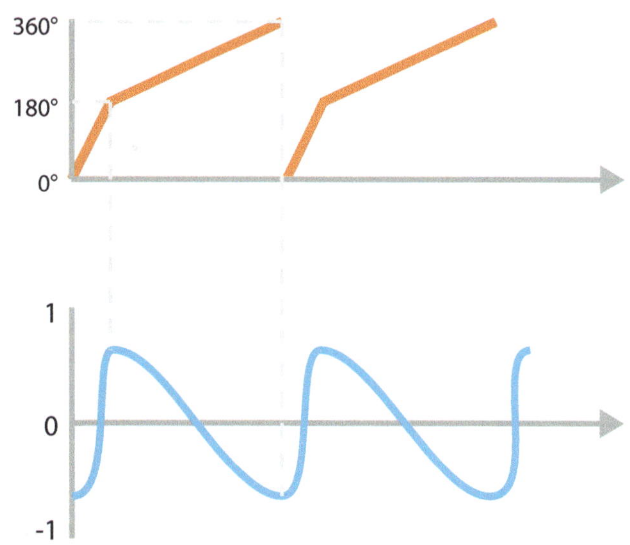

The game of creating interesting waveforms gets interesting when we begin to experiment with these lookup speeds to create different distorted waveforms. Each new possibility brings a different timbre. In the classic Casio synthesis system, there are several waves generated with phase distortion to choose from. On top of that, we can combine up to four of these waves to create even more complex waves.

* **WAVETABLE/TABLE LOOKUP SYNTHESIS**

This is a kind of synthesis that relies on tables of pre-existing values to create sound. The tables generally store many values representing one period of various waveshapes. The musician will select a waveshape and the player will then playback this one period of data at different rates to get different frequencies, or different amplitudes to get various amplitudes. Waveshapes can be sine, sawtooth, square, or any waveshape that you want. See also page 192.

Another important feature is the presence of envelopes, or instructions, for both the table lookup speeds and the final amplitude envelope. The table lookup speed instructions determine the phase distortion, while the latter determines the amplitude ADSR envelope, like the one we saw in subtractive synthesis. Both of these options make the output wave more complex and allow the sound to come "alive."

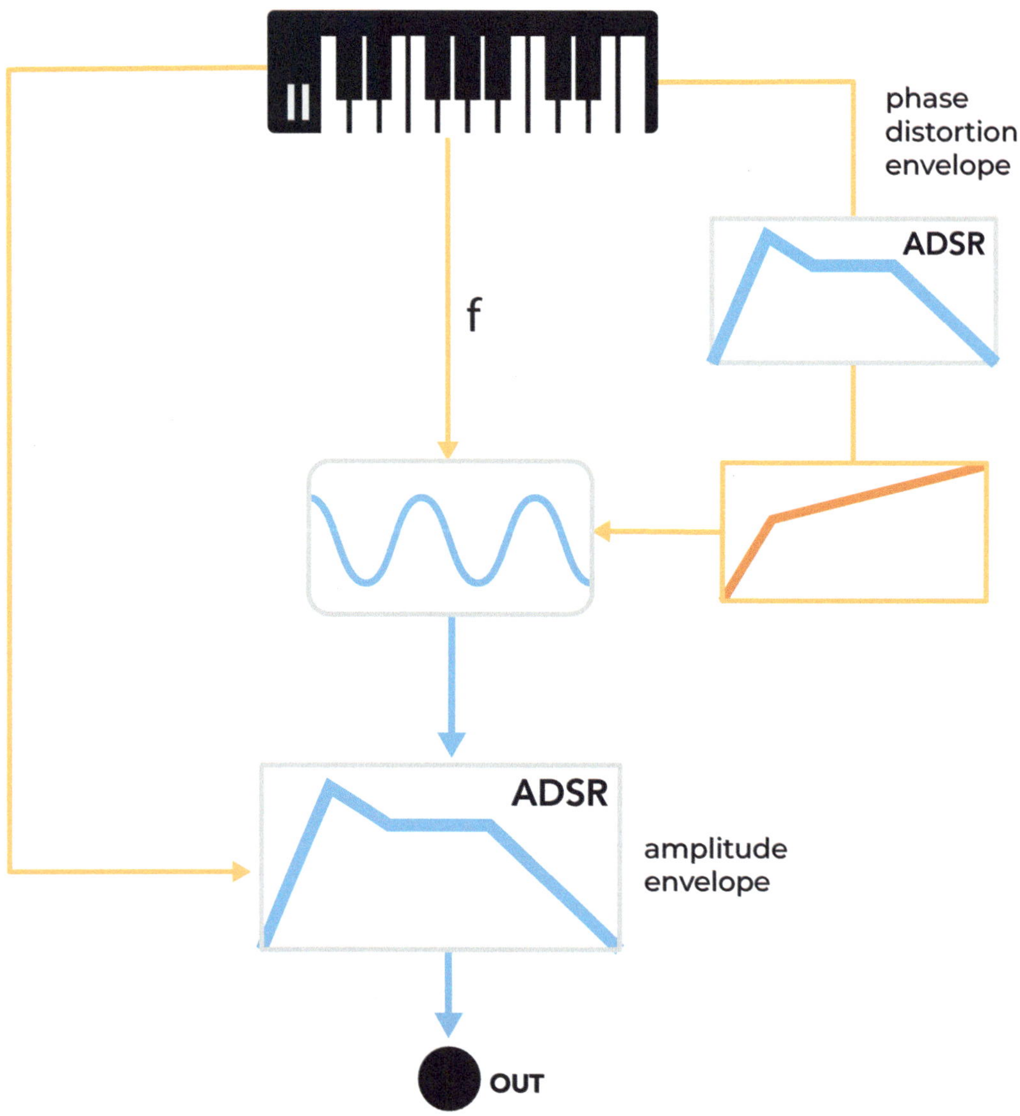

Casio CZ ~ pdhalf csound ~ virtualCZ ~ phase distortion plugin

PHYSICAL MODELING

Unlike the synthesis techniques that we have seen so far, **physical modeling synthesis** is not a simply a single algorithm, or single concept, but a family of algorithms or concepts that share the same principle—to observe the physical behavior of real acoustic instruments, mathematically model the physical phenomenon, and mimic the physical behavior virtually to recreate the sound. Clearly, as with all synthesis, the goal is not necessarily to faithfully reconstruct the timbres of real instruments, but to also be able to create new sounds by incorporating novel mathematical models. Once I have mathematically modeled an instrument using physical model synthesis, I can "play" with the parameters and stretch the limits of what we might imagine as acoustic instruments. For example, we can develop guitars with strings reaching one kilometer long, flutes made of uranium, or even marimbas with 1/8 inch keys.

Physical modeling synthesis usually focuses on an acoustic instrument's three stages of sound generation: the Exciter, the Resonator, and the Environment. Let's take a guitar as an example and investigate these three stages.

The Exciter is the fingers or a pick/plectrum. Other governing aspects for us to potentially model are the hand or finger technique, the pick material, and the pick dimensions.

The Resonator is essentially the body. The governing parameters include the size, shape, and material, to name a few.

The Environment dictates where I place a microphone. This is also the mathematical point in space where the output is taken from. Is this point close to the strings or close to the body? Far away or close? What kind of room is the guitar in? Is it empty? What are the wall materials and reverberation time?

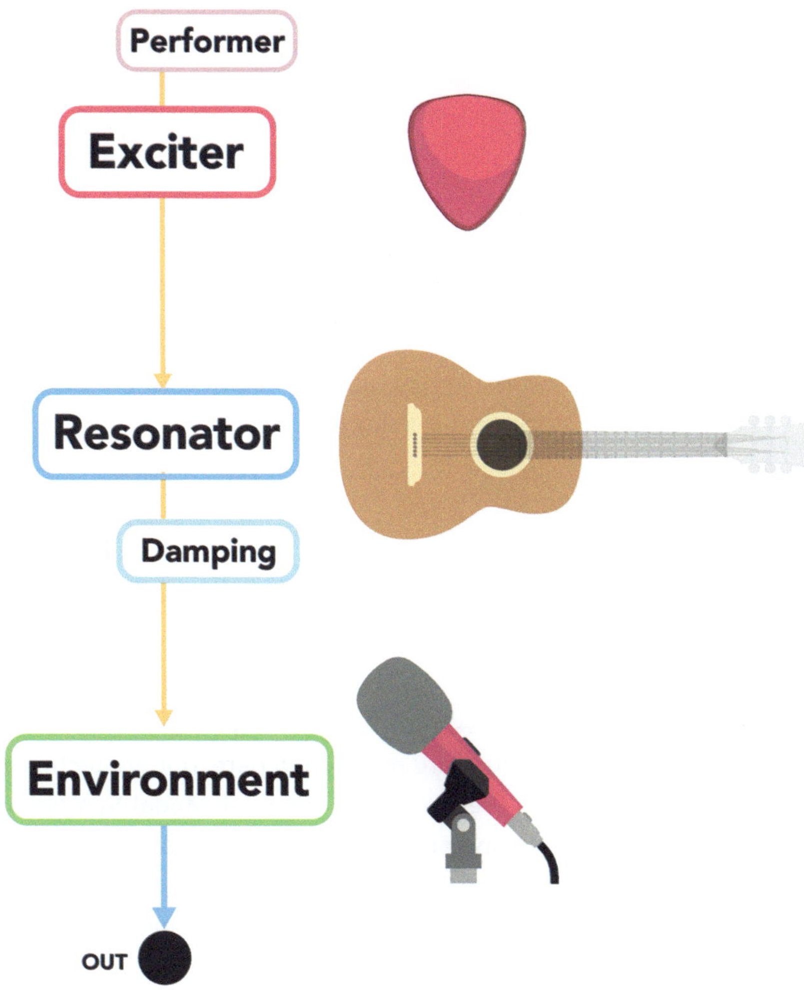

In the Exciter stage, just as we discussed needing to include the hand or finger technique, this is where the Performer's technique and playing style can be modeled. This is where the lips, the mouth, the arm, the hands, and other physical aspects of the performer can be accounted for.

And finally, at the tail end of the Resonator stage, we can include a Damping stage that attenuates the propagation, thereby filtering the sound. This stage depends on the resonating part's material, size, and shape.

All these stages have a unique set of parameters that, when varied, allow us to model the size, material, and shape of each stage into our algorithm, customizing our final sound.

A simple example of physical modeling synthesis is the **Karplus-Strong (KS)** algorithm. Originally conceptualized in 1983, the KS algorithm reproduces the physical mechanisms of a plucked or struck string. Conceptually simple and efficient, the only components needed for this are a noise generator, digital delay lines, and a low-pass filter.

1. **White noise** is generated
2. This excitation is fed directly into a **delay line**
3. The output of the delay is input into a **filter** (usually a first-order low-pass filter)
4. The filtered signal goes to the output and is simultaneously fed back into the delay line, where steps 2-4 are repeated

What happens is that the noise is modified with a comb filter, made by the combination of delay and feedback (as you will recall from the chapter on delay, page 117). The harmonics in the higher frequencies gradually fade away due to the work of the low-pass filter. To make a physical comparison, the struck string starts with a noisy vibration pattern, then the vibrations settle into a pitch. The higher frequencies begin to die off and the sonic richness also starts to thin out, and the note fades away to nothing.

To create a specific pitch with the KS algorithm, we use the same formula that we encountered earlier when discussing comb filters. Pitch is mainly determined by the time length of the delay line. By taking 1000 and dividing that by our desired frequency, i.e., **delay = 1000/frequency**, we can calculate the delay time, in terms of milliseconds, necessary to create our desired pitch. This delay time approximately corresponds to a certain number of samples at a given sampling frequency. The formula associated with this is D = Fs/Fo where Fs is the sampling frequency, Fo is the frequency of the desired pitch, and D is the number of samples to delay the signal by. It is worth noting that we are limited to D being an integer number, as we cannot have partial samples in digital audio. This means that the KS algorithm may not actually be able to recreate an exact frequency, as we cannot have a fractional or a partial number of samples in real audio.

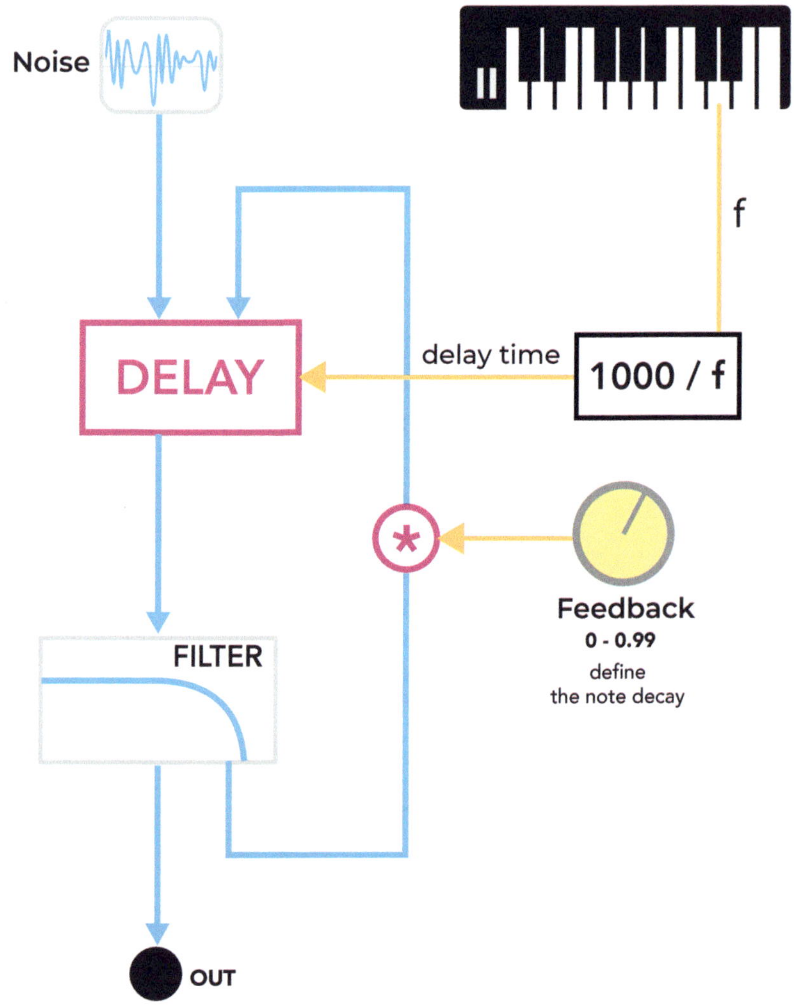

As we said at the beginning of this section, there are many approaches to physical modeling synthesis. Except for the simple Karplus-Strong implementation, many of these techniques employ very complex procedures to design and implement. The following types of physical modeling techniques are mentioned here, but are technically beyond the scope of this book to explain. These techniques include the **Mass-Spring Model**, **Modal Synthesis**, the **MSW Model** (McIntyre, Schumacher, and Woodhouse), and the **Waveguide Model**. Commercially, physical modeling synthesizers are widespread as plugins and in DAW software, and less popular within standalone synthesizers. The most prominent of this kind of hardware device is the Yamaha VL1, which was built originally in 1993 but did not ultimately achieve commercial success.

.using your favorite programming language, create a Karplus-Strong algorithm and a system for playing notes in a scale. Add an automatic arpeggiator of random notes within a musical scale of your choice. Make the note playback speed variable

.create a song for an acoustic instrument and its corresponding synthesizer that uses physical models. With regards to the synthesizer, work on the parameters that simulate situations that may be impossible to reproduce with a real instrument. For example, experiment with the size of the body or tube, with the distance between the various components, with varying manufacturing materials, and with different positions of pickups or microphones. ***Theme: "Mother and Child"***

IRCAM Modalys ~ IRCAMAX ~ Yamaha VL1 ~ karplus strong synthesis ~ Phyzmod vst

GRANULAR SYNTHESIS

Are you familiar with Seurat's pointillist paintings? The colored dots on a canvas, viewed from a certain distance, reveal shapes and figures. A similar thing happens with **Granular Synthesis,** a synthesis theorized many years ago that was only able to be implemented more recently due to digital audio computing. This synthesis algorithm centers on the idea of creating complex sounds from many simple short sounds called grains. A grain is a very small sound fragment that, when combined and played sequentially and/or superimposed at varying speeds, phases, and volumes, generates a single fused timbre. Sometimes this collection of synthesized grains can be described as a cloud of sounds.

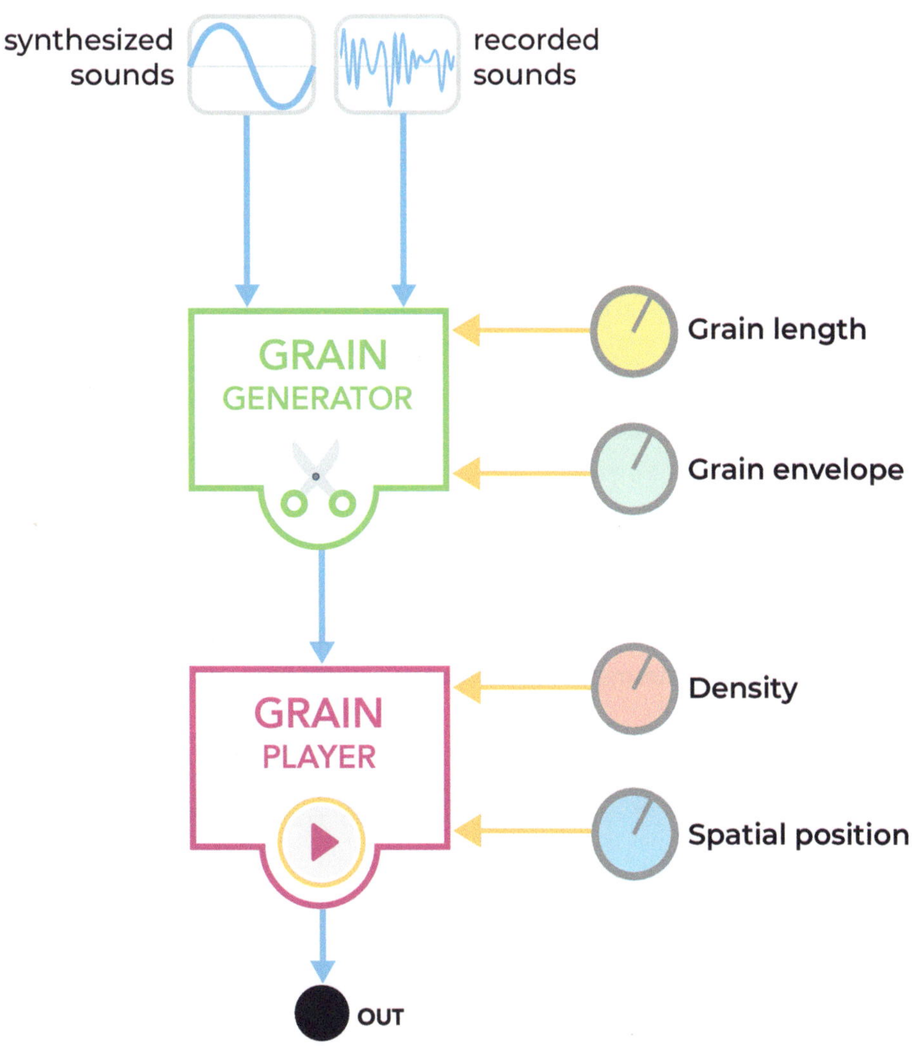

These sound grains can be derived from various sources, from recorded sounds to other synthesized sounds. We set the **length** of the grains (generally between 1 and 100 ms) and apply an amplitude **envelope** to them, which typically has a symmetrical attack / decay. The selection of the type of amplitude envelope can play a large role in the sonic character of our final timbre.

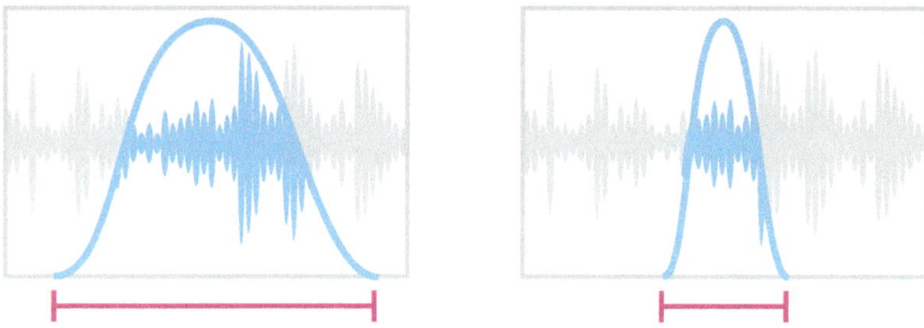

SYMMETRICAL ENVELOPES

Gaussian: this is a "gentle" amplitude envelope because it has relatively slow attack and decay, thus allowing for clouds with a mellow sound. The attack and decay curve can be sharper or shallower, thus revealing more or less sound from the original sound grain.

Trapezoidal: this amplitude envelope has sharp corners. These corners create more scratchy timbres because the resultant sound is rich in high frequencies. The overall trapezoidal envelope can also be more or less narrow.

Pulse: this envelope is a special type of Gaussian envelope that is very narrow; therefore, only a tiny portion of the sound is used.

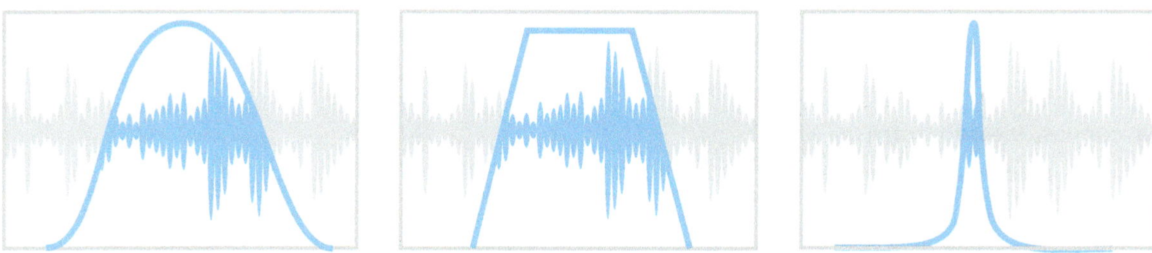

Gaussian — Trapezoidal — Pulse

ASYMMETRICAL ENVELOPES

Finally, there are asymmetrical envelopes, which have immediate attacks and slow decays or vice versa, and can even have random noise-like envelopes. By not having symmetry, these envelopes can create extremely sour and scratchy sounds.

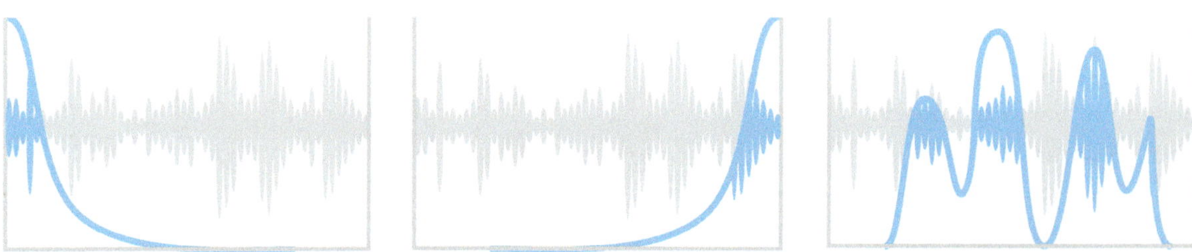

Fall — Rise — Noise

Once the grains have been generated, we move to the playback portion. This is where the final timbre is actually constructed. We can play the grains in various ways with different parameters, with each particular setting resulting in a unique result.

There are four types of grain playback:

- **Synchronous (Synchronous Granular Synthesis):** When playing back a series of grains, the time gap or offset between the grains is constant
- **Quasi-synchronous (QSGS):** In this case, the time gap between the grains is almost, but not exactly, constant
- **Asynchronous (ASGS):** The time gap between the grains, during playback, is not constant
- **Pitch-synchronous (Pitch-Synchronous Granular Synthesis):** In this form of granular synthesis, the time gap between the grains corresponds to a frequency that is synchronized with the pitch of the grains

When we play the grains in synchronous mode, the pitch of our resulting timbre will be more perceptible and will be affected by the time gap I specify between grains, also called the density. As we move away from synchronous mode, the resultant pitch becomes increasingly less defined and the sound approaches a texture with chaotic characteristics. In the case of granular pitch-synchronous synthesis, we have a variable (not constant) time gap that depends on the note I want to hear. If you press a G, the synthesizer adjusts the pitch of the grains and the time gap between the grains to create the timbre and harmonic structure of a G note.

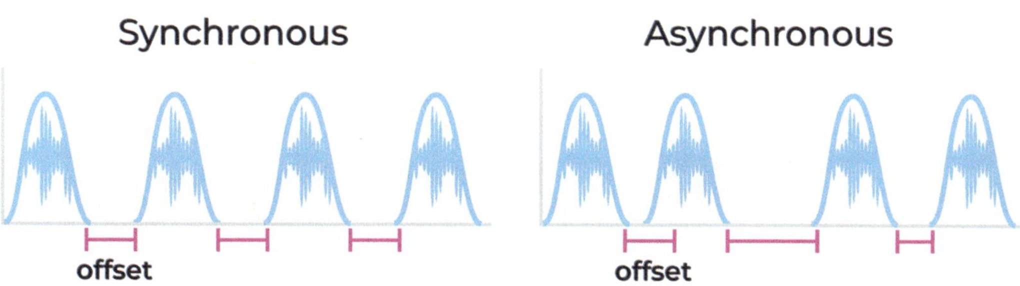

I can set the following parameters for a grain player:

Grain density is the number of grains that the player plays at the same time. Imagine that a player starts with a single violinist; if I increase the number of violinists, I can increase the number of violin notes my song can have simultaneously, leading to a greater density of violin notes. This happens in grain players whose quantity, or number of sound instances, is increased to increase grain density.

Spatial position determines where to place the grains the players play within the space. We can position these grains in a left and right stereo space or within a three-dimensional space. I can, for example, arrange the grains of the sound cloud around the listener as if the listener were inside the cloud itself. For this and the other parameters for granular synthesis, a sense of randomness is very important in order to obtain interesting sonic results, especially when the randomness is bounded within some predetermined limits. For example, if I can randomize the position of the grains, not within the entire listening space, but limited to the possible places behind the listener's head, I can achieve these potentially interesting results.

As stated above, granular synthesis was really only practically possible after the advent of digital audio. This kind of computationally based synthesis ultimately became popularized with commercial software (e.g., ***Granulator for Ableton Live***) and also within the growing software apps for smartphones and tablets (***SpaceCraft*** and ***Borderlands Granular***).

More recently, standalone hardware-based instruments, such as the ***Tasty Chips Electronics GR-1*** (2019), are also seeing the incorporation of granular synthesis. These hardware devices can remind us of *Barry Truax*'s early experiments in his song *Riverrun* (1986), where he created dedicated synthesis hardware: the ***DMX-1000 Digital Signal Processor.***

.extract a 30-second sample from a classical song of your choice. Put the sample in a granular synthesizer and create a song by scrubbing along the sample and varying the granulation parameters. An overall crescendo of grain density should drive the song's structure. ***Theme: "Drops"***

.generate a haiku using an AI chatbot with the theme "grains of a granular synthesizer." Record your voice reading the haiku and use it as the source material for a granular synthesizer. Create melodic and rhythmic parts and arrange the the grains into a composition that reflects the content of the haiku

.create the sound of a thunderstorm that gradually becomes a hailstorm and then subsides. Use only a granular synthesizer to achieve this, carefully choosing the original sounds from which you extract the grains

Barry Truax Riverrun ~ Robert Henke Granulator ~ Tasty Chips GR-1

SAMPLING SYNTHESIS

You may have intentionally or unintentionally utilized sampling synthesis many times before because it is the basis of many electric keyboards that simulate piano sounds. To some, sampling synthesis is not even considered a kind of sound synthesis because it does not originate with simple elements, such as sine waves or filters. However, we will include it here with the other synthesis methods because, in essence, it is used to generate sounds.

Sampling synthesis is based on reproducing previously recorded notes upon pressing, for example, keyboard keys. It is therefore used primarily to recreate the sound of an existing instrument rather than to create a new timbre. However, as we shall see, there are methods of customization that allow us to greatly modify the original recorded samples that come from the instrument. The first step of sampling synthesis is to record, or sample, the various sounds needed in a composition or performance. In a sense, this method has some similarities with granular synthesis, but the time scale that we are working with differs greatly, with sound grains in granular synthesis ranging from 1-100 ms, and with sound samples in sampling synthesis extending to lengths of several seconds longs. Here in sampling synthesis, the note that is produced is a single sample, rather than a series of grains reproduced as a cloud of sounds. Finding samples can be done with standalone recordings or downloading free or paid sample packages.

The recording of notes, known as sampling (not to be confused with what happens in the analog-to-digital processs), can involve different levels of accuracy. The accuracy is dependent on the number of samples that are recorded from

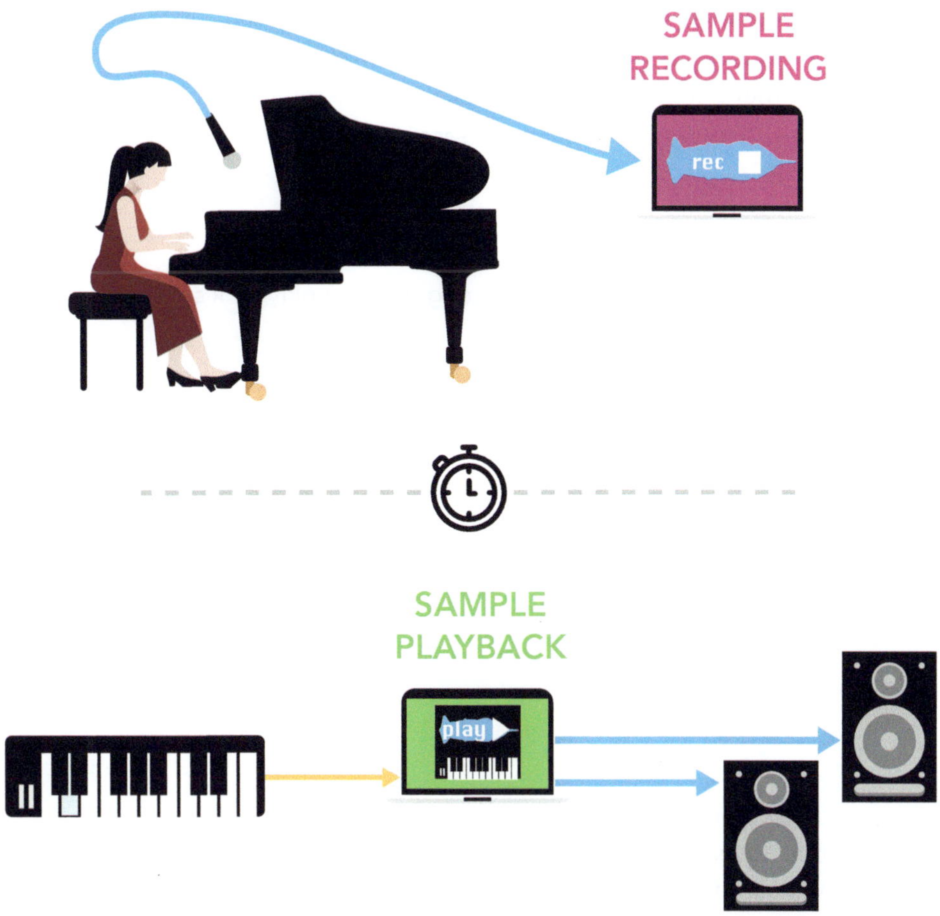

the original instrument. The more diverse the samples are (e.g., varying pitches, dynamics, articulations, etc.), the more faithful the playback will be to the original instrument.

To represent the entire frequency and timbral range of an instrument, different sampling techniques can be employed, each having different levels of accuracy and efficiency. For example, if too few samples are taken, then the samples cannot truly match the variety of timbres an instrument can produce. If many samples are taken, the sonic accuracy may be improved at the expense of the sheer number of samples needed.

Single-sampled is the method where only one sample is recorded, which will be used, during playback, to generate all the notes of the instrument. It's the simplest case because it requires little work at the sampling stage. It does potentially require, though, considerable manipulation in order to recreate all the pitches of a given instrument. Having only one sample does not provide the variety of timbres possible for an instrument; thus, this kind of sampling leads to output sounds that may not be very faithful to the original instrument, especially when we try to play notes very far from the sampled note. If I record a C4 and want to play a G6, the computer must transpose the note by 19 semitones. This fact will inevitably lead to a variation in timbre because the harmonic structure of the high notes does not necessarily line up exactly with the harmonic structure of the low notes.

Multi-sampled is when a sample is recorded for each note of the instrument, achieving greater timbral fidelity and variety, because the computer does not have to make any transpositions of notes.

Multilayer-sampled is often the best method because not only is every note of an instrument recorded, but each note is also recorded at different dynamics. There is very strong agreement and fidelity to the sound of the original instrument. The reason we utilize this method is that the timbre of an instrument can also vary depending on what dynamic, or amplitude, level the notes are played. With this type of sampling, I can capture and reproduce the differences in timbre between a soft C4 and a C4 at a very loud volume.

Once we have all the samples (either recorded by us, downloaded, or purchased), we can set up our sampler, a device or software program that plays back our samples. The sampler can also handle the transposition of notes in the single-sampled technique mentioned above or, in the case of the multi-sampled method, it chooses the sample played based on the input note. Also, in the multilayered-sampled method, the sampler selects samples depending on dynamics and pitch.

Samplers often also give you the ability to make small changes to the playback settings, allowing you to refine your synthesized output sound.

Crop allows you to choose the start and end point of the sample during playback.

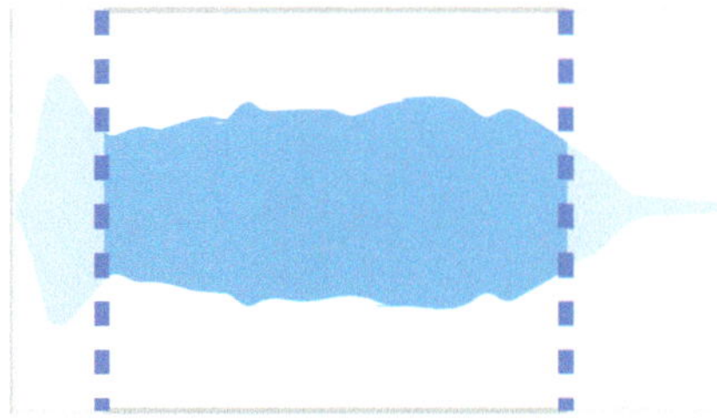

Envelope (ADSR) allows you to superimpose an amplitude envelope to each sample during playback. In this way, I can, for example, distort the envelope of a marimba by softening its attack to make it less percussive or decrease the release of a guitar string to transform it into tuneful percussion.

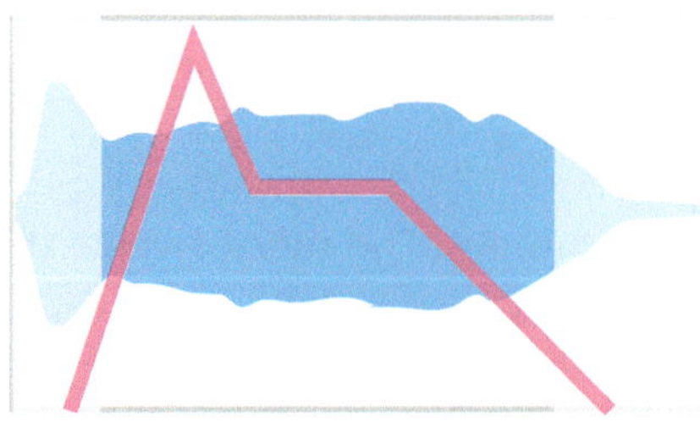

Loop is the function of the sampler that takes a portion of the sample and plays it back, or loops it, continuously as long as the MIDI key is pressed and sustained. This function is important and necessary when I want to hold a note longer than the original length of the sample, allowing me to hold a note for potentially many seconds. Clearly, the sampled sound has an endpoint and has a finite time length. If we take a stable part of the note's sustain, we can extend the overall length of our note, to as long as we want, by internally looping the assigned potion. We then resort to looping an internal part of the sample.

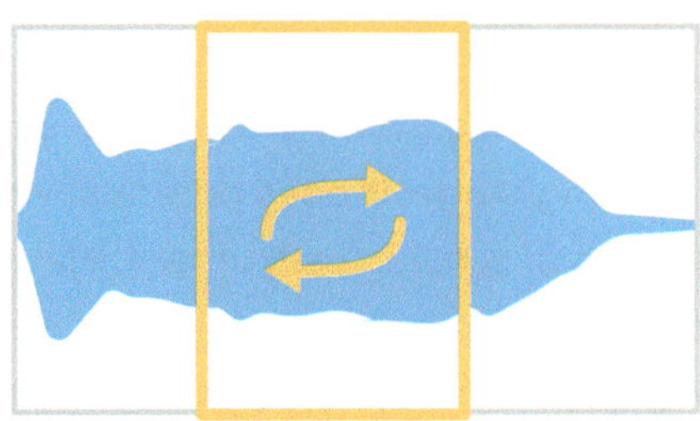

End point is the parameter that marks the time point within the sample that tells the sampler where to go after we release the MIDI key. With this parameter, we can, for example, give a natural tail to a synthesized instrument because, when we release the MIDI key, the sampler jumps to the end point of the original sample and incorporates this tail into the tail of my synthesized sound.

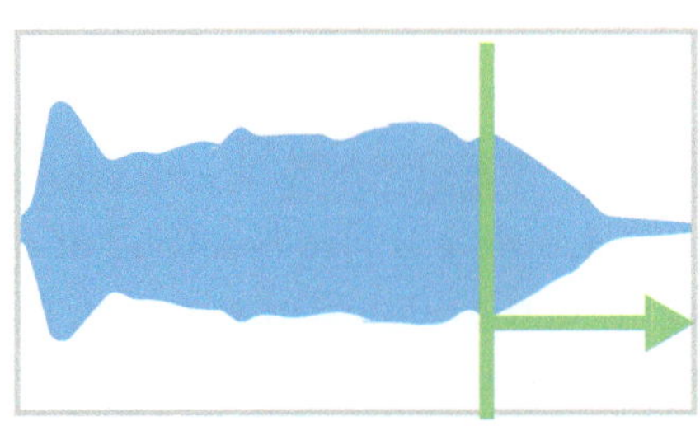

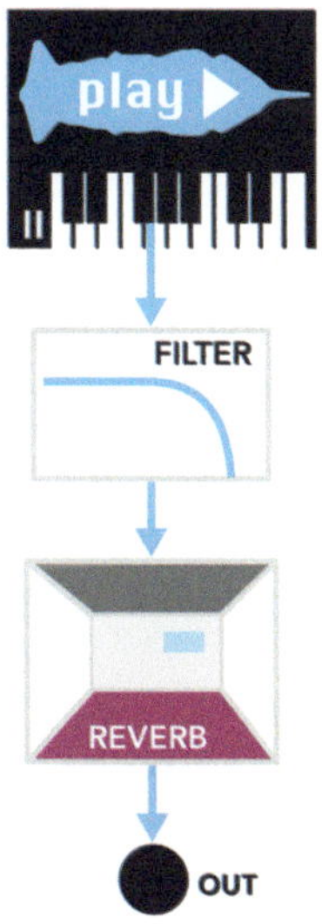

At the end of the sampler's workflow, as with other types of synthesizers, we can find one or more **effects** that help refine the synthesized sound we just created.

The most classic effects are **filters**, adjusting certain unwelcome frequencies, and **reverb**, simulating the instrument's sound in a particular real environment.

We find hundreds of commercial instruments, both hardware and software, that use sampling synthesis techniques. In terms of hardware implementations, imagine all the keyboards you have seen that simulate pianos, organs, and strings. For software-based samplers, one of the most prominent synthesizers is the ***Kontakt***.

Many of the devices we find commercially allow us to load our own ***samples*** into samplers. These kinds of samplers vary in price, quality, and synthesis techniques. Some projects, such as orchestral projects, require more fidelity and utilize multilayered-sampling techniques.

One instrument worth mentioning in particular here is the ***Mellotron***. This keyboard instrument was produced in 1970 and helped define the progressive rock sound of the 1970s. It is interesting because it is conceptually based on sampling synthesis where a key pressed corresponds to a pre-recorded note being played. In this case, the notes for each note of an instrument were recorded on tape. If we wanted to change instruments, we needed to replace the whole set of tapes. This made the ***Mellotron*** an impractical instrument compared to today's samplers. Still, for the time, it made it possible to create the sound of an orchestra without having to paying dozens of orchestral players. This revolutionary feature was not the sole reason the Mellotron is considered an historically important synthesizer. The reason for its importance stems from the fact that the slight imperfections in recording and playback of the tapes did not ultimately recreate accurate orchestra sounds. Instead these unique sounds, different from a real orchestra, became ironic timbres, which we still find emulated and used in hundreds of music and moving picture productions each year.

.record a C note of your voice, put it into a sampler, and try to recreate the mellotron sound with a hypothetical vocal tape. Pay particular attention to filtering and pitch movement. For the former, use a regular equalizer, and for the latter, try experimenting with a flanger. Recording into a DAW, play with your instrument of choice, ***"Strawberry Fields Forever" by The Beatles***

.record 10 versions of the same note on an instrument of choice. Put them into a sampler and create a system that randomly plays one of the 10 versions at 70 BPM in 16th notes

.record an 8-10 second musical phrase of your choice. Create or manipulate an existing sampler to get different reading points from your recorded sample. Create a performance in which the computer generates readings from different, random points in the sample, and you interact with your live instrument by imitating, harmonizing, and doing counterpoint. ***Theme: "Like a parrot"***

Mellotron ~ Strawberry Fields Forever The Beatles ~ MLR monome ~ Spitfire Labs

WAVETABLE SYNTHESIS

Wavetable synthesis generically relies on reading through tables of pre-existing values to create sound. The tables generally store values that represent one period of various waveshapes. By reading through the list of values that denote a particular waveshape at different speeds, this synthesis algorithm is able to generate different pitches while retaining the timbral structure that comes from the waveform itself. This type of technique is also called **look-up table synthesis**.

It is also possible, instead of being limited to one waveform or table, to read through several tables containing different waveforms simultaneously. The result creates a timbre that can come "alive," potentially varying its characteristics as the note is played. To make the sound come alive, a morphing envelope (ADSR, LFO, automated envelopes, manually driven envelopes) is used to move between waveshapes. The timbral shifts can take place in steps (i.e., abrupt transitions) or in a continuous and gradual manner. Today when we talk about wavetable synthesis, we refer to precisely this multiple-table approach. An example of a hardware wavetable synthesizer is the *PPG Wave* and a software example is *Ableton*'s *Wavetable*.

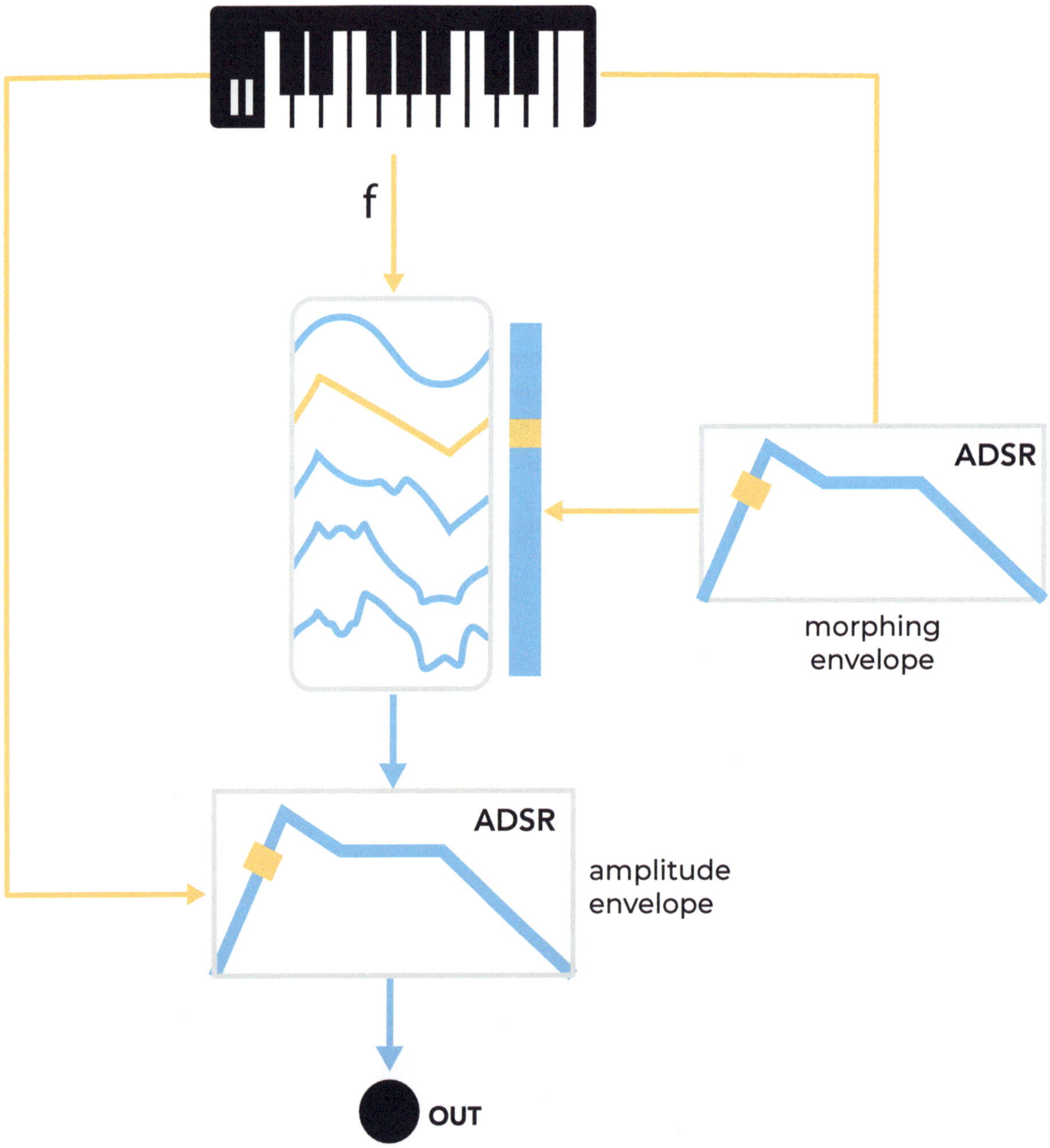

VECTOR SYNTHESIS

A variation of this approach is **vector synthesis**. In this scenario, instead of moving only in one dimension through a table, we have a two-dimensional plane, which has, at its four corners, four different tables. By using a joystick or similar device, we can send X and Y values as we move through the plane in two dimensions, morphing between the four different timbres created by the tables. An example is the *Sequential Circuits Prophet-VS*.

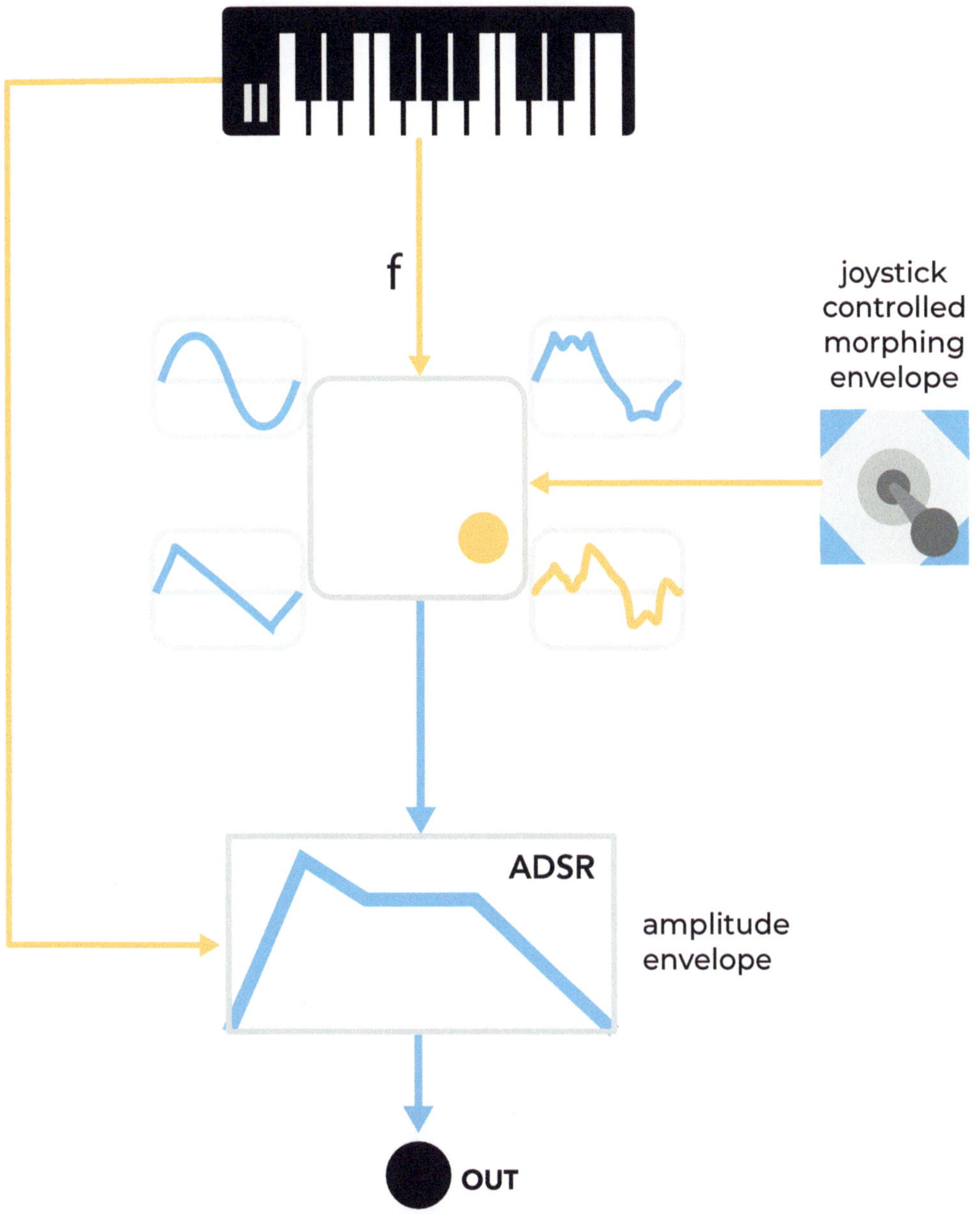

.create a vector synthesis algorithm from scratch in your DAW to make a new timbre. Choose four different instruments as your sources and map a MIDI controller to crossfade between the instruments based on the position of the joystick or potentiometers. With the timbre you just invented, create a short performance. ***Theme: "Solar eclipse"***

PPG Wave ~ Wavetable Ableton ~ Arturia Pigments ~ Prophet-VS ~ Korg Wavestation

SOFTWARE

DAW

Reaper - www.reaper.fm FREE to EVALUATE
Ableton Live - www.ableton.com
Pro Tools - www.avid.com/pro-tools
Cubase - www.steinberg.net/cubase
Logic Pro - www.apple.com/it/logic-pro
Soundtrap (web) - www.soundtrap.com

MUSIC NOTATION

Musescore 2 - musescore.org FREE
Finale - www.finalemusic.com
Sibelius - www.avid.com/sibelius

MUSIC PROGRAMMING SOFTWARE

Pure Data - puredata.info FREE
Max - cycling74.com
Max for live - www.ableton.com/en/live/max-for-live
VCV Rack 2- vcvrack.com FREE

ANALYSIS

EAnalysis - logiciels.pierrecouprie.fr/?page_id=402
Acousmographe - https://inagrm.com/en/showcase/news/203/acousmographe

VIDEO EDITING

Openshot - openshot.org FREE
Shotcut - shotcut.org FREE
Adobe Premiere pro - www.adobe.com/products/premiere.html
Final cut pro - www.apple.com/final-cut-pro
Davinci Resolve - www.blackmagicdesign.com/products/davinciresolve

AUDIO UTILITY

Spear - www.klingbeil.com/spear FREE
Audacity - www.audacityteam.org FREE
Blackhole - existential.audio/blackhole FREE
Audiosculpt - https://forum.ircam.fr/projects/detail/audiosculpt/

FREE RESOURCES

SLIDES

+

INTERACTIVE GRAPHICS

PLAY

www.tommasorosati.it/en/play-with-sound/

audio E-learning:

learningsynths.ableton.com | learningmusic.ableton.com | musiclab.chromeexperiments.com

free VST Instruments and effects:

plugins4free.com | www.spitfireaudio.com

free multitrack songs download:

www.telefunken-elektroakustik.com/livefromthelab | www.cambridge-mt.com/ms/mtk

convolution reverb IRs:

fokkie.home.xs4all.nl/IR.htm | www.echothief.com

Spatialization:

SpatGRIS | Envelop spat | Anaglyph vst

Soundmaps:

timberfestival.org.uk/soundsoftheforest-soundmap | soundcartography.wordpress.com | www.montrealsoundmap.com | www.sonotecabahiablanca.com/wp/mapa-sonoro | www.firenzesoundmap.org | freesound.org/browse/geotags

BIBLIO-GRAPHY

Pierre Schaeffer - **Treatise on Musical Objects: An Essay Across Disciplines (1966)** - University of California Press, 2017

R. Murray Schäfer - **The Soundscape: Our Sonic Environment and the Tuning of the World** - ed. Inner Traditions/Bear & Company, 1993

Curtis Roads - **The Computer Music Tutorial** - ed. MIT Press, 1995

Luigi Agostini - **Creare paesaggi sonori** - Edizioni Lulu.com, 2007

Alex Ross - **The Rest Is Noise: Listening to the Twentieth Century** - Picador, 2008

Andrea Cremaschi, Francesco Giomi - **Rumore bianco: introduzione alla musica digitale** - ed. Zanichelli, 2008

Iannis Xenakis, Sharon E. Kanach - **Music and architecture : architectural projects, texts, and realization** - Pendragon Press, 2008

Autori Vari - **Dizionario enciclopedico universale della musica e dei musicisti (DEUMM)** - diretto da Alberto Basso, 16 vol, Utet, 2010

Enrico Cosimi - **Manuale di musica elettronica. Teoria e tecnica dei sintetizzatori** - ed. Tecniche Nuove, 2011

Leonello Tarabella - **Musica Informatica** - ed. Maggioli, 2014

Vincenzo Lombardo, Andrea Valle - **Audio e multimedia** - ed. Apogeo Education, 2014

Dennis DeSantis - **Making Music: 74 Creative Strategies for Electronic Music Producers** - ed. Ableton AG, 2015

V.J. Manzo, Will Kuhn - **Interactive Composition: Strategies Using Ableton Live and Max for Live** - ed. Oxford University Press, 2015

David Felton, Greg Scarth, Chris Barker, Oliver Curry, Marc Adamo - **The Secrets of Dance Music Production** - ed. Jake Island Ltd, 2016

Alessandro Cipriani, Maurizio Giri - **Electronic Music and Sound Design - Theory and Practice with Max 8 - Vol.1** - ed. ConTempoNet, 2019

Alessandro Cipriani, Maurizio Giri - **Electronic Music and Sound Design - Theory and Practice with Max 8 - Vol.2** - ed. ConTempoNet, 2020

Mark Fell - **Structure and Synthesis - The Anatomy of Practice** - Urbanomic, 2021

THANKS TO

TOMMASO

My students from the "Licei Musicali" of Prato and Pisa with whom I also went to Saturn

My US students at Indiana University Indianapolis for helping me pronounce "choir"

Fabio De Sanctis De Benedictis, who introduced me to the music I like to make today

The other teachers (Roberto Neri, Alberto Gaetti, Marco Ligabue, Alfonso Belfiore, Mauro Grossi, Marco Liuni, Tommaso Dini...), for telling me the things written in this book (and so much more) for the first time

My professors at IU, Indianapolis, especially Timothy Hsu (helping me to find guanciale), Scott Deal, and Daniel Walzer

Nicoletta Andreuccetti for allowing me to work and learn with her compositions

My Ph.D peers, especially John Best, Miguel Carballo, Bhawna Rathi, Harry Chaubey, Jerelle Austin, and Peter Metzger

Samuele Strufaldi (+ Francesco Gherardi), companion/s of sound and metaphysical conjectures

Scilla, without whom I would not be in motion

To Davide Lufrano, great musician, companion in music, life, and even more easy things

TIMOTHY

My family, who has been a constant source of inspiration and energy.

My wonderful colleagues and friends at Indiana University – Indianapolis, Department of Music and Arts Technology

Dr. Daniel Walzer for his support and networking

The remarkable students at Indiana University – Indianapolis, in particular, Bhawna Rathi and Tommaso Rosati who are pioneers in the IU-Indianapolis AcousTech Lab

My amazing former choral and technology students, friends, colleagues at the Georgia Institute of Technology

INDEX

A

A/B 67
acousmatic music 14, 104
ADC (Analog to Digital Converter) 78, 83, 86, 150
additive synthesis 168-170
aftertouch 96
aliasing 91, 150–151
all-pass (filter) 105, 111, 113, 132–134
AM (Amplitude Modulation) 168, 172–173
Ambisonics 156–157
amplitude 30–34, 39
amplitude spectrum 39
analog signal 46, 73, 78, 83, 85, 87, 89, 90, 150, 170
anti-aliasing filters 91
aperiodic wave 24
arrangement 12
asynchronous (ASGS) 187
attack (ADSR) 38, 170, 180
attack (compressor) 140-141, 144
AU (Audio Unit) 9–10
audio interface 46, 52, 78, 83–86
auditory system 19, 30, 32, 33, 62, 115, 133, 154, 158
auto-wah 112
AUX 73-74

B

balanced signal 53–54
band-pass (filter) 107, 110–112
bandwidth 107-108, 110, 113
beats 36
bell (filter) 108
bidirectional 61, 64, 94
binary code 82–83, 86, 89
binaural 158
bit 34, 82–84, 88, 89
bit crushing 150–151
bitrate 82–83
boundary layer microphones 57
bytes 82

C

cable 46–54, 94
- RCA 48, 51
- TS 47–48, 51, 84
- TRS 48, 51, 84, 94

cardinal sine 90
cardioid 57, 59, 63–65, 67
CBR (Constant Bit Rate) 83
ceiling (limiter) 144
center frequency 105, 107–108, 110, 112
channel voice messages 95
chorus 114, 123–124
C:M ratio (FM) 175–176
coincident pair 62-64
comb filter 117–118, 134
composition 12, 196
compressor 12, 82, 140–145
- compression ratio 141
- downward compression 140
- multiband compressor 143
- threshold 141
- upward compression 140

computer 8–9, 13, 78–84, 86, 94, 98, 101, 130, 156, 159, 164, 167, 189
connector 47–48, 51, 81, 94
constant power pan 160
control change 96, 98
critical frequency (all-pass) 111, 113
cutoff 59, 106–112, 170
CV (Control Voltage) 3, 166
cycle 22–24, 34, 36, 87, 90, 181

D

DAC (Digital to Analog Converter) 78, 83, 89
DAW (Digital Audio Workstation) 9–10, 31, 34, 46, 156, 159, 160, 184, 193
decay (ADSR) 38, 170, 180
decibel (dB) 31–32, 34, 141, 142
- dBFS 31, 34, 144
- dB FS (full scale) 31, 34
- dBmV 31
- dB SIL 31–32
- dB SPL 31, 34, 127
- dBu 31, 51
- dBW 31

de-esser 144
delay 114–124, 131–132, 134, 143, 184
deviation (FM) 176–177
diaphragm 54–56, 59, 61
DI-Box 46, 53
- Direct Inject Box 53

digital signal 46, 75, 78, 83, 86, 89, 150, 167
distortion 58-59, 62, 70-72, 91, 147-152, 168, 179-182
DJ set 13, 93
dry-wet 1115-124, 131, 134
dynamic envelope 37–38, 165–166, 168, 170
dynamic loudspeaker 76
dynamic microphone 54, 56, 58
dynamic range 84, 88, 89, 117, 140, 142, 145
dynamics 30, 37, 95, 145, 162, 189, 190

E

early reflections 128, 131
echo 114-118, 125-126, 129
EG (envelope generator) (FM) 178
elastic medium 19–23, 30, 53
electric piano 50-52, 69, 71
envelope follower 139
equalizer, EQ, equalization 12, 47, 74-75, 105, 108, 109
equal temperament 28
expander 145
- downward expansion 145
- upward expansion 145

F

Faraday's Law 54, 56, 69-70, 76
FFT (Fast Fourier Transform) 38, 138
figure-8 61, 156–157
filter 39, 59, 73, 74, 77, 91, 93, 105–114, 117–118, 120, 127, 131–134, 139, 143, 144, 155, 165-166, 170–171, 183-184, 191
  filter order 109
flanger 114, 122–123
Fletcher-Munson diagram 33, 88
FM (Frequency Modulation) 168, 174–179
foldover (distortion) 91
Fourier 38, 138
frequency 20, 22–29, 33, 35–44, 55, 59, 70, 77, 86–87, 90–91, 105–113, 117, 120, 122–123, 125, 131–135, 138, 143–144, 148, 150–151, 155, 159, 166, 170–178, 184, 187, 189
frequency response 55, 57–58, 62, 77, 105, 109, 155
fused reverberation 128, 131
fuzz 149

G

gate 146
  noise gate 146
grain density 187
granular synthesis 168, 185-187

H

harmonic 38–44, 51, 71, 148-149, 151, 168, 174, 177, 179–181, 184, 187, 189
harmonic spectrum 39–40, 131, 175
HDD (hard disk drive) 80
headphones 12, 46, 73, 74, 76, 78–79, 83-86, 157–158
high-pass (filter) 59, 105–106, 108-110, 120, 133, 143
high-shelf (filter) 108
HRTF (Head-related transfer function) 155–156, 158
humbucker 70
hypercardioid 60

I

IFFT (Inverse Fast Fourier Transform) 138
IFT (Inverse Fourier Transform) 138
ILD (Interaural Level Difference) 154, 156, 158, 160
impedance 51–53, 84
  Hi-Z 52, 84
  Lo-Z 52, 84
impulse response 128, 135-136, 138
infrasound 25
inharmonic 38–39, 43, 168
inharmonic spectrum 40, 175
inverse square law 31, 127-128, 133
ITD (Interaural Time Difference) 154, 156, 158

K

Karplus-Strong (KS) 184
knee (compressor) 142

L

Larsen effect 54–56, 59–60
LFO (Low Frequency Oscillator) 112–113, 122–124, 166, 170
limiter 140, 144
linear synthesis algorithms 168
live electronics 15, 104
liveset 16
lookup table (synthesis) 181-182, 192
loudness 30-34, 36
low-pass (filter) 91, 105–106, 108–110, 112, 120, 133, 143, 170, 184
low-shelf (filter) 108, 109

M

magnetic pickup 51-52, 69, 71-72
mass-spring model 184
mastering 9, 12, 78, 139, 141, 144
meter 34, 74
microphone 46-69, 73, 74, 79, 84, 129, 156-157
microprocessor 80
MIDI 8–10, 93–100, 102, 190
  .mid files 99
  MIDI clock 97
  MIDI controller 98, 100
mixer 9, 47, 49–53, 55, 73–77, 83-84, 98, 159-160
mixing 9, 12, 63-64, 140
modal synthesis 184
modular (synthesizer) 167
modulation index (FM) 176–177
MP3 9, 82–83
MPE 93, 100
M/S (Mid-Side) 61, 64, 156
MSW model 184
multiple echo 116-118
multitap delay 118-120, 123, 131
multitap multiband delay 120
music notation software 8, 12

N

near-coincident pair 62, 65-67
nonlinear synthesis algorithms 168
NOS 66
notch (filter) 107, 110
note OFF (MIDI) 96
note ON (MIDI) 96
Nyquist frequency 87, 90-91, 150, 175
Nyquist-Shannon sampling theorem 87

O

omnidirectional 57, 60, 67, 156–157
operating system 79, 81–82, 94
operators (FM) 177-178
ORTF 65
OSC (Open Sound Control) 93, 101–102
overdrive 70, 148–149, 152, 179
oversampling 91
overtones 39–40, 43, 170

P

PAD 59
pan (mixer) 63-67, 73-74
panning 63-67, 160-162
parabolic reflector 62

period 22–24, 35, 42, 179, 181
periodic wave 23-24
phantom power (+48V) 54–57, 74, 84
phase 34–39, 41, 49, 51, 62–65, 67, 105, 111, 113, 130, 132–133, 181–182
phase distortion synthesis 181–182
phaser 113
phase spectrum 38–39
phon 33
physical modeling 183–184
pickup 51-52, 54, 69–72
ping pong delay 121
pitch bend (MIDI) 96
pitch-synchronous granular synthesis 187
polar pattern 59-61
polyphonic aftertouch 96
pop filter 61
power amplifier 77
preamplifier 50-52, 55-57, 74, 83-84
precedence effect 115
predelay 128, 131, 134
pressure zone microphones (PZM). *See boundary layer microphones*
production 12
program change (MIDI) 97
psychoacoustic 30, 115, 154

Q

Q (filter) 106–112
quantization 86, 88-90, 150
quasi-synchronous granular synthesis (QSGS) 187

R

RAM 80
real time 96, 104, 130, 135, 152, 159, 164, 180
recording 9, 12, 55-57, 59, 61-66, 90, 104, 156-157
release (ADSR) 38, 170, 180
release (compressor) 140-141
resampling 150-151
reverb, reverberation 125-138, 155
  convolution reverb 135-138
  electromechanical reverb 130
    plate reverb 130
    spring reverb 130
  stereo reverb 133
RM (Ring Modulation) 168, 172–173
RT60 128, 134

S

sample and hold 90
sampling 86-87, 90-91, 150-151, 167
sampling frequency (rate) 87, 90-91, 115, 150-151, 175, 184
sampling synthesis 188-191
sawtooth wave 41, 166, 170, 181
semi-modular 167
send/return 73-74
shelf (filter) 108-109
shockmount 61
sidebands 172–173, 175–177
signal levels 50-51
  instrument level 51
  line level 51
  mic level 50
sine wave 23, 33, 35–36, 38–39, 41–42, 44, 87, 148–152, 166, 168-169, 172–173, 179-181
single coil 70
software 8-10, 12, 78-83, 94, 98-99, 100-102, 156, 159, 164, 166-167
spaced pair 62, 67
spatialization 12, 14, 62, 133, 153-162
speaker 14, 31, 47-48, 52, 54, 56, 72, 76–79, 85, 120, 129, 157-160
spectrum 37–41, 58, 90–91, 105, 107, 111, 117, 131, 137-138, 148–149, 170, 173, 175–176
speed of sound 21, 23, 127
square wave 41, 123, 148–149, 151, 166, 170
SSD (solid state drives) 80
stereo microphone techniques 62-67
subtractive synthesis 106, 166, 168, 170-171
subwoofer 77, 159
supercardioid 60
sustain (ADSR) 38, 96, 165, 180
synchronous granular synthesis 187
synthesis 78, 93, 106–107, 152, 163–193
SysEx 97
system message 95, 97

T

table lookup *See lookup table (synthesis)*
THRU (MIDI) 95
timbre 37-44, 147, 164
transducer 19, 47, 53, 69, 130
triangle wave 41, 166, 170
tweeter 77, 120

U

ultrasound 25

V

VBR (Variable Bit Rate) 83
VCA (Voltage Control Amplifier) 166, 170–171
VCF (Voltage Control Filter) 166, 170–171
VCO (Voltage Control Oscillator) 166, 170–171
vector synthesis 193
vibrating body 19–20, 22, 30, 56
VST 9–10

W

wah-wah 112
wave (sound wave) 19-24, 30–31, 34–36, 46–47, 53–59, 76, 87, 115, 125, 127, 155
wavelength 23, 125
waveshaping 152, 168, 179-180
wavetable synthesis 181, 192
white noise 24, 43–44, 117, 184
windscreen 62
woofer 77, 120

X

X/Y 63

T - #0203 - 060125 - C208 - 297/210/10 - PB - 9781032796826 - Matt Lamination